WORLD ORDER AFTER LENINISM

WORLD ORDER

ORDER

after Leninism

Edited by
Vladimir Tismaneanu,
Marc Morjé Howard,
and Rudra Sil

HERBERT J. ELLISON CENTER FOR RUSSIAN,
EAST EUROPEAN, AND CENTRAL ASIAN STUDIES
UNIVERSITY OF WASHINGTON,
SEATTLE

in association with

UNIVERSITY OF WASHINGTON PRESS
SEATTLE AND LONDON

Design by Pamela Canell
10 09 08 07 06   5 4 3 2 1

University of Washington Press
P.O. Box 50096, Seattle, WA 98145, U.S.A.
www.washington.edu/uwpress

Library of Congress Cataloging-in-Publication Data
Tismaneanu, Vladimir.
World order after Leninism / by Vladimir Tismaneanu,
Marc Morjé Howard, and Rudra Sil.— 1st ed.
p. cm.
"Essays in honor of Ken Jowitt."
Includes bibliographical references and index.
ISBN 0-295-98628-x
1. Communist state. 2. Post-communism. 3. Political
culture—Communist countries. 4. Political culture—
Former communist countries. 5. Communism. I. Howard,
Marc Morjé. II. Sil, Rudra, 1967– III. Jowitt, Kenneth. IV. Title.
JC474.T497 2006   335.43—dc22   2006002428

This book is printed on New Leaf Ecobook 50, which is
100 percent recycled, containing 50 percent post-consumer
waste, and is processed chlorine free. Ecobook 50 is acid free
and meets the minimum requirements of ANSI /NISO Z39–
49—1992 (R1997) (Permanence of Paper).♾♻

Essays in honor of Ken Jowitt

CONTENTS

III *Political, Economic, and Social Change:*
     Beyond Eastern Europe

WORLD ORDER AFTER LENINISM

INTRODUCTION

Ken Jowitt's Universe

RUDRA SIL AND MARC MORJÉ HOWARD

T his volume is intended as a tribute to an extraordinary scholar who
has been a teacher, mentor, or colleague—as well as a friend—to all
of the authors featured here. Ken Jowitt is professor emeritus of political science at the University of California, Berkeley, and is currently Pres
and Maurine Hotchkis Senior Fellow at the Hoover Institution at Stanford.
Jowitt received his B.A. in 1962 from Columbia University and his Ph.D.
in 1970 from the University of California, Berkeley, where he taught before
retiring in 2002.

Jowitt's writings have spanned three decades and influenced several generations of scholars attempting to gain some analytic purchase on the rise,
transformation, and decline of communism worldwide. He is best known
for his original and incisive analysis of the phenomenon most call "communism," but which Jowitt insisted on calling "Leninism" in order to
emphasize the distinctive organizational character of the party created by
Vladimir Lenin. Jowitt's most important contributions on the nature, transformation, extinction, and legacy of Leninism were compiled in his provocatively titled volume, *New World Disorder: The Leninist Extinction.*

Jowitt's distinctive understanding of the Leninist phenomenon began
to take shape in his first book, *Revolutionary Breakthroughs and National
Development: The Case of Romania, 1944–65.* In this book, Jowitt challenged
efforts to characterize communism as either an antimodern phenomenon
or an alternative route to modernity. Instead, he drew upon a detailed exam-

ination of the first two decades of Communist Party rule in Romania to suggest that Leninism represented a distinctive kind of modernity wedded to a revolutionary transformation of an economy, a society, and a political community. In a subsequent monograph, *The Leninist Response to National Dependency,* Jowitt went on to locate the novelty of Leninism in the "charismatic impersonalism" evident in Leninist party organization, as opposed to the procedural impersonalism characteristic of modern organizations in the West. According to Jowitt, Lenin's genius lay in his ability to combine seemingly irreconcilable features into his "party of a new type":

> Lenin's innovation was to create an organization and membership effectively committed to conflicting practices—command and obedience with debate and discussion; belief in inexorable laws of historical change with empirical investigation of social development; heroic action with a persistent concern for the scientific and sober operation of an economy and society; and an emphasis on individual revolutionary heroism with an emphasis on the superordinate impersonal authority of the Party, itself the central heroic actor and focus of emotional commitment.[1]

This synthesis represented only the "genetic" features of Leninism, however. In a 1978 article in *World Politics* titled "Inclusion and Mobilization in European Leninist Regimes,"[2] Jowitt proceeded to identify and explain the "developmental" features of Leninist regimes. Rather than minimizing the significance of change in such regimes, as proponents of the "totalitarian school" were wont to do, and rather than interpreting change as evidence of deradicalization and development, as proponents of modernization theory suggested, Jowitt interpreted change in terms of three discrete core tasks that a revolutionary regime had to undertake at different stages:

> *transformation:* a new revolutionary party wrests political and military control from a preexisting regime in order to transform the old society

> *consolidation:* the new revolutionary regime seeks to insulate itself from the political, economic, and cultural threats of a society that still cannot be trusted

> *inclusion:* the party seeks to integrate itself with unofficial, nonparty sectors of society without yielding its authoritative claims to the "correct line."

These distinct stages not only constitute a general model of organizational change in revolutionary settings (a model that some of Jowitt's students have applied to phenomena beyond the Leninist world), but they map on to the actual histories of Leninist regimes rather nicely. In the first and most authoritative embodiment of Leninism, the Soviet Union, the leaderships of Vladimir Lenin, Joseph Stalin, and Nikita Khrushchev corresponded neatly to the changing core tasks associated with the three stages.

Under Leonid Brezhnev, however, the Soviet Union also demonstrated the distinctive challenges of the inclusion stage: for the first time, the revolutionary regime faced the absence of a combat task vis-à-vis society while having to simultaneously defend its mobilizational role and build an inclusive political community. With this change came threats to the party's own internal discipline, as personal ties between party cadres and members of the unofficial sectors of society set the stage for the organizational corruption of the party, marked by the erosion of the "charismatic impersonalism" at the heart of Leninism. Jowitt laid out how this process was concretely manifested in the case of Soviet Leninism in a 1983 article titled "Soviet Neotraditionalism: The Political Corruption of a Leninist Regime."[3] The analysis of clientelism and the organizational corruption in the era did not fit neatly into any of the prevailing treatments of either the Soviet Union or the communist world writ large, but it proved to be remarkably prescient. Given the proliferation of "neotraditional" corruption accompanying the Communist Party's attempts at inclusion under Brezhnev, Jowitt identified the KGB as the organization that would most likely emerge as the central locus of efforts to reconstruct the relationship between regime and society.[4] In doing so, Jowitt essentially anticipated the rise of former KGB chief Yuri Andropov who, during his brief stint, did indeed set out on a mission to root out corruption and revitalize the party, a mission that would soon be taken in new directions by Mikhail Gorbachev.

Although the rapid succession of reforms initiated by Gorbachev would set the stage for the extinction of Leninist regimes, Jowitt's writings continued to be original and revealing. While many students of Eastern Europe and the Soviet Union tended to view Gorbachev's reforms as deviations from Leninism, Jowitt viewed Gorbachev's strategy as motivated by an effort to restore the original revolutionary vigor of Bolshevism—but a Bolshevism essentially reflecting a Menshevik view of history and society that would have the unanticipated consequence of removing both the economic and political underpinnings of whatever legitimacy the Communist Party retained in the Soviet Union.[5] With the fall of the Berlin Wall, while some euphorically proclaimed the final triumph of liberal capitalist democracy as the "end of history," Jowitt warned of the potential dangers of rushed efforts to build new institutions in a highly uncertain and turbulent environment. In such an environment, with the order of the cold war suddenly displaced by competing ways to characterize and reconfigure the new world order, he emphasized the sense of anxiety likely to pervade post-Leninist societies.[6]

Most famously, Jowitt noted the complications likely to result from a "Leninist legacy" that was quite inhospitable to liberal capitalist democracy and that would be accompanied by emotional fragmentation, ethnic and territorial fragmentation, demographic fragmentation, and political fragmentation, thus favoring trends towards authoritarianism.[7] On a global scale, he argued that "the Leninist defeat will lead to a reconfigured world," and that the process of reconfiguration would be marked not by a widely accepted "new world order" but by "shifting and contested boundaries (. . . territorial, ideological, cultural, economic, and political) and by insecure identities."[8] While Jowitt's worst fears may not have materialized in each and every post-Leninist society, the analysis drew attention to mechanisms that many other students of postcommunism were failing to take into account, mechanisms that now seem more relevant as anxieties, tensions, and frustrations within and beyond the former Leninist world come to be more profoundly felt after the initial rush to proclaim the decisive triumph of liberal capitalism.

Jowitt's engagement with the emergence, transformation, and extinction of Leninism has set the stage for a new book he is writing, tentatively entitled *Frontiers, Barricades and Boundaries*. This book departs from where the collection of essays in *New World Disorder* left off, identifying the changes in international political geography in the post–cold war era and the various sorts of challenges to American and Western institutions that have been emerging over the past decade. He has also become an acclaimed commentator on American foreign policy. Although sympathizing with efforts to make the world (particularly the Middle East) more stable and recognizable, Jowitt has warned that attempts to rebuild nations without attention to the configuration of preexisting social relations will only lead to deeper conflicts and further turmoil. Extending the logic underlying his treatment of the "Leninist legacy" to the American attack on the Iraqi Baathist regime, Jowitt warned that while removing Saddam Hussein from power may be justified on any number of grounds, "the process of invasion, occupation, and attempted construction of a democratic nation in Iraq is likely to lead either to heightened authoritarian rule or civil violence in the rest of the Middle East—or both. A poison dart indeed." For those who were counting on a revitalized Iraqi society led by a liberated middle class, Jowitt went on to note:

In no way do the Iraqi middle classes resemble the proto-liberal capitalist classes of seventeenth-century Western Europe with their preferences for, and understanding of, a legally framed market economy and individual autonomy. As for Iraqi society in general, it is fragmented into hostile tribes and clans based on kinship, religion, and ethnicity. In such an environment, creating civility will require Promethean effort. Creating a civil society and democratic government will take a miracle.[9]

Over the past decade, Ken Jowitt has had perhaps his greatest impact as a highly sought-after speaker on world affairs, delivering widely acclaimed lectures and speeches around the world. These include the presidential address at Whitman College, the Princeton Lectures, and talks given at the Commonwealth Club, the World Presidents' Organization, and the Defense Intelligence Agency. He has also served as the Jean Monnet Visiting Scholar at the European University Institute in Florence, and appears occasionally on television programs such as CNBC's *Hardball*. As his audiences will readily attest, Professor Jowitt's lectures and talks have always been dynamic and have never failed to simultaneously illuminate, provoke, and entertain.

No Festschrift for Ken Jowitt would be complete without some mention of his extraordinary qualities as a teacher. During his years at Berkeley, Professor Jowitt guided the intellectual development of dozens of scholars now teaching at major research universities worldwide or serving in international organizations and think tanks. Jowitt taught two popular graduate seminars on comparative (post)communism and nation building. In his undergraduate lecture courses, Professor Jowitt was an inspiration to thousands of students, many of whom (including one of the editors of this volume) were inspired to become political science majors and pursue doctoral studies in the discipline after taking his introductory course on comparative politics. His lectures were incomparable in their intensity and energy, earning him ovations at the end of every class. While most of us worry about whether our students will remember anything they learn in our classes after the final exam, it is telling that students who took Professor Jowitt's course would recall key concepts and arguments from Jowitt's lectures years later. Professor Jowitt was also an avid supporter of student athletes, encouraging them to stay in school and earn their degrees in spite of the enormous pressures of juggling the demands of intercollegiate athletics and Berkeley's rigorous undergraduate degree requirements. It is no wonder then that Professor Jowitt won awards for distinguished teaching on a number of occasions and was dean of undergraduate studies at Berkeley from 1983 to 1986.

The essays that follow are by scholars who have been fortunate to have had Professor Jowitt as a teacher and colleague. The essays represent original substantive contributions in their own right, but they also address the analytical concepts and substantive issues to which Jowitt has devoted his intellectual energies. We view these essays as falling primarily into one of four overlapping categories: (1) the nature of Leninism and its legacy; (2) the politics of identity and social transformation in Eastern Europe and the former Soviet Union; (3) the challenges and dynamics of political, economic, and social change in areas beyond Eastern Europe; or (4) the methodological foundations of Jowitt's work, such as his Weberian understanding of social science and his use of the comparative method.

Part one of the volume encompasses essays addressing the nature of Leninism and its legacies. Vladimir Tismaneanu's essay, "Lenin's Century: Bolshevism, Marxism, and the Russian Tradition," departs from the premise that Marxism would have remained little more than a sociological doctrine had Lenin not transformed its salvationist weltanschauung into a global political praxis. This is what enabled Bolshevism to acquire an intellectual and political reality, a total and totalizing philosophical, ethical, and practical-political direction within the world revolutionary movement. At the same time, coming to terms with Lenin's legacies requires recognizing that Bolshevism in the Soviet Union found its causes, origins, and most propitious ground in the radical segments of Russian political culture, a culture that reflects a love for the ultimate, universally cathartic, redeeming revolution. Nevertheless, as Jowitt accurately perceived, Leninism represented a new form of political radicalism, irreconcilable with the Western individualistic liberal tradition, that rested on a charismatic vanguard party that could substitute for more traditional religious referentials in times of deep moral and cultural crisis.

The next two essays shift the focus to the legacies of Leninism as these have shaped developments in postcommunist Europe. In chapter 2, "The Leninist Legacy Revisited," Marc Morjé Howard takes a fresh look at Jowitt's influential but controversial essay "The Leninist Legacy" with the benefit of more than a decade of hindsight. In revisiting Jowitt's claims about the ways in which legacies of Leninist regimes would hinder smooth transitions to liberal capitalist democracy, Howard argues that while only a few of Jowitt's most apocalyptic predictions about Eastern Europe have come to pass, this is because of the surprisingly assertive and supportive role played by the European Union (EU)—a development that Jowitt actually called for in his 1991 essay, but (like most observers at the time) did not expect would be forthcoming. Nonetheless, even in the eight or more postcommunist countries that will soon be "adopted" by the EU, Jowitt's overall description of the Leninist legacy and its effects on individuals and societies in many ways still holds true. Howard concludes that "The Leninist Legacy" continues to have its own "legacy"—namely, a lasting if indirect influence on scholarly debates about the relative importance of historical versus contemporary factors in explaining postcommunist developments.

In his essay "Transition to What? Legacies and Reform Trajectories after Communism," Grigore Pop-Eleches attempts to trace the different economic and political reform trajectories of postcommunist countries to differences in Leninist and pre-Leninist legacies. Contrary to the early optimistic expectations of a uniform transition from communism to Western-style democratic and capitalist institutions, the changes of the last fifteen years suggest a growing divergence among the former communist "comrades." Pop-Eleches finds that, while a distinct Leninist legacy is still noticeable in the prevalence of noncivic popular attitudes and the weakness of civil society organizations and political parties, the divergence of national regime trajectories is best explained by differences in Western integration incentives and precommunist legacies. Thus, whereas the new EU members (and a few of the more advanced current candidates) have made significant progress in reforming their political systems, in countries with fewer integration prospects and more difficult legacies the long-expected normalization has resulted either in distinctly non-Western economic and political arrangements or in uneasy and volatile hybrids due to the tensions between formal Western institutions and local cultural and social conditions.

Part two examines the regions of the world where Leninism first took root—Eastern Europe and the former Soviet Union—but focuses on longer-term historical processes shaping identity politics and social transformation in these regions. In his essay "Institutions and the Development of Individualism: The Case of Western Poland after World War II," Tomek Grabowski argues that the rise of individualism (a culture based on the moral primacy of individuals over groups) requires strong institutions. But these must be institutions of a peculiar type: they must socialize individuals to adopt group norms without inculcating in the targets of socialization any feeling of inferiority vis-à-vis the group and its standard-bearers. That is a rare and difficult balance to achieve. The Catholic Church in the Polish Western Territories after World War II proved to be such an institution. As a result of a unique set of circumstances, the Church in western Poland broke away from the time-honored traditions of Polish Catholicism. As did its Protestant counterpart in Western Europe centuries earlier, it placed individual conscience above group conformity. The fact that the culture of individualism exists today in western as opposed to eastern or central Poland, Grabowski argues, can be attributed to a significant degree to the socializing activity of the Church.

Oleg Kharkhordin's essay, "The Soviet Union as a Reign of Virtue: Aristotelian and Christian Influences on Modern Russian Ethics and Politics," examines the adaptation of the "ethics of virtue" by the Bolsheviks. Kharkhordin argues that what Aquinas did for Western Christianity—adding three theological virtues to the list of four cardinal ones and thus integrating Aristotle into Christianity—was similarly done by generations of nameless monastic scribes in Russia, who had achieved the same effect *unintentionally*. This inculcation of Aristotelian virtue into the most basic moral intuitions of Orthodox Christianity in Russia played itself out after 1917, when virtue ethics (as opposed, following Alasdair MacIntyre, to ethics of principle) became predominant. The tradition of republican virtue that the Bolsheviks inherited from the French Revolution was grafted on to a vast sea of mundane moral intuitions about religious virtue shared by peasants. The outcome was a tendency to pay attention to particularities of the case in consideration rather than to a general rule that has to be applied—in this case, to model narratives that exemplified virtues rather than to theories of morals, and an emphasis on desirable character traits rather than internal values. This predominance of the ethics of virtue, rather than the ethics of principle, continues to influence developments in post-Soviet Russia.

In the following essay, "Slobodan Milošević: Charismatic Leader or Plebiscitarian Demagogue?" Veljko Vujačić seeks to interpret Milošević's leadership appeals in the historical context of the crisis in Serbia and Yugoslavia in the late 1980s. Elaborating on Max Weber's ideal-type of charismatic authority, with the help of ideas drawn from the work of Jowitt and Pierre Bourdieu, Vujačić argues that Milošević originally exhibited a potential for becoming a charismatic leader. Building on Jowitt's insight that charismatic leaders typically reconcile latent predispositions that are seen as mutually irreconcilable, Vujačić proceeds to identify those latent predispositions in Serbia, and shows how Milošević attempted to build mass support by skillfully combining political appeals to very different social constituencies. For a variety of reasons, however, Vujačić argues that Milošević ultimately failed to become a truly charismatic leader, and developed a system of plebiscitarian rule instead.

The essay coauthored by Gail Kligman and Katherine Verdery, "Social Dimensions of Collectivization: Fomenting Class Struggle in Transylvania," uses ethnographic material to explore how class relations emerged through an attack on the status character of village social organization. Their analysis is very much part of the Weberian conceptual universe that so importantly influenced Jowitt's thinking about the distinctiveness of Leninism. Kligman and Verdery take as their point of departure Jowitt's discussions of the significance of collectivization as a defining feature of Leninist strategy and the paucity of research on the social rather than economic dimensions of collectivization. Kligman and Verdery's study focuses on the means by which Leninist cadres-in-formation sought to provoke class struggle in two villages in Transylvania, located in Romania, the country that launched Jowitt's career as a student of Leninist regimes. The essay draws on data from interviews and archival research from a larger collaborative project to show some of the processes whereby "peasant extended patriarchal households," as Jowitt labeled them, were undermined as "units and models of socio-economic and political power."

Part three looks at the dynamics and challenges of political, economic, and social transformation beyond Eastern Europe. In her essay "Stages of Development in Authoritarian Regimes," Barbara Geddes seeks to extend Jowitt's insights about the developmental stages of Leninist movements to the trajectories of authoritarian rule found elsewhere. Based on data gathered from 160 post-1945 dictatorships, Geddes argues that when authoritarian regimes initially come to power, leadership within the junta or other governing entity tends to be collegial; hierarchies and routines for making and implementing decisions are not yet clear; personnel within the junta often change in rapid succession; and citizens, especially those with personal links to members of the governing group, often have considerable access and ability to influence decisions. However, Geddes goes on to note that in about three years, authoritarian regimes that survive tend to go through remarkably similar changes that essentially represent efforts at the core task of consolidation. In this time, a clear hierarchy will have been established and decision making within the junta will have become less collegial. Struggles will have occurred within the junta as individual members attempt to consolidate their personal rule. Although these efforts to personalize power are not always successful, they often are. The citizen coalition supporting the dictatorship will have narrowed and become more defined. By the end of three years, only certain citizens will be able to influence government decisions. Geddes concludes with a theory of her own to explain the consolidation of authoritarian rule and why some authoritarian seizures of power end in a reasonably stable dictatorship but others are quickly overthrown in their turn.

Yong-Chool Ha's essay, "From Neotraditionalism to Neofamilism:

Responses to 'National Dependency' in Newly Industrialized Countries," extends Jowitt's category of neotraditionalism to make sense of patterns of political economy and social change in East Asia. Taking as his point of departure Alexander Gerschenkron's arguments about the challenges of economic backwardness, arguments that Jowitt popularized for thousands of students in lectures and seminars, Ha notes that studies of late industrialization have tended to overemphasize the role of the state in guiding industrialization while neglecting the *social* dimensions of relative backwardness. Ha draws upon Jowitt's conceptualization of "neotraditionalism" to bridge the gap between political economy and political sociology in East Asia. Using empirical evidence from South Korea from the period extending from the mid-1960s through 1980, Ha examines how the state, in attempting to negotiate the roles of economic and societal actors in the course of industrialization, unintentionally reinforced traditional primary social ties in a novel institutional environment (in much the same way that personal clientelist ties emerged in the course of the inclusion stage of Leninism). Ha argues that, in place of class, a new amalgam of modernity and tradition was created that could be appropriately labeled "neofamilism."

Calvin Chen, in "Leninism, Developmental Stages, and Transformation: Understanding Social and Institutional Change in Contemporary China," considers the institutional features of China's post-Mao reforms. While some emphasize the intractability of institutions like the *danwei,* or work unit, as evidence of China's lingering Leninist orientation, others cite the entrenchment of market practices as a sign of a coming "Leninist extinction." Both camps, however, fail to fully appreciate the connection between post-Mao trends and the unfolding of what Jowitt might refer to as the "developmental stages" of Leninist (and post-Leninist) regimes. Chen argues that recent changes in the organization of the party-state and Chinese society can be better understood not only as a result of the party's inability to handle the task of inclusion but also as an effort to promote a number of newly created local institutions. Focusing on township and village enterprises (TVEs) in the Chinese countryside, Chen employs Jowitt's dynamic framework for analyzing organizational change to show how the shifting imperatives of transformation, consolidation, and inclusion may be identified with the different strategies that employers and managers deploy to cope with the fundamental tasks of production in light of the social milieu from which their labor force is drawn. But Chen also notes that alongside these distinct stages are some universal imperatives that accompany organizational growth, especially given the sheer number of people to be managed in a large-scale TVE. Thus, the logic of Leninist development, combined with the logic of organizational growth, serves to explain shifting strategies for recruitment, personnel management, and work organization in China's s.

Part four addresses different methodological aspects that are explicit or implicit in Jowitt's approach to social analysis. In "Weber, Jowitt, and the Dilemma of Social Science Prediction," Stephen E. Hanson draws attention to the scientific status and predictive power of Jowitt's neo-Weberian approach to comparative politics. Hanson argues that at least one important reason no one has noticed the predictive accuracy of neo-Weberian theory is that there is actually no consensus among contemporary political scientists about the role of empirical prediction in testing theories. Indeed, a substantial number of scholars in the field have given up (explicitly or implicitly) the idea that what actually happens in the world has any role to play in evaluating a social scientific theory's value. Detached from the anchor of empirical testing, Hanson contends, the political science discipline floats in a sea of abstractions, with little relevance to "science" as it has been understood in the modern world since the Enlightenment. Ironically, at the same time, scholars interested in real-world political phenomena have increasingly tended to reject the ideal of "political science" altogether—thus ceding the symbolically crucial term "science" to the disciplinary mainstream. In light of these tensions within the discipline, Hanson argues for an alternative Weberian understanding of "prediction" in terms of three main ideal-types—traditional "wisdom," charismatic "prophecy," and rational-legal "scientific testing"—each tied to a particular conception of time. Hanson then proceeds to demonstrate how Weber's emphasis on the interpretive understanding of social action can improve scientific prediction in the latter sense.

Rudra Sil's essay, "The Evolving Significance of Leninism in Comparative Historical Analysis: Theorizing the General and the Particular," examines Jowitt's use of the comparative method in light of the particular intellectual environment in which it was conceived. From the 1950s to the 1970s, most approaches either viewed Leninist regimes as models of totalitarianism, as cases of industrialization under authoritarian rule, or as a set of individual nations each with unique historical or cultural traditions. None of these approaches, Sil notes, were as effective as Jowitt's in capturing the distinctiveness and boundedness of Leninism as a mode of political organization and a strategy of economic and social transformation. By essentially combining John Stuart Mill's methods of agreement and difference in an eclectic manner, Jowitt was able to identify the general characteristics shared by Leninist regimes in spite of their varied historical inheritances while specifying what was particular about Leninism vis-à-vis other models of authoritarianism and development worldwide. Sil argues that this strategy, while correcting for blind spots evident in mainstream approaches to comparative communism, remains valuable in the present intellectual climate as a means to overcome the stalemate between universal templates of "transition" and studies of individual countries. But Sil also calls for attention to two other comparative dimensions that Jowitt did not emphasize for analytic purposes at the time he was writing: (1) the particular variants of Leninism across space and their differential effects on specific aspects of post-Leninist society, and (2) the general characteristics shared by Leninist/post-Leninist and developing/transitional societies given the common influences and pressures these face in the post–cold war global environment. Combining these comparative frameworks, Sil concludes, allows us to better theorize the differences across individual Leninist regimes while demonstrating the contemporary relevance of Leninism as a category in making sense of an evolving global order.

Finally, the two essays in the concluding section are by two of Jowitt's closest friends and most distinguished colleagues, Stephen Holmes and Daniel Chirot. These essays offer broad, sweeping perspectives of Jowitt's work and its overall significance for making sense of Leninism as well as the character of world order after the Leninist extinction. Holmes, in his essay "Conjuring Up a Battlefront in the War on Terror," implicitly engages Jowitt's more recent writings on international political geography since the Leninist extinction, taking on contemporary issues of foreign policy and world affairs in the process. And Chirot, in his essay "The Power of Imaginative Analogy: Communism, Faith, and Leadership," recalls Jowitt's intellectual journey and notes the different ways in which his teaching and scholarship left an indelible mark on the study of the rise and fall of Leninism.

NOTES

1. Reprinted as chapter 1, "The Leninist Phenomenon," in Ken Jowitt, *New World Disorder: The Leninist Extinction* (Berkeley: University of California Press, 1992), 3.

2. Reprinted as chapter 3, "Inclusion," in Jowitt, *New World Disorder*.

3. Originally published in *Soviet Studies* 35, no. 3 (July 1983); reprinted as chapter 4, "Neotraditionalism," in Jowitt, *New World Disorder*.

4. "Neotraditionalism," in Jowitt, *New World Disorder*, 156–58.

5. "Gorbachev: Bolshevik or Menshevik?" in *Developments in Soviet Politics*, ed.

Stephen White, Alex Pravda, and Zvi Gitelman (Durham: Duke University Press, 1990); reprinted as chapter 6 in Jowitt, *New World Disorder.*

6. "The Leninist Extinction," in Jowitt, *New World Disorder,* chap. 7, especially 266–77.

7. "The Leninist Legacy," in Jowitt, *New World Disorder,* 296–99.

8. "A World Without Leninism," in Jowitt, *New World Disorder,* 310–11.

9. Ken Jowitt, "Rage, Hubris, and Regime Change," *Policy Review* 118 (April–May 2003): 33–43.

1 *Leninism and Its Legacy*

1

LENIN'S CENTURY

Bolshevism, Marxism, and the Russian Tradition

VLADIMIR TISMANEANU

arxism was, as Leszek Kolakowski once said, the greatest philosophical fantasy of modern times. All its radical hubris notwithstanding, Marxism would have remained a mere sociological doctrine had Vladimir Lenin not turned it into a most potent political weapon. This is the meaning of Antonio Gramsci's comparison between Lenin and Saint Paul—Lenin transformed the Marxian salvationist *weltanschauung* into a global political praxis. The bolshevik revolution was applied eschatological dialectics, and the Third International symbolized the universalization of the new revolutionary matrix. Lenin's crucial institutional invention (the Bolshevik Party) and his audacious intervention in the praxis of the world socialist movement enthused Georg Lukacs, who never abandoned his deep admiration for the founder of bolshevism. Referring to Lukacs's attachment to Lenin's vision of politics, Slavoj Zizek writes, "His Lenin was the one who, apropos of the split in Russian Social Democracy into bolsheviks and mensheviks, when the two factions fought over a precise formulation of who can be a Party member as defined in the Party programme, wrote: 'Sometimes, the fate of the entire working class movement for long years to come can be decided by a word or two in the party programme.'"[1] We need to remember that Leninism, as an allegedly coherent, homogenous, self-sufficient ideological construct, was a post-1924 creation: It was actually the result of Gregory Zinoviev's and Joseph Stalin's efforts to delegitimize Leon Trotsky by devising something called "Leninism" as opposed to the heresy branded as "Trotskyism." At the same time, bolshevism was an intellectual and political reality, a total and totalizing philosophical, ethical, and practical-political direction within the world revolutionary movement.[2] It was thanks to Lenin that a new type of politics emerged in the twentieth century, one based on elitism, fanaticism, unswerving commitment to the sacred cause, and complete substitution of critical reason through faith for the self-appointed "vanguards" of illuminated zealots (the professional revolutionaries). Leninism, initially a Russian then a world-historical cultural and political phenomenon, was in fact the foundation stone of the system that came to an end with the revolutions of 1989–91. Whatever one thinks of Lenin's antibureaucratic struggle during his last years, or about his initiation of the New Economic Policy (NEP), the thrust of his action was essentially opposed to political pluralism. The nature of the bolshevik "intraparty democracy" was essentially inimical to free debate and competition of rival political views and platforms (as Lenin himself insisted, the party was not a "discussion club"). The March 1921 "ban on factions" resolution, directly related to the crushing of the Kronstadt uprising, indicated the persistent dictatorial propensity of bolshevism. The persecution of the left-wing Socialist Revolutionaries and Mensheviks, not to speak of other foes, confirms that for Lenin and his associates, the "dictatorship of the proletariat" meant the continuous strengthening of their absolute control over the body politic. Tolerance for cultural diversity and temporary acceptance of market relations were not meant to question the fundamental power relationship—the party's monopolistic domination and the stifling of any ideological alternative to bolshevism.[3] In this respect, there were no serious differences between the members of Lenin's politburo—Trotsky, Zinoviev, and Nikolai Bukharin included. To put it briefly, there was no Leninism, no totalitarianism—at least not in its Stalinist version. The twentieth century was in fact Lenin's century. In other words, postcommunism means a continuous struggle to overcome the "remains of Leninism" or "the Leninist debris," a term I proposed as an elaboration on Ken Jowitt's illuminating concept of the Leninist legacy as a civilizational constellation including deep emotions, nostalgias, sentiments, resentments, phobias, collectivist yearnings, and attraction to paternalism and even corporatism.[4]

Jowitt is among the few political scientists who accurately understood the deep appeals of Leninism as directly related to the emergence of the vanguard party as a substitute for traditional charismatic, religious-type reference frameworks in times of deep moral and cultural crisis:

VLADIMIR TISMANEANU

Leninism and Nazism were each, in different ways, perverse attempts to sustain and restore a heroic ethos and life in opposition to a liberal bourgeois individualistic system. . . . the defining principle of Leninism is to do what is illogical, and that is to make the impersonal charismatic. Charisma is typically associated with a saint or a knight, some personal attribution, and what Lenin did was remarkable. He did exactly what he claimed to do: he created a party of a new type. He made the party charismatic. People died for the party.[5]

Thus, Jowitt's definition of Leninism links the ideological, emotional, and organizational components in a comprehensive dynamic constellation: "Leninism is best seen as a historical as well as organizational syndrome, based on charismatic impersonalism; a strategy based on an 'ingenious error' leading to collectivization/industrialization; and an international bloc led by a dominant regime, with the same definition as its constituent parts, acting as leader, model, and support."[6]

Leninism as a political and cultural regime, or as an international system, is undoubtedly extinct. On the other hand, the Leninist/Stalinist model of the highly disciplined, messianic sect-type organization based on the rejection of pluralism and the demonization of the "Other" has not lost its appeal—suffice it to remember Lenin's diatribes against the Mensheviks, the Socialist Revolutionaries, the "kulaks," the "bourgeois intellectuals," etc. In his view, their place, even when they disguised themselves as nonparty-affiliated individuals, was in jail.[7] This quasi-rational, in fact almost mystical identification with the party (conceived as a beleaguered fortress, surrounded by vicious enemies—therefore the barricade component of the story) was of course a main psychological feature of bolshevism (in whatever incarnation) before what Robert C. Tucker defines as its de-radicalization (what Jowitt would call the rise of the Aquinas temptation, in the figure of "modern revisionism," as Mao Zedong accurately defined Titoism and Khrushchevism). To be a Leninist meant to accept the party's claim to scientific knowledge (grasping the "laws of historical evolution") as well as its prophetic/oracular pretense; doubting the party's omniscience and omnipotence was the cardinal sin (as finally admitted by the Old Bolshevik Nikolai Rubashov, Arthur Koestler's hero in *Darkness at Noon*). Think of Lenin's famous statement in October 1917: "History will not forgive us if we miss this opportunity." As Leszek Kolakowski put it, "Party mindedness, the political principle revered by all Leninists, resulted in the infallible image bestowed on the general secretary."[8] Yuri Pyatakov, one of Lenin's favorites among the younger generation of the Bolshevik Old Guard, spelled out this identification with the party in most dramatic terms: "Yes, I shall consider black something that I felt and considered to be white, since outside the party, outside accord with it, there is no life for me."[9] Ideological absolutism, sacralization of the ultimate goal, suspension of critical faculties, and the cult of the party line as the perfect expression of the general will were embedded in the original bolshevik project. The subordination of all conventional moral criteria to the ultimate end of achieving the classless society was the main problem with Leninism. It shared with Marxism what Steven Lukes calls "the emancipating vision of a world in which the principles that protect human beings from one another would no longer be needed."[10] One of the best descriptions of the Communist mind can be found in the following testimony of Lev Kopelev, the model for Aleksandr Solzhenitsyn's character Rubin in his novel *The First Circle*:

> With rest of my generation I firmly believed that the ends justify the means. Our great goal was the universal triumph of Communism, and for the sake of that goal everything was permissible—to lie, to steal, to destroy hundreds of thousands and even millions of people, all those who were hindering our work or could hinder it, everyone who stood in the way. And to hesitate or doubt about all this was to give in to "intellectual squeamishness" and "stupid liberalism," the attributes of people who "could not see the forest for the trees."[11]

Lukes is therefore correct in emphasizing the structural-generative ideological and emotional matrix of communism that made its crimes against humanity possible: "The defect in question, causing moral blindness at a heroic scale, was congenital."[12] This same point is emphasized by Martin Amis, for whom Lenin "was a moral aphasiac, a moral autist."[13] The magic evaporated once the historically anointed leader ceased to be the custodian of absolute truth. This makes Khrushchev's onslaughts on Stalin at the twentieth Congress of the Communist Party of the Soviet Union (CPSU) on February 25, 1956 (the "Secret Speech"), and at the twenty-second Congress in October 1961 crucially important (as admitted by Mikhail Gorbachev in his conversations with former Prague Spring chief ideologue Zdenek Mlynař.[14] At the same time, it was precisely the charismatic impersonalism, as Jowitt argues, that provided the antidote to desperation at the moment Khrushchev exposed Stalin's crimes. This feature, indeed, crucially distinguished bolshevism from nazism: "The leader is charismatic in Nazism; the program and (possibly) the leader are charismatic in Leninism."[15] The Leninist ultimate goal was the elimination (extinction) of politics through the triumph of the party as the embodiment of an exclusionary, even eliminationist/exterminist general will.[16] Under conditions of monistic certitude, recognition of fallibility is the beginning of any ideological fundamentalism's extinction. But during the "heroic" times, throughout War Communism and the "building of socialism," the unity between *party* and *vozhd* (leader) was, no less than terror, the key to the system's survival. Homo Sovieticus was more than a propaganda concoction.

In her acceptance speech for the year 2000 Hannah Arendt Award, given jointly by the city of Bremen, the Heinrich Böll Foundation, and the Hannah Arendt Association, Elena Bonner writes, "One of Hannah Arendt's key conclusions was 'The totality of terror is guaranteed by mass support.' It is consonant with a later comment by Sakharov: 'The slogan "The people and the Party are one," painted on every fifth building, are not just empty words.'"[17] This is precisely the point: the internalization of Leninist forms of thinking by millions of denizens of the Sovietized world, and their readiness to accept paternalistic collectivism as a better form of life than risk-driven, freedom-oriented experiences. In my view, the major cleavage in today's Russian political culture is that between the Leninist heritage and the democratic aspirations and practices associated with the name of Andrei Sakharov and Russia's human rights movement. To quote Elena Bonner again,

> In the preamble to his draft for a Soviet Constitution, Sakharov wrote: "The goal of the peoples of USSR and its government is a happy life, full of meaning, material and spiritual freedom, well-being, and peace." But in the decades after Sakharov, Russia's people have not increased their happiness, even though he did everything humanly possible to put the country on the path leading to the goal. And he himself lived a worthy and happy life.[18]

As a political doctrine (or perhaps as a political faith), bolshevism was a synthesis between radical Jacobinism or Blanquism (elitism, minority rule disguised as "dictatorship of the proletariat," exaltation of the heroic vanguard); unavowed Russian "Nechaevism" (a radical-conspiratorial mentality); and the authoritarian-voluntarist components of Marxism.[19] Bolshevism places the emphasis on the omnipotence of the revolutionary organization and nourishes contempt for what Hannah Arendt once called "the little verities of fact"—e.g., Lenin's and Trotsky's fierce attacks on the "renegade" Karl Kautsky, who had dared to question the bolshevik repudiation of all "formal" liberties in the name of protecting the "dictatorship of the proletariat," never mind that Lenin borrowed from Kautsky his "injection of consciousness" theory.

Is this all over? Far from it—and this applies not only to the countries once ruled by Leninist parties, but also to nationalist socialist parties like Baath and charismatic fundamentalist, neototalitarian movements, including Osama bin Laden's Al Qaeda.[20] The Leninist (bolshevik) mental matrix is rooted in a political culture suspicious of open dialogue and democratic procedures, and hostile to spontaneous developments from below. Leninism is not only an ideology, but also a set of precepts and techniques meant to inspire revolutionary global activism and militantism opposed to bourgeois liberalism and democratic socialism. This is precisely the similarity, but also the main distinction between the two main onslaughts on liberal individualism: fascism is a pathology of romantic irrationalism, and bolshevism is a pathology of Enlightenment-inspired hyperrationalism.[21] I don't want to be misunderstood: as an offspring of nineteenth-century antibourgeois, often antimodern ideologies of resentment, fascism did not need bolshevism in order to emerge and mature (as demonstrated in Isaiah Berlin's fascinating essay on Joseph de Maistre and the origins of fascism).[22] The cult of race, the blending of pseudoscientism (social Darwinism) with the neopagan worshipping of blood and soil, and the resentful rejection of liberal values as "soulless arithmetic" predated Leninism. On the other hand, it is hard to deny that the triumph of bolshevism and the intensity and scope of the Red Terror, together with the traumatic effects of World War I and the widespread sentiment that "the world of yesterday" (Stefan Zweig) had irretrievably come to an end, catalyzed the Fascist offensive against the universalistic traditions of the Enlightenment. Fascism was no less a fantasy of salvation than bolshevism: both promised to rescue humanity from the bondage of capitalist mercantilism and to ensure the advent of the total community. The Leader, as a superman, of course, plays an essential role in such movements. To quote Paul Berman:

> Lenin was the original model of such a Leader—Lenin, who wrote pamphlets and philosophical tracts with the confidence of a man who believes the secrets of the universe to be at his fingertips, and who established a weird new religion with Karl Marx as god, and who, after his death, was embalmed like a pharaoh and worshipped by the masses. But il Duce was no less a superman. Stalin was a colossus. About Hitler, Heidegger, bug-eyed, said: "But look at his hands."[23]

Spontaneity *(stikhiinost')* has always been the Leninists nemesis (think of Lenin's polemics on the relationship between class and party, first with Rosa Luxemburg, then with the left-wing communists). Its counterpart was the obsession with *partiinost'*, the unbound acceptance of the party line

VLADIMIR TISMANEANU

(philosophy, sociology, and aesthetics had to be subordinated to the party-defined "proletarian interests," hence the dichotomy between "bourgeois" and "proletarian" social science). Much of this dogmatism stemmed from Russian authoritarian traditions and the lack of a culture of public debate. Remember Antonio Gramsci's reflections on Russia's "gelatinous" civil society and the omnipotence of the bureaucratic state? Wasn't Lenin himself, by the end of his life, terrified by the resurgence of the time-honored traditions of rudeness, violence, brutality, and hypocrisy that he had lambasted and against which the revolution was presumably directed?

Now, in dealing with the impact of Russian ideas and practices on the West, there is always a problem: What Russian tradition do we refer to? The Decembrist or the czarist-autocratic one? Chaadaev or Gogol? Turgenev or Dostoyevski? The liberal humanists who opposed the pogroms and the blood libel or the Black Hundreds? Vladimir Korolenko or Konstantin Pobedonostsev? The bolshevik apocalyptical scenario or the Menshevik evolutionary socialism? The terrorist rejection of status quo, the intelligentsia's perpetual self-flagellation and outrage, or the dissident vision of a liberated polis? And even within the dissident culture, there has always been a tension between the liberals and the nationalists, between the supporters of Andrei Sakharov and those of Igor Shafarevich. All these questions remain as troubling now as they were one hundred years ago. Once again, Russia is confronted with the eternal questions "What is to be done?" and "Who is to be blamed?" And, whether they admit it or not, all participants in the debate are haunted by Lenin's inescapable presence. Lenin was the most influential Russian political personality of the twentieth century, and for Eastern Europeans, Lenin's influence resulted in the complete transformation of their life worlds. It would be easy to simply say that Leninism succumbed in the events of 1989–91, but the truth is that residual bolshevism continues to be a major component of the hybrid transitional culture of post-Soviet Russia (and East Central Europe). The major theme of the Richard Pipes-Martin Malia controversy is thus important not only for our interpretation of Russian modern history but also for the discussion of the nature and future of left-wing, socialist politics in the twenty-first century: was it Russia that destroyed (compromised) socialism, as Pipes and, earlier, Max Weber put it, or rather was it revolutionary socialism that, because of its political, indeed metaphysical, hubris, imposed immense sufferings on Russia?[24] Thus, objecting to young Georg Lukacs's celebration of Lenin's takeover of power in Russia, Weber insisted on the impossibility of building up the socialism Karl Marx had envisioned in the absence of genuine capitalist, bourgeois, market developments: "It is with good reason," he wrote, "that the *Communist Manifesto* emphasized the *economically revolutionary* character of the bourgeois capitalist entrepreneurs. No trade-unions, much less state-socialist officials, can perform this role for us in their place."[25] Earlier than many later critics of sovietism, Weber concluded that the Leninist experiment would discredit socialism for the entire twentieth century.[26] So, is there a reason to consider Lenin's political praxis as a source of inspiration for those who look for a new political transcendence? Is it a blueprint for a resurrected radicalism, as suggested by Slavoj Zizek, who proposes the revival of the Leninist 1917 revolutionary leap into the kingdom of utopia? Reactualizing Lenin's defiance to opportunistic/conformist submission to the logic of the status quo is for Zizek the *voie royale* for restoring a radical praxis:

> *This* is the Lenin from whom we still have something to learn. The greatness of Lenin was that in this catastrophic situation, *he wasn't afraid to succeed*—in contrast to the negative pathos discernible in Rosa Luxemburg and Adorno, for whom the ultimate authentic act is the admission of the failure, which brings the truth of the situation to light. In 1917, instead of waiting until the time was ripe, Lenin organized a pre-emptive strike; in 1920, as the leader of the party of the working class with no working class (most of it being decimated in the civil war), he went on organizing a state, fully accepting the paradox of the party which was to organize—even recreate—its own base, its working class.[27]

Compare this exalted vision of Lenin to former communist ideologue Alexander Yakovlev's indictment of Lenin's essential role in the establishment of a dictatorial regime in which the working class was to suffer as much as other social strata the effects of utopian social engineering.[28] Can Leninism be separated from the institution of the vanguard party and be conceived as a form of intellectual and moral resistance to the conformist debacle of the international left at a moment of civilizational collapse (World War I)? The debate on Leninism bears upon the possibility of radical-emancipatory practice and the need to reconstruct areas of autonomy in opposition to the logic of instrumental rationality. The burning question remains whether such efforts are predestined to end up in new coercive undertakings, or whether Leninism was a peculiar, sui generis combination of Marxism and an underdeveloped political and economic structure. Indeed, as Trotsky insisted, the defeat of "world revolution"—after all, the main strategic postulate on which Lenin had built his whole revolutionary adventure—made the rise of Stalinism a sociological and political necessity. Here we may remember Isaac Deutscher's analysis:

VLADIMIR TISMANEANU

Under Lenin, Bolshevism had been accustomed to appeal to reason, the self-interest, and the enlightened idealism of "class-conscious" industrial workers. It spoke the language of reason even when it appealed to the *muzhiks*. But once Bolshevism had ceased to rely on revolution in the West, once it had lost the sense of its elevation above its native environment, once it had become aware that it could only fall back on that environment and dig itself in, it began to descend to the level of primitive magic, and to appeal to the people in the language of that magic.[29]

How does one make sense of the fact that, unlike all other Eastern European societies, Russia is the only one that seems unable to restore precommunist traditions and parties? Where are the Socialist Revolutionaries, Kadets, mensheviks, or even bolsheviks? The answer is that, whatever one says or thinks about the final disintegration of Leninism, it was a quite successful experiment in reshaping political community according to a certain interpretation of social science.[30] As Louis Althusser once put it, Leninism was not a new philosophy of praxis, but a new praxis of philosophy. In fact, this meant that a group of self-appointed revolutionary pedagogues managed to coerce a large population to accept their obsessions as the inexorable imperative of History. Indeed, as Vassily Grossman's novel *Life and Fate* poignantly reveals, there was no significant distinction between the way the denizens of the Soviet world and the subjects of the Nazi dictatorship experienced ideology and power (which, of course, does not mean that the ideologies were identical, but simply that what Steven Lukes calls "moral blindness" functioned in both systems).

Yet one needs to be very cautious in writing Leninism's definitive obituary. Yes, as a Russian model of socialism it is exhausted, but there is something in Leninism—if you want, its antidemocratic, collectivist pathos associated with the invention of the party as a mystical body transcending individual fears, anguishes, despair, loneliness, etc.—that remains with us. All political figures in post-Soviet Russia—all parties, movements, and associations—define themselves, and must do so, in relationship to Lenin's legacies. In this respect, as an organizational principle, not as a worldview, Leninism is alive, if not well. Ideologically it is extinct, of course, but its repudiation of democratic deliberation and contempt for "sentimental bourgeois values" has not vanished. This is because the cult of the organization and the contempt for individual rights is part and parcel of *one* direction within the "Russian tradition" (I have doubts that one can speak of *the* Russian tradition, or, together with Hélène Carrère d'Encausse, of *le malheur russe*, etc.). Russian memory includes a plurality of trends, and one should avoid any kind of Manichean taxonomy. It is doubtless that, as Nikolai Berdyaev noticed, there is something deeply Russian in the love for the ultimate, universally cathartic, redeeming revolution, which explains why Lenin and his followers (including the highly sophisticated philosophers Georg Lukacs and Ernst Bloch) did embrace a certain cataclysmic, Messianic, absolutist direction within the Marxian tradition.[31] At the same time, one should place Leninism in contradistinction to other versions of Marxism, at least as legitimate if not more legitimate than the bolshevik doctrine. It is not at all self-evident that one can derive the genocidal logic of the gulag from Marx's universalistic postulates, whereas it is quite clear that much of the Stalinist system existed in embryo in Lenin's Russia. Together with Robert C. Tucker, we should admit the heterogeneous nature of the bolshevik tradition itself and avoid the temptation of "retroactive determinism"—Stalin's Lenin was therefore only one of the possibilities implied in the Leninist project.

One can ask then, what was Lenin's unique, extraordinary innovation? What was the substance of his transformative action? Here, I think that Jowitt rather than Zizek gives the accurate answer. The charismatic vanguard party, made up of professional revolutionaries, was invented by Lenin over one hundred years ago, in 1902, when he wrote his most influential text, *What Is to Be Done?* Lars Lih, in his recent work, disagrees with the "textbook interpretation" of Leninism (the predestined-pedagogical role of the revolutionary vanguard, i.e., the Communist Party) and insists that many, if not most, Social Democrats at the beginning of the twentieth century were convinced of the need to bring consciousness to the class from "without."[32] According to Lih, the thrust of the anti-Lenin critique from other socialists was aimed not at *What Is to Be Done*, but rather at his "Letter to a Comrade," written in September 1902 and especially *One Step Forward*, published in spring 1904. But this "injection approach" (bringing consciousness from the outside, awakening a dormant proletariat) is not the thrust of Lenin's main revision of classical Marxism: it is not the educational action per se, but rather the nature of the pedagogical agent that matters in the story. This "party of a new type" symbolized what Antonio Gramsci later called the "New Prince": a new figure of the political that absorbs and incorporates the independent life of society up to the point of definitive osmosis/asphyxiation. It is, in the words of A. J. Polan, "the end of politics" via the ultimate triumph of political will. Vladimir Mayakovsky was right when he said, "When we say Lenin/We mean the Party/And when we say Party/We mean Lenin."[33] (This identification between party and leader started under Lenin and reached its ultimate expression under Stalin and Mao—in the Fascist experiments, the role of the party, and even that of ideology, was less significant.) The Leninist party is dead (it is quite ironical that the Gennady Zyuganov–style epigones of the Communist Party of the Russian Federation combine Slavophile orthodoxy, xenophobia, imperialism, and bolshevik nostalgia in a baroque nationalist-cum-egalitarian collectivistic blending). But the cult of the party as a sacred institution, the sectarian vision of a community of virtuous, ascetic, righteous individuals selflessly committed to improving the life of humanity and erecting Nikolai Chernyshevky's "Crystal Palace" *here and now* is not extinct. It explains the nature of the postcommunist transitions where the initiatives from below are still marginal, and the center of power remains, in many cases, as conspiratorial, secretive, and nondemocratic as it was in pre-Leninist and Leninist times. Is this bound to stay the same? My answer is tentatively negative; after all, the monolith was broken, the dream of communism as the secular kingdom of God has failed. The challenge remains, however, of coming to terms with Lenin's legacies and admitting that sovietism was not imposed by extraterrestrial aliens on an innocent intelligentsia, but rather found its causes, origins, and most propitious ground in the radical segments of the Russian political culture.[34] To put it simply, the Third International and the major schism within the world Marxist movement were the consequences of Lenin's defiant gesture, his seizure of power in the fall of 1917. "History will not forgive us if we don't do it" was, again, a personalization of an alleged historical necessity.

The twentieth century was one of revolutions and counterrevolutions, and the bolshevik takeover of power in October 1917 inaugurated a period of global ideological warfare that may have come to an end only with the collapse of the USSR in 1991 (the "age of extremes," as Eric Hobsbawm calls this epoch, or, to use George Lichtheim's term, later adopted by Ernst Nolte, "the European civil war").

In an important book, Claude Lefort, the distinguished French political philosopher and author of seminal studies on modern bureaucracy, Fascist and Communist totalitarianisms, the Jacobin tradition, as well as Machiavelli's thought,[35] proposes a deliberately controversial thesis. Engaging in a polemic with both François Furet *(Le passé d'une illusion)* and Martin Malia *(The Soviet Tragedy)*, Lefort maintains that bolshevism (or, in general, twentieth-century communism) was not simply an ideological mirage (illusion, chimera, delusion, etc.).[36] Ideology mattered enormously, as Solzhenitsyn, on whom Lefort wrote extensively, had demonstrated. But the ideological passion alone, or the frantic will to impose a utopian blueprint, cannot explain the longevity and intensity of the communist phenomenon. In the spirit of French sociology (Emile Durkheim and Marcel Mauss), it would be fruitful to regard communism as "total social fact." The totalitarian system can be seen not only as an emotional-intellectual superstructure but also as an institutional ensemble inspired by these passions. In other words, it is not the original Marxism as constituted in the Western revolutionary tradition that explains the Soviet tragedy but rather the mutation introduced by Lenin.

There is, undoubtedly, an authoritarian propensity at the heart of the Marxian project, but the idea of the ultracentralized, sectarian, extremely militarized party, a minority of knowledgeable "chosen ones" who possess the gnosis while preaching egalitarian rhetoric to the masses, is directly linked to Lenin's intervention in the evolution of Russian and European Social Democracy. Lenin's revolutionary novelty consists in the cult of the dogma and the elevation of the party to the level of uniquely legitimate interpreter of the revealed truth (a major distinction of right-wing revolutionary totalitarian movements). Indeed, Lenin carried to an extreme the idea of a privileged relation between "revolutionary theory" and "practice." The latter constitutes (substantiates) itself in the figure of the presumably infallible party, custodian of an omniscience ("epistemic infallibility," to use Giuseppe di Palma's term) that defines and exorcises any doubt as a form of treason.

In opposition to those authors who are still ready to grant Marxism and even Leninism a certain legitimacy in their claims to liberal-democratic pedigrees, it is essential to recognize (together with Lefort, but also with Cornelius Castoriadis, and, much earlier, Rosa Luxemburg, Karl Kautsky, Anton Pannekoek, and Boris Souvarine) that bolshevism is inherently inimical to political liberties. It is not a deviation from the democratic project but its direct and unequivocal opposite. Thus, Lefort quotes Alexis de Tocqueville: "To grant the epithet of democratic to a government that denies political freedom to its citizens is a blatant absurdity." The annihilation of democracy within the Leninist practice is determined by the nature of the party as a secular substitute for the unifying totalizing mystique in the political body of the absolute sovereign (the medieval king). In other words, the Leninist model breaks with the Enlightenment tradition and reasserts the integral homogenization of the social space as a political and pragmatic ideal. There is therefore no way to democratize Leninist regimes, precisely because the doctrine's original intention is to organize total domination.

Here lies the essence of the Leninist (or communist) question: the insti-

VLADIMIR TISMANEANU

tution of the monolithic, unique party that emerges as a "besieged fortress" after 1903 (the great schism between bolsheviks and mensheviks) acquires planetary dimensions after 1917. Marxism, converted and adjusted by Lenin, ceases to be a revolutionary doctrine aiming at grasping/conceiving *(begreifen)* reality, and becomes an ideological body that requires from militants a discipline of action that makes them "members of a collective body." Thus, bolshevism adds to nineteenth-century revolutionary mythologies something new: the inclusion of power in a type of representation that defines the party as a magical entity. It is thus important to keep in mind the significance of the political and symbolic structures of Leninism, the underpinnings that ensured its success as an ideological state (Weltanschauungstaat). No matter how we look into this story, Lenin's celebration of the party's predestined status, together with his obsessive insistence on conspiratorial forms of organization (the revolutionary "cells") and the cult of fanatic regimentation, have initiated a new form of political radicalism, irreconcilable with the Western individualistic liberal tradition or, for that matter, with antiauthoritarian, democratic (liberal) socialism. Zizek's proposed "return to Lenin" means simply a return to a politics of irresponsibility, a resurrection of a political ghost whose main legacies are related to the limitation, rather than the expansion, of democratic experimentation; after all, it was Lenin who suppressed direct democracy in the form of councils, disbanded the embryonic Russian parliament, and transformed terror into a privileged instrument for preserving power. Once again, when Hitler destroyed the Weimar constitutional system and abolished all "bourgeois freedoms," he imitated the bolshevik precedent of the permanent emergency syndrome as a justification for legitimizing the destruction of legality and the elimination, including the physical annihilation, of all those regarded as "objective" obstacles to the building of a perfect, organic community.

NOTES

1. See Slavoj Zizek, *Did Somebody Say Totalitarianism?* (London: Verso, 2001), 116.

2. See, in this respect, Bertram Wolfe, "Leninism," in *Marxism in the Modern World,* ed. Milorad M. Drachkovitch (Stanford: Stanford University Press, 1965), 47–89.

3. See Andrzej Walicki, *Marxism and the Leap into the Kingdom of Freedom* (Stanford: Stanford University Press, 1995), 269–397 (hereafter cited as *Marxism*).

4. See my book *Fantasies of Salvation: Nationalism, Democracy, and Myth in Post-Communist Europe* (Princeton, NJ: Princeton University Press, 1998).

5. Harry Kreisler, "The Individual, Charisma, and the Leninist Extinction," brochure, A Conversation with Ken Jowitt (Berkeley: Institute of International Studies, 2000).

6. Ken Jowitt, *New World Disorder: The Leninist Extinction* (Berkeley: University of California Press, 1992), 49.

7. See the quotations on Lenin and terror in Kostas Papaioannou's excellent anthology *Marx et les marxistes* (Paris: Gallimard, 2001), 314.

8. Leszek Kolakowski, *Main Currents of Marxism*, vol. 3, *The Breakdown* (Oxford: Oxford University Press, 1978), 90.

9. Piatakov quoted in Walicki, *Marxism*, 461

10. See Steven Lukes, "On the Moral Blindness of Communism," *Human Rights Review* 2, no. 2 (January–March 2001), 120.

11. Ibid., 121.

12. Ibid., 123.

13. See Martin Amis, *Koba the Dread: Laughter and the Twenty Million* (New York: Hyperion, 2002), 90.

14. Mikhail Gorbachev and Zdenek Mlynař, *Conversations with Gorbachev on Perestroika, the Prague Spring, and the Crossroads of Socialism* (New York: Columbia University Press, 2002).

15. Jowitt, *New World Disorder*, 10.

16. See A. J. Polan, *Lenin and the End of Politics* (Berkeley: University of California Press, 1984), 73. For the relationship between Leninism and Marxist eschatology, see Igal Halfin, *From Darkness to Light: Class, Consciousness, and Salvation in Revolutionary Russia* (Pittsburgh: Pittsburgh University Press, 2000).

17. Elena Bonner, "The Remains of Totalitarianism," *New York Review of Books*, March 8, 2001, 4.

18. Ibid., 5.

19. See Alain Besançon, *The Rise of the Gulag: The Intellectual Origins of Leninism* (New York: Continuum, 1981); and J. L. Talmon, *Myth of the Nation and Vision of the Revolution: Ideological Polarizations in the Twentieth Century* (New Brunswick, NJ: Transaction, 1991).

20. See Paul Berman, *Terror and Liberalism* (New York: Norton, 2003).

21. See Pierre Hassner, "Par-delà l'histoire et la mémoire," in *Stalinisme et nazisme: Histoire et mémoire comparées*, ed. Henry Rousso (Paris: Editions Complexe, 1999), 355–70. These topics have been luminously explored in the writings of François Furet, Cornelius Castoriadis, Ferenc Feher, and Claude Lefort.

22. See Isaiah Berlin, *The Crooked Timber of Humanity: Chapters in the History of Ideas* (New York: Knopf, 1991), 91–174.

23. Berman, *Terror and Liberalism*, 50.

24. See Martin Malia, *The Soviet Tragedy* (New York: Free Press, 1994); see also Mikhail Heller and Aleksandr Nekrich, *Utopia in Power: The History of the Soviet Union from 1917 to the Present* (New York: Summit Books, 1986); and Richard Pipes, *The Russian Revolution* (New York: Vintage, 1990).

VLADIMIR TISMANEANU

25. Quoted by John Patrick Diggins, *Max Weber: Politics and the Spirit of Tragedy* (New York: Basic Books, 1996), 239.

26. Ibid., 230.

27. See "Introduction: Between The Two Revolutions," in *Revolution at the Gates: Selected Writings of Lenin from 1917*, ed. Slavoj Zizek (London: Verso, 2002), 6.

28. See Alexander Yakovlev, *A Century of Violence in Soviet Russia* (New Haven, CT: Yale University Press, 2002); see also my review of Yakovlev's book, "Apostate Apparatchik," *Times Literary Supplement*, February 21, 2003, 26.

29. See Isaac Deutscher, "Marxism and Primitive Magic," in *The Stalinist Legacy: Its Impact on 20th Century World Politics*, ed. Tariq Ali (Harmondsworth, UK: Penguin Books, 1984), 113–14.

30. See Daniel Chirot, "What Was Communism All About?" (review essay on *The Black Book of Communism*), *East European Politics and Societies* 14, no. 3 (Fall 2000): 665–75.

31. Gorbachev's former chief ideologue, Alexander Yakovlev, writes about this in his otherwise uneven and vehement contribution to *Du passé nous faisons table rase! Histoire et mémoire du communisme en Europe*, ed. Stéphane Courtois (Paris: Robert Laffont, 2002), 173–210.

32. See Lars T. Lih, "How a Founding Document Was Found, or One Hundred Years of Lenin's *What is To be Done?*" *Kritika: Explorations in Russian and Eurasian History* 4, no. 1 (Winter 2003), 5–49.

33. Mayakovsky wrote these verses in his poem "Vladimir Ilyich Lenin," in Vladimir Mayakovsky, *Moia revolutsia* (Moscow: Sovremennik Publishers, 1974).

34. In addition to Jowitt's contributions, see Robert C. Tucker, *The Soviet Political Mind* (New York: Norton, 1971); and Robert Conquest, *Reflections on a Ravaged Century* (New York: Norton, 2000).

35. For an excellent analysis of Lefort's writings, see Dick Howard, *The Specter of Democracy* (New York: Columbia University Press, 2002), 71–82.

36. See Claude Lefort, *La complication: Retour sur le communisme* (Paris: Fayard, 1999).

2

THE LENINIST LEGACY REVISITED

MARC MORJÉ HOWARD

F ew articles or books—much less chapters in edited volumes—in the
field of postcommunist studies have had the impact of Ken Jowitt's
"The Leninist Legacy." Originally published in a book edited by Ivo
Banac,[1] Jowitt's essay raised a strident challenge to the newly ascendant "transitions to democracy" literature. In his piece, Jowitt strongly criticized self-
proclaimed "transitologists," who tended to stress general universal factors
in democratization, while overlooking (or ignoring) the particular effect
of the communist past on postcommunist transformation. In stark contrast
to the reigning optimism of the early 1990s, Jowitt argued that the emerging political and economic order in Eastern Europe would be considerably,
and negatively, shaped by the "inheritance" bequeathed by decades of communist rule. Moreover, he predicted that the "transitions" under way in most
postcommunist countries were more likely to result in fragmentation and
failure than in successful democracy and market capitalism.

Jowitt's essay (which was later reprinted in several different forms, most
notably in his 1992 book, *New World Disorder*[2]) has had a remarkable shelf
life, particularly since it addresses the events of a period of rapid change
and tremendous uncertainty shortly before the final collapse of the Soviet
Union and at the onset of the newly invigorated European Union. Indeed,
one is hard-pressed to think of other works published during that tumultuous time period that have been so consistently cited, from the time when
they were written to the present. Over the first few years after publication,

Jowitt's piece was widely discussed by Eastern Europeanists, who incorporated the concept of the Leninist legacy into their counterarguments to the transitologists about the distinctiveness of the communist and postcommunist experiences, as opposed to other "transitions" in Southern Europe, Latin America, and elsewhere.[3] At the time, the indisputable economic decline, political disarray, and cultural conflict in Eastern Europe during the mid-1990s all appeared to offer strong support for Jowitt's pessimistic argument, which many viewed as having been prescient, at least in part, and also courageous for its resistance to the excessive academic optimism surrounding the events of 1989.[4]

In recent years, however, Jowitt's argument has been portrayed more critically (sometimes explicitly, more often implicitly), as many scholars—whether specialists on Eastern Europe or other regions—have been emphasizing the *diversity* of postcommunist outcomes, measured along a series of different criteria.[5] These studies stress that while some countries have clearly struggled with the legacies of communism, others seem to have proceeded relatively unburdened along the path to democratic stability and consolidation. In other words, the emergence of "success stories"—particularly in Poland, Hungary, and the Czech Republic, but also in Slovenia and the Baltic states—has been thought to provide evidence that the Leninist legacy argument has not withstood the test of time.

Although academic fashion would seem to dictate that Jowitt's legacy argument is now passé, intellectual curiosity should encourage a closer reading of Jowitt's original essay, to see if his claims have been accurately portrayed (and, by extension, critiqued). Was his characterization of a singular, common legacy as simplistic as it is sometimes depicted, such that it is immediately falsified by the observation of variation within the postcommunist region? Were Jowitt's predictions as absolute and catastrophic as they are often presented? And what, if any, is the continuing relevance of his contribution?

This chapter takes a fresh look at Jowitt's argument, based primarily on a careful rereading and rethinking of the piece itself—with the benefit of more than a decade of hindsight. My purpose in doing so is to distance myself from the many ways in which Jowitt's piece has been summarized, analyzed, and critiqued by others, and to return to the source itself, in order to understand it *on its own terms.* I start by recapitulating the key points of Jowitt's argument about the Leninist legacy, as well as his predictions about its likely effects on Eastern Europe. Then I address the important—yet often misunderstood—issue of whether Jowitt's argument is meant to apply to all postcommunist societies in the same way and to the same degree, or whether he leaves room for variation in terms of processes, paths, and outcomes. Finally, I assess the extent to which "The Leninist Legacy" has held up empirically over the last fifteen years.

In short, after presenting the argument in a way that is faithful to its original words and intent, I then move to a more independent evaluation of its insightfulness and predictive accuracy. I argue that while Jowitt's detractors are correct in asserting that few of his most dire predictions about Eastern Europe have come to pass, this is because of the surprisingly assertive and supportive role played by the European Union (EU)—a development that Jowitt actually called for in his 1991 essay, but (like most observers at the time) did not expect would be forthcoming. Nonetheless, I suggest that even in the eight or more postcommunist countries that have recently been "adopted" by the EU, Jowitt's overall description of the Leninist legacy, and its effects on individuals and societies, still largely holds true. Finally, I conclude that "The Leninist Legacy" continues to have a lasting (albeit often indirect) influence on debates about the relative importance of historical versus contemporary factors in explaining postcommunist developments.

THE LEGACY ARGUMENT

Jowitt's depiction of the Leninist legacy contains a number of interrelated features. The most important involves the lasting distinction between public and private realms, which were central to everyday life in communist societies. As Jowitt writes, "The Leninist experience in Eastern Europe (and elsewhere) reinforced the exclusive distinction and dichotomic antagonism between the official and private realms."[6] In other words, with a public sphere that was entirely controlled by the Communist Party and its corollary organizational apparatus—including the secret police, the trade union, and many mass-membership organizations—most communist citizens developed a cautious relationship to public and formal activities. Private relations, in contrast, became even more vibrant and meaningful, since people could only speak openly in front of others they knew and trusted, and also because connections took on an important role in the shortage economy, where people had to rely on their family, friends, and acquaintances in order to get things done, rather than going through official channels.[7]

The corollary of this stark distinction between public and private was the development of a widespread behavior based on *dissimulation,* whereby individuals and groups became remarkably adept at publicly misrepresenting their private thoughts and actions. Jowitt argues that "dissimulation became the effective . . . bond between the domineering official and

MARC MORJÉ HOWARD

societal supplicant during the entire period of Leninist rule."[8] Dissimulation became a way of coping, getting by, and advancing one's career in a world in which the official presentation of public life had little to do with everyday private reality.[9]

Another consequence of the public/private division was "the central place of rumor as covert political discourse," which "had and continues to have a debilitating effect in political life. It divides, frightens, and angers those who participate in what amounts to a chronic mode of semihysterical (pre)political speech."[10] While, of course, rumors exist in all countries, the deep estrangement of communist societies from their institutions and leaders, along with chronic economic shortages and political deception, led to the emergence of rumor as a central part of political and social life.[11]

A final feature that constitutes Jowitt's Leninist legacy has to do with the fragmentation of the polity and society. According to Jowitt, "the Eastern European polities were fragmented, not integrated: fragmented into mutually exclusive official and private realms bridged by mutually deceptive presentations of their respective 'selves.'"[12] This societal fragmentation led people—elites and ordinary citizens alike—to think primarily in terms of narrow individual self-interest, rather than about the larger public good.[13]

Ultimately, Jowitt argues, what was lacking in communist societies was "a culture of impersonal measured action." Moreover, in the aftermath of what Jowitt calls the "Leninist extinction," the result is that postcommunist societies have "very little experience with regular, deliberate economic and political activity in a context of impersonal procedures." Even in extraordinary cases—such as Adam Michnik and Solidarity in Poland or Václav Havel and Civic Forum in Czechoslovakia—where the private ethics of several individuals were transferred to their leadership roles, Jowitt argues that these private virtues could not successfully be institutionalized in the public realm.[14] Overall, Jowitt characterizes the Leninist legacy as "a worldview in which political life is suspect, distasteful, and possibly dangerous; to be kept at bay by dissimulation, made tolerable by private intimacy, and transcended by private virtues or charismatic ethics."[15]

In terms of his predictions for the future, Jowitt emphasizes the "fragility" of democratic politics in postcommunist countries, which (with the possible exception of Poland) do not have "established successor elites" to lead their societies in a decisively democratic direction.[16] This absence, according to Jowitt, will likely increase the "maelstrom quality of life throughout the area." Jowitt also argues that "fragmentation"—in many different forms—will increase in the immediate future: the *emotional* fragmentation of the populations, the *ethnic and territorial* fragmentation of several countries (he mentions Yugoslavia, Moldova, and Czechoslovakia), the *demographic* fragmentation that will result from the brain drain of emigration, and the *political* fragmentation caused by the instability of ruling parties and coalitions.[17] In short, Jowitt argues that "today Eastern Europe is a *brittle* region. Suspicion, division, and fragmentation predominate, not coalition and integration. Sooner rather than later, attitudes, programs, and forces will appear demanding and promising unity."[18]

Jowitt does not simply assert that the new postcommunist democracies will be fragile because of the absence of public virtues and societal integration. He goes on to argue that antidemocratic forces will soon emerge, and that they will become much more powerful and influential than their democratic counterparts. And he adds that "Eastern European fragmentation offers a firmer foundation for transiting to some form of authoritarian oligarchy (in response to perceptions of anarchy) than to democracy."[19] More specifically, Jowitt views two organizations as having the potential to undermine postcommunist democracy: the Catholic Church and the military. As "the maelstrom develops," Jowitt argues, the national armies in particular will "become more self-aware, confident, and assertive."[20] In an oft-cited passage, Jowitt predicts that "it will be demagogues, priests, and colonels more than democrats and capitalists who will shape Eastern Europe's general institutional identity."[21]

ONE LEGACY OR MANY?

Since the title of Jowitt's essay invokes a singular legacy—*the* Leninist legacy—it is perhaps tempting to dismiss it as too great a generalization, as a homogenizing argument that assumes that all postcommunist countries are the same, and that they face identical problems and challenges. Yet a careful reading of his essay reveals a more nuanced perspective.

On the one hand, Jowitt does place greater emphasis on the underlying similarity within the post-communist region, particularly in response to a literature that ignored the countries' shared Leninist experience. For example, he writes, "I have obviously, if not explicitly, argued that the historical differences between countries and their current modes of transition from Leninism are not as important as the similarities."[22] On the other hand, he is certainly aware of national differences, as he adds, "Now for the necessary genuflection to national differences: they exist. It is clear that different types of fragmentation will predominate in different countries, and that some will have lower thresholds of violence."[23] Jowitt pays particular

MARC MORJÉ HOWARD

attention to the case of Poland, which he views as "the one genuine exception."[24] And he also stresses that the impact of such anti-democratic factors as the Catholic Church and the military "may vary decisively from country to country."[25]

In other words, Jowitt is much more *aware* of national differences than his critics have given him credit for; he simply chooses to *emphasize* the common underlying problems that he thinks most countries in the region are likely to face. For example, he argues quite clearly that "today the *dominant and shared* Eastern European reality is severe and multiple fragmentation."[26] And he predicts that "the likelihood is that most [experiments] will fail, but some will succeed, and many of those will have predominantly anti-democratic capitalist features. Whatever the results of the current turmoil in Eastern Europe, one thing is clear: the new institutional patterns will be shaped by the 'inheritance' and legacy of forty years of Leninist rule."[27] In short, while Jowitt clearly understands that there will be multiple legacies across countries, he still chooses to highlight one overarching, fundamental legacy that most postcommunist countries will share—even though that legacy may take on different forms in different countries.

PREDICTIONS

It is indisputable that Jowitt's most Jeremiah-like predictions have not become a reality, at least not in the "Eastern Europe" to which he devotes most of his piece. Indeed, most of the countries in Eastern Europe discussed in "The Leninist Legacy" have not followed Jowitt's predicted path. The brutal fragmentation of Yugoslavia did not lead to a regional conflict that spread through the Balkans. Czechoslovakia split up peacefully, not violently. The Catholic Church, along with all other forms of organized religion, remains an anemic, not a powerful, force throughout the region (perhaps even in Poland). And national armies have not become more assertive in seeking to unify their societies. In this sense, Jowitt's predictions from 1991 clearly have their limitations.

One should point out, though, that even though they were not published in his "Leninist Legacy" essay, Jowitt's arguments about "movements of rage" have been frighteningly accurate. Indeed, when one looks at much of the non-Western world, one finds what Jowitt defined as "violent nativist responses to failure, frustration, and perplexity."[28] The rise of Al Qaeda and its many corollaries in Afghanistan and around the world have shown that the "extinction" of communism has led to a world of more disorder and violence, as Jowitt had predicted, rather than liberal democracy.

Moreover, the "re-Sovietization" of regimes throughout Central Asia and much of the Caucasus region has followed a form and logic that fit Jowitt's legacy prediction quite well.

But not in "Eastern Europe" (or, rather, "Central Europe"—the now politically correct term[29]). This was certainly Jowitt's main mistake, and the one that has opened the door to so much criticism and "refutation." Had he argued that Central Europe, rather than Poland, would be the exception, scholars might been more forgiving when pointing out variation in Freedom House scores, which are thought to disprove the existence of a common legacy. But he *did* write about Eastern Europe, and he did so because of his desire to emphasize a shared past and a common culture, despite all of the other clear differences, many of which were already apparent in 1989 and historically.[30]

Nonetheless, it would be a mistake to dismiss the analysis of postcommunist societies in "The Leninist Legacy" solely based on the fact that violence and maelstrom have not engulfed Eastern Europe. On the contrary, a closer reading of Jowitt's essay shows that he actually identified one plausible, if at the time unlikely, way in which these serious problems could be averted, namely, if Western Europe would provide "a massive 'democratic subsidy'" to the countries of Eastern Europe.[31]

Jowitt goes on to elaborate this point at greater length. He asks, "Question: Is there any point of leverage, critical mass of civic effort—political, cultural, and economic—that can add its weight to civic forces in Eastern Europe and check the increasing frustration, depression, fragmentation, and anger that will lead to country- and regionwide violence of a communal type in Eastern Europe? Yes! Western Europe."[32] Revealing his pessimism about the likelihood of such a development, however, Jowitt adds, "The necessary, though not necessarily forthcoming, Western European response to the syndrome of Eastern European fragmentation is adoption; of Eastern Europe by Western Europe. . . .This would require enormous imagination, coordination, and intrusion on Western Europe's (and, in a significant way, the United States') part: a massive economic presence, provision for major population shifts on the European continent, and intracontinental party cooperation and action; all of which would substantially affect the current definition and operation of national sovereignty."[33]

Jowitt was certainly not alone in doubting that Western Europe would respond to the collapse of communism by expanding the still-struggling European Community (EC) to the east. On the contrary, the view of most analysts at the time was that the EC (which became the EU in 1992) had too many problems of its own, and that the French (and others) already

MARC MORJÉ HOWARD

had serious reservations about German unification, much less any further eastward expansion of the EC. It also appeared highly unlikely that the countries of the EC would be willing or able to change the "definition and operation of national sovereignty" that Jowitt argued would accompany any "adoption" of the postcommunist countries.

The fact that the EC/EU developed in an unlikely (some would say miraculous) way, with strong and consistent support for the incorporation of the countries of Eastern Europe, helps to explain why the outcome of Jowitt's most catastrophic predictions were averted. And since Jowitt not only explicitly mentions this (albeit slim) possibility but also calls for it as "necessary," its occurrence should certainly not be held against his argument. After all, Jowitt suggests that if this "adoption" were not forthcoming, "one alternative is for Western Europe to become liberal fortress Europe and deny its 'brother's keeper' responsibility. In that case, developments in Eastern Europe will degenerate in a frightening fashion."[34] Neither of these two developments—"fortress Europe" in the West or violent fragmentation in the East—occurred, but the former appeared likely in 1990–91, and Jowitt may well have been correct in asserting that the latter would have followed. Political elites in both Western and Eastern Europe certainly acted as though they shared such fears, and they therefore presented the theme of "Eastern enlargement" as the historic obligation of the EU. Indeed, one of the remarkable aspects of postcommunist politics—with, interestingly enough, the same underlying phenomenon taking place in otherwise quite different political situations—has been the virtual unanimity among otherwise intense political rivals about the need to do everything possible to join the EU (with NATO being viewed and used as a stepping stone toward that ultimate goal).

In short, although his dire predictions for Eastern Europe have not taken place—and in that sense one can say that he was "wrong"—Jowitt's analysis actually identifies the very reason that accounts for his failed prediction, and he strongly advocates precisely the policy development that later took place. The fact that his argument may have had at least some indirect resonance on a policy terrain that shifted fairly dramatically over the course of the 1990s could perhaps be viewed as an accomplishment, rather than a failure, of Jowitt's predictions.

CHARACTERIZATIONS

Leaving aside the issue of Jowitt's predictions for the future of Eastern Europe, his *characterizations* of postcommunist institutions and societies still have enormous relevance today. Even in some of the most "success-ful" postcommunist countries—whether one looks at political party sys-tems, market institutions, labor unions, or interest groups—the word "fragmentation" applies to each. Jowitt's depiction of Eastern Europe as a "brittle region," in which "suspicion, division, and fragmentation pre-dominate, not coalition and integration,"[35] still fits. There are of course wide differences between the countries in terms of institutional design and performance—as well as their precommunist and communist histories—but even with the support of their "adoptive parents" in the EU, they are all still struggling tremendously with their respective legacies, which result from a shared Leninist experience.

Moreover, one finds even stronger similarities among the societies of the region. Not only is participation in the organizations of civil society signifi-cantly lower in postcommunist Europe than in other regions of the world, but this phenomenon—in these otherwise institutionally diverse countries—can be explained by very similar historical and "experiential" causes that result from the shared social experience of life under communism.[36]

Indeed, Jowitt's characterization of the distinction and antagonism between public and private spheres still applies to people throughout the region, many of whom feel as alienated and detached from public activi-ties as ever. Rumor is still a widespread phenomenon, although certainly more so in some countries (especially Romania) than others. And one could even argue that the legacy of dissimulation is thriving today, as elites in particular have become "remarkably adept at publicly misrepresenting their private thoughts and actions"[37] by steadfastly exhibiting, without any apparent reservations, a positive and promising picture of their countries—often contrary to reality. In other words, while the new "object" of dis-simulation is the polar opposite of its predecessor, the inner objectives and behavior of elites may have remained very similar.

CONCLUSION: THE LEGACY OF "THE LENINIST LEGACY"

In addition to still being relevant for, and applicable to, postcommunist insti-tutions and societies, the arguments that Jowitt developed over a decade ago have had a lasting impact on the field of postcommunist studies. While many scholars have sought to disassociate themselves from his work because of its unrealized predictions about the future in Eastern Europe, his rebuttal to the reigning transitologists has, at least implicitly, reshaped the debate in the field of postcommunist studies. By going against the grain to draw atten-tion to the enduring legacy of the past, Jowitt directly or indirectly influenced

MARC MORJÉ HOWARD

other scholars, who formulated a new debate about how far back into the past one should go in explaining postcommunist developments, and whether the past or the present matters more for explaining the future. Some of them choose not to discuss his work explicitly,[38] and others give his contribution more credit,[39] but they all have had to confront the challenges that he raised to the reigning optimism of the early 1990s, when Adam Przeworski wrote that democratizing countries "are determined by a common destination, not by different points of departure."[40] Jowitt's overall contribution was to challenge scholars to address, grapple with, and take seriously Leninism as a "point of departure," and to investigate its lasting—even if varied and changing—legacy. Even when his work is oversimplified, misrepresented, or (perhaps worse) ignored, the influence of Jowitt's ideas remains strong. In this sense, just as Jowitt argued that Leninism, even after its disappearance, has left a lasting legacy in the postcommunist world, "The Leninist Legacy," even after it has stopped being cited directly, will likely continue to have a long-term influence on the field of postcommunist studies.

NOTES

1. Ivo Banac, ed., *Eastern Europe in Revolution* (Ithaca, NY: Cornell University Press, 1992), 207–24.

2. Ken Jowitt, *New World Disorder: The Leninist Extinction* (Berkeley: University of California Press, 1992), 284–305. The chapter was also published in Vladimir Tismaneanu, ed., *The Revolutions of 1989* (London: Routledge, 1999), and an abridged version was published as "The New World Disorder" in *Journal of Democracy* 2, no. 1 (Winter 1991), and later reprinted in Larry Diamond and Marc F. Plattner, eds., *The Global Resurgence of Democracy*, 1st and 2nd eds. (Baltimore: Johns Hopkins University Press, 1993 and 1996).

3. The specific elements of the legacy that scholars chose to emphasize were quite varied, including the nature and consequences of political opposition and crises; the simultaneity of postcommunist political, economic, and in some cases even national transitions; the particular institutional design of communist systems; and the attitudinal orientations and behavioral practices that developed under communism. But the historical emphasis and causal logic are similar, and the common argument is that without an understanding of the communist past, it is difficult to make sense of developments in the postcommunist present and future. See, for example, Grzegorz Ekiert, *The State Against Society: Political Crises and Their Aftermath in East Central Europe* (Princeton: Princeton University Press, 1996); Claus Offe, "Capitalism by Democratic Design? Democratic Theory Facing the Triple Transition in East Central Europe," *Social Research* 58, no. 4 (1991): 865–892; Valerie Bunce, *Subversive Institutions: The*

Design and the Destruction of Socialism and the State (Cambridge: Cambridge University Press, 1999); Steven L. Solnick, *Stealing the State: Control and Collapse in Soviet Institutions* (Cambridge, MA: Harvard University Press, 1998); Piotr Sztompka, "Civilizational Incompetence: The Trap of Post-Communist Societies," *Zeitschrift für Soziologie* 22, no. 2 (1993): 85–95; and Piotr Sztompka, "The Intangibles and Imponderables of the Transition to Democracy," *Studies in Comparative Communism* 24, no. 3 (1991), 295–311.

4. See, for example, Ellen Comisso, "Prediction Versus Diagnosis: Comments on a Ken Jowitt Retrospective," *Slavic Review* 53, no. 1 (Spring 1994): 186–92; Stephen E. Hanson, "The Leninist Legacy and Institutional Change," *Comparative Political Studies* 28, no. 2 (1995): 306–14; and Richard Rose, William Mishler, and Christian Haerpfer. *Democracy and Its Alternatives: Understanding Post-Communist Societies* (Baltimore: Johns Hopkins University Press, 1998).

5. See, for example, Jacques Rupnik, "The Postcommunist Divide," *Journal of Democracy* 10, no. 1 (1999): 57–62; Jeffrey S. Kopstein, "Postcommunist Democracy: Legacies and Outcomes," *Comparative Politics* 35, no. 2 (January 2003); Charles King, "Post-Postcommunism: Transition, Comparison, and the End of 'Eastern Europe,'" *World Politics* 53, no. 1 (2000): 143–72; Valerie Bunce, "The Political Economy of Postsocialism," *Slavic Review* 58, no. 4 (1999): 756–93; and M. Steven Fish, "Democratization's Requisites: The Postcommunist Experience," *Post-Soviet Affairs* 14, no. 3 (1998), 212–47.

6. Jowitt, "The Leninist Legacy," in *New World Disorder,* 287. Note that all page references in this chapter refer to the *New World Disorder* version of Jowitt's chapter.

7. For studies that draw on Jowitt's public/private distinction, see Alena V. Ledeneva, *Russia's Economy of Favours: Blat, Networking, and Informal Exchange* (Cambridge: Cambridge University Press, 1998); and Marc Morjé Howard, *The Weakness of Civil Society in Post-Communist Europe* (Cambridge: Cambridge University Press, 2003).

8. Jowitt, "The Leninist Legacy," 288.

9. See Oleg Kharkhordin, "The Soviet Individual: Genealogy of a Dissimulating Animal," in *The Global Modernities,* ed. Roland Robertson (New York: Sage, 1995); Oleg Kharkhordin, "Reveal and Dissimulate: A Genealogy of Private Life in Soviet Russia," in *Public and Private in Thought and Practice,* ed. Jeff Weintraub and Krishnan Kumar (Chicago: University of Chicago Press, 1997).

10. Jowitt, "The Leninist Legacy," 289.

11. See also Vladimir Tismaneanu, *Fantasies of Salvation: Democracy, Nationalism, and Myth in Post-Communist Europe* (Princeton, NJ: Princeton University Press, 1998).

12. Jowitt, "The Leninist Legacy," 290.

13. This is a theme that Jowitt developed in his earlier work as well. See in particular "Soviet Neotraditionalism: The Political Corruption of a Leninist Regime," *Soviet Studies* 35, no. 3 (July 1983): 275–97, which was also reprinted as "Neotraditionalism" in *New World Disorder,* 121–58.

14. Jowitt, "The Leninist Legacy," 291–93.

15. Ibid., 293.

16. Ibid., 294–95.

17. Ibid., 294–99.

18. Ibid., 298.

19. Ibid., 300.

20. Ibid., 301.

21. Ibid., 300.

22. Ibid., 299.

23. Ibid., 299–300.

24. Ibid., 299.

25. Ibid., 301.

26. Ibid., 300 (emphasis in original).

27. Ibid., 285.

28. Jowitt, "The Leninist Extinction," in *New World Disorder*, 275. This chapter was first published in *The Crisis of Leninism and the Decline of the Left: The Revolutions of 1989*, ed. Daniel Chirot (Seattle: University of Washington Press, 1991).

29. In fact, many scholars (and editors) now insist on using the lowercase for "central Europe" or "western Europe," to emphasize that the modifier is strictly geographic, not political or historical. But this overcorrection misses the point that those who work on regions such as "South Asia" or "Central America" continue to capitalize them. And, of course, this new academic "correct line" is also intended as an attempt to wipe away the political/historical dimension of Europe's geography—as if that were possible!

30. There is a certain disingenuousness to the way in which some people refute the legacy argument by setting up the expectation that all postcommunist countries are exactly the same and by suggesting that the big "surprise" that must be explained is that they are actually different. But an analysis of economic differences in the entire postcommunist region shows that, while these differences have certainly increased over the last decade or more, the "rank order" has for the most part remained unchanged. In other words, while the differences have certainly grown, they were already there. And to imply that all countries had the same starting point—much less the same geography—is misleading at best. For an analysis of the economic changes over the first postcommunist decade, see Valerie Bunce, "The Political Economy of Postsocialism," *Slavic Review* 58, no. 4 (Winter 1999): 756–93; for an analysis of the powerful effect of geography within the region, see Jeffrey S. Kopstein and David A. Reilly, "Geographic Diffusion and the Transformation of the Postcommunist World," *World Politics* 53, no. 1 (October 2000): 1–37.

31. Jowitt, "The Leninist Legacy," 301.

32. Ibid., 304.

33. Ibid., 304–5.

34. Ibid., 305.

35. Ibid., 298.

36. Howard, *The Weakness of Civil Society.*

37. These were the words I used above to summarize Jowitt's argument about dissimulation during the communist time period.

38. See, for example, Herbert Kitschelt, Zdenka Mansfeldova, Radoslaw Markowski, and Gábor Tóka, *Post-Communist Party Systems: Competition, Representation, and Inter-Party Cooperation* (Cambridge: Cambridge University Press, 1999); David Stark and László Bruszt. *Postsocialist Pathways: Transforming Politics and Property in East Central Europe* (Cambridge: Cambridge University Press, 1998); and Bunce, *Subversive Institutions.*

39. See, for example, Kopstein, "Postcommunist Democracy"; Juan J. Linz and Alfred Stepan. *Problems of Democratic Transition and Consolidation: Southern Europe, South America, and Post-Communist Europe* (Baltimore: Johns Hopkins University Press, 1996); and especially many of the contributions in *Capitalism and Democracy in Central and Eastern Europe: Assessing the Legacy of Communist Rule,* ed. Grzegorz Ekiert and Stephen E. Hanson (Cambridge: Cambridge University Press, 2004).

40. Adam Przeworksi, *Democracy and the Market: Political and Economic Reforms in Eastern Europe and Latin America* (Cambridge: Cambridge University Press, 1991), xii.

3

TRANSITION TO WHAT?

Legacies and Reform Trajectories after Communism

GRIGORE POP-ELECHES

The passage of sixteen years since the collapse of communism in Eastern Europe provides a good vantage point not only for assessing the social and political trajectories of ex-communist countries but also for revisiting one of the most original and influential perspectives on the "transition," Ken Jowitt's "The Leninist Legacy." This essay analyzes to what extent a common Leninist legacy persists in the social and political fabric of the former communist countries, and discusses how this legacy can be reconciled with the dramatic divergence of developmental paths among the countries in that region. Specifically, I will focus on the degree to which precommunist cultural and developmental differences survived the homogenizing influence of communism, and how these differences were exacerbated by the peculiar nature of the Western approach to conditionality and integration in the post–cold war era.

Before launching into an empirical assessment of the theoretical half-life of some of the predictions advanced in several essays of Jowitt's book *New World Disorder—The Leninist Extinction*, let us briefly recall the intellectual backdrop against which Jowitt's theories developed. Politically, the late 1980s and early 1990s were marked by the triumph of Western liberalism over its last great ideological challenger, Marxism-Leninism, leading many observers to predict a widespread institutional convergence to Western liberal capitalism resulting in what Francis Fukuyama termed "the end of history." In the economic sphere, the widely (if not universally) accepted

Washington Consensus expected that with the retrenchment of the state from economic planning, liberal capitalist institutions would naturally emerge regardless of structural differences. Meanwhile, in political science the predominant theoretical approach to the study of democratization, drawing largely on the Latin American and southern European experiences, rejected earlier efforts to identify the structural preconditions for democracy and focused instead on more proximate explanations, such as elite politics, institutional design, and democratic crafting.[1] While most authors acknowledged that structural differences existed and could potentially be relevant, their overall approach towards legacies nevertheless embodied Adam Przeworski's view that democratization is defined not by the point of departure but by the end goal—democracy.[2]

As such, Jowitt's unequivocal insistence that "the Leninist legacy is currently shaping, and will continue to shape, developmental efforts and outcomes in Eastern Europe"[3] stood out as a fairly isolated skeptical voice amid the "possibilism" of the early 1990s. In fact, Jowitt's claim that Western liberal capitalism was only one—and a rather unlikely—possible endpoint of the postcommunist transformation questioned the very utility of "postcommunist transition" as an analytical concept.[4] After all, transition implies a common evolution *away* from a starting point (communist-style command economies and one-party rule) and *towards* some presumed endpoint, defined more or less explicitly as Western-style liberal democracy and capitalism. Moreover, by predicting that prolonged turmoil and (predominantly antidemocratic) political experiments would likely emerge from the rubble of Leninism,[5] Jowitt questioned another central component of the transition discourse—the notion of a return to a (however vaguely defined) *normality*. This expectation of normality was an understandable psychological reaction to the trauma of communism and the chaos of the early postcommunist period, and was initially fueled by the optimism of the "return to Europe" rhetoric.

Seen from this perspective, the theoretical debate between Jowitt's legacy-based approach and the transitions-to-democracy school boils down to the question of the degree to which the political outcomes in the former communist countries can be characterized as being "normal," and to what extent this normality corresponds to the theoretical blueprints envisioned by the two approaches. This essay first offers a broad empirical assessment of the relative normality of different countries of the former Soviet bloc. Having established the unevenness of postcommunist normalization, the discussion then turns to the factors that can help us explain cross-national divergence. Finally, I will discuss the theoretical implications of

GRIGORE POP-ELECHES

these explanations for assessing the continued relevance of Leninist legacies in understanding the politics of postcommunism.

Before interpreting the nature of the political and socio-economic constellations after a decade and a half of change, it is worth noting that the
speed of political and economic change has indeed slowed down in many
postcommunist countries, implying the achievement of a steady state—
a crucial component for "normal" polities and economies. Nevertheless,
as recent events in Georgia and Ukraine suggest, many of the postcommunist regimes, particularly in the Balkans and the non-Baltic Soviet
Union, are far from stable, let alone consolidated. Such instability, which
has important contagion potential, is likely to be exacerbated by broader
international crises, such as Afghanistan in the case of the Central Asian
republics. Given that political elites still suffer from a profound legitimacy
deficit even in the region's more democratic countries, fundamental challenges to the existing political order—whether in the form of extremist/
anti-systemic political parties or movements of rage (like the miners'
revolt in Romania in 1999)—should not be completely discounted.[6]

With regard to outcomes, the events of the last fifteen years have made
it abundantly clear that normality has taken very different shapes in different countries. Thus, eight ex-communist countries have recently joined
the European Union (EU), and two others—Romania and Bulgaria—are
slated to join in 2007–8, which can be interpreted as a confirmation of their
political and economic institutional convergence with Western norms.
However, for most other countries the long-expected normalization has
resulted either in distinctly illiberal economic and political arrangements
(especially in Belarus and Central Asia) or in uneasy and volatile institutional hybrids (such as in Russia, the Ukraine, and Bosnia). Just as importantly, these cross-national differences are not merely a reflection of
different speeds on a common one-way street leading towards Western liberal capitalism but are indicative of qualitative differences between the end
points of the postcommunist transformations. Thus, at first glance, one
could conclude that Jowitt's skeptical appraisal of post-Leninist democratic
prospects was largely accurate for much of the Balkans and the former Soviet
Union, whereas the eight first-wave EU candidates and (to a lesser extent)
Bulgaria and Romania conform more closely to the optimistic expectations
of the transitologists. However, such a conclusion is unsatisfactory, both
because counting correctly predicted cases is a blunt analytical instrument,

and because in any case Jowitt's legacy-based predictions did not preclude the potential for liberal democracy, especially if the nascent democratic forces were to receive substantial foreign support through Western adoption.[7]

COMMON LENINIST LEGACIES

The question about whether ex-communist countries are still set apart by the Leninist legacies is primarily a question of cross-regional analysis. While an extensive analysis of the sort is beyond the scope of this essay, I will nevertheless provide a few glimpses into how postcommunist politics differ from those of other regions. In particular, I will draw on comparisons with two sets of countries: established Western democracies, whose social and political models have exerted a defining influence on postcommunist reforms, and may therefore be considered the ideal standard of "normality" by which to judge transition countries; and Latin American countries, whose authoritarian past and economic vulnerability arguably make them a more appropriate "control group" for evaluating the specifically Leninist influence on Eastern European social and political development. This latter comparison, while at odds with the Western aspirations of Eastern Europeans, addresses an increasingly common view that the standards by which to judge ex-communist countries should be those of developing countries at similar levels of development.[8]

Starting from the admittedly very broad perspective of civil and political rights, as reflected by the Freedom House scores for 2003, we find that only twelve of the twenty-seven countries of Eastern Europe and the former Soviet Union were considered "free," nine were deemed "partly free," and the remaining six "not free,"[9] a tally that compared negatively not only to Western Europe but also to the Latin America/Caribbean region, where almost two-thirds of the countries received a "free" rating, and only two (one of them being Cuba) were coded "not free." Thus, a postcommunist democracy deficit seems to persist even after more than a decade of "transition," though surprisingly little of this deficit can be ascribed to democratic breakdowns along the lines predicted by Jowitt (military coups, the antidemocratic role of the Catholic Church, and novel political experiments). However, a closer look at the political patterns within these three broad categories reveals some interesting nuances about the links between Leninist legacies and the extent of political freedoms. First, it is worth noting that most of the ex-communist region's authoritarian leaders were very straightforward "Leninist legacies," in the sense that Nursultan Nazarbayev in Kazakhstan, Saparmurat Niyazov in Turkmenistan, Ilham Aliyev in Azerbaijan, and Islam Karimov in Uzbekistan had all been leaders of their respective republics during Soviet times. Even where former communists were more willing to abide by democratic rules, the survival and remarkable political success of Leninist personnel produced significant political resentment and "emotional fragmentation" along the lines predicted by Jowitt.[10] The resulting tensions undermined the quality of democracy and in extreme cases (such as in Georgia, Albania, and Armenia) contributed to serious political violence.

Second, it is important to remember that, particularly among the "partly free" polities—and even among some of the region's democratic "pioneers"—there is significant subnational heterogeneity in the degree to which different citizens experience democracy. The first type of such heterogeneity is of an ethnic nature, and harks back to what Jowitt refers to as the legacy of "ethnic and territorial fragmentation" inherited from the communist regime.[11] Many of the restrictions on minority rights in post-communist countries—such as the restrictive citizenship laws against Russians in Estonia and Latvia or against Serbs and Croats in Slovenia—are direct consequences of the disintegration of multinational communist states, and to a large extent represent retaliations for earlier abusive minority policies under Leninism. Other forms of ethnic/racial discrimination—most prominently the treatment of the Roma throughout Eastern Europe—is neither formally codified nor a direct outgrowth of communist policies but nevertheless reflects the broader "pluralism deficit" that plagues postcommunist societies. While ethnic tensions and discriminatory practices are obviously not a post-Leninist monopoly, the specific form and nature of these conflicts arguably continues to bear the indelible imprint of the communist approach to the "nationality question." The second type of heterogeneity is territorial, and refers to the uneven penetration of democratic norms into different parts of many transition countries. Even abstracting from the most obvious examples of this type—such as breakaway territories in Moldova and Georgia, or some of the more remote Russian regions—the general weakness of the postcommunist state implies strict limits on the ability of the central government to ensure respect for democratic principles at the local level. As a consequence, the actual civil and political rights of many citizens depend less on the democratic inclinations of the national government and more on the decisions of local leaders, who often rule in a much more traditional and authoritarian manner. Of course, the existence of such "brown areas" is hardly a unique post-communist phenomenon (after all, Guillermo O'Donnell developed the term in reference to Latin America[12]). However, the social and political relations in postcommunist brown areas preserve much of the peculiar mixture of traditional and modern elements characteristic of Leninism. As a consequence, whereas an inhabitant of the capital may enjoy civil and political rights comparable to those of Western Europe, a villager from a remote rural area is likely to have experienced few if any changes in political leaders and practices compared to fifteen years ago.[13]

Another prominent socio-political legacy of communism, the "ghetto political culture," resulted from the Communist Party monopoly over the political realm and was characterized by popular avoidance and mistrust of politics.[14] While the communist-era political apathy was certainly overcome in most countries by the initial burst of political enthusiasm in the period between the fall of communism and the first competitive elections, the increasing popular disaffection with electoral politics—reflected most clearly in the rapidly declining voter turnout rates—suggests that the early participatory exuberance may have been only a temporary deviation from the long-term alienation between citizens and political elites. On the other hand, judging by the data from the 1995–97 *World Values Survey,*[15] the low regard of postcommunist citizens for key political institutions (the government, parliament, and political parties) was on average only slightly worse than in advanced Western democracies, and somewhat more positive than the evaluations of Latin American citizens, which suggests that the legitimacy deficit may be part of a broader crisis of political representation in the last decade, rather than a symptom of the Leninist legacy.

The development of postcommunist political parties presents a similarly mixed picture of the ability of transition countries to overcome the anomic political legacy of Leninism. Thus, the heterogeneous mixes of individuals who competed in the founding elections were hardly parties in their own right—in fact many avoided the party label (preferring vague names such as Civic Forum in the Czech Republic, National Salvation Front in Romania, Public Against Violence in Slovakia, Solidarity in Poland, etc.) and even proclaimed their reluctance to engage in factionalist party politics. Whereas in subsequent elections more mainstream political parties began to dominate politics (at least in the parliamentary and semi-presidential systems of Eastern Europe), more recently we have witnessed a revival of "unorthodox" political formations (ranging from personalist parties such as the National Movement Simeon II in Bulgaria in 2001 to the extreme-right Greater Romania Party in Romania in 2000 and the agrarian-populist Samoobrona in Poland) whose main appeal was their rejection of an increasingly unpopular mainstream political elite. This electoral volatility, which is considerably higher than in Western Europe or even Latin America, is symptomatic of the weak institutionalization and shallow social roots of postcommunist parties, which in turn are clearly rooted in the diffuse, poorly articulated social and political cleavages inherited from the communist regime.[16]

Another significant and lasting Leninist legacy is the pervasiveness of paternalism in postcommunist politics. The remarkable organizational and electoral strength of communist successor parties should be interpreted not as a sign of the vitality of leftist ideology in the region (either in its communist or "refurbished" social-democratic versions) but rather as an expression of the deep-rooted appeal of paternalist politics in societies where individualism had been traditionally weak and was further undermined in the Leninist period. This argument is supported by the fact that, except in the Czech Republic, in Eastern European democracies with relatively weak showings by communist successor parties, the paternalism demand was met by national-populist parties, such as Vladimír Mečiar's Movement for a Democratic Slovakia in Slovakia and Franjo Tudjman's Croatian Democratic Union in Croatia. Among the former Soviet republics, where traditional authority patterns were even more prevalent both before and during communism, the role of paternal figures in postcommunist politics has been even more pronounced, as reflected in the ruling style of leaders such as Vladimir Putin and Eduard Shevardnadze (not to speak of Alexander Lukashenka or Nursultan Nazarbayev)

The discussion so far suggests that, as far as political attitudes and institutions are concerned, Leninist legacies are still discernible even though many of the shortcomings are starting to resemble the "normality" of other developing regions, such as Latin America. However, whereas formal political institutions can change almost overnight, and popular attitudes towards the political system can also respond quite rapidly to changes in leadership, other Leninist legacies are arguably more deeply ingrained in postcommunist societies, and can therefore be expected to change more slowly. One of the most important examples can be found in Jowitt's discussion of the distorted relationship between the public and the private, which can be traced back to the communist reinforcement of the traditional zero-sum mentality, and manifests itself in a deficit of "public virtues"[17] and a weakness of civic culture[18] in both communist and postcommunist societies.

This public virtues deficit is visible at the level of both the elite and the general population, thereby creating a vicious cycle that is difficult to break without significant external assistance. At the elite level, the widespread use of public office for private gain has become one of the most salient political issues in postcommunist countries in the context in which communist-era disregard for public property and collective good was reinforced by the immense corruption opportunities inherent in the rapid privatization of large parts of the state sector. Indeed, corruption is not only pervasive in most of Eastern Europe and the former Soviet Union,[19] but there is little evidence that things are even moving in the right direction, despite numerous domestic and international anticorruption initiatives.[20] Compared to advanced Western democracies, ex-Leninist countries show a substantial gap in controlling corruption, as reflected by the perceptions of both business people and citizens.[21] On the other hand, the same sources suggest that, at least in its pervasiveness, postcommunist corruption is remarkably similar to corruption in Latin America with respect to regional averages[22] and to the large intraregional cross-national corruption differences.[23] While these broad cross-regional findings should be taken with a grain of salt, they nevertheless question the strength of a Leninist (as opposed to a postauthoritarian, low/middle-income country) corruption-boosting effect.

Surprisingly, the more significant symptoms of the post-Leninist syndrome can be found at the level of the average citizen. According to the 1995–97 *World Values Survey,* compared not only to Western Europeans but even to Latin Americans, postcommunist citizens were on average significantly more likely to engage in a variety of activities that are at odds with the public interest, such as avoiding transportation fares, buying stolen goods, or cheating on taxes. While such actions may pale in comparison to the "sins" of high-level corruption, they nevertheless create a degree of complicity between elites and ordinary citizens, which helps to perpetuate the system in a way reminiscent of the complicity with the communist regime. The second public virtues deficit is of an organizational nature, and has to do with the underdeveloped "art of association" in ex-communist countries. When it comes to membership and participation in a variety of civic and political organizations (including churches, charities, professional and sports associations, unions, and political parties) Eastern Europeans appear to be considerably more reticent than citizens of other regions: thus, only 55 percent of ex-communist respondents reported belonging to any organization, compared to 71 percent in Latin America and 85 percent in Western democracies.[24] The disparity is even larger with respect to active rather than passive membership, with only 20 percent of Eastern Europeans reporting associational activity, well below the regional averages of Latin America (50 percent) and the West (57 percent). Thus, it appears that despite the widespread (and justified) focus on corruption, the burden of the Leninist legacies is reflected more clearly in the lack of public virtues at the level of ordinary citizens, possibly because they have been less directly affected by the "civilizing" pressures of Western conditionality. While this deficit is understandable as a reaction against the forced "collective" activities of the communist period, it nevertheless represents a significant obstacle to the development of stable democracies in Eastern Europe and the former Soviet Union.

The discussion so far has identified a number of important areas in the social and political development of the former Soviet bloc that still bear the clear imprint of the common Leninist legacy, including civic attitudes, civil society development, and paternalist politics. From this point of view, Jowitt's emphasis on shared legacies holds up well after sixteen years of "transition," especially compared to the optimistic tabula rasa expectations of the transitology school.

LEGACY DIFFERENCES AND THEIR POLITICAL CONSEQUENCES

The dramatic and systematic divergence of postcommunist national trajectories raises an important theoretical challenge to the logic of an explanation that emphasizes primarily the *dominant and shared* Leninist legacy among the former communist "comrades."[25] In itself, the mere existence of democratic success cases and of cross-national differences is not necessarily problematic for Jowitt's theory, given its emphasis on the contingent and experimental nature of political developments in the fragile new democracies of Eastern Europe. Moreover, Jowitt does acknowledge the existence of national differences with respect to the predominant type of fragmentation and violence thresholds. However, given his clear emphasis on commonalities, Jowitt does not pursue these ideas much beyond discussing the potential differences in the roles of the army and the Catholic Church, neither of which has played an important antidemocratic role so far. The remainder of this essay is therefore devoted to discussing the key drivers of this divergence, and their implications for our understanding of the role of legacies during the postcommunist transformations.

Since the collapse of communism, the countries of the former Soviet bloc have diverged dramatically in their social, economic, and political trajectories. As mentioned earlier, reasonably stable and functional democratic institutions have arisen in East Central Europe and the Baltics, and political liberalization occurred later and was more susceptible to political instability in the Balkans (e.g., in Albania and Macedonia), whereas in most of the former Soviet Union democracy is either significantly flawed (such as in Russia and Ukraine) or completely absent (as in Central Asia, Azerbaijan, and Belarus). Similar and largely overlapping geographic clusters can be observed with respect to the extent of economic reforms, political-party and civil-society development, corruption, ethnic and political violence, and state capacity. While such a brief overview can hardly do justice to some of the interesting nuances and exceptions, I would argue that without great loss of generality, we can conclude that sixteen years of postcommunist transformations have resulted in a number of very different types of "normality" in the former Soviet space.

How can we account for these profoundly different outcomes in the relatively short time span since these countries embarked on their postcommunist journey from what in many ways looked like fairly similar starting points? In answering this question, I will discuss several types of historical legacies that have affected postcommunist countries differently. While some of these legacies have deep historical roots and may be difficult or even impossible to reverse in the short term, focusing on concrete factors rather than adopting the vague and often unstated assumptions of geographical shortcuts[26] should facilitate a more nuanced and realistic assessment of democratic prospects in the former Soviet bloc.

The first cluster of largely precommunist legacy differences consists of several regionally distinct cultural and religious patterns. Even a brief survey of the postcommunist region reveals that the historically important European Kulturgefälle persists in the postcommunist period: whereas, with the exception of Croatia (and temporarily Slovakia), the Western Christian countries have been consistently the most democratic in the region, the Eastern Orthodox countries have had a bumpier political reform path (ranging from fragile democracies in Bulgaria and Romania to outright authoritarianism in Belarus), and in the predominantly Muslim countries (with the partial exception of Albania) democratic progress has been very limited. Of course, religious heritage also overlaps almost perfectly with imperial legacies, with the countries in the Central European sphere of influence inheriting not only Western religions but also Western institutions and civic values which set them apart from the regions dominated by the Russian or the Ottoman Empire.[27]

Even though communist rule had eroded the large prewar modernization and development differences both within and between the countries of the region, important cross-national differences survived with respect to levels of economic development, urbanization, and education. Once again, these differences largely followed the familiar west–east/south gradient, from the fairly affluent, highly urbanized, and educated Czech Republic to the much poorer and predominantly rural areas in Central Asia and the southern Balkans, thereby contributing to social settings with very different potentials for developing civic attitudes and organizations. These differences in the strength of civil society played an important role in driving the uneven democracy patterns: whereas Eastern Europeans were for the most part able to check the authoritarian impulses of powerful leaders such as Lech Wałęsa, Ion Iliescu, Vladimír Mečiar, and Franjo Tudjman, in large parts of the Soviet Union political leaders met with much weaker organized social and political resistance.[28] To the extent that powerful leaders in such countries were challenged in their attempts to consolidate political power, such challenges often resulted in violent factional conflict, ranging from isolated political assassination attempts in Armenia and Macedonia to civil wars in Albania, Georgia, and Tajikistan.

After the collapse of communism, the newly liberated countries also faced a third set of problematic legacies—the state- and nation-building challenges characteristic of postcolonialism. Even where the upheaval associated with this difficult process did not deteriorate into outright ethnic violence, democracy was often delayed (and its quality diminished) by the centrality of the "nationality question." Just as clearly, the nature and intensity of the nation and statehood conflicts varied substantially across countries, and was highly correlated with the emerging regime patterns. Thus, of the only six ex-communist countries with unchanged borders since 1989, Poland and Hungary were consistently among the region's democratic frontrunners, Bulgaria and Romania also outperformed their Orthodox and Balkan peers, Mongolia stood out as a democratic outlier in Central Asia, and even Albania's conflict-ridden democracy was arguably above expectations. Meanwhile, ethnic conflict has seriously undermined democracy in the former Yugoslavia, where Serbia, Croatia, and Bosnia had less democratic regimes than the relatively liberal nature of the Yugoslav regime would have predicted. On the other hand, despite some nontrivial blemishes in the first part of the 1990s, the political development of Estonia and Latvia shows that democracy is not impossible even in newly independent states with high ethnic fragmentation.

Turning to some of the more proximate legacies, variations in political reforms in the 1980s and the modes of extrication from communist rule exerted a surprisingly weak influence on postcommunist reform paths: while Hungary's and Poland's gradual political opening may have given them a democratic head start, and the Czech Republic did equally well despite its unreformed Stalinist regime in the 1980s, most former Yugoslav republics seem to have benefited little from the more liberal nature of Yugoslav communism. Similarly, differences in economic liberalization played only a minor and temporary role after 1990, arguably because even the more advanced reformers of late communism did not fundamentally alter the logic of the socialist system, especially when compared to the depth of post-communist transformations. What mattered much more for both economic reforms and democratization were the structural economic distortions inherited from the communist regime, especially the prevalence of energy-intensive and polluting Stalinist-type heavy industry. While such indus-trial dinosaurs were a general feature of Soviet bloc economies, they were particularly prevalent in the countries/regions that had been less industri-alized at the outset of communism, especially in the Soviet Union. Since these factories were particularly poorly prepared for free-market compe-tition, the regions whose livelihood depended on them tended to support ex-communist and populist leaders and parties, thereby further reducing the prospects of democracy in some of the less-developed countries.

As the preceding discussion has shown, in addition to the powerful Lenin-ist legacy shared by former Soviet bloc comrades, the collapse of commu-nism left behind several important and strongly correlated cross-national legacy differences with respect to cultural/religious traditions, degrees of modernization, state- and nation-building challenges, and structural eco-nomic distortions. Thus, the countries of East Central Europe were not only historically and culturally closer to the West than their eastern and south-ern brethren, but were also richer, more modern, and less ethnically diverse, with longer statehood histories and relatively less distorted economies at the outset of the transition. Even though no single factor can fully account for the cross-national regime patterns since the collapse of communism, the various overlapping legacies jointly account for most of the variation in the extent of democracy across the region, and so far there is no evidence that the power of these legacies diminishes over time.[29] Of course, it is possible to point to exceptions from this "iron law of history": Belarus's authoritarian regime is at odds with its relatively benign legacies, whereas Mongolia and Moldova exceeded legacy-based expectations. How-ever, these exceptions are not only rare but have a remarkable tendency to correct themselves, as suggested by the authoritarian backsliding in Kyr-gyzstan, a one-time democratic overachiever, and the recent improvements in erstwhile democratic underachievers such as Slovakia, Croatia, and Serbia.

INTERNATIONAL FACTORS AND WESTERN INTEGRATION

Whereas the significant and lasting cross-national developmental differ-ences discussed in the previous section led to important variations in the

GRIGORE POP-ELECHES

democratic receptiveness of domestic social and political environments, the divergence of postcommunist regime patterns was further encouraged by the uneven nature of Western interventions in the region. As Jowitt had predicted in "The Leninist Legacy," the fate of postcommunist democracy was closely intertwined with the extent to which the liberal democratic West fulfilled its role of a constructive "Norman" entity able to shape the world in its own image. In theory the (at least rhetorically) open-ended integration promise should have had an equalizing effect on political and economic developments in the postcommunist space by encouraging the adoption of Western institutional blueprints. In practice this potential for overcoming the Leninist legacy and reducing the effects of structural differences may be realized among the countries that for developmental and historical reasons are close to the "deep integration" threshold (the eight new EU members, Romania, Bulgaria, and potentially Croatia and Serbia). The joint effect of close international scrutiny and substantial structural funding may help reduce the gap between Western and Eastern Europe, as well as between different Eastern European countries.[30] Despite the official "open-door" integration promise, however, the actual integration prospects of different countries have varied substantially. Even abstracting from Central Asia, which is not even geographically a part of Europe, it was clear from early on that by virtue of their geographic location, historical ties, and socioeconomic and political baggage, the short-to-medium-term integration prospects of many Balkan and former Soviet countries were rather limited. As a consequence, the reform incentives associated with the promise of European integration were considerably weaker both for the political elites and for the populations of the more peripheral postcommunist countries, which in turn meant that the immediate benefits of adopting Western economic and political standards were likely to be lower at the periphery. These weaker incentives may explain why voters and politicians alike were less willing to embrace reforms, especially when such reforms produced palpable economic and political costs in the short run.

However, the international influence on postcommunist political developments has not been limited to Western integration promises but has included concerted international efforts to monitor elections, human rights, and minority policies. In extreme cases, particularly in the case of the former Yugoslavia, the West has been willing to take an even more activist stance against extreme deviations from Western standards of civil and political rights. However, in this respect, too, there exists a geographic bias in Western involvement, in the sense that minority rights violations prompted military interventions in Kosovo but not in Chechnya, while civil wars triggered a belated but considerable Western peacemaking and reconstruction effort in Bosnia but not in Tajikistan, Transdniestr, Nagorno-Karabakh, or Abkhazia. While the Western reluctance to intervene militarily in parts of the former Soviet space may reflect concerns about not crossing Russian strategic interests in its own "backyard," it nevertheless contributed to the widening gulf between democratic practices in different parts of the former communist bloc. Along similar lines, one should note the different democratic standards applied by the West in its conditionality towards different transition countries. Thus, whereas Western governments made repeated efforts to marginalize Mečiar in Slovakia, they were willing to accept and even support Yeltsin in Russia or Akayev in Kyrgyzstan, even though the latter two leaders were guilty of more significant violations of democratic norms than was Mečiar. Besides strategic interests and lesser-of-two-evils considerations, these different standards arguably reflect deep-seated Western views about the types of political institutions and practices that can be expected to take root in different parts of the former communist bloc.

ONE OR SEVERAL LEGACIES? THEORETICAL IMPLICATIONS AND CONCLUSION

How can the wide diversity of postcommunist regime outcomes be reconciled with Jowitt's emphasis on the common and shared nature of the Leninist legacy in Eastern Europe and the former Soviet Union? There are two approaches to answering this question. The first answer starts from the assumption that the only potentially problematic cases to be explained are the instances of reasonably stable democracies in the region, whereas the remaining fragile democracies, hybrid regimes, and full-blown authoritarian systems are fully consistent with Jowitt's post-Leninist vision of the region. In this respect, the incentives provided by European integration appear to be crucial, given that (with the partial exception of Slovakia) the eight recently admitted EU members have been the region's most consistently democratic countries. Of the other four Eastern European countries ranked as "free" by Freedom House in 2003, Bulgaria and Romania have undoubtedly received an important "democracy boost" due to the prospects of EU membership (expected by 2007), whereas the more recent and fragile political opening in Croatia and Serbia-Montenegro also bears the imprint of Western interventions and incentives. Therefore, it appears that the countries which have so far been able to overcome the Leninist legacy obstacles to democratic stability were those fortunate enough to be included in the "adoption plan" of the European Union. Beyond this striking cor-

GRIGORE POP-ELECHES

relation, even a cursory look at Eastern European political developments in the last sixteen years reveals the crucial importance of Western pressures on a broad range of vital components of democracy, such as minority rights, freedom of the press, and free and fair elections.

While such an explanation successfully reconciles regime diversity with the existence of powerful, shared Leninist legacies, it suffers from two drawbacks. The first one is relatively minor, and concerns the question of how to account for Mongolia's surprisingly vigorous democracy, which can hardly be attributed to hopes of Western integration. The second and theoretically more difficult problem is that the countries with the best initial Western adoption prospects were not chosen at random but represented the ex-communist countries with the most promising historical legacies in the region. The resulting selection bias makes it difficult to disentangle the effects of Western integration incentives from those of different initial conditions. Nevertheless, several observations indicate that legacy differences matter even beyond their crucial role of identifying likely candidates for Western integration. Thus, even among the countries with real integration perspectives, democracy was on more solid ground in the ethnically homogeneous, richer, and economically less distorted countries of the group (Hungary, Slovenia, the Czech Republic, and Poland), compared to the structurally and historically more disadvantaged EU aspirants (Slovakia, Bulgaria, and Romania). Furthermore, in early 1990 Serbia and especially Croatia were more prosperous and more integrated with the West than Bulgaria and Romania, which suggests that the rockier regime trajectory of the former can be better explained by their complicated ethnic and statehood legacies than by differences in Western integration prospects. Finally, the wholesale adoption of Bosnia by the international community in the second part of the 1990s has so far produced modest results in overcoming the difficult legacies of ethnic conflict.

The second answer to the question of how to reconcile Jowitt's emphasis on the common nature of the Leninist legacy with the diversity of post-communist regime outcomes acknowledges the importance of cross-country legacy differences but treats them within the framework of Jowitt's analysis of the nature of Leninist regimes. More specifically, the "commanding heights" approach to economic development, which focused on priority sectors at the expense of nonessential areas, and the "production mentality," which regarded cultural transformation as a secondary and derivative accomplishment to economic change,[31] played an instrumental role in the survival of precommunist legacy differences. Since rural areas were particularly likely to suffer from such benign neglect,[32] it is easy to see that traditional social, cultural, and political relations survived to a larger extent in the less-developed, predominantly rural countries of the former Soviet bloc. Moreover, the type of traditional relations that were reproduced by the communist system were likely to differ between sub-regions, which may explain why the countries with more functional inter-war democracies were generally more democratic after the collapse of communism. Even in the industrial sector, where the Leninist cultural and political penetration was greater, one would expect a longer half-life of tra-ditional work and social patterns in countries and regions where the over-whelming majority of industrial workers come from a rural background. Along similar lines, Jowitt's insight, that in Romania the public-private sep-aration under the communist regime mirrored and reproduced the tradi-tional Eastern Orthodox separation of religious ritual and private life,[33] implies that in Western Christian countries without such sharp traditional dichotomies, communist modernization efforts may have yielded more legal-rational power relations and a more complementary relationship between the public and private realm, thereby leaving behind a somewhat attenuated Leninist legacy. Finally, the region's long-standing ethnic and territorial tensions were not resolved by several decades of proletarian inter-nationalism, not only because the nationality question, like that of cul-ture, was of secondary importance on the ideological agenda but also because heavy-handed efforts to promote civic identities at the expense of ethnic ones, combined with substantial interregional economic trans-fers, provided steady fuel and popular legitimacy for nationalist claims to ethnic self-determination.

The remarkable persistence of a uniquely Leninist imprint on a wide range of political developments, particularly the prevalence of noncivic popular attitudes and the weakness of civil society organizations and political par-ties, set ex-communist countries apart not only from their Western democr-acy models but also from other developing regions, such as Latin America. On the other hand, the significant divergence of national regime trajecto-ries is more difficult to reconcile with Jowitt's emphasis on the common and shared nature of Leninist legacies. However, of the two key drivers of diver-gence identified here , one—Western integration incentives—was actually acknowledged by Jowitt as a potential way to overcome the burden of Lenin-ist legacies, whereas the second—historical legacy differences—although downplayed in Jowitt's predictions, can actually be fruitfully analyzed within his theoretical framework of the nature of Leninist regimes. Therefore, the legacy of Jowitt's theoretical contribution to understanding postcommu-nist political developments extends beyond the well-known role of a historically grounded skeptical antidote to the democratic optimism of transitologists, since it provides an important framework for understanding the complicated interaction between ideological blueprints and pre-existing social and cultural conditions.

NOTES

1. See, for example, *Transitions from Authoritarian Rule: Comparative Perspectives*, ed. Guillermo O'Donnell, Philippe C. Schmitter, and Laurence Whitehead (Baltimore: Johns Hopkins University Press, 1986); Giuseppe Di Palma, *To Craft Democracies: An Essay on Democratic Transitions* (Berkeley: University of California Press, 1990); Terry L. Karl and Philippe C. Schmitter "Modes of Transition in Latin America, Southern and Eastern Europe," *International Social Science Journal* (May 1991): 269–84; and Adam Przeworski, *Democracy and the Market: Political and Economic Reforms in Eastern Europe and Latin America* (Cambridge: Cambridge University Press, 1991).

2. Przeworski, *Democracy and the Market*, xii.

3. Ken Jowitt, *New World Disorder: The Leninist Extinction* (Berkeley: University of California Press, 1992), 286.

4. Of course, in the postcommunist context, "transition" acquired a broader meaning than the "democratic transition" discussed by the transitology school, since it included at least three crucial dimensions: political, economic, and nation/state-building tasks.

5. Ken Jowitt, *New World Disorder*, 285.

6. Instability could be exacerbated if Western democratic conditionality suffers from the growing rift between the United States and Western Europe.

7. Ken Jowitt, *New World Disorder*, 304–5. This argument is discussed in more detail in Marc Howard's contribution to this volume, so I will not dwell on it here.

8. For a forceful argument in this sense, see Andrei Shleifer and Daniel Treisman, "A Normal Country," *Foreign Affairs* 8, no. 2 (2004).

9. The situation looks even worse once we include occupied/disputed territories such as Transnistria, Chechnya, and Kosovo.

10. Jowitt, *New World Disorder*, 296–97.

11. Ibid., 297.

12. Guillermo O'Donnell, "Delegative Democracy," *Journal of Democracy* 5, no. 1 (1994): 55–69.

13. For an interesting case study documenting such continuity in a Romanian village (Nucsoara), see Alina Mungiu-Pippidi, *Secera și buldozerul. Scornicești și Nucșoara. Mecanisme de aservire a țăranului român* (Iasi: Polirom, 2002).

14. Jowitt, *New World Disorder*, 288.

15. World Values Survey Group, *World Values Survey, 1995–97* (Ann Arbor, MI: Institute for Social Research, 1998).

16. Ibid., 294–95.

17. Ibid., 292.

18. Ibid., 304.

19. According to the 2001 *New Europe Barometer,* of the ten Eastern European EU candidates, Slovenia was the only country where a minority of respondents (42 percent) believed that most or almost all public officials were corrupt. For the other countries, these distrust ratings ranged from 54 percent in Hungary to 80 percent in Slovakia, 89 percent in Romania, 92 percent in Latvia, and 95 percent in Lithuania. Richard Rose, *A Bottom-Up Evaluation of Enlargement Countries: New Europe Barometer 1* (Aberdeen, Scotland: CSPP Publications, University of Aberdeen, 2002).

20. Thus, judging by the evolution of Transparency International's Corruption Perception Index (CPI) between 1997–98 and 2001, among the Eastern European countries only Hungary showed real progress, whereas several countries—including Poland, the Czech Republic, and Romania—actually slipped in the rankings. Transparency International, "Corruption Perception Index 2001," http://www.transparency .org/cpi/2001/cpi2001.html.

21. For the former, I relied on data from various years of Transparency International's Corruption Perception Index (CPI), while for the latter I used survey data from the *1995-7 World Values Survey.*

22. On the 1 to 10 (most to least corrupt) CPI scale, the average score for postcommunist countries was 3.6, compared to 3.7 for Latin America/Caribbean countries, and 7.9 for Western established democracies. Similarly, a *1995-7 World Values Survey* question about the pervasiveness of political corruption, scored from 1 (low) to 4 (high), revealed identical regional averages of 3.0 for Eastern Europe and Latin America, compared to 2.4 for Western countries.

23. Whereas Chile and Estonia had 2001 CPI scores that were superior to those of Italy, countries such as Bolivia or Ukraine "clustered" around the bottom of the scale among some of the world's more corrupt regimes.

24. Based on data from the *1995-7 World Values Survey.*

25. Jowitt, *New World Disorder,* 300.

26. One prominent example of such essentialism is the pejorative use of the term "Balkans," which, as Maria Todorova has argued quite eloquently, has been turned into "one of the most powerful pejorative designations in history, international relations, political science and, nowadays, general intellectual discourse." See Maria Todorova, *Imagining the Balkans* (London: Oxford University Press, 1997), 7.

27. Janos discusses the different foundations of political authority (legal-rational in Western Christianity versus traditional in Eastern Orthodoxy) and Lal points to the differences in the relationship between church and state, and the higher degree of separation between them in Western Christianity. See Andrew C. Janos, *East Central Europe in the Modern World: The Politics of the Borderlands from Pre- to Postcommunism* (Stanford: Stanford University Press, 2000); Deepak Lal, *Unintended Consequences: The Impact of Factor Endowments, Culture, and Politics on Long-run Economic Performance* (Cambridge, MA: MIT Press, 1998).

28. These two mechanisms may explain the trajectory of several postcommunist leaders in the former Soviet republics—most notably Boris Yeltsin in Russia and Askar Akayev in the Kyrgyz Republic—who failed to deliver on their early democratization promises. In both cases, the most serious political challenge to the president's authority came from largely unreformed communist parties, which not only limited the bargaining power of domestic democracy advocates but also contributed to a more lenient Western attitude toward the democratic lapses of the two regimes.

29. For a more systematic elaboration of this claim using cross-national statistical data for the twenty-eight ex-communist countries, see Grigore Pop-Eleches, "The Enduring Curse of the Past: Initial Conditions and Post-Communist Reform Trajectories," paper prepared for the 2003 annual meeting of *APSA*, Philadelphia, August 28–31, 2003.

30. The Irish economic miracle of the last two decades provides some hope, although results were more modest in Spain, Portugal, and particularly Greece.

31. Jowitt, *New World Disorder*, 60–61.

32. Ibid., 81.

33. Ibid., 83–84.

II *Identity and Social Transformation*
in Eastern Europe and Russia

4

INSTITUTIONS AND THE DEVELOPMENT
OF INDIVIDUALISM

The Case of Western Poland after World War II

TOMEK GRABOWSKI

W ill Poland succeed in the European Union (EU)? Will the EU
benefit from Poland's membership? And, more fundamentally,
what kind of a social, political, and cultural animal is Poland?
Is it a Western country? Or is it closer, say, to Turkey, and, by admitting
Poland, has Europe let a large chunk of Asia in?

Today, in the aftermath of the EU's historical enlargement, the wildest
and most extreme opinions about the newcomer can be heard. Officially,
European bureaucrats maintain that there is no problem. To be admitted,
they say, the newcomers had to fulfill certain uniform criteria including,
for instance, making sufficient progress in synchronizing their laws with
those of the EU. Since Poland had done that, it means that it was ready;
there is nothing more to say.

Beneath this veneer of official optimism, however, there is a good deal
of uncertainty and even fear. And I do not mean just for the average European "man in the street"; I also mean for the continent's elites. Jokes float
around about Poland's medieval Catholicism and her old-fashioned nationalism. There is talk about the Polish peasant, unwashed and primitive, and
about Polish workers, ready to swamp the labor market of neighboring
countries. *The Economist* has outlined the nightmare scenario: Poland will
be a thorn in Europe's back, because it will combine the worst features of
the old members; it will be poor and backward, like Greece; it will demand

huge subsidies for its farmers, like France; it will be skeptical about integration and scandalously pro-American, like Britain; and it will be corrupt, like Italy.[1]

The reality is more complicated. Poland is a hopeful newcomer. It has a potential for being a productive and dynamic member of the European community. But the secret about Poland is that culturally, it is one of the most heterogeneous countries ever admitted to the EU. The country sits on a cultural fault line. On the one hand, it is one of the few postcommunist countries where an authentic, recognizably liberal culture shows strong signs of life. On the other hand, there is ample evidence pointing to the exceptionally strong, authoritarian, and backward-looking undercurrents in Polish society, which brew under the surface of its ostensibly liberal democratic institutions. To put it somewhat crudely, you have in one and the same country parts that are a bit like Ukraine, and parts that are quite like Belgium. The two Polands are in conflict; its outcome hangs in the balance.

The fault line is to a significant degree (although not exclusively) geographical. It divides the country along the north-south axis. If you want to see modern, dynamic, and tolerant Poland, go west—to Wrocław, Opole, or Gdańsk. If you want to see illiberal and authoritarian Poland, go east—to places such as Lublin, Rzeszów, Białystok, or even, perhaps, Warsaw.

The aim of this essay is to shed some light on the origins of this divide. In particular, I want to explain why western Poland achieved a breakthrough to cultural individualism and eastern Poland did not. With that goal in mind, I focus especially on the role of institutions as midwives of individualism, both in general, and in the Polish case. My central argument is that organized Catholicism played a key role in bringing individualism to western Poland, but that it was a highly anomalous, local version of Catholicism.

THE CENTRALITY OF INDIVIDUALISM

When we talk of a country's "readiness for Europe," we usually make assumptions about culture. Some of the fears I just mentioned boil down to the question of culture—to the feeling that Poland may be culturally too different, too alien for Western Europe. We need to be specific here. The central fact about Western Europe is that it is a liberal democratic space; the sociopolitical "essence" of Europe is liberal democracy. Hence, to assess Poland's chances of success in the EU, in ways which go beyond wishful thinking and prejudices, we should start by asking, What kind of a culture supports liberal democracy?

Let's begin impressionistically—with Alexis de Tocqueville. Writing in

TOMEK GRABOWSKI

the 1830s, Tocqueville was trying to understand why liberal democracy was successful in the United States but not in France. His main claim was that

> the reign of freedom cannot be established without that of mores, nor mores founded without beliefs. . . . In the United States the dogma of the sovereignty of the people is not an isolated doctrine . . . on the contrary, one can view it as the last link in a chain of opinions that envelops the Anglo-American world as a whole.

What is this "chain of opinions"? asked Tocqueville. And he observed that according to a near-universal consensus among the Americans,

> Providence has given to each individual, whoever he may be, the degree of reason necessary for him to be able to direct himself in things that interest him exclusively. Such is the great maxim on which civil and political society in the United States rests. The father of a family applies it to his children, the master to his servants, the township to those under its administration, the province to the townships, the state to the provinces, the Union to the states.

Even America's dominant religion, says Tocqueville, manifests the same attitude: Protestantism "submits the truths of the other world to individual reason . . . and it grants that each man freely take the way that will lead him to Heaven."[2] Here, according to Tocqueville, lies the key to America's success with democracy.

What is Tocqueville saying? He is saying, in effect, that liberal democracy requires more than a certain set of institutions or a certain level of economic development. It requires more than free elections, a free press, or an independent judiciary. In order for liberal democracy to be sustainable, a society needs a culture whose members believe in their own capacity to discern what is best for them; in other words, who trust their own reason and judgment. This is the "chain of opinions" that he talks about.

Why is such a culture important? For one thing, only people with moral and intellectual self-confidence make competent citizens. A citizen is someone willing and able to bring his own voice to debates about issues of general importance. This means, among other things, that *he does not instinctively defer, on such issues, to the opinions of others, be it his friends, parents, workmates, bosses, or priests.* Only citizens can fill the formal institutions of democracy with substance. They are noisy and inquisitive. They demand equal treatment; they scrutinize the behavior of their leaders, whom they treat as their equals, and they expect that the leaders live up to certain standards. Without citizens' engagement, governments cease to be both responsible and responsive. Thus democracy needs a culture of citizenship. And a culture of citizenship, in turn, needs individualism.

The question of individualism—its meaning, origins, and sustainability—is one of the abiding concerns of Ken Jowitt's work. "An effective liberal capitalist democracy," he observed at the beginning of the 1990s, "rests on the foundation that is not marketization or privatization; it is individuation. The individual is the basis of liberal capitalist democracy. The question [in any society attempting democratization] is whether you can in fact create a culture in which the individual is the primary actor, as citizen, as entrepreneur, and as a source of moral conscience."[3]

Individualism, is, of course, a contested concept. Some view it as an ideology. In this vein, Steven Lukes distinguishes four elementary ideas "variously expressed and combined" in the term "individualism": (1) the supreme dignity of the individual human being; (2) autonomy; (3) privacy; and (4) self-development. Others view individualism as a peculiar social condition or tendency toward a withdrawal from public life into private life; as such, it is almost synonymous with "egoism" or social anomie. To Marxists, "bourgeois individualism" conjures up the image of political institutions and ideological justifications associated with the liberal state. To Michel Foucault and his disciples, individualism or "modern subjectivity" is a set of practices centered on personal self-perfection and self-fashioning. The only consensus that holds (and it is a significant one) is that individualism is, for better or worse (depending on one's partisan proclivities), a distinct marker of Western liberal capitalist societies—or that, at least, it has developed to the highest degree in the West.

Following Jowitt, who builds on the classical tradition of Emile Durkheim, by "individualism" I will understand a cultural order based on the moral primacy of individuals over groups. In individualist cultures, the individual—not the group—is viewed as the primary actor—as citizen, as entrepreneur, and as a source of moral conscience. A modal member of such a cultural order has an autonomous sense of self-worth that is not reducible to his group memberships and social statuses. Instead, self-worth may come from a number of alternative sources, such as personal achievement (the memory of past struggles and victories) or religion (which declares that each individual, with his unique qualities, is the subject of God's love irrespective of his social station). This autonomous self-worth is, chiefly, what in turn gives a modal member of an individualist order ethical self-confidence: a belief in his capacity for forming a judgment.

The contrast between the individualistic culture and the other major type

TOMEK GRABOWSKI

of cultural order, corporate culture, is substantial. In corporate cultures, the group, not the individual, is the primary unit of action, responsibility, and conscience in society. Whereas individualist cultures encourage their members to question received opinions and to exercise their own judgment, corporate cultures emphasize the individual's inherent weakness, together with his moral and intellectual insufficiency vis-à-vis the group. The members of such cultures are expected to treat key moral precepts of the community as sacred dogmas. The sum total of their group memberships and social statuses normally provides them with the only basis of self-worth that they have. Ninety percent of world cultures, past and present, have been organized on the corporate principle. (This does not mean that "pure" individualist or corporate societies exist anywhere. Each real society is to some degree a mixture of both elements.) Individualism is, historically speaking, an aberration.[4]

Poland has a potential for being a productive and dynamic member of the European democratic community primarily for one reason: it is blessed with the presence of a genuinely individualist current in its culture. But this cultural current is, for a large part, regionally based. The main engine behind the Westernization of Poland—its main asset and a calling card when it comes to claims to European modernity—is roughly the western half of the country.

The east-west divide in today's Poland can be observed on multiple levels, from political and economic patterns to social attitudes to forms of religiosity to voting behavior:

- In the June 2003 referendum on EU membership, regional residence was the single most powerful predictor of the vote. In the western and northern provinces, the rate of support for the EU was *on average* almost twenty percentage points higher than in the eastern provinces.[5] Central Poland was an intermediate case. This is an extraordinary result. For one thing, it is the inhabitants of the western borderlands that should be more afraid of German power, of "the Germans coming and buying our land, our factories, and destroying out culture." Instead, it is the easterners (many of whom have never met a German industrialist) who are much more anti-European and xenophobic.
- In the 2005 parliamentary and presidential elections, the votes split along regional lines. The west and northwest voted for the pro-European, liberal, Civic Platform, and for its presidential candidate, Donald Tusk. The victorious presidential contender, Lech Kaczyński, together with his nationalist Eurosceptical Law and Justice party, won in the east and the southeast.
- According to research on attitudes, the Poles in western Poland are significantly

more individualistic than the Poles in the east. This applies to religious attitudes in particular. An extensive research into Polish Catholic religiosity conducted in the 1990s has revealed the existence, as the authors put it, of "two Polands." In the east and south-east, "Catholicism manifests itself in a greater participation in the Church's organized life and in greater deference to the Church's teachings. The north and the west are the areas where self-declared Catholics have a greater critical distance to the Church's rules and prohibitions, and are much more open to alternative views."[6]

- Economically, the west has done much better, too, after 1989. For instance, it has consistently attracted more foreign direct investment, and has higher rates of medium- and small-scale entrepreneurial activity, than the east (but not necessarily less unemployment). Again, central Poland is an intermediate case.[7]
- There are marked differences in the style and substance of urban politics between the two parts of the country. In the west, urban politics is more pragmatic and more driven by local issues. In the east, local politicians tend to mechanically replicate, in their struggles, nationwide conflicts. In the west, a liberal center (broadly defined) has as a rule clung to power, whereas in the east, control of local councils has typically alternated between postcommunist and right-wing parties.

What accounts for this present-day disparity? Why did western Poland make the (apparent) leap to individualism, while eastern Poland did not? More generally, how does a switch from a corporate order to an individualistic one occur?

THE GENESIS OF INDIVIDUALISM:
THE THREE HISTORICAL "MOMENTS"

Roughly, a cultural breakthrough of this kind involves a confluence of three "historical moments" that occurs very rarely. These moments are a widespread uprooting, a frontier experience, and an institutional intervention. It is this sort of confluence which led to the rise of the individualist cultures in Western Europe and North America and, on a smaller scale, in western Poland after World War II; while its absence foreclosed similar breakthroughs throughout much of the world, including Poland's hinterland, to this day.

The first historical moment necessary for the emergence of the individualist culture is a social uprooting on a wide scale. The resilience of the corporate way of life depends ultimately on the viability of the smallest unit of society—the kinship group. This is where basic orientations to life are

TOMEK GRABOWSKI

collectively elaborated and passed on, and where persons find the ultimate shelter from even the most threatening circumstances of life. This is also where the most inventive strategies of cultural resistance originate. As long as this basic fabric of kinship is preserved, culture can change only so much—there can be secondary adaptation and individual defections, but there can be no switch from one fundamental type of culture to another. Only a widespread uprooting, in other words a destruction of these smallest building blocks of society, will leave people truly defenseless vis-à-vis the threatening new circumstances and therefore capable of fundamentally rethinking their basic orientations. The point is not new. It was made long ago by students of modernization. More recently, Alan Macfarlane has persuasively demonstrated that the rise of English individualism (England being the first recognizably individualist society in history) was predicated in part on the uprooting of the traditional peasant family.[8]

A second critical moment in the rise of individualism is the presence of a frontier experience. The person who has contributed most to our understanding of the cultural importance of frontiers was Frederick Jackson Turner. According to Turner, a frontier is a place of exorbitant social and material opportunities for personal advancement, far beyond what any settled society can provide. It is also a place with weak or nonexistent institutions and, because of that, it is a dangerous place, where risks and uncertainties are extraordinary. Frontier environments privilege a peculiar type of a person: fiercely independent and rebellious, enterprising and ruthless, with a strong ego, oblivious to the needs of others.[9] The appearance of such self-reliant characters—more specifically, of a critical mass of such characters in a limited space—is a key stepping-stone on the way to individualism. As do members of an individualist culture, self-reliant frontiersmen posses a sense of self-worth irreducible to their group memberships and social statuses. One example of frontier environments was the urban areas in northwestern Europe at various times between the eleventh and the sixteenth centuries. Another, of course, was the American West after the Civil War. Both areas were the incubators of individualism.[10]

Poland, too, went through its uprooting and its frontier experience. The geographical locus of both was the so-called Western Territories, a vast area acquired from Germany in 1945. The mass-scale uprooting was the legacy of the war as well as of the brutal resettlement policies of the victorious Allies. The frontier experience of the 1945–1948 period resulted from the wholesale destruction of the centuries-old German cultural legacy by the advancing Soviet army (which created an almost inexhaustible supply of farms, businesses, and houses for the taking) combined with the frightening weakness of the Polish state in the Territories. By the late 1940s, the Western Territories saw the rise of a social character type familiar from other frontier settings: a large group of greedy, aggressive, unsentimental upstarts who were achievement-oriented and proud of their self-reliance.[11]

Here, finally, we get to the third necessary moment: an institutional intervention. The emergence of the new, self-reliant character type is not yet tantamount to the rise of individualism as a culture. Self-reliance is merely a character disposition. Individualism, on the other hand, is a cultural order organized around the idea of the moral primacy of the individual over the group. The members of an individualist culture have, like the self-reliant character, a sense of worth independent of their group memberships. In addition, however, they are *also* oriented in their actions to larger standards and principles, which include the idea of right and wrong, and obligations to other human beings, to the community, and to the nation. The former aspect—an independent sense of self-worth—may come from personal experience and struggle on the frontier. The latter element—standards—cannot arise from personal experience. Standards are, by definition, passed on exclusively in socialization and in the course of interactions with other members of the culture.

Therefore, if the movement towards individualism is to continue, an institution must appear on the frontier—either from the outside, or founded by the self-reliant characters themselves—to take control of the situation and to announce that the frontier is over. It must declare what is permissible and what is not, and impose limits on legitimate behavior. It must effectively "convert" the Clantons—that is, those Clantons who want to and can be converted—into Wyatt Earps. In medieval European cities, that role was played by one social institution above all: Protestantism.

But for such a conversion to occur, the institution in question must possess very peculiar features. It must combine respect for individual dignity with the ability to impart wider standards. This is by no means an easy feat. Institutions generally tend to be very good at socializing in group norms, but they tend to threaten individual efficacy in the process. Those institutions that will eventually succeed in establishing themselves in frontier environments can easily destroy the incipient individualist spirit. To take but one example, this is what happened in the Soviet Trans-Ural provinces after their pacification by the Communist Party under Stalin. These provinces used to be a frontier environment as late as the 1920s, with plenty of self-reliant characters roaming around. Yet by the 1940s, most traces of Soviet individualism had become extinct.[12]

The central dilemma may be put as follows: how to teach group norms

TOMEK GRABOWSKI

without inculcating in the target of the teaching a sense of the individual's smallness and inferiority vis-à-vis the collectivity and its standard-bearers— including moral educators themselves? In other words, how to, on the one hand, uphold the value of the individual and acknowledge a self-reliant person's self-worth, and, on the other hand, pass on norms and obligations that, inevitably, entail submission to something larger than any single person? On the face of it, this looks like squaring a circle.

Yet a solution has occasionally been found. Protestantism, again, provides a requisite matrix. Protestantism contained what, on the face of it, looked like incompatibles. On the one hand, it laid a unique emphasis on the rights of conscience or private judgment and hence on an individual's— as opposed to a community's—moral worth. On the other hand, it did so in the context of an equally strong emphasis on the absolute, normatively binding obligations and duties owed God (like the Ten Commandments).

But the institution need not be a religious one. In France, a version of a secular ethic based on Immanuel Kant that was widely promulgated by the educational institutions at the turn of the twentieth century contributed crucially to the consolidation of individualist culture in that country. The Kantian system, like Protestantism, squares the apparent opposites. It elevates individual moral insight above any group wisdom. At the same time, it demands that we treat others in the same way that we would like to be treated—and builds an entire system of obligations on this basis.[13]

THE POLISH CASE

Poland, too, had its uprooting and its frontier experience, but the fact that the culture of individualism exists today mostly in western as opposed to eastern and central Poland can be largely attributed to the socializing impact of the Catholic Church. And here, Jowitt's point about the underappreciated role of Fortuna in great historical transformations applies particularly well. For the Polish Church to become an institution promoting individualism was nothing short of a miracle. Very little in the historical trends before and immediately after 1945 suggested such a possibility. The Polish Church had traditionally been the carrier of authoritarian and corporate ethos, a ruthless persecutor of any openings into more critical, spiritual, or humanist versions of Catholicism. This was so in the interwar period and, to a large extent, in the first twenty years after the war.[14] Not in western Poland, though. Between 1945 and 1955, the Western Territories saw the birth of a highly anomalous version of Catholicism, a Catholicism concerned more with individual efficacy than with group conformity.

One document gives us an early glimpse of the things to come. In the fall of 1945, Teodor Bensch, a priest and a head administrator of the Varmia region (one of the five new provisional church districts in the Western Territories) issued a public appeal to the priests in his district. It reads in parts as follows:

> The great task of rebuilding a ruined religious life requires more than routine work, a work as usual. The fires of faith, of hope and Christian love are half-extinguished. Senile lips will not set these fires ablaze again. Exceptional times call for exceptional people. May God help us spiritually rise to the occasion. For a gigantic work awaits us. To effectively combat the specter of unlimited greed which has descended upon us. To courageously condemn lies, dishonesty, and pillage. . . . To rescue for God the neglected youth that was brought up in the rotten moral climate of war. Can anyone doubt what qualities of mind and heart such a work requires? To work miracles and to sanctify souls: this can be done only by a priest with a gift of heart coming from God Himself; a priest of unshaken faith, of great and selfless love; a priest who understands the need for suffering and self-denial.

"Let us use the everyday meditation and prayer," he continues, "to awaken in us faith in the supernatural dignity of man and in his eternal destiny. Let's not forget that despite the stain of sin, every person, even the most depraved person, carries within himself a gift of holiness." He finishes with the following appeal:

> In the name of these principles, I ask and appeal to my fellow priests: Under no circumstances, even with the best of intentions, do not reprimand or reprobate anybody from the pulpit by name. Refrain from malice and slander. Do not spread rumors or engage in personal quarrels and parochial intrigues.[15]

It is a remarkable document. What a contrast with the self-satisfied, ossified, and hierarchical world of standard Polish Catholicism! Many elements of modern, reformed Christianity are present here. They include an emphasis on unconditional love, on forgiveness, and on second chances. There is also an unmistakable focus here on fundamental moral precepts, not on ritualistic details. There is, furthermore, rhetorical simplicity, which creates a powerful and direct emotional effect. Another idea running through the sermon is that in order to reach the faithful, the old methods, based on scaring them, on beating them into submission, must be abandoned. Yet the sermon is far from exceptional; by the end of the

TOMEK GRABOWSKI

decade similar motifs came to dominate the tenor of the entire western Church.

The newly created western chapters of the Church were strikingly different from the old chapters. They replaced authoritarian practices with dialogue and persuasion in the spirit of free inquiry; collectivism, with spiritual individualism; and the traditional emphasis on group-maintaining ritual, with stress on personal ethic. This was the kind of Catholicism that was capable of supporting a culture of individualism; while it taught wider standards, rooted in Christian universalism, it did so on terms consistent with an individually based self-worth independent of group membership or social status.

THE CAUSES AND MANIFESTATIONS OF THE WESTERN ANOMALY

One key factor in the metamorphosis of the Polish Church from a corporate to an individualist culture was the absence of a functioning hierarchy in the western Church in the first postwar decade. Between 1945 and 1956, the western Church failed to form itself into anything resembling a normal organization. Its structure was most unusual. First, the status distinctions within the body of clergy—the entire extensive hierarchy—disappeared or lost their meaning.[16] Second and more specifically, the consecutive layers of overseers—the topmost layers above all—did not form, or remained token and powerless.[17] The priests in the west were thus free agents, unhinged from the Church as a corporate body. As a result, they became unusually responsive to the conditions on the ground, and both willing and able to radically revise their pastoral approach.

This inability to form a hierarchy stemmed in large part from the Vatican's actions and inactions. Unwilling to antagonize West German political circles, Pope Pius XII was not interested in granting legal status to the Polish Church's possessions in the west, for that would have legitimized the Soviet-sponsored division of Germany and the changes in her international borders.[18] The chief result of the Vatican's manifest hostility was the inaction and timidity of both western Church administrators and their superior, the Polish primate—especially the new and inexperienced primate, Stefan Wyszyński, who took over in 1948. Afraid of displeasing the Pope, these Polish officials abandoned most constructive organizational steps in the west, such as nominating priests to their posts; developing new bishop's curiae, cathedral chapters, and bishops' courts; creating new parishes; and adjusting existing parish boundaries to take into account the new demographic realities in the Western Territories. There were no bishops in the Territories until 1956. A further deterrent in this regard was Pius's decree of 1949, which confirmed the Pope's prerogatives in matters of ecclesiastical appointments, and automatically excommunicated any church officials who usurped them.[19]

This absence of hierarchy, leading, among other things, to a lack of penalties for unorthodoxy, created a room for bottom-up creativity and experimentation. Unshackled from rigid rules and organizational routines, a priest both could—and had to (since he had no prop in the form of a functioning organization)—listen to local secular community leaders and respond in new ways to the social environment which demanded radically reformed pastoral methods.

Another cause of the metamorphosis was the bankruptcy of the Church's old ways on the western frontier. Over and over again, a western priest would stumble on the unpleasant fact that his pastoral methods, and consequently his very figure, seemed strangely irrelevant, even ridiculous, in the new settler communities. For instance, social pressure and shaming—his favorite methods of ensuring conformity—were rendered ineffective by the settlers' lack of wider group identifications.[20] His focus on external observances and rituals was counterproductive: because of the tremendous sociocultural heterogeneity of the new settler communities, various groups of settlers had conflicting notions of what a "correct" ritual was.[21] His rigid emphasis on minutely prescribed social forms looked ridiculous in a situation where personal security was the settlers' basic concern; as a priest, he was now expected, above all, to do something about widespread social demoralization. In addition, his habitual authoritarianism was under attack from self-reliant settlers who demanded to be respected and treated like equals.

Frustration and a sense of failure were palpable among priests in the west. Bolesław Kominek says that these priests soon knew that the methods from eastern and central Poland were inapplicable in western realities:

> We worked very hard to make sure that eastern traditions were not replicated in our territory. We sensitized our priests to the new existential [social and political] conditions [in the Western Territories]. We fought hard against automatic or mindless imitation of the pastoral traditions from Lviv or Vilnius. . . . From the start, we educated them in a pastoral style that was new and specifically ours.[22]

In many ways, the last type of failure just mentioned—the failure of authoritarianism—was most important in finding a way out of the crisis. The lack of hierarchy made a priest dependent (much more than usual) on ordinary believers, their interests, and values. Without help from the

TOMEK GRABOWSKI

believers, the priest could not accomplish much, from securing his means of subsistence to advancing the process of church rebuilding. Yet it so happened that the people who could help him the most were also those who hated authoritarianism the most; these were the most enterprising, energetic, and successful members of the new communities, that is, the self-reliant frontiersmen par excellence. As his habitual authoritarianism carried him nowhere, a priest groped for an alternative method, one that was acceptable to the self-reliant settlers and could secure their cooperation.

The Communist Party took advantage of the western clergy's vulnerabilities, and, using a carrot-and-stick approach, pried them further away from the mainstream Church. The majority of western priests became entangled, one way or another, with pro-regime splinter groups such as the association PAX. Between 1949 and 1956, in public statements and confidential documents alike, regime functionaries boasted that in the Western Territories the remolding of priests into a "progressive force" loyal to the socialist state was most advanced.[23]

Although PAX was the Trojan horse of Polish Catholicism, its message was innocent enough. It mercilessly exposed the obscurantism of Polish Catholicism of the past. It constantly contrasted "the conservative theology of the Polish bishops with the new currents of thinking coming from the pens of the . . . progressive French priests-theologians."[24] The journals and other public forums organized by PAX served as a platform for the discussion of these and other, little-known currents within Western European Catholicism. Thus, thanks to PAX, and irrespective of its collaborationist stance, a major reevaluation of the intellectual and social legacy of Polish Catholicism was under way.

It was largely out of these failures and pressures that the new spirit was born. The Church that was trying to establish itself in the formerly German territories in the west was essentially a weak, embattled organization fighting for its survival. It was in no position to resist pressures from either the settler population or the Communist regime, each of which, in its own way, demanded that the Church reform its ways. In their search for more effective methods—a sine qua non of remaining relevant in the new settler communities— western priests stumbled on a solution. They elaborated, through trial and error, a set of new and more effective practices, centered on the notion of the return to the original spirit of Christianity. It was a type of Christianity that Maurice Ashley has described in a different (English) context as one which "set more store upon a decent life than on the sacraments and ritual."[25] This new spirit was reflected, for instance, in the sermons of Bolesław Kominek; in the moral self-help books written by Aleksander Zienkiewicz; in the curriculum of the Wrocław Theological Seminary; in Professor Wiesław Gawlik's teachings on conscience; in the work of Józef Wojtukiewicz, the director of the Catholic institute in Wrocław and later in Varmia; in the biblical scholarship of Eugeniusz Dąbrowski; and in the life work of other prominent western priests such as Bensch, Andrzej Wronka, Andrzej Bardecki, Józef Majka, and many others. Below I illustrate in more detail two specific aspects of the western Church's novelty: its authoritative (as opposed to authoritarian) didactic style and its interest in internalization.

An Authoritative Posture

The traditional Polish Church was overwhelmingly authoritarian in its didactic approach. The hierarchy and the clergy claimed an unconditional power over, and sharply distinguished themselves by status barriers from, the lay believers. In his articulation of standards, a typical priest expected nothing short of complete and blind obedience. In the west, this authoritarianism was largely replaced by an authoritative posture: an attempt to teach standards through persuasion and debate.

Writing about the Wrocław theological seminary in the mid-1950s, historian Jan Krucina observes that, unlike seminaries in central Poland at the time, its guiding spirit was that of open-ended debate, questioning of dogmas, and "bold discussions."[26] One practical expression of this critical spirit was the radical upgrading of philosophy, putting it on a par with theology. The professors in the seminary adopted the principle that "philosophy precedes theology; that, furthermore, even later [during the course of the study], when taking into account the Revelation, philosophy does not dissolve into theology but remains an autonomous path for human understanding and for the development of human spirit. . . . Practicing philosophical skills emboldened [the students] to pose questions and debate issues."[27]

A similar approach of open-ended discussion ruled in other seminaries in the Western Territories—in Opole, Varmia, and Gorzów. In the Varmia seminary, the professors concluded that "old, time-honored methods could not be continued. New methods were necessary. [Their elaboration] was a product of discussions and conflicts."[28] In Opole, the rector inaugurated a new style. He "emphasized the formation of intellectual independence and decisiveness in students; a mentality which is not driven by imposed ideas but which, after making a judgment about the correctness of ideas, tries to work them through and to make them one's own."[29]

A good example of this new approach are the sermons of Aleksander

TOMEK GRABOWSKI

Zienkiewicz, for many years a teacher of religion in Wrocław high schools. These sermons have the structure of an argument: there is a readily discernible distinction between claims and premises. The author dialogues with an imaginary listener, anticipating and addressing his concerns. The language is simple and conversational. Zienkiewicz incorporates into his sermons various reservations and counter-arguments, including occasionally the most fundamental ones, such as those that question the basis of his (the Church's) authority.[30]

Internalization

Another component of change in the Polish Church was a shift in emphasis from compliance with standards to the internalization of standards. Traditionally, the Polish Church had been distinctly oriented to external compliance. This meant three closely related things. First, the focus was on proper social forms and not on the subjective meaning of actions. The required proof of membership in the Catholic community consisted of doing and saying the proper things, and making the proper gestures on the appropriate occasions. It did not matter if the things said and done felt genuine or not. Second, the Church was oriented to enforcing conformity through readily available, ever-present sanctions, such as shaming, meted out by the priest or by the wider community, rather than toward helping a person to acquire the criteria of judgment which would make him follow standards even in the absence of external sanctions. Third, the focus of Church teaching was on behavior in the public view, not in private—in standardized, stereotyped, and scripted circumstances, not in novel, unpredictable (or unscripted) circumstances arising in private interactions.[31]

In this respect, too, western priests accomplished a stunning about-face. The new emphasis can be seen, for instance, in the often-repeated opinion among priests in the west that the model of Catholicism understood mostly as a ritual was obsolete and irrelevant. Rather, religion must be a matter of belief, of a true spiritual experience. Church historian Stefan Wójcik points to the same shift away from social forms and in the direction of subjective motivations when he observes that the task of the Wrocław seminary was primarily the formation of a proper human being, and only secondarily the education for priesthood, with its specialized liturgical knowledge.[32]

Also, the priests became interested in inculcating the criteria of judgment that a person would use regardless of sanctions. Kazimierz Dola, writing about the priests in the Opole area, points out their awareness that the "the external stimuli, such as social environment, institutions, the pulpit, school and even family, were disappearing" as guarantors of moral conduct. Instead, they based their work on the premise that "religiosity and religious practices must increasingly become a matter of personal deliberations and decisions. . . . A pastor must facilitate with words and by personal example a process in which, by autonomous decisions, the faithful make a choice in favor of God and the Church."[33]

These new priorities were centered on, and bounded by, the idea of conscience. Western priests understood conscience as an internalized system of values which did not necessarily have obvious or unitary behavioral correlates, the adoption of which was a matter of free choice; following this "voice" became independent of social sanctions or pressures, and could indeed require going against social pressures.

We can glimpse the way western priests thought of conscience from the lectures of Wiesław Gawlik, a logician and professor of the Wrocław seminary. Conscience, writes Gawlik, is a sensation of command and prohibition, of approval and disapproval. It is a universal faculty of individual mind, like thought, feelings, or memory. Conscience is the supreme path to knowing God, as opposed to listening to the voice of humanity, represented by religious rites and practices, or to contemplating God through his external acts of creation. It is the direct voice of God in each of us. "In the same way as sunshine implies that there is sun in the sky, or as a nightly knock on the door implies that someone in the darkness behind the door wants to be let in, so the Voice of Conscience not only commands us, but necessarily raises our mind to the idea of an invisible Teacher." Conscience must not be confused with the voice of society, in the form of internalized norms, commands, and prohibitions. The voice of conscience and the voice of society often coincide, but this does not make them identical. "Conscience is the voice of God to such a high degree" that its commands override all other considerations.[34]

A Catholicism based on argument, on free inquiry; a Catholicism stressing individual moral efficacy and not group conformity; a Catholicism extolling individual worth and reason—these were, in the Polish-Catholic context, revolutionary doctrinal and pedagogical innovations. As Protestantism did it in its time, this western form of Catholicism solved the problem of a postfrontier society. It was able to teach norms in terms consistent with high individual personal efficacy. On the one hand, it supported individual ego. Instead of assaulting individual self-esteem and intelligence, it started with the reality of high individual self-esteem, grounded it in religious notions of God's love for man, and built obligations on this basis. On the other hand, it taught wider standards, which,

TOMEK GRABOWSKI

if internalized, could effectively attenuate the antisocial proclivities of the self-reliant character.

This little-known metamorphosis lay at the root of what was to be, two decades later, the ultimate contribution of the Church to the rise of individualism as a culture. In a nutshell, in 1956, the Gomulka regime conceded an unusual degree of autonomy to the entire Polish Church, thus saving not only the mainstream Church but also the western church, from marginalization. Subsequently, Church leaders in Warsaw found it expedient to shield and support the western anomaly, creating the conditions for its preservation and growth. Later, in the 1960s and 1970s, as the first signs of a crisis of official ideology coincided with the revival of Catholicism throughout Poland, the western innovation, heretofore still limited in its impact, began to spread violently, as first-generation settlers in the west revived their tenuous links with Catholicism.

It is among their children, or among the second generation of the Polish inhabitants of the Western Territories, that the western model of the Church had its greatest impact. The Church was their primary socializer, filling the moral vacuum created by weak family ties and by the ineffective, increasingly opportunistic Communist Party. Ultimately, the Church extended its influence to large social groups in the Western Territories, especially in the cities. Hundreds of thousands of people, including the future activists of Solidarity and today's local politicians, grew up under its formative influence. Here lies the direct source of the cultural "miracle of the Western Territories" whose political and social consequences we observe today.

CONCLUSION

Poland sits on a civilizational fault line. It is also an area of historical indeterminacy. Its maelstrom of values and political currents (liberalism, Catholic fundamentalism, fascism, and peasant populism, to mention only a few) testifies to the country's turbulent history. Liberalism exists, but it contends with strong illiberal, authoritarian strands in culture. The future is unclear.

This is where membership in the EU can make a crucial difference. By providing Polish democracy with standards to emulate, with political support, and, yes, with money, the EU should help tilt the balance. In that respect, Poland is different from a host of other European countries. On the one hand, it is different from a country like Norway. It will make no difference for Norway's democracy whether the country becomes an EU member or not. If anything, the EU, with its bureaucracy, statism, and secrecy, may slightly weaken Norway's culture of citizenship. On the other hand, Poland is also different from a country like Greece, where even a long-standing EU membership was not enough to alter its essentially illiberal culture. Despite a huge transfer of resources from Brussels and the build-up of its highways and telephone lines, Greece has remained what it was before joining: a country run by powerful families, village elders, and corrupt politicians, where one Papandreou regularly succeeds another in power. But in a culturally fractured country like Poland, a powerful external support can enable the Polish liberals to gradually convince the country that they are not an exotic minority but a part of the dominant civilization.

NOTES

I am indebted to Ken Jowitt for so many ideas in this chapter that to mark each borrowing in the text would be impractical. Individualism, Protestantism, frontier, and the connection between the postwar western migrations, the Church, and Poland's modernization—on all these and many other issues, Jowitt's inspiration has been determinative. So has that of Shari J. Cohen and Carrie A. Timko-Santos, who will undoubtedly recognize many of their thoughts in the text below. The argument presented is further developed in my forthcoming book, *A Freak of Culture: Frontiers and Institutions in the Making of Individualism.*

1. "A Nervous New Arrival on the European Union's Block," *The Economist,* August 30, 2003, 16–18.

2. Alexis de Tocqueville, *Democracy in America,* ed. and trans. Harvey C. Mansfield and Delba Winthrop (Chicago: University of Chicago Press, 2000), 11, 381.

3. In Tomek Grabowski, "Nowy Światowy Nieład: Rozmowa z Kenem Jowittem," *Gazeta Wyborcza,* February 27–28, 1993, 12.

4. This and the previous paragraph draw on Jowitt's diverse writings and his lectures at the University of California in the 1990s. However, he might not agree with everything that is said here.

5. "Powiaty Europy," *Gazeta Wyborcza,* June 10, 2003, 20.

6. "Polski Katolicyzm Anno Domini '92," *Polityka,* December 12, 1992.

7. See, for instance, *Encyklopedia Geograficzna Świata: Atlas Polski* (Kraków: Opres, 2000), 79, 107, 120–21.

8. Alan Macfarlane, *The Origins of English Individualism* (Oxford: Basil Blackwell, 1978).

9. Frederick Jackson Turner, *The Frontier in American History* (New York: Holt, 1920), 37, 269–72.

10. On early modern Western European urban areas as frontier environments,

see Erik H. Erikson, *Young Man Luther* (New York: Norton, 1958), 59; and Henri Pirenne, *Medieval Cities* (Princeton, NJ: Princeton University Press, 1948), especially 114–29, 148–49, and 152–61.

11. See, for instance, Padraic Kenney, *Rebuilding Poland, 1945–1950* (Ithaca, NY: Cornell University Press, 1997).

12. On the destruction of fledgling individualism in Stalin's Soviet Union, see Leon Trotsky, *The Revolution Betrayed* (Detroit: Labor Publications, 1991), 84–86, 137–38, 174–91.

13. Raymond Aron, *Main Currents of Sociological Thought: Durkheim, Parento, Weber* (New York: Basic Books, 1967), 5.

14. Ewa Morawska, "The Polish Roman Catholic Church Unbound," in *Can Europe Work?* ed. Stephen E. Hanson and Wilfried Spohn (Seattle: University of Washington Press, 1995).

15. Quoted in Jan Obłąk, "Dzieje diecezji warmińskiej w okresie dwudziestolecia (1945-1965)," *Nasza Przeszłosc* 22 (1965): 214–15.

16. Ryszard Marek, *Kościól rzymsko-katolicki wobec Ziem Zachodnich i Północnych* (Warsaw: PWN, 1976), 61, 69–73.

17. Marek, *Kościól*, 214–15.

18. See Bolesław Kominek, *W służbie Ziem Zachodnich: Z teki pośmiertnej* (Wrocław: Wydawnictwo Wrocławskiej Księgarni Archidiecezjalnej, 1977), 104–17.

19. Marek, *Kościól*, 53.

20. Czesław Strzeszewski, "Najbardziej potrzebne czynniki etyczno-społeczne na Ziemiach Zachodnich," in *Kościół na Ziemiach Zachodnich*, ed. Jan Krucina (Wrocław: Wydawnictwo Wrocławskiej Księgarni Archidiecezjalnej, 1971), 90.

21. Wincenty Urban, *Duszpasterski wkład księży repatriantów w Archidiecezji Wrocławskiej w latach 1945–1970* (Wrocław: n.p., 1970), 25–45.

22. Kominek, *W służbie*, 84.

23. See Stefan Wójcik, "Życie i działalność Księdza Infułata Kazimierza Lagosza," in *Kościół katolicki na Dolnym Śląsku w powojennym 50-leciu*, ed. Ignacy Dec and Krystyn Matwijowski, eds. (Wrocław: Instytut Historyczny Uniwersytetu Wrocław skiego, 1996), 91.

24. Andrzej Micewski, *Cardinal Wyszyński* (San Diego: Harcourt Brace Jovanovich, 1984), 271.

25. Maurice Ashley, *England in the Seventeenth Century* (Baltimore: Penguin, 1967), 238.

26. Jan Krucina, "Formacja teologiczna alumnów," in *Pięćdziesiąt lat Wyższego Seminarium Duchownego we Wrocławiu*, ed. Ignacy Dec and Krystyn Matwijowski (Wrocław: Instytut Historyczny Uniwersytetu Wrocław skiego, 1997), 54–55.

27. Ibid., 53–54.

28. Quoted in Obłąk, "Dzieje diecezji," 223.

29. Kazimierz Dola, "Kościół Katolicki na Opolszczyźnie w Latach 1945–1965," *Nasza Przeszłosc* 22 (1965): 105.

30. Aleksander Zienkiewicz, *Miłości trzeba się uczyć* (Kraków: Wydawnictwo Apostolstwa Modlitwy, 1988).

31. Morawska, "Polish Roman Catholic Church," 52.

32. Stefan Wójcik, *Katechizacja w warunkach systemu totalitarnego* (Wrocław: Instytut Historyczny Uniwersytetu Wrocławskiego, 1995).

33. Dola, "Kościól Katolicki," 112.

34. Wiesław Gawlik, "Poznanie Boga przez sumienie u Newmana," *Znak,* no. 179 (1969): 172–73.

5

THE SOVIET UNION AS A REIGN OF VIRTUE

Aristotelian and Christian Influences
on Modern Russian Ethics and Politics

OLEG KHARKHORDIN

I t was at one of Ken Jowitt's lectures that I first heard Thomas Aquinas
mentioned in relation to Russia.[1] This sounded strange—what could this
philosopher have to do with a country where only about thirty pages of
Summa Theologiae were translated, and where the only existing treatise on
Aquinas was written by a Polish communist? Jowitt, however, did not mind
compellingly combining the seemingly incompatible—this was his definition of charisma.

This article will explore a link between *Doctor Angelicus* and Russian
communism, though not in the way Ken would necessarily put it. I would
claim that what Aquinas did for Western Christianity—adding three theological virtues to the four cardinal ones and thus integrating Aristotle
into Christianity—was similarly done by generations of nameless monastic scribes in Russia, who had unintentionally achieved a similar effect. This
inculcation of the Aristotelian virtue ethic into the most basic moral intuitions of Orthodox Christianity in Russia played itself out after 1917, when
virtue ethics (as opposed, following Alasdair MacIntyre, to the ethics of
principle—for example, to the Kantian system[2]) became predominant. The
tradition of republican virtue that the Bolsheviks inherited from the French
Revolution was grafted onto a vast sea of mundane moral intuitions on
religious virtue shared by the peasants. The outcome was attention to particularities of the case in consideration rather than to a general rule that
has to be applied to all cases, a yearning for narratives that depicted model

virtues rather than produced a theory of them, and, finally, an emphasis on desirable character traits rather than internal values. This predominance of the ethics of virtue, rather than the ethics of principle, still influences the post-Soviet situation.

1

Western students of Soviet morals for a long time characterized the specificity of this ethical system as aimed at training certain traits that constitute a model moral character rather than learning and applying universal ethical rules. For example, an analysis of the 1961 Moral Code of the Builder of Communism, adopted by the Twenty-second Party Congress together with the last version of the party program, shows that though the code enumerates certain "principles," "the emphasis clearly is placed on morally praiseworthy attitudes, sentiments and predispositions, making it a statement of exemplary character rather than of conduct rules."[3] Indeed, such principles as proletarian internationalism can be seen as a restatement of the virtue of *caritas* (love for other Christians), no matter what their ethnic origin is, while unflinching communist resistance to enemy doctrines has its corollary in Christian enmity toward devilish machinations, no matter what their provenance. According to standard analyses of Soviet ethics, the ultimate criterion of the morality of an act was whether it contributed to the building of communism or not—that is, whether and to what extent it corresponded to the ultimate goal of political development. The Moral Code of the Builder of Communism, then, was a "device of the party leadership to promote those *traits* which it deems more important to molding society in the direction it wishes."[4]

Katerina Clark described Socialist Realism as a system not of aesthetic but of didactic concern par excellence, which aimed at moral transformation rather than at aesthetic insight. Clark has also recently outlined a set of personal features of the fearless leader captured by standard epithets of the Socialist Realist novel that were intended to be emulated by readers of the novel (and, by extension, by viewers of Socialist Realist films as well): these included temperance and perseverance, then rigidity of faith, and, finally, care for the masses. Hot-headedness was allowed as well, but such passionate outbursts were usually ascribed to disciples, who would eventually master their intemperance and would come to be self-possessed and self-controlled believers.[5] Although Clark registers the preponderance of two character traits—temperance and love/*caritas*—other virtues, such as prudence, courage, and justice, can be found in didactic novels as well.

OLEG KHARKHORDIN

Learning these qualities was easy. As my own analysis of communist books of guidance has demonstrated, the main way to fashion one's self was to choose and follow an exemplary hero, resolving difficult moral situations with the help of personal identification with this model figure: what s/he would have done in such a case? Preaching by example, stemming from the medieval *imitatio Christi*, rather than its corollary, preaching by word, came to dominate the arsenal of moral practices of the Soviet civilization.[6]

Attention to model character traits suggests that Soviet morality was a morality of virtue rather than a morality of principle. Alasdair MacIntyre's *After Virtue* and the ensuing discussion on how virtue ethics are opposed to ethics of principle articulated this now-famous distinction between the morality of appropriate action that eschews general rules and the morality of law that is predicated on the application of a standard universal rule to any situation of everyday life. If Aristotle and Aquinas are key figures for the first type of moralizing, Immanuel Kant and John Rawls would be central for the second. In this respect, Soviet morals were more Aristotelian than Kantian in nature.

For example, Soviet people grew up habitually criticizing the "coldness and inhumanity" of laws. They demanded instead that a judicial decision "takes into consideration the particular condition of a given individual" *(voidet v ego polozhenie)*, that it shows its full humanity in accounting for all the minute details of the situation, the act, and individual under consideration. Harold Berman noted long ago this intense personalization of Soviet justice by comparing the criminal codes of the Anglo-American world and of the USSR. In the USSR, negligence was defined as a criminal failure by a particular defendant to consider consequences, while in the United States, a person could be indicted for negligence if s/he failed to consider any of the factors that any rational person should have taken into account.[7] In the Soviet case, this American standard was clearly not enough—judicial investigation was supposed to determine whether this particular standard of rational behavior could be applicable to the person in question, given his or her education, background, standpoint, and mood at the time of the crime, and so on.

Thus, a feeling of total appropriateness underlay the functioning of justice; it was not possible to satisfy the people's sense of justice simply by claiming that the predetermined rules were applied in an equal way. Everyone was sure that such a general application could not guarantee real equality of treatment, given the differences between individuals. The same applied to moral judgment in everyday debates—no single general criterion could be used to evaluate the morality of a given action. Only a consideration of the context of an act—the particularities of the person who had carried it out and the specificity of consequences—could provide a totally just evaluation of an act. In short, the appropriateness of action for a given context, not its conformity with a general rule, was the main way to assess its moral rightness. Soviet ethics was a form of virtue ethics.

Soviet politics were no less Aristotelian than Soviet morals, since it relied on elements of quasi-Aristotelian reasoning to an unprecedented extent, and it is surprising that so many political theorists of Soviet civilization overlooked this basic fact. At the least, Soviet politics relied on those elements that Thomas Hobbes thought to be Aristotelian when he decided to scrap them for good. One can briefly enumerate the three pre- or anti-Hobbesian features that clearly distinguish the Soviet political system from that of modern liberal democracies. First, this politics had a clearly set goal, a telos of political development that Aristotle sets up for the polis by saying that people get together to live in city-states not just in order to live but in order to "live well." Hobbes, who represents the foundation of our modern understanding of politics, singled out this very definition as the root of all evil. In his opinion, because some vicious philosophers (and here he implies Aristotle and Aquinas) had posited a certain summum bonum as the goal of the development of politics, seditious ministers of the English revolution (who had their own idea of the good for the country) fomented dissent and then open rebellion by clashing with the royalists who had another vision of the good. Hobbes would then argue that a modern state is different from the previously conceived types of political union in that it eschews imposing the desired goal of development. In short, modern politics is about avoiding the sum of bad things, *summum malum,* rather than seeking summum bonum, that is, the modern state should guarantee the pursuit of the good to every citizen, but specifically in the private sphere, while its public activity should simply guarantee law and order, thus preventing the "war of all against all."[8] Thus, post-Reformation Europe guaranteed freedom of conscience and the pursuit of religiously defined good in the private realm, while no common perception of the good life as a shared goal of society's aspirations was to be pursued by public authorities. Now, this is exactly opposite to the Soviet understanding of politics. The Soviet Union had a clearly defined goal—the building of a communist society—and thus considered itself morally superior to the liberal West, where politics was all about lowly motives of self-preservation and ensuring for each an opportunity for the private pursuit of avarice and similar sins.[9]

Second, the communist project relied on a decisive feature lying at the foundation of teleological politics of the common good—what Aristotle

OLEG KHARKHORDIN

called *homonoia*, what his Latin detractors translated as *concordia*, and what in Russian became *edinoglasie*, unanimity—which, given the Bolshevik fear of factional strife, ushered in an intense effort to weed out all types of schismatics and factionalists.

Third, given that Aristotle often insisted that friendship was more important than justice,[10] one is hardly surprised that citizens of the Soviet Union were supposed to be friends in the common undertaking of building a better future. No other major modern country besides the USSR officially ascribed to its citizens the title of "comrades."[11] Of course, the link to the Aristotelian model came through a long chain of descent. The Bolsheviks copied the vocabulary of Western European socialism of the 1830s and 1840s and of the French Revolution, with both these vocabularies and their shared notion of *fraternité* being heavily indebted to Rousseau's vision of people united in the general will. This vision itself was inherited from Montesquieu and Machiavelli, with their notion of republican virtue that was a handy redefinition of Aquinas's notion of the Christian virtue of the prince, itself a product of a medieval interpretation of Aristotelian politics. Of course, Aristotle did not demand periodic revues of virtues of comrade-citizens (even though some commentators define care for citizens' virtues as a central feature of the Aristotelian view of the polis[12]), but when the Bolsheviks institutionalized regular purges, they might have brought this logic to its conclusion.

Given these Aristotelian qualities of the Soviet system, one is puzzled by two questions: where did they come from, and do they still matter after the collapse of the communism?

2

The Bolsheviks were never enamored with Aristotle per se, since he was just one small part of the ancient heritage they were supposed to make available to each person in his or her individual development. Their language was mostly suffused with appeals to Robespierre, Gironde, Thermidor, and other imagery of the French Revolution, which relied on Rousseau and the notion of civic virtue, a point well stressed almost fifty years ago by Jacob Talmon.[13] But I would suggest that the Bolsheviks' version of the discourse of civic virtue, hardly comprehensible to the masses of illiterate peasants, managed to strike a chord with these masses because it had hit a rock bottom of popular discourse on virtues that they habitually received during liturgy—catechistic expositions of the basics of the Orthodox Christian faith and transmissions of stories from saints' vitae.

Russian Church literature is pervaded by discourse on virtues all the way up to 1917 and after, while secular works with this term (*dobrodetel'* in Russian) in the title tend to become scarce after the end of the eighteenth century. Checking computer catalogues of major libraries reveals that theatrical plays with titles such as "Virtuous French Lady" or "Virtue Rewarded"[14] and secular books with titles like "Virtuous Soul, or Rules of Moral Guidance"[15] had become fairly rare by the beginning of the nineteenth century and almost petered out by the middle of it. Perhaps translations of Kant and the spread of German idealism in general (with its ethics of principle) contributed to this development. Perhaps Russian revolutionaries and the learned society of the nineteenth century wanted to stress that they were radically distant from the stale discourse on virtues of the official Church or from the Masonic interpretation of virtues characteristic of the eighteenth-century Russian Enlightenment. Perhaps attention to the inner life of the individual was replacing the usual didactic enumeration of visible personal qualities called virtues. All of these may have been reasons, but the end result is the same: virtue survived as a central concern mainly in church discourse.

But where did the Russian Church get this discourse on virtues? To answer this question, one has to engage in a detective story similar to Umberto Eco's *The Name of the Rose* —trying to discover the traces of a villain who introduced an Aristotelian type of ethics into mainstream Russian Church culture. In Latin Christianity, everything seems more or less straightforward: Thomas Aquinas wrote a commentary on Aristotle's *Nicomachean Ethics,* adding three theological virtues (faith, hope, and love) to the ancient four "cardinal virtues" (prudence, justice, temperance, and courage). In so doing, he authorized not only the subordination of pagan virtues to Christian ones, but he also attempted an integration of these pagan virtues into a Christian view of life as an open-ended quest for salvation. And who was the Russian or Slavonic Aquinas? Given the prevalence of discourse on virtue in the Russian Church and the many texts of the Greek Church fathers translated into Slavonic in the eleventh through fourteenth centuries, how and in what form did virtue make its entry into the Russian discourse on ethics? That is, who of the saintly authors adapted Aristotle's discourse on virtues for Christian use, and how was it then transmitted to the Slavonic world?

3

Aristotle had a rather unhappy fate in Russia. After the disintegration of Kievan Rus', very few people, if any, could read Greek, so that in 1518 the

OLEG KHARKHORDIN

grand prince had to invite to Muscovy a monk from Mount Athos, Maxim the Greek, to translate some extant Greek manuscripts into Russian. The first full versions of Aristotelian treatises became available in Latin translations only with the spread of the Ruthenian literary influence in the mid-seventeenth century. Because of their connection with Catholicism and Jesuit colleges in Poland, however, these were viewed with suspicion by their contemporaries. For example, one of the leaders of the Russian Schism, Archpriest Avvakum, deliberately rejected philosophical syllogism as "an external whore" (vneshniaia bliad'),[16] arguing that checking a theological argument by the criterion of its logic and conformity to a syllogistic structure is a trick of the devil. In 1664 he writes, "Christ did not teach dialectic or rhetoric because a rhetor and a philosopher cannot be a Christian. . . . For Hellenic wisdom is the mother of all devilish dogmas."[17] His insistence that pagan philosophers are to be rejected as sources of Christian wisdom parallels the preoccupation of a majority of the early church fathers, who witnessed the uneasy coexistence of pagan philosophy taught in Byzantium's secular schools with the public preaching of Christianity in the churches. Indeed, the fathers found many heretics of their day pushed into their mistaken stances by faithfully applying syllogistic inquiry to the scriptures. As a result of this, the fathers knew Aristotle, but there was a tacit contract not to cite him when criticizing Peripatetic philosophy.[18]

Some quotations from Aristotle were available in the *Pchela*—a medieval Russian translation of *Melissa*, a Byzantian collection of the remarks and maxims of philosophers and church fathers. The Greek original was part of the florilegium tradition, but the Russian translation endowed this collection with a different function—it became a source of didactic wisdom on the salvation of the soul, and was copied endlessly in the fifteenth and sixteenth centuries.[19] It would have been extremely difficult to guess the content of the *Nicomachean Ethics* simply on the basis of these didactic aphorisms. Also, some of these alleged citations from Aristotle reflected not his philosophy but Christian views ascribed to him later in order to employ his authority. But since Russian scribes frequently dropped the names of authors when rewriting a manuscript, the problem of ascribing to Aristotle some of the pieties he did not pronounce died out in subsequent versions of this collection.

The main reception of systematic Aristotelian philosophy before the Ruthenian influence of the seventeenth century came through the interpretation of the works of St. John of Damascus.[20] His *Dialectics* contained a prolonged exposition on the categories of Aristotle, without ever mentioning the philosopher by name. But the book depended on Aristotelian logic rather than on ethics, and virtues are discussed only passim, as a small part of the chapter on freedom of the will.[21] When Prince Andrei Kurbsky translated Damascene's *Dialectics* into Russian in the sixteenth century, he mulled over the categories of logic, not of ethics, even though he may have read the *Nicomachean Ethics* as well.[22] His introduction to Damascene's translation, though, used Maxim the Greek's translations of excerpts from St. Gregory of Nazianzus's funeral oration for St. Basil the Great,[23] and this may show us a more effective route of transmission of Aristotelian ethics into Russian life.

Fedor Karpov, a sixteenth-century boyar famous for his learned exchange with Maxim the Greek on astrology and for some letters to the Moscow metropolitan Daniel (where he quoted Aristotle on politics), is perhaps the sole example of direct knowledge of Aristotle on the part of a subject of Muscovite czardom. He definitely used book 10 of the *Nicomachean Ethics,* and possibly books 9 and 5 of *Politics.*[24] Karpov's exposure to Aristotle was exceptional within Muscovy; he was engaged in diplomatic service and could have encountered Aristotle in Latin translations with some of his contacts. Most of his contemporaries could examine only a pseudo-Aristotelian treatise, a Slavonic translation of a book from the mirror of princes genre, which is written as a series of advices from Aristotle to his disciple Alexander the Great, and which came to be known in Latin as *Secretum Secretorum.* Curiously enough, the Slavonic version was translated from Hebrew at the end of the fifteenth century and was used by the first officially condemned heretics of Russian history—the Judaizers.[25] Given its Hebrew provenance, this version of *Secretum Secretorum* contained some added excerpts from Maimonides (also an Aristotelian thinker who adapted Aristotle for Judaism). The effect of this treatise on Muscovy's morals is hard to evaluate, largely because the twenty or so extant copies of the Slavonic *Secretum Secretorum* contain advices on medicine and divination together with advices on political or moral issues.[26] Here Russian history abandons its similarity to *The Name of the Rose* but becomes more like another seminal novel, Milorad Pavic's *The Khazar Dictionary,* and it requires a well-qualified researcher capable of doing work in Hebrew, Arabic, Latin, and Slavonic to evaluate rival versions of what may have happened during this most curious episode of medieval crosscultural translation.[27]

4

Dmitrii Bulanin, Viktor Zhivov, and Francis Thomson have noted the absence of documented traces of direct transmission of Hellenistic philosophy to Russia, since (according to a now widely accepted thesis first proposed by Georgii Fedotov) the entire corpus of Slavonic translations available to a Kievan and then Muscovite reader up until the seventeenth century and the Ruthenian breakthrough was roughly comparable to the collection of a typical provincial Greek monastery, such as the monastery of St. John on Pathmos, for which we have the thirteenth-century records of its holdings.[28] Indeed, the majority of available literature in Slavonic was of a didactic and liturgical character. But even the first translations carried with them a description of some doctrine of Christian virtues. The first *Izbornik* (a book of Christian wisdom allegedly addressed to Prince Sviatoslav, but actually just a Kievan copy of the text translated from the Greek original for the Bulgarian King Simeon at the end of the tenth century) from 1073 already carries a description of ancient cardinal virtues. I. I. Sreznevskii even mentions it in his dictionary article on *doblest'* (courage): "There are four types of virtue: prudence *(mudrost')*, justice *(pravda)*, temperance [or, rather, in its Christian version, "chastity," in the sense of not submitting to one's passions—i.e., *tselomudrie*], courage."[29] The *Izbornik* from 1076 includes St. Basil the Great's exhortation, "How should a man live?" which details monastic virtues but was mistakenly addressed by a Kievan scribe to the laity.

The most popular genre of medieval Russian literature was miscellanea, which copied quotes from different existing books and put them side by side in a new book. Precisely because each such book was almost an encyclopedia of Christian knowledge, a monk with such a book in his possession could go and found a new hermitage of saintly living. William Veder calls the structural principle of these books "kaleidoscopic,"[30] but they may also be called "constellations" (to use the term of Walter Benjamin): these books are products of authoritative quotation where hardly anything was added by the profane hands of a scribe, the only resemblance of authorial intention being an arrangement of cited sources. Thus, we cannot find a single Russian-authored treatise commenting on the *Nicomachean Ethics*, but we find many manuscripts faithfully copying the original set of Slavonic translations together with citations from some added translations, mainly done in the thirteenth and fourteenth centuries. Postmodernists would marvel at this "death of the author": the Aquinas effect was achieved by a mass of hardly identifiable scribes who managed to adapt and integrate the Aristotelian ethics as thoroughly as Aquinas had, but without any dogmatic treatises. They merely copied simple sets of exhortations and admonitions originally translated from Greek, frequently broken into smaller sets of quotes or even into one-liners, with all these new elements being regrouped into new constellations.

Of course, a manuscript might have been used for other purposes than learning virtue. Furthermore, the presence of a book, even in a substantive number of extant manuscripts, does not mean that it was read. Evidence of efforts of authorial creativity and direct appeal to individual morals appears only with the development of sermon writing for elite audiences in the mid-seventeenth century. Paul Bushkovitch documented the usual concerns of such popular sermon writers as Epifanii Slavinteskii and Simeon Polotskii. Both of these Ruthenians-turned-Muscovites dropped the ascetic list of virtues and exhorted listeners (or readers) to fight two main vices of the Muscovite court—pride and greed—opposing to them the Christian virtues of humility and charity. That is, Slavinteskii and Polotskii copied their Ruthenian predecessors, but dropped from their consideration ancient cardinal virtues such as justice, concentrating on the Christian virtues most important for court life. However, the cardinal virtues of the Aristotelian epoch were not forgotten altogether: in a rare sermon Slavinteskii directed to the monks in the 1650s, he enumerates the usual four Hellenistic virtues, and then adds a Christian one—humility (smirenie),[31] in effect doing what Aquinas did to the set of virtues when he added three theological virtues to the four ancient ones. Now, one should not take Epifanii to be a grand innovator, since his spiritual teacher, Bishop Petr Mohila, the founder of the first religious academy in Kiev, already included the three theological virtues of Aquinas—faith, hope, and love—in his version of the Orthodox catechism published in the 1620s.[32] Mohila, of course, was just incorporating into Orthodox thought what he had learned from his Catholic teachers in Poland, where he had picked up both Aquinas and Aristotle. Once Ukrainians and Belorussians had firmly set themselves up in Moscow, Aristotle (in Latin and in Catholic interpretations) became a staple diet for at least two generations of the elite of the Russian clergy, until the "St. Petersburg takeover" tried to purge this Muscovite spirit and to introduce elements of Protestantism into Orthodoxy instead.[33]

But, one might argue, the sermons of the Ukrainians would not have struck such a chord with the Russian soul if it were not already prepared to listen to exhortations on virtue and to denunciations of vice. The pre-seventeenth-century sources of exhortation to virtuous living are more or less clear: the two most widely cited and excerpted church fathers in Russia were St. John Chrysostom and St. Ephraim the Syrian, both preoccupied with virtue.[34] Apart from this, one could have access to miscellanea, three different types of which—*The Golden Chain, Izmaragd,* and *Pchela*— are prevalent.

Let us take a closer look at the first version of *Pchela* in comparison to

OLEG KHARKHORDIN

later ones.[35] It is especially interesting, since its opening sections follow the order of the cardinal virtues. The first section, a general introduction on virtues, lists quotes from Solomon, St. Gregory of Nyssa, Socrates, Diogenes, and Aristotle. In chapter 2, on prudence, we have didactic sentences from an unnamed apostle, Jesus, son of Sirach, Socrates, Diodorus, Aristotle, and Favorinus; on chastity (temperance), we have Job, Plutarch, Alexander the Great, Epictetus, Menedemus, and Xanthus; on courage, Socrates, Alexander the Great, Leonidas, King of Sparta, and Aristotle; on justice, Philip of Macedon, Menander, Hyperides, and Pythagoras. Chapter 5 is about the virtue of friendship (yet another Aristotelian topic), and only then comes a chapter on charity. In the later version, this florilegium was transformed into a very pious reading by changing the order of the presentation of the chapters and placing all sentences on cardinal virtues at the end of the manuscript; of the sixty-eight chapters in the second version, justice is mentioned only in chapter 12 (rather than chapter 5), and all other Hellenistic virtues and the general introduction are almost at the end of the book. The book opens with chapters (taken from the back of the first version) on power, charity, grace, prayer, providence, laudation, war and peace, memory, and so on. The rearrangement, one might guess, suited the goals of an ancient scribe presenting the book of wisdom to a Christian prince concerned with the problems of rule and piety rather than to a Byzantian student of rhetoric.

Georgii Fedotov, who tried evaluating how the secular audience received writings on virtue like the *Pchela,* suggested considering the twelfth-century epistle of Vladimir Monomakh. Of course, it is clear that only the elite thought about Christian virtues at that time, and this famous grand prince of Kievan Russia is one of the best examples of this very selective reception. Only in the seventeenth century would many people start caring about what Monomakh cared about in the twelfth; still, the pattern of reception is interesting. Monomakh repeats what he could get from the 100 words of pseudo-Gennadius included in the *Izbornik* of 1076, that a prince should have the virtues of obedience, humility, repentance, and mortification.[36] But then he shifts his attention to justice, a main concern for a ruler, and advises his sons on this most important of princely virtues, adding a secular flavor to an otherwise trite Christian exposition. One of the reasons Aquinas had to tolerate the cardinal virtues and deal with Aristotle in thirteenth-century Western Europe was that the Church had to somehow accommodate the barbaric people of Northern Europe, who still lived according to the heroic virtues so well described by Homer and more or less successfully adapted by Aristotle for a fine Athenian society. By merging such heroic warrior virtues as temperance and courage with such theological virtues as charity and hope, Aquinas was opening the way for successfully integrating Germanic tribes into the new Christian order.[37] Monomakh was doing the same, by adapting strict monastic concentration only on matters of faith to make it fit his princely concerns.

Where did the Greek fathers get their knowledge of Aristotle and virtues? Plato and the Stoics are mentioned more frequently, since they could be rather well-integrated into Christianity. Aristotle, on the contrary, became suspect after the first heretics, so many Christian authors discuss Aristotelian topics without mentioning his name. Some early authors— like Clement of Alexandria (third century), an originator of apophatic theology and the first to seriously concern himself with a discursive justification of Christian morals—could still be open in their use of Aristotle: "It is in the area of ethics that Aristotle most directly influenced Clement. Here Clement does not parade Aristotelian theories and distinctions simply to display his erudition, rather they form an integral part of his thought. In two broad areas of ethics, that concerning the 'good life' and that dealing with volition and wrongdoing, Aristotle's influence is clear."[38] Later fathers could hardly do the same.

Werner Jaeger agrees with Aristotelian influences on Clement, but in his opinion the most decisive introduction of Aristotle into Christian morals happens in the writings of St. Basil the Great. But in Basil's multivolume oeuvre, Aristotle's name appears only three times. In *Contra Eunomius* (1.5.43), he says that a Christian does not need the syllogisms of Aristotle, and in 1.9.8 he adds that Eunomius used them. In epistle 135 he evaluates Aristotle and Theophrastus as literary pragmatists who, in his opinion, were better in this respect than Plato. Still, Basil "had postulated a Christian ethics, and his commentary on the Psalms shows clearly that he wanted to use them as such. On closer inspection we see that behind this interpretation there stands Basil's own experience with Aristotle's *Nicomachean Ethics,* that he had no doubt studied carefully during his stay at the school in Athens. He then felt the need for a Christian equivalent and thought that the Psalms came closest to it."[39]

One of many questions for future study is the transmission of the discourse on ethics from the Alexandrian school (Clement of Alexandria and Origen) to the Cappadocians (Basil the Great, Gregory of Nazianzus, and Gregory of Nyssa). André-Jean Festugiere noted that only Athens and Alexandria had Aristotle in original manuscripts rather than in doxography— that is, in collections of concise statements on the opinions of philosophers popular in Byzantium. Thus, it is highly doubtful that anyone but Origen read Aristotle's treatises in manuscript form. David Runia adds Clement to this list. However, these two were virtually unknown in Russia, while the Cappadocians were a favorite object of quotation pilfering; some of their works (like Basil's "How Should a Christian Live?") were copied by generations of scribes. Clearly, the task of tracing the hidden Aristotelianism of the fathers is a daunting task.

5

In 1926, Emelian Iaroslavskii, then the head of the central control commission prosecuting the misconduct by the party members edited a book entitled *What Should a Communist Be Like?* The book was part of the discussion on party ethics at the time, and included a number of articles on communist morality, notably the discussion between Western European communists and their Russian counterparts, together with some articles by popular communist zealots such as Sofia Smidovich, Nadezhda Krupskaia, and Martyn Liadov. In 1935, a similar book, with the title *What Does the Party Demand from a Communist?* (republished in 1936 in a corrected edition) had already ceased to present the issues as a discussion, and opted instead for a clear, concise catechism of the moral qualities of a communist. The 1943 edition, *What Does the Party Demand from a Communist During the Great Patriotic War?* shifted the emphasis in that it added warrior virtues to the list of theological ones (*soznatel'nost'* [conscience] and *skromnost'* [modesty] were moved a bit to make way for *muzhestvo* [courage]) but it did not change the essential character of the appeal: St. Basil the Great was speaking through the lips of St. Emelian Iaroslavskii, who by that time had already published 5 volumes of writing against Christianity.

Parallel to this high moral discourse, which hardly influenced the masses, Bolshevik moral precepts were being integrated into the standard secondary-school program of Russian literature. A Maiakovskii verse for children started with a line known by generations of Soviet citizens: "A child came to his father and asked, 'Father, what is good and what is bad?'" *(Krokha syn prishel k otsu. . . .)* The father then enumerates a series of typical situations that detail virtuous and vicious qualities. A more advanced version of Maiakovskii was offered for teenagers, in the famous poem "Lenin": "To a youth thinking about a model from which to make his own life, I say: Make it from that of Felix Dzerzhinsky!" *(Iunoshe, obdumyvaiuschemy zhitie, sdelat' by zhizn' s kogo. . . .)* The structure of setting up and following a moral exemplar is clearly outlined here. In short, a list of virtues is given by a father to a son not in the form of a doctrinal treatise but in a series of model characters (and rhyming makes it easier to remember). St. Pavel Korchagin replaces St. Paul, while St. Oleg Koshevoi replaces Prince Oleg—the alleged founder of Kievan Rus'. The new society is based on communist virtue, obvious moral exemplars, and educative Socialist Realist vitae and sermons—saintly zeal rules the day.[40]

Now, could these ways of moralizing, deeply impregnated in everyday life, have disappeared in the twenty or so years after the collapse of the USSR? Given that the integration of Aristotelian ethics of virtue into the Russian culture had taken centuries of insistent effort, it would be hard to believe its erosion has happened so quickly. Let us consider the two implications of this conjecture.

First, attention to virtues rather than to stale survey studies of values may allow us to redirect Russia's quest for a new type of ethic that may found a better future. For example, a study of the ethos of those whom contemporary Russians call "bandits" and whom Vadim Volkov in his fascinating book has analyzed as "enforcement partners"[41] shows that these virtuosos of violence share a certain way of life that cherishes personal qualities rooted in sports' teams activities of the Soviet past. Self-restraint in talk and action, courage sometimes bordering on total disregard of death, friendship in helping a warrior-comrade—all these qualities are part of the ideological self-representation (that is, misrepresentation) that these communities share.

Now, instead of unmasking the bandits' discourse as misrepresentation (a task for a critical sociologist), a virtue theorist might try doing what Aquinas did to the Christianity of the thirteenth century, founding the Christian virtues on the bedrock of the cardinal virtues of the hero-warrior that so well suited the Germans and the Irish of those times. In a twelfth-century society with the absence of institutional mechanisms of conflict resolution, noted Alasdair MacIntyre, this was an ingenious way of integrating warring tribes into the world of Christian morality and more or less predictable behavior. One can imagine that a new ethos can be articulated in a similar way in postcommunist Russia.

The second implication of this study for contemporary concerns is an opportunity to compare radical virtue regimes and their sequels on the basis of a single common denominator—a reception and adaptation of Aristotelian ethics. One of the reasons for Aquinas's creativity in adapting Aristotle to Christian purposes was the need to wrestle the main intellectual weapon from the Arab conquerors—a serious threat at that time. Indeed, Al-Farabi and Al-Ghazali made Aristotle palatable to Islam long before he became part and parcel of Western Christianity, and Maimonides did the same for Judaism. Now, given that the ethics of virtue was the common

OLEG KHARKHORDIN

denominator of all of these moral traditions, a well-founded comparative study of the revolutionary politics of virtue, and a concomitant reconceptualization of certain contemporary problems, like the Israeli-Arab conflict, become possible. It was not for nothing that the main Taliban government agency was called the Ministry of Virtue and Vice.

NOTES

I started thinking of writing this article in the spring of 2001, having walked past Ken's office after teaching a class on Aristotle at Berkeley. I am grateful to Viktor Zhivov, Alexander Etkind, and Mikhail Krom for their discussion of the weaknesses of the argument during a seminar we had in the fall of 2001. Jeff Weintraub's contribution was invaluable, as ever. And my final thanks go to the editors of this volume, who have pressed me to finish this think piece, which over the years has been discussed at Yale, Harvard, EHESS in Paris, and many other universities.

1. See, e.g., Ken Jowitt, *New World Disorder: The Leninist Extinction* (Berkeley: University of California Press, 1992), 181, 189.

2. Alasdair MacIntyre, *After Virtue* (London: Duckworth, 1981). See also *After MacIntyre*, ed. John Horton and Susan Mendus (Notre Dame, IN: University of Notre Dame Press, 1994).

3. Kit R. Christensen, *The Politics of Character Development* (Westport, CT: Greenwood, 1994), 118.

4. Richard T. De George, *Soviet Ethics and Morality* (Ann Arbor: University of Michigan Press, 1969), 103.

5. Katerina Clark, "Socialist Realism With Shores: The Conventions for the Positive Hero," in *Socialist Realism Without Shores*, ed. Thomas Lahusen and Evgeny Dobrenko (Durham, NC: Duke University Press, 1997).

6. Oleg Kharkhordin, *The Collective and the Individual in Russia* (Berkeley: University of California Press, 1999), and chapter 6 of Caroline Walker Bynum, *Docere verbo et exemplo: An Aspect of Twelfth Century Spirituality* (Missoula, MT: Scholars Press, 1979).

7. Harold Berman, *Justice in the USSR*, 2nd ed. (Cambridge, MA: Harvard University Press, 1962), 258.

8. See, e.g., Norberto Bobbio, *Thomas Hobbes and the Natural Law Tradition* (Chicago: University of Chicago Press, 1989).

9. This heroic ethic and positing of the common goal of the good life is not uniquely Soviet, of course. In the twentieth century, another notable example is the Third Reich, but this paper eschews consideration of the complicated relationship between the Soviets and the Third Reich, as well as the question of an Aristotelian community defined in terms of racial purity.

10. As, for example, he says in the beginning of chapter 8 of the *Nicomachean Ethics:* "Friendship also seems to hold cities together, and lawgivers seem to be more concerned about it than justice. . . . [For] when people are friends, justice is unnecessary, but when they are just they need friendship as well" (1155a22–27).

11. One other example is, of course, the Nazi notion of Parteigenosse, but it applied only to party members, and was never universalized to cover all citizens of Nazi Germany.

12. John M. Cooper, "Political Animals and Civic Friendship," in *Friendship: A Philosophical Reader,* ed. Neera Kapur Badhwar (Ithaca, NY: Cornell University Press, 1993).

13. Tamara Kondratieva, *Bolcheviks et Jacobins: Itineraire des analogies* (Paris: Payot, 1989). J. L. Talmon, *The Origins of Totalitarian Democracy* (London: Secker & Warburg, 1952).

14. Anne de la Roche-Guilhen, *Dobrodetelnaia frantsuzhinka, ili istoriia o Agnesie Soro, zhivshei vo vremia Karla VII* (St. Petersburg: 1791). Liubov Krichevskaia, *Slepaia mat', ili nagrada ispytannoi dobrodieteli: Drama* (Kharkov: 1818). See also, e.g., *Dobrodetelnoi volshebnik: dramaticheskaia opera v piati deistviiakh* (Moscow: 1787).

15. Aleksei Artemiev, *Dobrodetelnaia dusha, ili Nravouchitelnyia pravila v polzu i nauchenie iunoshestva* (St. Petersburg: 1777).

16. Victor Zhivov, "Religioznaia reforma i individualnoe nachalo v russkoi literature XVII veka," in *Iz istorii russkoi kultury,* vol. 3 (Moscow: Iazyki russkoi kultury, 2000), 477.

17. Francis J. Thomson, "The Distorted Russian Perception of Classical Antiquity: The Causes and Consequences," reprinted in *The Reception of Byzantine Culture in Mediaeval Russia* (Ashgate, UK: Variorum, 1995), 347.

18. David T. Runia, "Festugiere Revisited: Aristotle in the Greek Patres," *Vigiliae Christianae* 43:1 (1989).

19. Dmitrii M. Bulanin, *Antichnye traditsii v drevnerusskoi literature, XI–XVI vv.* (Munich: Otto Sagner, 1991), 62–66.

20. See V. P. Zubov, *Aristotel'* (Moscow: AN SSSR, 1963), 332. W. F. Ryan, "Aristotle in Old Russian Literature," *Modern Language Review* 63, no. 3 (1968).

21. Ioann Damaskin, *Polnoe sobranie tvorenii* (St. Petersburg: 1913), 237.

22. Vasilii Kalugin, *Andrei Kurbskii i Ivan Groznyi* (Moscow: Iazyki russkoi kultury, 1998), 100, repeats Kurbsky's statement that he had read Aristotelian ethics, but there is scant evidence to prove this point. See Bulanin, *Antichnye Traditsii,* 81; and Georgii Florovskii, *Puti russkago bogosloviia* (Paris: 1937), 32.

23. Dmitrii Bulanin, *Perevody i poslaniia Maksima Greka* (Leningrad: Nauka, 1984), 39n39.

24. Alexander Klibanov, *Dukhovnaia kultura srednevekovoi Rusi* (Moscow: Aspekt Press, 1994), 210, 214.

25. W. F. Ryan, "Aristotle and Pseudo-Aristotle in Kievan and Muscovite Russia," in *Pseudo-Aristotle in the Middle Ages,* ed. Jill Kraye et al. (London: Warburg Institute, 1986), 106, comes to the conclusion that it was a "dominating text ascribed to Aristotle in the Muscovite period."

OLEG KHARKHORDIN

26. Ryan claims that the unprecedented autocratic rule of Ivan the Terrible can be explained by adherence to advices contained in the mirror of princes that he owned. Czar Alexei Mikhailovich, father of Peter the Great, also had a copy of this work. W. F. Ryan, "The *Secretum Secretorum* and the Muscovite Autocracy," in *Pseudo-Aristotle: The Secret of Secrets*, ed. W.F. Ryan and Charles B. Schmitt (London: Warburg Institute, 1982).

27. Moshe Taube has approached this problem with adequate skill, but there is no publication yet; see http://www.aatseel.org/program/aatseel/1998/abstracts/Moshe_Taube.html (accessed September 12, 2005). The "Judaizers literature" also included a Russian version of Al-Ghazali's "Intentions of Philosophers," another treatise with Aristotelian themes.

28. Fedotov, *Russian Religious Mind*, vol. 1; Bulanin, *Antichnye traditsii;* Zhivov, "Religioznaia reforma"; Thomson, "Distorted Russian Perception."

29. I. I. Sreznevskii, *Materialy dlia slovaria drevne-russkago iazyka*, vol. 1, col. 672 (St. Petersburg: Tipografiia Imperatorskoi Akademii Nauk, 1893–1912).

30. William R. Veder, "Old Russia's 'Intellectual Silence' Reconsidered," in vol. 2 of *Medieval Russian Culture*, ed. Michael S. Flier and Daniel Rowland (Berkeley: University of California Press, 1994).

31. Paul M. Bushkovitch, *Religion and Society in Russia: The Sixteenth and Seventeenth Centuries* (Oxford: Oxford University Press, 1992), 152.

32. Georgii Florovskii, *Puti russkago bogosloviia* (Paris: 1937), 49,

33. Ibid., chap. 4. Gregory Freeze also states that up until 1760 a (miniscule) number of students of diocesan seminaries, who managed to master Latin grammar and made it to the end of the normative six-year program, learned Aristotle's logic and Aquinas's theology. After that, the 1760s seminaries began using a philosophy textbook by Baumeister (essentially an adaptation of Christian Wolff) instead of Aristotle, while Prokopovich and new Russian Church hierarchs' treatises replaced Aquinas. Gregory Freeze, *The Russian Levites: Parish Clergy in the Eighteenth Century* (Cambridge, MA: Harvard University Press, 1977), 93–94.

34. This was Fedotov's opinion, shared by many others; he never gave grounds for this largely intuitive claim, however. Interestingly enough, these two were among the three ancient church fathers (the third one was Gregory of Nazianzus) that autodidactic peasants perused in their reading groups in 1904; see Vera Shevzov, *Popular Orthodoxy in Late Imperial Rural Russia* (Ph.D. diss, Yale University, 1994), 656, 661.

35. Translated in the twelfth and thirteenth centuries, the earliest manuscript being from the fourteenth century, there are about twenty extant copies. Dmitrii Bulanin, ed., *Slovar' knizhnosti i knizhnikov Drevnei Rusi*, vol. 2, part 1 (Leningrad: Nauka, 1987), 382–84. For full text, see V. Semenov, ed., *Drevnerusskaia "Pchela" po pergamennomu spisku* (St. Petersburg; 1893).

36. Fedotov, *Russian Religious Mind*, 245–57.

37. MacIntyre, *After Virtue*, 165–67.

38. Elizabeth A. Clark, *Clement's Use of Aristotle: The Aristotelian Contribution to*

Clement of Alexandria's Refutation of Gnosticism (Lewiston, NY: Edwin Mellen Press, 1977), 27.

39. Werner Jaeger, *Early Christianity and Greek Paideia* (Cambridge, MA: Belknap, 1961), 59, 96.

40. See an enthusiastic account in Ella Winter, *Red Virtue: Human Relationships in the New Russia* (New York: Harcourt, Brace and Company, 1933).

41. Vadim Volkov, *Violent Entrepreneurs: The Use of Force in the Making of Russian Capitalism* (Ithaca, NY: Cornell University Press, 2002).

6

SLOBODAN MILOŠEVIĆ

Charismatic Leader or Plebiscitarian Demagogue?

VELJKO VUJAČIĆ

INTRODUCTION

I n *The Leninist Response to National Dependency,* Ken Jowitt advances a
highly suggestive proposition about charismatic leadership. According
to Jowitt, the innovative aspect of charisma lies in the ability of the charismatic leader "to dramatically reconcile incompatible commitments and
orientations. It is in this sense that the charismatic is a revolutionary agent—
someone who is able in certain social circumstances institutionally to
combine (with varying degrees of success for varying degrees of time) orientations and commitments that until then were seen as mutually exclusive. It is the extraordinary and inspirational quality of such a leader that
makes possible the recasting of previously incompatible elements into a
new unit of personal identity and organizational membership, and the
recommitment of (some) social groups to that unit."[1] Jowitt illustrates this
observation with several examples. Christ's peculiar innovation consisted
in the reconciliation of the conflicting imperatives of "ethnic and parochial
Judaism" with the "the incorporation of the gentile world" into a new unit
of organization and membership—the Church. Analogously, Hitler reconciled traditional ethnic German nationalism with the "supra-ethnic exclu-
sivity" of Nazi Aryanism, and institutionalized this ideological amalgam
into a new unit of membership—the Nazi Party. Jowitt's foremost example,
however, is Lenin's "party of a new type," which he views as an innova-

tive amalgam of individual heroism and organizational impersonalism. The creativity and imagination with which Jowitt has applied his central intuition about the Leninist party as an innovative amalgam of charismatic-mobilizational, rational-procedural, and (neo)traditional political-cultural orientations to the developmental history of Leninist regimes is well known. For the purposes of this article, however, it is Jowitt's specification of two additional conditions of charismatic success that is of central interest.

First, Jowitt observes, since charisma is politically innovative by definition, a charismatic leader will have difficulty mobilizing social constituencies unless he (she) possesses "qualities that, at least in a formal or structural sense, are consistent with the defining features of the society he wishes to change." Thus, it was Christ's "status as a rabbi and student of Mosaic law that made him intelligible to others," which gave him insider status; similarly, Hitler's participation in the German war effort gave him the credible status of a German nationalist, rendering him culturally intelligible to his following. Finally, while Lenin's commitment to organizational impersonalism was culturally innovative in the Russian socio-cultural context, his status as a "teacher-headmaster" and "wise old man" made him recognizably "Russian" in the cultural sense.[2]

Secondly, Jowitt argues, the political-cultural match between leaders and followers must be institutionally embodied in the charismatic organization. In the case of Leninist parties, the emphasis on hierarchy, collectivism, self-sacrifice, and the personal authority of the cadres are critical political-cultural features that render the party organization intelligible to the mass following, as they are congruent with the status orientations of traditional peasant societies. On the other hand, the stress on impersonal criteria in judging cadre performance, empirical study of the class struggle, and rational discussion of the party line are culturally innovative elements that help account for the success of Leninist parties among newly mobilized constituencies in societies undergoing rapid social mobilization (e.g., intellectuals, students, and workers of peasant origin).[3] It follows from this that while charismatic leaders and their organizations foster a radical break with traditional socio-cultural orientations, the incorporation of some elements of tradition into an innovative ideological-institutional framework is a necessary condition of their ultimate success. Thus, the affinity between tradition and charisma is rooted not only in the personal character of these two types of authority—as Weber had it—but also in the political-cultural and institutional imperatives of acquiring an initial charismatic following by incorporating elements of tradition.

Jowitt's criteria of charismatic success are meant as a supplement to and

VELJKO VUJAČIĆ

not a refutation of Weber's basic point that charismatic leaders arise in periods of profound institutional crises, when standard responses to recurrent challenges are no longer effective. As Weber writes, in such times, recognition of the leader's charismatic qualities becomes a matter of "complete personal devotion" born of "enthusiasm, or of despair and hope."[4] The decisive point here is that it is the subjective recognition of the charismatic claims of the leader by the following—not the extraordinary personal qualities of the leader as such—that help explain the emergence of the "charismatic bond."[5] The point deserves to be reiterated, in view of both the numerous attempts to psychologize charisma and the rejection of the concept of charisma altogether on the grounds that the unpredictability of its emergence does not make it a useful tool for social-scientific research. At the risk of erring in the direction of excessive sociologization, we should take note of the observation by Pierre Bourdieu: "Let us then dispose once and for all of the notion of charisma as a property attaching to the nature of a single individual, and examine instead, in each particular case, sociologically pertinent characteristics of an individual biography. The aim in this context is to explain why a particular individual finds himself socially predisposed to live out and express with particular cogency and coherence, ethical or political predispositions that are already present in a latent state amongst all the members of the class or group of his addressees."[6] Although overly deterministic in the sense that it risks denying the creative aspects of charismatic leadership, Bourdieu's formulation correctly addresses our attention to the latent aspirations of the potential charismatic following, and nicely complements Jowitt's central observation about the reconciliation of "mutually incompatible commitments and orientations" as central to understanding charismatic appeals.

Jowitt's (and Bourdieu's) theoretical observations enable us to address a key lacuna in Weber's theory of charismatic authority, namely the unresolved problem of the sociological origins of charisma. Taken together, these observations enable us to assemble the essential elements for a *definition of the charismatic situation*. Although such a definition cannot enable us to predict the rise of charismatic leaders, parties, or movements, it can help us retrospectively conceptualize their point of sociological origin in the societies in which they arose. To systematize these observations in a somewhat more formal fashion, we might define a charismatic situation as one in which (1) profound institutional crisis is accompanied by the repetitive failure of existing institutions to solve it by employing standard means; (2) a variety of social constituencies with well-defined "latent ethical and political predispositions" are available for political mobilization; (3) a leader (and/or party) emerges offering a potentially novel fusion of mutually incompatible orientations and commitments into a "new unit of organization and membership"; (4) the leader's (and/or party's) appeals are "at least formally congruent" with traditional political-cultural orientations, rendering them culturally recognizable to potential constituencies (here it deserves to be pointed out that tradition should not be equated with the existence of traditional society, but can also refer to the congruence between leadership appeals and select elements of unique national and even transnational traditions, e.g., fundamentalist Islam); and (5) elements of tradition are incorporated into the new institutional-ideological amalgam, and subordinated to the larger transformative goals of the charismatic leader/party/movement.

A qualifying remark is in order. The existence of a charismatic situation and of leaders who have the potential to be recognized as charismatic is not sufficient to guarantee that truly charismatic leadership will emerge. Most importantly, just as the followers have to recognize the leader as charismatic, the leader has to develop a sense of mission which, if interiorized by his followers, will result in their "inner transformation," i.e., identity-altering political (and/or religious/cultural) experiences. Pressures for routinization, temptations of opportunism, and the permeable boundary between charisma and personal rule, however, might result in the rapid devolution of charisma in the direction of tradition, even when a formal commitment to a modernizing agenda is an essential element in the leader's (party's) agenda. In addition, a plebiscitarian leader of the masses might temporarily succeed in reconciling mutually incompatible commitments and orientations without necessarily placing them on a new institutional foundation. When this happens, the leader's initial charismatic gains are rapidly wasted, resulting in the loss of support on the part of some (but not all) critical constituencies whose latent aspirations he (she) has failed to satisfy.

The example of Slobodan Milošević, a leader who came to personify the latent aspirations of different constituencies in Serbia in the critical period of the demise of the Yugoslav federation, briefly illustrates the latter dynamic. There is little doubt that Milošević came to power in a "charismatic situation" as defined above; that he possessed elements of genuine charisma and acquired a strong mass following; that he succeeded in temporarily reconciling commitments and orientations that were previously seen as mutually incompatible; and, finally, that he was "culturally recognizable" to his following. Yet, despite the possession of these characteristics, Milošević does not qualify as a charismatic leader. Most importantly,

Milošević did not embrace a transformative charismatic mission, failed to forge mutually incompatible orientations and commitments into more permanent units of organization and membership, and did not incorporate critical elements of tradition into an innovative framework. As a result, his rule did not leave a lasting institutional legacy on a par with such genuine charismatic leaders as Juan Peron or Charles de Gaulle.

LATENT PREDISPOSITIONS AND THE EMERGENCE OF A CHARISMATIC SITUATION IN SERBIA IN THE 1980s

In outlining the emergence of the charismatic situation in Serbia in the mid-1980s, it is imperative to begin with a brief outline of the crisis of Yugoslav federalism. This crisis had its roots in the rapid decentralization of authority from the federal center to the republics and autonomous provinces (Kosovo and Vojvodina) in the late 1960s. Although envisaged as an integral part of a broader reform strategy, the process of decentralization was fraught with unintended consequences. Most importantly, the rise of the Croatian mass movement under the auspices of a reformist-nationalist leadership (1968–1971) raised the question of Yugoslav state integrity in dramatic form. Marshal Tito's response to this challenge was a purge of the Croatian "nationalists," and of recalcitrant republican elites in Slovenia ("technocrats") and Serbia ("liberals") as well. Paradoxically, the reimposition of ideological and party controls was not accompanied by institutional centralization, but rather by the further devolution of authority to the republics and autonomous provinces in the 1974 constitution. In adopting this strategy, Tito counted on his personal authority, the Yugoslav People's Army (JNA), a renewed ideological emphasis on "brotherhood and unity," and a complicated system of functional representation to hold the country together. The institutional downside of this strategy, however, became apparent in the early 1980s when Tito's death left a political vacuum at the center, and the federal state was reduced to a collection of elites acting as the pseudo-representatives of the various republics and autonomous provinces. The crux of the issue was that the institutional imperative of achieving consensus gave republican and provincial elites veto power over all major federal decisions, impeding necessary political and economic reforms.[7] The crisis of the foreign-debt-ridden and inefficient Yugoslav economy further exacerbated this situation, as it gave rise to repeated conflicts between the more developed republics and autonomous provinces, which contributed disproportionately to the federal state (Slovenia, Croatia, and Vojvodina), and their less-developed counterparts, which expected the policy of transfer payments to continue. At the same time, however, even the elites of the less-developed republics and autonomous provinces (Bosnia, Macedonia, Montenegro, and Kosovo) resisted any interference from the federal center in "their internal political matters."

The position of Serbia in this emerging system of Yugoslav confederalism was unique. Historically, Serbia and the Serbs were associated with the central Yugoslav state both politically and ideologically. If in the interwar period, however, this association had been placed on a firm institutional and ideological foundation (the Serbian dynasty as the dynasty of the unified state, the domination of ethnic Serbs in the political elite, and the incorporation of Serbian cultural themes into the ideology of Yugoslavism), the communist regime made a sharp institutional and ideological break with "greater Serbian hegemony." Institutionally, the dissociation of Serbian and Yugoslav identities was manifested in the creation of the Socialist Republic of Serbia that was envisaged as a quasi-national state of titular nationality on a par with other Yugoslav republics; ideologically, any form of "greater Serbian nationalism" was permanently discredited. In order to further reduce Serbia's potential for hegemony, Tito's regime carved out two autonomous provinces within Serbia (Vojvodina and Kosovo), refused to create corresponding autonomous regions for Serbs in Croatia and Bosnia, and promoted the institutional and ethnic separation of Montenegro from Serbia. After the mid-1960s, "socialist Yugoslavism," too, was discredited under the pretext of the struggle against "bureaucratic centralism" and "unitarism," ideological sins identified with Serbian cadres.[8] Finally, once the "Serbian liberals" were purged in the early 1970s, the modernizing form of Serbian particularism (i.e., one centered on the Republic of Serbia, not on the Serbian nation in Yugoslavia as a whole) was discredited for good, leaving the next generation of Serbian party leaders in a quandary: if the Serbs were not allowed to be "socialist Yugoslavs" and could not concentrate on the narrower interests of the Republic of Serbia, what form of Serbian national identity was ideologically acceptable?[9]

The decentralizing policies of Yugoslav communists were already subjected to criticism by leading Serbian intellectuals in the early 1970s. As Belgrade professor of law Mihailo Djurić argued at the time of the passing of the 1971 constitutional amendments, "The borders of today's Socialist Republic of Serbia are neither the national nor the historical borders of the Serbian people." If these "administrative," "arbitrary," and "unsustainable" borders between republics and autonomous provinces were "to be understood as the borders between national states," Djurić warned, about 40 percent of all Serbs would find themselves outside the jurisdiction of Serbia proper. The number of Serbs thus left outside of the borders of Serbia equaled the number of all Croats in Yugoslavia or the number of all Slovenes, Macedonians, and Bosnian Moslems in Yugoslavia combined.[10]

Djurić's criticism of the constitutional amendments earned him a one-year prison term. By the late 1970s, however, when the decentralizing effects of the 1974 constitution came into full effect and the autonomous provinces of Kosovo and Vojvodina practically acquired the status of republics, the terrain of political struggle shifted to party committees. The efforts of Serbia's leading party politician of the time, Dragoslav Marković, to institutionally reintegrate Kosovo and Vojvodina into Serbia, however, came to no avail. More than that, in the early 1980s the Serbian party leadership suffered repeated political humiliations by the "confederal bloc" led by Slovenia, Croatia, and Vojvodina in federal party meetings.[11] Although Milošević's predecessor at the helm of Serbia's party organization, Ivan Stambolić, partially succeeded in persuading the Yugoslav party leadership to initiate a process of constitutional revision that would enable Serbia to reassert control over its two autonomous provinces, the political process was too slow to keep pace with the increasingly troublesome Kosovo crisis. This crisis lingered on from the time of the 1981 Kosovo riots, but exploded in 1986 and 1987, when Serbian emigration from Kosovo assumed dramatic proportions and the leaders of the new grassroots movement of the Kosovo Serbs threatened to organize a mass exodus of the remaining Serbian population from the province.[12]

The relative institutional weakness of Serbia, however, was only one element in the overall status of Serbs in the Yugoslav (con)federation. Equally important was the fact that many Serbs had developed a positive identification with the Yugoslav communist state through their participation in the Partisan movement. This Partisan constituency was especially pronounced among Serbs in Croatia and Bosnia who formed the bulwark of Tito's movement and were relatively overrepresented in the army officer corps, the Federal Ministry of the Interior, and the party and government structures of Croatia and Bosnia.[13] This, then, was a latent elite constituency with a vested interest in a strong federal state, and one that, moreover, had bitter memories of wartime massacres in the Independent State of Croatia.[14]

At least initially, however, the decisive terrain on which the Serbian national question was fought was Serbia itself. Here, in addition to the dramatic Kosovo crisis, the intellectual revival of liberalism and nationalism was most important. In the six years after Tito's death (1980–86), intellectual dissent took a variety of forms: challenges to Tito's personality cult;

the proliferation of "flying universities," attempts to found new journals as vehicles for an emerging independent public opinion, the publication of personal memoirs, novels, and historical works breaking official taboos concerning Yugoslavia's past, and social scientific critiques of the inefficient, corrupt, and decentralized political system. Serbia's writers and historians were particularly active in exposing the illegitimate methods which the Communist Party used to stifle political parties in the postwar period, questioning the commitment of Tito's Partisans to fighting the Nazi invader (as opposed to waging an internal war against the Serbian Chetniks), and opening up painful questions about the past, notably about the genocide of Serbs in the Independent State of Croatia. As a result, a wholesale questioning of the official historical narrative occurred, presenting the communist regime with the increasingly difficult dilemma of restoring the credibility of the dominant ideology.[15]

One of the most widely shared ideas that emerged from this intellectual reckoning was the notion that the pathological political and economic consequences of Yugoslavia's decentralization were not the result of infighting in the communist elite or other historically contingent factors, but part and parcel of a deliberate policy to weaken Serbia. In this reinterpretation of the communist project, the weakening of Yugoslavia's federal center and of Serbia as the historical bulwark of the unified Yugoslav state was seen as a continuation of the interwar policies of Yugoslav communists. Acting under Comintern instructions, the argument went, Yugoslav communists (including "deluded" Serbian internationalists among them) deliberately sought to destabilize the interwar kingdom by supporting peripheral nationalist movements in Croatia, Macedonia, and Kosovo, and delegitimizing the Yugoslav state as an artificial creation of the Versailles treaty. The systematic demonization of Serbs as "oppressors" and "unitarists" was integral to this ideological project, as testified by the repeated invocation of "greater Serbian hegemony" as the allegedly main culprit for Yugoslavia's nationality problems. In making this accusation the cornerstone of their ideological view and translating it into a policy that institutionally crippled Serbia, the communists were curtailing the Serbs' right to national self-expression, denigrating the disproportionate contribution of Serbian communists to the Partisans' National-Liberation War, and encouraging the fragmentation of the Yugoslav state. This argument was most clearly articulated by sociologist Ljubomir Tadić, and also found its way into the key document of an emerging Serbian particularism, *The Memorandum of the Serbian Academy of Sciences and Arts* (1986).[16]

By 1986, therefore, the Serbian party elite found itself challenged on multiple fronts: resistance from the "confederal bloc" and constitutional deadlock on the Yugoslav level; the defiance of the elites of Vojvodina and Kosovo in Serbia itself; an emerging grassroots movement of the Kosovo Serbs that exposed the impotence of the federal state in resolving the ethnic crisis in Kosovo; and the mounting challenge posed by a vigorous liberal and nationalist opposition. The severe problems faced by the Yugoslav economy in the early 1980s posed an additional threat to regime stability. Here, too, Serbia's situation was unique. Despite the presence of backward regions in Serbia itself (not to mention Kosovo, Yugoslavia's poorest region), Serbia was officially treated as a "developed republic" and a donor of federal aid to undeveloped regions. Throughout the early 1980s, the theme of Serbia's "falling behind" was repeatedly voiced in the speeches of Milošević's predecessor, Ivan Stambolić, who called into question the continued viability of Serbia's considerable contributions to the federation.[17] The problem of Serbia's economic stagnation also figured prominently in the Memorandum, where it was largely attributed to the artificially low prices imposed on Serbia's raw materials and energy sources, communist nationality policy, and a form of "unequivalent exchange" that favored Slovenia and Croatia.[18] Whatever the preferred interpretation, however, it was clear that the Serbian economy was under particularly severe strain on account of its sizeable state-dependent working class, high unemployment (15–17 percent in the 1981–1985 period), and migrant outflow from rural to urban areas.[19] Under these conditions, not only the working class, but also middle-class specialists and bureaucrats faced a considerable erosion in their standard of living, all the more difficult to accept in view of their high consumption levels financed by foreign loans in the 1970s. The inflation of university degrees further exacerbated the relative deprivation caused by unrealistic social expectations in a deteriorating economic environment. Not accidentally, the best Yugoslav (not only Serbian) sociologists began speaking of blocked social mobility, the advent of a "closed society," and the overproduction of specialists as chronic social-structural problems that needed urgent remedy if Yugoslav society was to survive the challenges that lay ahead.[20] As far as the Serbian party leadership was concerned, its political-economic dilemma consisted in the necessity of curtailing the autonomy of Kosovo and Vojvodina, while at the same time pursuing liberalizing economic policies and supporting the reform program of the federal government.[21]

By the mid-1980s, therefore, the Serbian party leadership was facing political defeat on all fronts: (con)federal, domestic (internal opposition), ethnic (in Kosovo), and economic. Expectations of the gradual "withering away" of the communist regime were rife in Belgrade, where a vigorous intellectual opposition was demanding the institutionalization of the rule of law, the legalization of political parties, the reassertion of Serbia's control over Kosovo, the strengthening of the federal state, and new solutions to the dramatic economic crisis. Nothing in the fairly dull biography of the party secretary of Belgrade's city committee (1984–86), Slobodan Milošević, suggested that he was the leader who would turn this political situation around. Yet, in intraparty circles in which, on account of his self-discipline, Milošević came to be known as "our little Lenin," a coterie of cadre followers was developing, preparing the ground for his rise to leadership.

The first intimation of Milošević's distinct leadership style occurred at the Eighteenth Session of the Central Committee of the League of Communists (CCLC) of Serbia (in November 1984), in which the increasing frustration of Serbia's party leadership with the "Vojvodina autonomists" broke out into the open. In this context, Milošević's speech stood out for its boldness. Attacking the "bureaucratic-etatist" forces that stood in the way of Yugoslavia's "unified market" by promoting "economic autarchy" as a means of consolidating their political independence, Milošević accused the provincial elites of promoting "economic backwardness" by pursuing the illusory goal of "protecting their workers" from world market competition, defending an untenable status quo, and masking their "undeserved privileges" with the help of ideological slogans. Milošević unfavorably contrasted the entrenched conservatism of provincial party officialdom with the demands for changes voiced by the "party membership," and especially the working class in Serbia's large enterprises. In an unusually bold statement for a communist official, Milošević directly questioned the traditional Yugoslav party line on the dangers of "unitarism":

> If someone is threatening us by saying that, by opening these questions, we are entering into a political crisis then so be it, because this is a division on the question: unity or separatism. In this crisis separatism will not pass, because the whole people is for unity. A leadership that cannot see this loses the trust of the people and should lose it. If the politics of disintegration and separatism does not leave the stage, this society has no perspective, it must disintegrate. We have to be aware that whenever we speak about unity, the opponents of necessary changes in the political system proclaim us to be unitarists and impute to us absurd intentions— that we want to abolish the republics and autonomous provinces, that we want to lower the aid to undeveloped regions, etc. But these insinuations, this kind of abuse can no longer pass. For a start, we must rid ourselves of the complex of unitarism. Serbian communists never fought for unitarism. On the contrary,

every such attempt was condemned. Serbian communists have been burdened unjustly and for a long time with the complex of unitarism and a feeling of guilt for the behavior of the Serbian bourgeoisie in the past, although it is well known that in this respect the Serbian bourgeoisie had the support of the whole bourgeoisie, and against itself the whole Yugoslav proletariat, whether its national origin was Serbian, Macedonian, or Croatian.[22]

Milošević's confrontational tone, unabashed defense of Yugoslav unity, rejection of the "complex of unitarism," and explicit recognition of the need to rebuild the party's legitimacy by regaining the support of "the people" offered an early intimation of his distinct political style. At the same time, it is noteworthy that Milošević portrayed himself as a champion of economic change and spoke of the need for a "unified Yugoslav market" in practically the same sentences in which he argued for intraparty unity. During the next two years, Milošević presented himself as a tough Titoist party conservative, adopting strong confrontational language vis-à-vis the domestic opposition (the "bourgeois right"), while at the same time posing as a champion of market-oriented economic reforms. If his "Leninist will" endeared him to party conservatives, his reformist sponsor, Ivan Stambolić, who promoted him to the leadership of the Serbian party in 1986, also thought him a devoted follower.[23]

Milošević's populist breakthrough, as is well known, came on April 24, 1987, in the small town of Kosovo Polje, when the new leader of Serbia's communists suddenly turned from a dull, grey apparatchik into a political hero. Standing on the balcony of the Kosovo Polje House of Culture, Milošević observed the tumultuous crowd of Serbs who wanted to speak to the party leader of Serbia without the mediation of Kosovo Albanian or Serbian officials whom they saw as politically bankrupt. When the local police began using truncheons to disperse the crowd, the president of Serbia's communists, visibly shaken, walked toward the mass gathered in front of the building, and suddenly pronounced a phrase which instantly turned him into a hero: "From now on, no one will dare to beat you! No one has the right to beat you!"[24]

What followed was a thirteen-hour meeting during which Milošević patiently listened to the *cahiers de doléances* of the Kosovo Serbs. Nothing like that had ever happened in the communist *ancien régime*. Politicians had always spoken in dull phrases about self-management and enemies of the party, or the latest and completely incomprehensible reorganization of the already tremendously complex Yugoslav political system. Even the word "crisis," increasingly found in their speeches, could provoke only protracted yawns. Most importantly, they had always spoken at, never with or to, the people.

By contrast, the encounter of Serbia's party boss with the Kosovo Serbs was both direct and dramatic. Old men and women, grieving mothers and war veterans, came to the podium, expressing anger and frustration at the impotence of Serbian and Yugoslav authorities, who did nothing to protect the Serbian minority in Kosovo. Stories of arson, of threats to life and property by local Albanians, and of mistreatment by the local party, judicial, and police authorities dominated the proceedings. The boldness of these testimonies in what was still a very controlled communist regime suggested a level of desperation and impotence that had turned into anger.[25]

As the meeting came to a close, Milošević delivered a powerful speech in which he appealed to Serbs and Montenegrins

> to stay here [in Kosovo], because this is your land, here are your houses, fields and gardens, your memories. You are not going to leave your land just because life has become difficult, because you are suffering from injustice and humiliation. It was never in the spirit of the Serbian and Montenegrin people to withdraw in the face of difficulties, to demobilize itself when it should fight, to become demoralized when the situation is hard. You should stay here both because of your ancestors and your heirs. Otherwise, your ancestors would be ashamed, your heirs disappointed.

Milošević ended his speech with an imperative statement in which he made clear to the Kosovo Serbs that "all of Yugoslavia is with you. It is not a question of Kosovo being a problem of Yugoslavia, but that Yugoslavia is also Kosovo. Yugoslavia does not exist without Kosovo! Yugoslavia disintegrates without Kosovo! Yugoslavia and Serbia will not give up Kosovo!"[26]

Despite his repeated emphasis on Titoist ideals (brotherhood and unity), the Yugoslav idea, and the need for the coexistence of Serbs, Montenegrins, and Albanians in Kosovo, Milošević's speech was highly nontraditional for a communist. This was particularly true of that part of his speech in which he appealed to the traditional heroism of Serbs and Montenegrins in the face of *injustice* and *humiliation,* and spoke of the significance of *land, memories,* and *ancestors.* By linking the question of dignity in the face of injustice to a historical tradition of Serbian *heroism,* to *land, memories,* and *ancestors,* Milošević was speaking in a new political language— the language of nationalism.

Milošević's Kosovo Polje speech almost instantly turned him into a hero of the masses. At a time when institutional gridlock was paralyzing the

Yugoslav federation and other communist leaders spoke in the frozen language of a half-dead ideology, Milošević's direct appeal to the people over the heads of other party officials struck a powerful chord. Like Weber's prototypical charismatic leader, Milošević appeared as a prophet endowed with a "gift of grace," capable of delivering his people from suffering by performing the "miracle" of returning the holy land of Kosovo to the fold of Serbia. And, in complete accordance with Weber's model, the personal devotion of his followers was based on the recognition of his charismatic qualities arising out of "enthusiasm, or of despair and hope."

A year later, the "Milošević revolution" was in full swing. In summer 1988, masses of people came out on the streets to express their support for constitutional changes which would bring the two autonomous provinces, Kosovo and Vojvodina, under the control of the Socialist Republic of Serbia. Although the regime played a considerable role in the organization of these "rallies of solidarity" with the Kosovo Serbs, there was a distinct impression that "the people" had come out into the open, spontaneously expressing grievances and demands that had never been voiced before. Even a cursory glance at the major slogans of the "rallies of solidarity" reveals the complexity of Milošević's appeals: here extreme nationalism, populist adoration for the leader, frustrated aspirations for social justice and reform, and nostalgia for the glorious days of Yugoslavism were all mixed in new and unpredictable forms. Thus, calls for revenge ("Out with immigrants from Albania!" "We will hang Vllasi!"—the Albanian communist leader) went hand in hand with Yugoslavist slogans ("We don't want civil war!" "Down with nationalists!"), and celebration of the leader ("Slobodan our hero, Serbia will die for you!"), with anticommunist sentiments and demands for social justice ("Central Committee, aren't you ashamed to hear the people crying?" "Down with the red bourgeoisie!").[27] At the same time, as he pursued "class war" in party committees and the "anti-bureaucratic revolution" in the street, Milošević made his first overtures to the Serbian Academy of Sciences and the Serbian intelligentsia. Suddenly, books deemed reactionary only a few years earlier could be published, with former class enemies from the "bourgeois right" transformed into les amis du peuple. Nor was the technical intelligentsia with meritocratic aspirations left out: for them, Milošević had promises of economic reform. In this fashion, Milošević attempted to satisfy the latent aspirations of his "articulate audiences" for political participation without turning them into potentially threatening publics.[28]

Perhaps the best illustration of Milošević's contradictory appeals is offered by his speech at the celebration of the six hundredth anniversary of the Battle of Kosovo on June 28, 1989, undoubtedly the moment of his greatest triumph as a leader. Admonishing Serbs to remember the main values bequeathed to them by the legacy of the Kosovo battle—unity, courage, and heroism—Milošević proceeded to state:

> Today, six centuries later, we are once again in battle, and facing battles. They are not armed battles, although the possibility of those cannot be excluded. But, regardless of what they are like, battles cannot be won without determination, courage, self-sacrifice. Without those virtues which were present in Kosovo a long time ago. Our main battle today is for the realization of economic, polit-ical, cultural, and general social prosperity. For a faster and more successful catching up with a civilization in which people will live in the 21st century. For this battle we need courage. To be sure[,] of a somewhat different kind.[29]

Milošević concluded his speech by underscoring that in Kosovo, Serbs not only defended themselves, but all of Europe as well. For this reason, accusations of Serbia's "anti-Europeanism" were unfounded. Serbia had always been in Europe and would remain so, but "on its own terms, with dignity."

Milošević's simultaneous appeal to very different constituencies (not just "nationalism") was key to his political success: Yugoslavia, unity, and Titoism for the party orthodox and army officers; Serbia ("land, memories, ancestors, heroism") for the nationalists and state support for the Kosovo Serbs; reform, rehabilitation, and "Europe" for the intellectuals; and social justice and protection for state-dependent workers and pensioners. When analyzed from this point of view, Milošević appears as the conciliator of the "greater Serbian" aspirations of Serbian nationalists and the Yugoslav orientations of army officers, party officials, and others; of technocratic aspirations for economic reform and of workers' aspirations of social justice; and, finally, as an orthodox communist who violated traditional norms of party behavior by giving free rein to mass activity and thereby satisfying the aspirations for political participation of an audience disgusted with the ineffectiveness of institutions without giving that audience true representation. By engaging in such appeals, Milošević found an ingenious solution to the central institutional dilemma of communist parties in the period of "neo-traditionalist" corruption and decay: the absence of a credible "combat task" that could provide the cadres with a sense of mission and the party with a novel foundation of legitimacy in an increasingly threatening environment.

The "Milošević solution" to this problem was anticipated long ago by Ken Jowitt when he noted that one way for communist parties to offer their "articulate audiences" a sense of political membership without giving up political monopoly was to "proliferate ethno-national combat tasks," elevate the army to the status of a new collective heroic agent, and substitute "the national unity of elite and citizens" for the political equality between them.[30] Milošević's solution fits the bill almost to perfection: his political language overflowed with terms such as "mobilization," "battle," "heroism," "differentiation" ("purges" in Yugoslav communist jargon), and "unity."[31] The pervasiveness of *combat metaphors* conveyed both Milošević's true Leninist determination in the class struggle and his strong preference for nonroutine crisis politics at the expense of institutionalized procedure. "Unity" on the other hand, was a term that served as a substitute for political participation and citizenship: thus, there was "the unity of all communists," "the unity of all the citizens and working people of Serbia," "the unity of all progressive socialist forces in Yugoslavia," and even "the unified Yugoslav market" as the necessary precondition for economic reform. In all these different forms of "unity," everyone—Serbs and Yugoslavs; communists and noncommunists; the party and the people; workers, peasants, and the "honest intelligentsia"; proponents of the central plan as well as market reformers—could find their place. Underlying all these forms of "unity," however, was the quintessential "unity of the leadership and the people," which served as a functional substitute for citizenship.

CONCLUSION

The foregoing brief and inevitably schematic analysis would seem to suggest that, in some important respects at least, Milošević indeed qualifies as a charismatic leader. First, there is little doubt that Milošević came to power in a "charismatic situation" and acquired a genuine mass following. Secondly, Milošević successfully appealed to different social constituencies with mutually incompatible latent dispositions. Thirdly, Milošević did incorporate elements of Serbian tradition into his political rhetoric, and ingeniously combined them with pro-Yugoslav sentiments which had resonance among many Serbs. Fourthly, Milošević's authoritarian-statist style did build on elements of traditional Serbian political culture, even if those have sometimes been exaggerated in existing scholarship. Despite the presence of all these elements, however, we would be hard-pressed to call Milošević a genuine charismatic leader. Rather, Milošević is best thought of as a party apparatchik who ingeniously used a charismatic situation to establish himself as a populist leader, and then consolidated (as Lenard Cohen has correctly observed) a combination of "personal and bureaucratic dictatorship" on that foundation. Cohen is likewise correct in noting that this process was in evidence as early as 1989–90, when Milošević began downplaying the "mobilizational and populist" aspects of his new regime, and also in documenting the evolution from "bureaucratic" to "personal authoritarianism" over time.[32]

What arguments can be induced to support this interpretation? First, after 1989, Milošević dismantled the grassroots movement of the Kosovo Serbs, which was an indispensable element in his takeover of power in Vojvodina (in October 1988) and Montenegro (in January 1989): henceforth, mass rallies could occur only at his explicit command. Secondly, instead of using his mass popularity to become "a dictator in the field of elections," Milošević rejected free elections and the multiparty system as a matter of principle, opting instead for a stage-managed communist-style election for the Serbian presidency in November 1989.[33] As a result, already by 1990, the patriotic terrain was being taken over by genuine nationalists like Vuk Drašković, while the liberal intelligentsia began forming opposition parties. Milošević's apparatchik-style fear of the "masses" became obvious in June 1990, when police force was used against opposition demonstrators on what turned out to be the first of many occasions. It would not be long before the police would grow into an overblown praetorian guard, even more powerful than the army. The "plebisictarian" component of Milošević's dictatorship, on the other hand, was left to the state-owned media and reserved for select occasions such as referenda and election campaigns.

Nor did Milošević forge "mutually incompatible orientations and commitments into a new unit of organization and membership." The Socialist Party of Serbia (SPS, formed in July 1990) was an opportunistic adaptation in the face of inevitable elections (after 1989), formed through a fusion of the renamed communist party and the front-like Socialist Alliance, whose considerable institutional sources the regime illegally appropriated. Moreover, by the mid-1990s, Milošević began purging even his Socialist Party, and moved the locus of power to a "neo-traditional coterie" of personal clients and "businessmen" gathered in the Yugoslav United Left (JUL), the marginal party formed by his wife, Mirjana Marković. As a result, the regime evolved into a "family dictatorship," moving from one crisis to the next, and relying increasingly on its praetorian guard and media monopoly to maintain control.[34]

Wasn't Milošević, however, a Serbian nationalist? Contrary to widespread perceptions, in the first presidential elections (in December 1990), Milošević campaigned on a "bureaucratic-populist" platform, promising the

VELJKO VUJAČIĆ

preservation of the socialist paternalist state to the nomenklatura and state-dependent classes ("with us there is no uncertainty"), and warning against the danger of "the darkest nationalism" coming from the right.[35] Unlike a "charismatic warrior" who leads the masses by personal example, Milošević announced his decision to go to war in a secret committee meeting, and deliberately did so in the immediate aftermath of the greatest crisis of his regime—the demonstrations of March 9, 1991. The selective rhetorical appropriation of elements of Serbian tradition in his speeches remained just that—selective and rhetorical. In contrast to Vuk Drašković, for instance, Milošević refused to embrace the Chetnik legacy, did not attempt to create a "Serbian national army," and showed little concern for the waste of Serbian lives in Croatia and Bosnia; unlike Vojislav Šešelj of the radical right, Milošević never explicitly endorsed the idea of a "greater Serbia," and his defense to this effect at the Hague Tribunal is procedurally correct, if cynical. The formation of the Federal Republic of Yugoslavia was a similarly opportunistic move (why not "Serbia and Montenegro?") designed to appropriate the institutional resources of the federal state for Serbia and claim international recognition. Certainly, no genuine Serbian nationalist would have been capable of so ruthlessly cutting off the Bosnian Serbs as Milošević did in the 1993–94 period, of allowing the Serbian Krajina to fall to the combined Croat-Moslem offensive in a mere four days without offering even symbolic support (in August 1995), of dispersing several hundred Serbian refugees throughout Serbia so that they would not pose a political threat, or of sacrificing the considerable Serbian population of Sarajevo in one stroke of a conference pen (in Dayton, 1995). Finally, a truly charismatic leader would have used the considerable surge of patriotic sentiment in Serbia at the time of the Kosovo conflict (March–May 1999) to provoke continuous NATO bombing and a potentially embarrassing ground offensive, sacrificing, if need be, the regime for the greater national cause.

Milošević's record on "economic reform" was even more abysmal. A self-professed champion of economic change, Milošević did his best to undermine the highly popular federal prime minister, Ante Marković, financing his own first election campaign (in 1990) with money "borrowed" from the Yugoslav National Bank. In subsequent years, Milošević proved himself a truly "neo-traditional" communist cadre, financing his regime through a combination of war booty, sanctions-busting smuggling operations, financial speculation in times of record-high inflation (1993), organized theft from his own citizenry, and loans from "allies" like China.[36] In the end, the ever narrower economic base of the regime alienated even Milošević's most faithful constituencies—state-dependent workers and the traditionalist rural strata—who were willing to accept ever-lower standards of living both for material (job security) and idealist reasons (sacrifice for the nation) much longer than the urban middle class (what remained of it).

If the foregoing analysis is correct, the Milošević example offers an excellent illustration of plebsicitarian, not charismatic leadership. The boundary between the two is not always easy to tell: like charismatic leaders, plebiscitarian demagogues come to power in periods of institutional crises, make direct appeals to the masses over the heads of existing officialdom, and attempt to bridge the gap between a variety of social and political constituencies. Unlike charismatic leaders, however, plebiscitarian demagogues do not embrace a transformative charismatic mission, fail to forge "mutually incompatible orientations and commitments" into more permanent "units of organization and membership," and use tradition opportunistically and selectively. As a result, although such leaders may stay in power for a long time, they do not leave behind a lasting institutional or symbolic legacy.

NOTES

1. Ken Jowitt, *The Leninist Response to National Dependency* (Berkeley: Institute of International Studies, University of California, 1978), 35.

2. Ibid., 46–47.

3. In this respect, see the classic study by R.V. Burks, *The Dynamics of Communism in Eastern Europe* (Princeton, NJ: Princeton University Press, 1961).

4. Max Weber, *Economy and Society,* vol. 1 (Berkeley: University of California Press, 1978), 242.

5. Douglas Madsen and Peter G. Snow, *The Charismatic Bond: Political Behavior in Time of Crisis* (Cambridge, MA: Harvard University Press, 1991).

6. Pierre Bourdieu, "Legitimation and Structured Interests in Weber's Sociology of Religion," in *Max Weber, Rationality, and Modernity,* ed. Scott Lash and Sam Whimster (London: Allen & Unwin, 1987), 119–36.

7. Steven Burg, "Political Structures," in *Yugoslavia: A Fractured Federalism,* ed. Dennison Rusinow (Washington, DC: Wilson Center Press, 1988), 9–23.

8. Dejan Jović, "Yugoslavism and Yugoslav Communism: From Tito to Kardelj," in *Yugoslavism: Histories of a Failed Idea, 1918–1992,* ed. Dejan Djokić (Madison: University of Wisconsin Press, 2003), 157–82.

9. Audrey Helfant Budding, "Serb Intellectuals and the National Question, 1961–1991" (Ph.D. diss., Harvard University, 1998), 134–35.

10. Mihailo Djurić, "Smišljene smutnje,"*Anali pravnog fakulteta u Beogradu* 3 (May–June 1971): 230–33.

11. Dejan Jović, *Jugoslavija: Država koja je odumrla* (Zagreb: Prometej, 2003).

12. Nebojša Vladisavljević, "Nationalism, Social Movement Theory, and the Grass Roots Movement of the Kosovo Serbs," *Europe-Asia Studies* 54, no. 5 (July 2002): 771–91.

13. As Burks, *The Dynamics of Communism in Eastern Europe,* 122, demonstrates, as late as 1943, fifteen out of twenty-seven Partisan divisions "appear to have been made up of Serbs, primarily *prečani*" (i.e., Serbs from Croatia and Bosnia).

14. For a further elaboration of this point, see Veljko Vujačić, "Institutional Origins of Contemporary Serbian Nationalism," *East European Constitutional Review* 5, no. 4 (Fall 1996): 51–61.

15. For a comprehensive discussion of the revision of history, see Jasna Dragović-Soso, *Saviors of the Nation: Serbia's Intellectual Opposition and the Revival of Nationalism* (London: Hurst and Company, 2002), 115–62.

16. See, for instance, his interview in the philosophical journal *Theoria* 2, no. 4 (1982), reprinted in Ljubomir Tadić, *U matici krize, 1968–1998* (Belgrade: Čigoja, 1999), 14–52; also see Ljubomir Tadić, *O velikosrpskom hegemonizmu* (Belgrade: Politika, 1992). For an excellent analysis of *The Memorandum,* see Audrey Helfant Budding, "Systemic Crisis and Nationalist Mobilization: The Case of the Memorandum of the Serbian Academy," in *Cultures and Nations of Central and Eastern Europe: Essays in Honor of Roman Szproluk,* ed. Zvi Gitelman et al. (Cambridge, MA: Harvard Ukrainian Research Institute, 2000), 49–69.

17. Ivan Stambolić, *Rasprave o SR Srbiji, 1979–1987* (Zagreb: Globus, 1988).

18. See Kosta Mihailovič and Vasilije Krestić, *Memorandum SANU. Odgovori na kritike* (Belgrade: SANU, 1995), 99–149, for the authorized and official version of the *Memorandum.*

19. Susan Woodward, *Balkan Tragedy: Chaos and Dissolution After the Cold War* (Washington, DC: Brookings Institution, 1995), 64.

20. Josip Županov, *Marginalije o društvenoj krizi* (Zagreb: Globus, 1983); Mladen Lazić, *U susret zatvorenom društvu* (Zagreb: Naprijed, 1987); Danilo Mrkšić, *Srednji slojevi u Jugoslaviji* (Belgrade: SSO Srbije, 1987).

21. Woodward, *Balkan Tragedy,* 78.

22. Slobodan Milošević, *Godine raspleta* (Belgrade: BIGZ, 1989), 30–36.

23. Ivan Stambolić, *Put u bespuće* (Belgrade: Radio B92, 1995).

24. Slavko Ćuruvija, "I on se tresao kao prut," *Borba,* 19 January 1993, is a first-hand account of the event which makes clear that Milošević was scared of the masses, and that his reaction was unexpected and largely spontaneous. Ćuruvija's witness account belies the widely accepted view that Milošević deliberately stage-managed the Kosovo Polje situation. See, for instance, Laura Silber and Alan Little, *Yugoslavia: Death of a Nation* (London: Penguin, 1995), 39.

25. For the full transcript of the meeting between Milošević and the Kosovo Serbs, see *Borba,* May 8, 9, and 11, 1987.

26. Milošević's Kosovo Polje speech can be found in Slobodan Milošević, *Godine raspleta*, 140–47.

27. Despite its "revolutionary bias," excellent empirical material on the rallies in Vojvodina can be found in Sava Kerčov, Jovo Radoš, and Aleksandar Raiš, *Mitinzi u Vojvodini 1988 godine* (Novi Sad: Dnevnik, 1990).

28. For this distinction, see Ken Jowitt, "Inclusion and Mobilization in European Leninist Regimes," *World Politics* 28, no. 1 (October 1975): 69–96.

29. *NIN*, July 2, 1989.

30. Ken Jowitt, "Soviet Neotraditionalism: The Political Corruption of a Leninist Regime," *Soviet Studies*, 35, no. 3 (July 1983): 275–97.

31. An excellent early analysis of Milošević's "combat rhetoric" is Kosta Čavoški, *Slobodan protiv slobode* (Belgrade: Dosije, 1991).

32. Lenard Cohen, *Serpent in the Bosom: The Rise and Fall of Slobodan Milošević* (Boulder, CO: Westview Press, 2001), 100. Characteristically, however, Cohen cannot make up his mind entirely, since he subsequently speaks of the "routinization of charisma" (115–18). The present author also earlier thought of Milošević as a charismatic leader, but has since changed his mind for the reasons outlined below. See Veljko Vujačić, "Serbian Nationalism, Slobodan Milošević, and the Origins of the Yugoslav War," *Harriman Review*, December 1995.

33. See Milošević's interview in *Le Monde*, 12 July 1989, translated in *NIN*, July 16, 1989, for his rejection of the multiparty system, and Cohen, *Serpent in the Bosom*, 118, for the staged presidential election.

34. Slobodan Antonić, *Zarobljena zemlja: Srbija za vlade Slobodana Miloševića* (Belgrade: Otkrovenje, 2002), has documented seven major regime crises in a ten-year period (1990–2000).

35. *NIN*, November 23, 1990.

36. Mladjan Dinkić, *Ekonomija destrukcije* (Belgrade: Stubovi kulture, 1997), extensively documents the politics of "economic destruction."

7

SOCIAL DIMENSIONS
OF COLLECTIVIZATION

Fomenting Class Warfare in Transylvania

GAIL KLIGMAN AND KATHERINE VERDERY

> Collectivization is more than an effort to economically and politically
> undermine landlords and kulaks; it is more than an effort to industri-
> alize. It is an attack on the social institutions and cultural orientations
> of peasant society. . . . The distinctiveness of Leninist strategy may lie
> in collectivization as a particular means of undermining the peasant
> extended household and village.[1]

In his little-known but, as always, thought-provoking publication *The Leninist Response to National Dependency* (1978), Ken Jowitt pointed to the significance of collectivization as a defining feature of Leninist strategy and lamented the paucity of research on its social dimensions. Although in recent years this neglect is slowly being remedied, most of the work done on the topic pertains to the Soviet Union, with a few notable exceptions,[2] and comes largely not from Jowitt's discipline, political science, but from history. Yet some of Jowitt's central insights in that publication retain their fruitfulness for thinking about this most far-reaching of the changes of socialism.[3] He understood that collectivization was not merely an aspect of the larger policy of industrialization but an assault on the very founda-tions of rural life, and he identified as a central feature of that assault the transformation of the "status order" on which life in peasant communi-ties was based.

Jowitt contends that in presenting village-level stratification as class differentiation, Lenin made an "ingenious error" having deadly consequences for Russian peasants. Because Lenin believed that villages were rife with class exploitation, his revolution would overturn rural inequalities by persecuting the exploiters—the wealthy peasants (kulaks)—a task in which he expected the poor and landless peasant classes to play a significant part. But, in fact, as Jowitt correctly observed, inequality in villages did not form a class structure; rather, it constituted a status order, in Weber's sense: what mattered was not primarily differences in people's relation to the means of production but the complex of attitudes and behaviors related to differential prestige and control over social relationships. To unleash class struggle in this context was to tear village social structure apart, imposing upon it a representation of social reality whose actualization would require dismantling the world in which Russian peasants lived. As Jowitt put the problem:

> The kulak is *not* [as Lenin thought] an alien in the village who is seen primarily as an economic exploiter, but he is a key figure in the corporate household and village system of social identification, organization, and power. Leninism errs in its understanding of his character and role, but it does so in a way that leads to strategies and policies that undermine the kulak, the peasant household, and the village community as defining institutions in a peasant-status society.[4]

Our essay builds upon this insight into why collectivization proved so dramatic for those who underwent it. We examine a particular set of social dimensions in Romania's collectivization, emphasizing the process whereby Leninist cadres-in-formation sought to provoke class struggle in two villages in Transylvania. Eradicating class inequality meant forcing people into classes that did not initially exist. How did this process unfold? What were its instruments, and what were their effects? Drawn from a large comparative project,[5] the essay uses data from interviews and archival research to show some of the processes whereby "peasant extended patriarchal households," as Jowitt labeled them, were undermined as "units and models of social, economic, and political power" in our two communities. Unlike most of the other essays in this volume, ours is primarily ethnographic, but our subject—how class relations emerged through an attack on the status character of village social organization—is very much part of the Weberian conceptual universe from which Jowitt drew so much inspiration. We also honor the long-standing engagement with comparative historical and ethnographic research that is so evident in all of his work.

GAIL KLIGMAN AND KATHERINE VERDERY

After World War II, the new Romanian government that emerged under the Soviet-backed Romanian Workers Party (PMR) faced a number of daunting tasks, among them the reshaping of political consciousness and the rapid industrialization of an economy that had been largely agrarian. (In 1948, 75 percent of Romania's population, or about 12 million people, were employed in agriculture.) Collectivization was to be a primary means for accomplishing these goals. It would help to form the "new socialist man" by eliminating "traditionalism" in the rural sector and subjecting the peasantry to intensive surveillance.[6] In addition, it would enable the regime to establish greater control over the food supply (so as to promote industrial development by holding down food prices and forcing surpluses out of agriculture) as well as to ensure a proletarianized labor force from villages as industry developed. Collectivization was therefore crucial to several aspects of the PMR's plans, all of which meant radically disrupting the way of life of Romania's predominantly rural population.

The apparatus of communist rule in Romania, however, was still in the process of consolidating itself and of forming the cadres upon whose actions it would depend. Given the resources available to the PMR at that time, collectivization would depend entirely on the actions of local cadres—that is, the policy was so far-reaching that the center could not effectively oversee it.[7] Party membership was approximately 1,000 in 1944, and its speedy increase to 710,000 a mere three years later indicates primarily that many of those people were "communists" in name only.[8] Despite the presence of Soviet advisors, then, the PMR regime was not sufficiently well entrenched to control the behavior of thousands of new activists—most of them little schooled in the ideas and practices of Soviet-style communism—whose job it would be to turn life upside down for those 12 million villagers. Thus, collectivization, so crucial to success in creating a communist Romania, would be based on the interaction among a massive and generally recalcitrant peasantry, an undisciplined and largely uneducated mass of activists, and the party center, itself riven with factional conflicts and always subject to orders from the Soviet Union. Simply from a structural point of view, collectivization faced great odds.

The policy was gradually implemented through a complex interplay of government directives and local actions, with considerable variation across the country in such respects as its timing, the extent of resistance it provoked, the degree of repression employed, and the success of the resulting collectives in meeting their aims. Early in the process of creating a socialist economy, the party decided to impose obligatory delivery quotas *(cote)*, successors of the wartime requisitions used to meet the heightened food requirements of the army. These quotas were intended to help feed people in regions suffering from famine as well as residents of cities marked for industrial development; they were also to serve as part of Romania's war reparations to the Soviet Union. Extracting them from the peasantry necessitated establishing with villagers a relation that was more intrusive and more intimate than that of any prior regime. The party-state sought to insinuate itself directly into rural communities and even into families, breaking down existing social relationships and creating wholly new alliances and enmities between newly formed groups, while completely refashioning villagers' sense of who they were. The prevailing kinship relations through which village social life had been organized were to be replaced by "class warfare," intended to usher in a new social order based in collective ownership and group labor.

VILLAGE SOCIAL ORGANIZATION

What did village life in Romania look like as the communists came to power? We must briefly characterize it in order to show its relation to the process of creating classes that would soon begin. Jowitt summarizes it in this way:

> Romania's basic social units, organizational models, and cultural matrices were the peasant household and village community. These were corporate units of identity and membership; "indivisible," clearly bounded units in competition over finite resources and based on personal-affective ties subordinating economic considerations and manipulating them in the light of their own status-based meanings.[9]

Village households consisted of patriarchal extended families, their relations with one another based on social standing that was recognized in terms of both material wealth and symbolic and social capital. The moral universe of these villagers was not egalitarian; some people were more "visible" *(văzuți)* than others. A variety of terms distinguished those accorded greater and lesser status honor (to retain Jowitt's Weberian phrasing): the rich were not just *văzuți* but *gazde* (property owners and household heads) or *bogați/bogătani/bogătași* (rich). (We will use the term *gazda*, pl. *gazde*.) Beneath them were "middle" peasants *(oameni de mijloc* or *mijlocași)*, and, at the bottom, the "poor" *(săraci)*, "lacking" *(lipsiți)*, "landless" *(fără pământ)*, etc. These categories had moral entailments: being rich was understood as a sign of virtue and hard work; being poor indicated lack of character, laziness, or bad habits such as drinking (rather than, say, simple bad luck). Such qualities were thought to be inherited through the corporate family line. Villages differed in the amount or quality of land one had to have in order to be considered "rich," but as Martha Lampland has shown for Hungary, a crucial ingredient was having enough land to be able to control one's own labor process and not have to work for others.[10]

The question of labor is particularly important for the discussion to follow. Rich peasants generally had too much land to work with family labor alone; at peak periods they drew upon their neighbors, kin, and ritual kin. Indeed, a *gazda* was socially defined by not working alone, by having the resources that enabled him to mobilize others; ritual kinship was one common way of doing so. Ritual kinship often linked families of unequal means, the junior couple *(fini)* providing labor, deference, and perhaps votes for village office while the senior couple *(naşi)* mediated disputes and provided loans, protection, and favors. A couple with many ritual kin might call a work party and invite their *fini* (along with others of lesser means) to come and help with the harvest, after which all would be treated to food and drink. The entire affair—the large numbers of people visibly working in one's fields, the audible party and quantities of food afterwards—signified the *gazda's* high status. This kind of "big man" arrangement is common to many societies throughout the world. One did not have to be rich to have others working with one, however, for families might associate with each other to make the job of plowing or harvesting easier. These simple labor exchanges might involve neighbors or kin, whether close or distant; they signified that a family had land to work, could organize the work of themselves and others on it, and therefore were people of good moral character. In these kinds of communities, that was what counted.[11]

TWO TRANSYLVANIAN VILLAGES

The two villages from which our data come, Kligman's field site, Ieud (Maramureş Region, northern Transylvania), and Verdery's, Aurel Vlaicu (Hunedoara County, south-central Transylvania), are very different villages, although they share the common Transylvanian history that distinguishes them from other villages in Romania's southern or eastern parts.[12] Ieud is in a hilly region with poor soil that often served as a reservoir for migrant labor into more fertile areas; in part for this reason, it was not as fully integrated into the feudal order as Vlaicu, a village in the Mureş floodplain known for its good soil and its use of migrant labor. According to local perception, both the different ecologies and the "free" versus "serf" histories of places like these affected the character of their people, Maramureşeni being considered more rebellious and former serfs in the Mureş plains more subservient. After World War II, Maramureş was one of several Romanian regions in which partisans resisted the extension of communist power into Romania, retreating into the hills and launching raids, meanwhile hoping that "the Americans" would come and liberate the country; many people from Ieud participated in these actions. In Vlaicu, by contrast, the main form of resistance was vociferous opposition to the planned collective on the part of rich peasant families, led by one Ioan Vlaicu, the brother of Romania's famous aviator for whom the village is named.[13] Ieud and Vlaicu also differed in their religious composition, Ieud having long been a bastion of Greek Catholicism, whereas Vlaicu was (except for its minority of Germans) almost entirely Romanian Orthodox. The communists' forced unification of the Greek Catholic and Orthodox churches in 1948 had a profound effect in Ieud and none at all in Vlaicu; the same was true when Romania's Greek Catholic Church was revived after 1989.

These differences in the two villages' religious and political histories accompanied differences in their collectivization. Ieud's collective was among the first inaugurated in Maramureş—a region that was only partially collectivized—as punishment for its resistance to communist rule. Owing to its poor terrain, the forced formation of a collective made virtually no economic sense. In Vlaicu, collectivization was delayed until late in the process (Vlaiceni attribute the delay to the Vlaicu family), but its good agricultural profile made it a logical candidate for collectivizing. The process was much more violent in Ieud than in Vlaicu, where relatively few people were arrested and none killed, while in Ieud three men were mortally shot and more than 100 villagers were arrested, of whom at least five died in prison.

Notwithstanding their differences, the two settlements were similar in their social worlds and moral universes as sketched in the previous section. Interviews and archival sources reveal the application of similar techniques in collectivizing them, as well as similar reactions to the process. For purposes of this essay, then, we will present data from Ieud and Vlaicu interchangeably, indicating in the text or a footnote which village is the source. We proceed with an account of how classes were created and class "exploiters" persecuted, and we present evidence of how villagers either protected their status honor, refusing the "impersonalization" that Jowitt sees as the heart of Leninist strategy in the countryside, or consciously relinquished it. We conclude with some observations on the inherent contradictions of class warfare and the resilience of village social institutions in its wake.

GAIL KLIGMAN AND KATHERINE VERDERY

> In constructing socialism, the goal followed by the members united in
> the collective farm is, through well-organized work done together and
> using shared means of production, to assure our victory over the chia-
> buri, exploiters and enemies of the working people, to do away forever
> with the darkness and backwardness of small individual farms, and to
> obtain instead the most production possible.[14]

Fomenting class warfare was central to the party's radical agenda of transforming peasant social organization and the moral universe in which peasants lived; collectivization provided the means to pursue it. Class warfare
was predicated on class categories then unfamiliar to those whose fates
would be determined by them. The party created a new classification system consisting of three categories of peasants—poor *(sărac)*, middle
(mijlocaş), and rich exploiters *(chiabur)*—that roughly paralleled the earlier referents of village social stratification mentioned above, but with radically altered social connotations. Rich peasants or *gazde*, who until then
had been accorded high status honor in their communities based largely
on their material and symbolic capital, now became *chiaburi* who exploited
the labor and lives of poor peasants.

The term *chiabur*, a word whose Turkish root means "rich" or "noble,"
was unknown in local parlance in our two regions.[15] As one eighty-six-year-
old former *gazda*-become-*chiabur* in Ieud explained, "The regime introduced this word. We didn't know what a *chiabur* was."[16] A key feature by
which the party intended to distinguish *chiaburi* from poor and middle peasants was their exploitation of salaried labor for thirty days or more per year
and/or their ownership of other means of production.[17] Recall that *gazde*
or rich peasants had enough land to need the help of others in working it,
whether through salaried or other reciprocated forms of labor. As a former collector of quotas, then in his eighties, commented, "Peasant *chiaburi*
worked along with their servants. They didn't hang around with their hands
in their pockets, no."[18] Another former *chiabur*, in his mid-eighties, elaborated further:

> If a man had a lot of land that he couldn't work alone, then he hired poor peas-
> ants. Here there was a class warfare when those who had been servants rose
> against the wealthier peasants. "Look, you, that *chiabur*, he exploited you!" They
> said that so one would hate the other. The poor who had worked for *gazde* were
> the first to join the collective. They [party cadres] told them, "Hey, we'll take

their land and it will be yours, you'll work here, just by the village, and we'll send them to work up in the hills, far off."[19]

A former party first secretary also commented retrospectively on the political construction of exploited labor: [20]

> There was a limit, from so many to so many days worked with the paid help of others. . . . It was an absurdity, not normal. No one considered anyone a *chiabur* in the way the party intended. You can't define a man as being something out of the ordinary because he employed the help of who knows whom for thirty days or more. But they [party leaders] needed to find a reason to label them as exploiters.

The reshaping of social categories and relations in everyday village life was fundamental to fomenting class warfare, which was designed to support and promote those labeled poor peasants *(săraci),* to convince and ally middle peasants *(mijlocaşi)* with them, and to demonize and discipline rich ones *(chiaburi).* Party initiatives in virtually all domains of activity differentiated villagers according to these class assignments, privileging the poor and punishing the wealthy. A "strictly secret" document that circulated in 1949 at the regional administrative level in Maramureş exemplifies this practice:

> The new law on agricultural taxes is formulated according to political interests: to protect poor and middle peasants and to give a strong blow to the wealthy. This law is applied in the context of increasing class warfare in the villages.[21]

How class warfare resonated among villagers depended on their socioeconomic position at the time. Some poor peasants who had been servants spoke bitterly about *gazde* and class disparities in the period before socialism. They noted that while most then-labeled *chiaburi* worked hard alongside their workers, there nevertheless had been some "bad" *chiaburi* who maltreated their workers, a point with which former *chiaburi* concurred.[22] (Most people today continue to use the term *chiabur* rather than the more neutral *gazda.*) Poor peasants who were sent to party school reminisced about learning of class exploitation and class consciousness, then returning to their villages motivated to seek justice through promoting class warfare. One person in his eighties who had been a servant asked rhetorically, "What did *gazde* ever do for the world? Nothing. . . . Everything they did, they did for themselves."[23] The communists, he added, created schools and encouraged education for all.

GAIL KLIGMAN AND KATHERINE VERDERY

Not all poor peasants reacted in this way, however. Some were the ritual kin of *chiaburi* and did not readily turn against them.[24] Others felt sorry for them and were moved by their plight. In Ieud, under the cover of darkness, loyal poor peasants risked bringing food to the families of *chiaburi* whose stocks had been depleted by increased requisitions, or risked hiding some grain and flour for them. One Vlaicu villager, discussing how his family sometimes gave loans to *chiaburi,* reported such an instance: "A *chiabura* came to our house, sat on the step, and said, 'If you won't lend me money for my quotas, I'll drown myself in the Mureş.'"[25]

Gazde, by contrast, represented themselves and were often represented by others, including poor peasants, as having been "good people" (esteemed). One former *gazda/chiabura,* a peasant woman in her late seventies, reflected:

> A good person was someone who was sensible, who reasoned about things, who respected everyone, no matter their status; he had goodness in him. . . . if a poor person helped you, you didn't take advantage of him, you paid him what he was owed. People educated their kids then, not like now.[26]

They saw themselves and were perceived by others as having been hardworking—the reason for having what they had—and as being widely respected for it. These attributes of wealth and character were, after all, the basis for their status honor.

Yet to foment class warfare required that *gazde* be the first to be denounced as *chiaburi.* While the number of *chiaburi* increased markedly in 1952 in response to directives from Bucharest, the criteria applied at the local level were often determined more by personal grudges than by official guidelines.[27] As a former member of the State Commission for Planning, in the Ministry of Agriculture, pointed out, "The laws were written in a civilized form, very nice, but how they were applied was another matter. It isn't all the same what is written on paper and what happened."[28]

Indeed, *chiabur* was quintessentially a weapon, rather than referring to actual characteristics of actual persons. Like "enemy of the people," of which it was a subset, it could be applied to people of all kinds, the point being to create public examples, attribute resistance to them (for example, for withholding grain or engaging in counterrevolutionary actions), and punish them for it. Some people labeled *chiabur* may have done the things or had the characteristics they were accused of doing or of having, but most did not. Moreover, the category's elastic boundaries made it possible for people to be moved in and out of *chiabur* status in response to denunciations, changed policies, petitions for dechiaburization, or revenge.[29] A former head of the agricultural section of the Orăştie district offices gave an example:

> I had a *chiabur*, Ştefănie din Beriu. The secretary of the people's council was in very bad relations with him, and Ştefănie told me why: the secretary asked him for a sow and he refused to give him one. So I was there right in that period when they were making people *chiaburi,* and the secretary denounced him. I talked to someone at the party offices about getting him out, but the secretary of the people's council in Beriu had it in for him. After we would [remove Ştefănie from the list], he'd put him right back on again.[30]

The potential for local-level abuse caused central authorities to intervene in hopes of controlling "mistaken identities," and to demand justification for what they felt were inadequately substantiated categorizations of alleged *chiaburi.* To illustrate, in an exchange between center and periphery, the former questioned authorities in Ieud about two individuals, requiring more detailed information about their situations. They were admonished that

> if the persons named were designated chiaburi based only on their wealth, then you have committed a grave abuse of the party line. . . . Those named, if they do not have means of exploitation, then they are poor or middle peasants, given that they have large families and live in a mountainous region where the land is poor. . . . In our work, we have to use all our force and the laws of proletarian dictatorship against the chiaburi, but not against poor or middle peasants under any circumstances.[31]

The response made clear that the two nevertheless had been rightly categorized: "D.I. is part of the exploiting class [exploiting labor more than thirty days in the year]; D.V. has 6 hectares of land of the best quality, a cow, 2 horses, 12 sheep, a thresher, a mill, a small timber mill operated by water."[32]

As we have seen, to further its goals, the party-state created *chiaburi* as a class enemy and then, in anticipation of their being the most likely to resist its consolidation of power, explicitly targeted them for gradual annihilation by imposing exorbitant taxes and quotas, arbitrary arrests, land confiscation, and the like. In implementing these practices, the party-state expected its representatives—whether national, regional, or local—to set good examples and to be able to account for the propriety of their actions.[33] The new socialist order being formed against the propertied class required

GAIL KLIGMAN AND KATHERINE VERDERY

a new socialist morality that would guard against the myriad tactics of the *chiaburi* to undermine it.

Toward that end, "good" communist citizens were admonished to be vigilant in their search for saboteurs. In Maramureş, the regional newspaper, *Graiul Maramureşului* (The Talk of Maramureş), warned, "Peasant workers must be ever vigilant in their efforts to discover and expose all attempts of the chiaburi to impede their struggle for a better life."[34] Those who attempted to thwart the regime's progress were publicly denounced. For example, again, as reported in *Graiul:*

> The chiabur F.I.C. [from Ieud] tried to avoid providing the wool quota. Although he has 42 sheep, he declared only 15 and that he is a middle peasant. He sent 27 of his sheep to his brother in village X to hide them. But, his ruse was discovered in time by the vigilance of those who work [for a living].[35]

Similar discoveries were publicized about *chiaburi* who tried to evade taxes. One packed the family's valuables into a chest and hid it in the barn, "believing that he could fool the collector. But he only fooled himself, his ugly deed exposed by a poor peasant while a fiscal agent found the chest in the barn."[36]

Those responsible for collecting produce or taxes ranged in manner from the overly zealous who sought to empty the cupboards of *chiaburi* to those "who were decent, who did not fleece you." The latter turned a blind eye, collecting almost everything but leaving just enough to feed the children something. As in all walks of life, there were "good" or "bad" collectors and fiscal agents. One former *chiabur,* now in his eighties, recounted how "they found one kilogram of *mămăligă* [cornmeal flour] hidden behind an icon. So that the children would have nothing to eat, they took the flour and spread it across the floor."[37] A former collector, now deceased, remarked that they took "everything fine from the house—the rug, the thickest woven woolen blanket."[38] The methods used to enforce compliance were perceived to be arbitrary in application. As a peasant woman now in her late sixties related, "Whoever they wanted to destroy, they did; whoever not, they didn't."[39]

CLASS STRUGGLE, STATUS HONOR, AND IMPERSONALIZATION

The preceding section has illustrated the party's devices for trying to turn a status order into a class-stratified one so as to destroy the exploiting "class." Yet, despite the vigilance of "good communists," *chiaburi* were thought to continue in their attempts to discredit and impede collectivization through spreading rumors, making threats, and engaging in diverse forms of sabotage. In the early years of communist rule, the high status honor of *chiaburi* in the communities in which they lived continued to resonate to considerable effect. One report about how *chiaburi* were resisting collections stated, "There is a rumor circulating that the sky will darken and it will rain fire. The result of this. . . . they [the villagers] have bought candles."[40] Another *chiabur* allegedly threatened that "using an axe, he will cut into pieces whoever goes near his property."[41] Yet another claimed, "All who join the collective will be taken to Siberia."[42] Others instructed poor and middle peasants to resist the production plans for all phases (e.g., planting on time, harvesting on time).[43] Even the village midwife, "who received a salary from the state," told a poor peasant woman suffering from an eye problem "and who had joined the collective that if she did not withdraw from it, she would go blind!"[44]

Peasants made into *chiaburi* were also able to defend themselves and their "status honor" through other means, notably legal-administrative ones.[45] During the 1950s, they filed petitions for dechiaburization to remove themselves from this undesirable category. Thus, even as party directives or their own ambition encouraged cadres to produce more *chiaburi* during the early 1950s, shifts in policy within the central committee provided room for people to contest the status of *chiabur*. On May 11, 1953, the president of the people's council of the Orăştie district in Hunedoara County reported to regional authorities that alongside his 623 *chiaburi* for that year, he had 484 contestations, of which 422 had not yet been resolved.[46] In a report on June 4, 1953, this same man reported the results of a meeting held to examine petitions for dechiaburization: cadres had analyzed a total of 53 contestations, reconfirming *chiabur* status in 29 cases, reversing it in 24, and holding over 10 for further research.[47] If in 1952 the Orăştie district had 1,029 *chiaburi*, in 1953 that number had fallen to 623, and in 1954, to 443.[48] The changes partly reflected Stalin's death, as well as struggles within the PMR over how to collectivize and how best to use *chiaburi* in doing so. Then, with the renewal of the collectivization campaign in 1956, we see the making of yet more *chiaburi*, and more contestations.

A person contesting his status would send a petition to the commune or district office, perhaps including "letters of reference" from other villagers; there, it would provoke an inquiry, the district administration sending out a delegate to research the case and return with a recommendation to the district party authorities. A complete contestation file might include the petition, some "letters of reference," the recommendation of the delegate, the decision of the district people's council, and occasionally communications from the region.[49] From such files we can see how status honor was being negotiated in response to the assault that cadres were making on it with their attempt to create classes. Here is an example.

The justification for classifying L. A. as a *chiabur* in 1952 reads as follows: "L.A. Possesses at present 8.63 ha. land. Had servants until 1948. Uses a salaried labor force for more than 30 days per year."[50] Two years later L.A. filed a contestation,[51] "it being affirmed that I had a servant until 1949 and that I didn't work my 8 ha. of land on my own."[52] He claimed that the information was completely false, that he hadn't had a servant since 1925, and that he had been classified a *chiabur* "only from the personal hatred of certain people of bad faith who reported on me out of spite." He continued that in 1948, his fellow villager comrade P. I. insisted that without any obligation, he take in P. I.'s nephew from a large and poor family in the mining town of Petroşani:

> He stayed for five months in which time I bought him clothes and shoes out of the goodness of my heart, and he left very satisfied with the help I had given him. This help that I gave to someone needy was seized upon by some of my enemies who affirmed that I had help in working my land, that is, a servant.

At the end of his petition, he presented a list of thirty-two Vlaiceni (many of them his ritual kin) who would vouch that he had never had servants or exploited anyone. On April 28, 1954, the district delegate wrote a report using almost exactly the same words as L. A.'s contestation, recommending that he be removed; two days later the president of the district council approved it.

What do this file and others like it show us about the attempt to replace status honor by class position? First, L. A. was at pains to show that he was not as important as he was made out to be. Here, he had a lot of explaining to do: he was one of Vlaicu's most influential men, from one of its most influential families. As mayor in the 1920s, he had managed to acquire a substantial amount of land that was supposed to go to war veterans and poor people. (This is clear from maps of the terrain of Vlaicu after the 1921 land reform.) At his funeral in 1973, nearly the whole village was present; people talked about how many villagers used to go to work his fields in "work parties," how many ritual kin (*fini*) he had, and so on. Like the contestations of several other *chiaburi*-designates, his strove to explain why someone who appeared to be his servant really was not. Others tried to explain away their use of extra hands at harvest as being "what any normal peasant does." All of them sought to resignify behavior that used to be seen as a sign of high status into behavior common to most villagers. Thus, in his contestation L. A. tried to erase what had made him visible in the village by passing himself off as just like others: he had negotiated away his status honor so as to avoid the class label *chiabur*.

For example, the criteria for *chiaburi* singled them out for using other than family members to work their land—precisely the thing that had marked L. A. as a man of high status in his earlier years. Wealthy peasants had always been recognizable for *not* working alone with their families but with servants, kin, and others; now they were having to present themselves as if they had worked alone. They were compelled to adopt the terms of the party and respond to them. In petition after petition they rehearsed a new vision of themselves and their social relations, seen through a new lens not of status honor but of class warfare. The documents cited also highlight the inventiveness of the petitioners, who employed numerous techniques for trying to evade official categories, such as claiming that they owned less land than they actually had, dividing their land into several plots and attributing those to other family members, or pointing out that their land was inherited or was their wife's dowry (i.e., they had not purchased it) and thus should not qualify them for *chiabur* status, etc.

Second, the process of making and unmaking *chiaburi* involved a struggle between individualizing (or decontextualizing), on the one hand, and "communalizing" (or contextualizing), on the other. The criteria given in lists of *chiaburi* individualized a person—always a single name, customarily the male household head—while assigning him a set of characteristics specific to him (and significant to the party)—he had a servant, owned a lot of land, had a mill, etc.. The contestations and their supporting references from fellow villagers then attempted to reposition the person in his community, making his behavior appear normal and like that of others, and to establish a context in which the petitioner could be seen as *not* being what the party's description of him claimed—not having servants but helping poor people; not exploiting labor but exchanging work like any other peasant at harvest time; not owning a tavern but serving the commune. In making *chiaburi*, the party strove to individualize and decontextualize them—to "impersonalize" them, in Jowitt's term—while those made into *chiaburi* reversed that procedure. For many, the status of *chiabur* thus became a kind of negotiation rather than an outright imposition.[53] Moreover, we see from these documents the failure of the party's efforts to create a certain kind of solidarity among poor and middle peasants against wealthy ones,[54] efforts they hoped would speed collectivization by expelling so-called *chiaburi* from community life. As we discussed above also, the

GAIL KLIGMAN AND KATHERINE VERDERY

class struggle that chiaburization was to promote gave way, in many cases, to expressions of community solidarity with those labeled *chiabur,* as fellow villagers supported them with favorable letters of reference.

CONCLUSION

> The Leninist "error" leads to *collectivization . . . an attack on the political economy of elite organization in a peasant society. . . .* Not simply elites, but the basic institutions of a status society—the peasant corporate household and the village community—are broken through—not eliminated, but decisively transformed and given new roles in the social, economic, and political order.[55]

Jowitt maintains that collectivization may have been "the most distinctive feature of Leninist regime strategies," the significance of which was "more in its social than its economic impact."[56] Although we would contend that, over the long run, collectivization had a profound economic impact, we concur with Jowitt about its pervasive social consequences. In this essay, we have brought comparative empirical evidence both to support this claim and to illustrate the processes through which the undermining of local social organization occurred. Although Leninist strategy did not destroy village life outright, it did reduce its familial organization to a subordinate role. As Jowitt pointed out, "The question is not whether the peasant extended patriarchal household has been completely eliminated, but whether it has maintained or lost its integrity as the institution providing personal identity, exercising social, economic, and political influence, and acting as the cultural model of authority and interpersonal relations."[57] We have demonstrated how Leninist strategy succeeded in breaking open peasant communities to the intrusions of the party-state, using class warfare as a weapon that transformed neighbors, ritual kin, and family members into "enemies" and "exploiters." This powerful discourse legitimated the ongoing inversion of social relations, making *gazde* into *chiaburi* and poor, uneducated peasants into local cadres.[58] Class warfare simultaneously refashioned the relationship between the party-state and socialist citizens—both in the making—and created communist authority in the micropractices of daily village life.

Yet, as we have also demonstrated, the structures and social relations that collectivization and class warfare had assaulted proved very durable and resilient, both during and after this tumultuous period. Cadres found that they could push forward with collectivization only if they recognized—

or appropriated—the local status order. To complete collectivization, they were compelled to bring in high-status peasant families—*chiaburi*—whose kin and ritual kin would then follow suit. For example, a former head of the agricultural section in the Orăştie district council, who had been active in the campaign to convince people to join the collective, observed:

> If we were looking for someone to be president or for some other cadre slot . . . the others would come and say to me, "Help us get X to join. Persuade his relatives and his ritual kin." They should have as many relatives as possible and be people of influence in the village. After a while, people got sick of the business with *chiaburi* and stopped paying so much attention to whether people had been *chiaburi* before.[59]

Thus, the party-state was ultimately forced to make compromises with the social order it was seeking to relegate to the dustbin of history, just as those resisting that trajectory made compromises with the party-state.[60]

This dynamic draws attention to the problems of a Leninist analysis predicated on a narrow view of class, rather than on a more Weberian one that links class with status and recognizes the complex cultural dimensions of the relationship between them. In this sense, Jowitt was right on target in pointing to the significance of the Leninist Party's elision of class and status in pursuing its goals. Ironically, he was perhaps a bit too Leninist in his confidence in the party's organizational efficacy and did not fully appreciate the impact of local-level (re)action on the party's ability to implement its initiatives. The process of creating its "impersonal-charismatic" organizational structure[61] and of instituting its goals was, as we have shown, a two-way street. Yet this insight is indebted to Jowitt's embrace of ethnography and his inimitable capacity to inspire and indeed provoke more nuanced understandings of the communist experience.

NOTES

We first thank Ken Jowitt for being himself. Over the years, we have benefited enormously from his provocative intellect, critical insights, collegiality, and steadfast friendship. Our research for this article formed part of a large collaborative project that we co-organized on collectivization in Romania, 1949–1962. We are grateful both to its participants, whose work enriched ours, and to the National Council for Eurasian

GAIL KLIGMAN AND KATHERINE VERDERY

and East European Research, the National Endowment for the Humanities, and the National Science Foundation, in particular, for their generous support.

1. Kenneth Jowitt, *The Leninist Response to National Dependency* (Berkeley: Institute of International Studies, University of California, 1978), 59, 63.

2. For example, István Rév, "The Advantages of Being Atomized," *Dissent* 34 (1987): 335–50.

3. This essay draws upon papers we contributed to a volume published in Romanian; see Gail Kligman, "Crearea autorității comuniste: Luptă de clasă și colectivizare la Ieud, Maramureș," and Katherine Verdery, "Chiaburii vechi și noi: Închiaburirea și deschiaburirea țăranilor din Aurel Vlaicu," both in *Țărănimea și puterea: Procesul de colectivizare a agriculturii în România, 1949–1962*, ed. Dorin Dobrincu and Constantin Iordachi (Iași, Romania: Editura Polirom, 2005).

4. Jowitt, *Leninist Response*, 58–59.

5. The broader project, entitled "Transforming Property, Persons, and State: Collectivization in Romania, 1948–1962," was funded by the Center for European and Russian Studies at UCLA, the National Science Foundation (grant no. BCS 0003891), the National Endowment for the Humanities, and the National Council for Eurasian and East European Research (contract no. 816–12g). It took place between April 1999 and April 2004 and included (besides ourselves) a total of eighteen scholars, most of them Romanian historians, anthropologists, and sociologists. Each scholar conducted research through oral history interviews and a variety of archives, with the goal of arriving at a synthetic picture of how collectivization proceeded across Romania. The project resulted in the volume edited by Dorin Dobrincu and Constantin Iordachi, *Țărănimea și puterea.*

6. Gheorghe Onișoru, *Instaurarea regimului comunist în România* (Bucharest: 2002), 90–91.

7. The same was true of decollectivization after 1991. See Katherine Verdery, *The Vanishing Hectare: Property and Value in Postsocialist Transylvania* (Ithaca, NY: Cornell University Press, 2003), chap. 3. Verdery's research on decollectivization shaped the way we approach its obverse.

8. See Ioan Chiper, "Considerations on the Numerical Evolution and Ethnic Composition of the Romanian Communist Party, 1921–1952," *Totalitarian Archives* 10 (Spring–Summer 2002), 11. Chiper also discusses alternative figures for membership in the PRC in 1944 and settles on the figure of about 1,000.

9. Jowitt, *Leninist Response*, 21.

10. Martha Lampland, *The Object of Labor: Commodification in Socialist Hungary* (Chicago: University of Chicago Press, 1995), 35–46.

11. Gail Kligman, *The Wedding of the Dead: Ritual, Poetics and Popular Culture in a Transylvanian Village* (Berkeley: University of California Press, 1988), chap. 1, and Katherine Verdery, *Transylvanian Villagers: Three Centuries of Political, Economic, and Ethnic Change* (Berkeley: University of California Press, 1983), chaps. 5–6.

12. See Verdery, *Vanishing Hectare*, 34–35.

13. See Verdery, *Transylvanian Villagers*, 226–27.

14. See DJAN (Direcția Județeană a Arhivelor Naționale) Maramureș, Fond Comitetul Raional PMR Vișeu, dos. 42/1952, vol. V, f. 50.

15. The Turkish word *kibar* also refers to someone well raised, from a good family, or cultivated. The Turkish word's connotations paralleled the status-based meaning of *gazdă*, while the party's usage of *chiabur* transformed it to mark the class distinction between "exploiter" and "non-exploiter." Another new term—*tovarăș*, or "comrade"—marked status equality in the socialist public sphere. *Tovarăș* (f. *tovarășă*) as a form of address replaced "Domnul" (Mr.), "Doamna" (Mrs.), etc.

16. Interview with I.S., July 2003, Ieud, Maramureș.

17. For a fuller discussion of the party's definition of *chiabur*, see "Indiciile de Baza pentru Identificarea Gospodăriilor Chiaburești," in DJAN Deva, Fond 16, "Comitetul regional PMR Hunedoara," dos. 430/1952, f. 252–63. Other means of production included mills, threshers, and the like. We emphasize that the amount of land owned by someone labeled *chiabur* was not a defining criterion. Land possessed could vary from five to more than fifty hectares, reflecting the elasticity and instrumentality of the category itself.

18. Interview with P.V., summer 2002, Ieud, Maramureș.

19. In rural areas, servants worked in the fields. Interviews with P. V. and I. S., summer 2002, Ieud, Maramureș. Poor peasants were often given plots of land "in exchange" for that confiscated from *chiaburi*. *Chiaburi* were publicly humiliated as they trudged long distances to the land they received in turn.

20. Interview with P.G., summer 2002, Baia Mare, Maramureș.

21. See *Circulara* 72, June 7, 1949, Maramureș, Romania. Class differentiation not only applied to quotas and taxes, but affected purchasing costs. For example, as one eighty-four-year-old peasant recollected, wood was cheapest for poor peasants (20 *lei* for a load); for middle peasants, 30; for *chiaburi*, 50.

22. One former servant recounted how, as a poor youth in Ieud, he was forced to work off a fine that should have been levied against the *gazda* for whom he worked and whose orders he was following when he was caught illegally sawing wood in the forest. He also referred to a *gazda* who hired a poor person to serve a prison term in his stead. Interview with D. V., September 2000, Giulvăz, Timiș.

23. He became the president of the collective farm and secretary of the party in Ieud. Pointing to a head scar, he also noted that in 1949 villagers beat the few of them who were communists. Interview with D. V., September 2000, Giulvăz, Timiș.

24. See David Kideckel, "The Socialist Transformation of Agriculture in a Romanian Commune, 1945–62," *American Ethnologist* 9 (1982): 320–40. In Ieud, former *chiaburi* have remained lifelong friends with those who risked their own lives to support them during the trying years of collectivization.

25. Interview with P. B., summer 2000, Aurel Vlaicu.

26. Interview with B. S., summer 2000, Ieud, Maramureș.

27. See Robert Levy, "Primul val al colectivizării: Politici centrale și implementare regională, 1949–1953," in *Țărănimea și puterea: Procesul de colectivizare a agriculturii în România, 1949–1962*, ed. Dorin Dobrincu and Constantin Iordachi (Iași: Editura

GAIL KLIGMAN AND KATHERINE VERDERY

Polirom, 2005). Similarly, personal vendettas accounted for local abuses with regard to collections; e.g., see DJAN Maramureș, Fond 10, dos. 33/1952, f. 61. On the dramatic increase in the number of persons labeled *chiabur*, see also Kligman, "Crearea autorității," and Verdery, "Chiaburii vechi." Contestations are discussed below in the section "Class Struggle, Status Honor, and Impersonalization."

28. Interview with B. G., summer 2002, Sighetul Marmației, Maramureș.

29. On the elasticity of the category and contestation of it, see, for example, Kligman, "Crearea autorității," and Verdery, "Chiaburii vechi." Although *chiaburi* and "enemies of socialism" were viewed as synonymous, a poor or middle peasant could also be reclassified as an enemy, as often happened in Ieud, if he "had a past hostile to the democratic regime, was the leader of one of the historic parties [Liberal or Peasant parties], or of the legionary-fascist party, was knowingly involved in anti-communist activities." See CNSAS (Consiliul Național pentru Studierea Arhivelor Securității), FP (Fondul Penal) 248, dos. 2, f. 17.

30. Interview with M. H., summer 2002, Geoagiu.

31. See CNSAS FP 248 dos. 2, f. 17.

32. See CNSAS FP 248 dos. 2, f. 22.

33. Party documents attest to local cadres acting inappropriately, drinking too much, womanizing, and otherwise failing to demonstrate proper socialist morality.

34. See Gh. Chindriș, "Chiaburii din plasa Iza sunt demascați și dați în judecată," *Graiul Maramureșului*, April 16, 1950, 3.

35. See N. Timiș, "Demascarea unui mârșav chiabur din Ieud," *Graiul Maramureșului*, July 31, 1949, 3.

36. See Goth Mihai, "Țăranii muncitori din comuna Ieud demască uneltirile chiaburești," *Graiul Maramureșului*, February 26, 1950, 5.

37. Interview with B. G., summer 2002, Sighetul-Marmației, Maramureș.

38. Interview with P. V., summer 2002, Ieud, Maramureș.

39. Interview with B. P., summer 2002, Ieud, Maramureș. Humiliating parents in front of their children was a typical—and sadistic—tactic of subordination.

40. See Arhiva Primăria Ieud, "Raport despre mersul schimbului de teren în c. Ieud, în vederea formării GACului PMR, j. Maramureș," February 25, 1950.

41. Interview with D. V., summer 2002, Ieud, Maramureș.

42. See CNSAS FD (Fond Documentar) 7, dos. 10, f. 293.

43. See, for example, DJBN Bistrița-Năsăud, fond 38, dos. 1 and 2 (regular reports, Sfatul Popular al Regiunii Rodna).

44. See CNSAS FP 248, dos. 2, f. 9.

45. Petitions constituted a significant form through which persons established or contested socialist identities. The party-state required all persons to petition the collective farm to join it, for example. On the language of petitions and petitions as a form of subordination to party authority, see Kligman, "Crearea autorității comuniste."

46. DJAN Deva, MISR (Ministerul de Interne, Sfatul Raional) Orăștie, dos. 10/1951 (n.p.).

47. DJAN Deva, MISR Orăștie, dos. 20/1953 (n.p.). The totals add up to 63, not 53.

48. DJAN Deva, MISR Orăștie, dos. 10/1951 (n.p.).

49. DJAN Deva, MISR Orăștie, dos. 7/1954 (n.p.).

50. DJAN Deva, MISR Orăștie, dos. 37/1952 (n.p.).

51. DJAN Deva, MISR Orăștie, dos. 7/1954 (n.p.).

52. DJAN Deva, MISR Orăștie, dos. 7/1954 (n.p.).

53. However, the label *chiabur* was not negotiable for those who simultaneously were labeled "enemies of the people" or "engaged in counterrevolutionary activity."

54. See Bogdan Tănăsescu, *Colectivizarea între propagandă și realitate* (Bucharest: Editura Globus, n.d.), 29.

55. Jowitt, *Leninist Response*, 58.

56. Ibid., 63.

57. Ibid., 65.

58. A biting popular verse that circulated in the early 1950s echoed the world turned upside down: "My oh my, Stalin, what have you done? You have made sausages from horsemeat, and from Gypsies, cadre!" Villagers often adapted instrumentally to changes in the status order, asking the head of the collective farm rather than former *gazde* to serve as godparents. In this manner, villagers personalized the charismatic impersonal authority of the party.

59. Interview with M. H., summer 2000, Geoagiu.

60. The extent to which changes were formal rather than social has been addressed by others than Jowitt, including ourselves. Mihail Cernea was among those noting that brigades replacing families as basic work units was one such example. The family became a tool of the party-state in its efforts to further its own goals. Nevertheless, the party-state relied on the family to do so. Many have argued that the party-state did not destroy familism as an organizing principle but rather appropriated it to its own ends.

61. Jowitt, *Leninist Response*, 48–50.

GAIL KLIGMAN AND KATHERINE VERDERY

III *Political, Economic, and Social*

Change: Beyond Eastern Europe

8

STAGES OF DEVELOPMENT
IN AUTHORITARIAN REGIMES

BARBARA GEDDES

W hat do you get if you cross charismatic insight with rational
choice? The result does not sound pretty but, as I show below,
the progeny can be useful beasts. They can carry heavy loads
when it comes to explaining political processes.

For most of recorded history, most human beings have lived under dictatorial rule. Nevertheless, most theories of government explain leadership
selection, policy making, and institutional choice in democracies. Most studies that do deal with authoritarianism seek to explain its beginning or end-
ing rather than the way authoritarian governments work. Kenneth Jowitt's
research on Leninist regimes is a major exception. Jowitt's central intellectual task has been to build an understanding of the nature of Leninist
regimes. As a pure type, the Leninist regime has died out. Except in China,
where some Leninist characteristics persist despite a mostly successful transition to ordinary noncommunist single-party rule, only a handful of mixed
systems adapted to very isolated ecological niches survive. But Jowitt's
insights into the developmental stages that Leninist regimes pass through
continue to have relevance in the twenty-first century because many other
forms of authoritarianism survive in the world, and Jowitt's ideas help to
explain them too.

In his earlier work, Jowitt dealt with two different aspects of the Leninist innovation: the characteristics that contributed to its transformative

capacity and the developmental changes that Leninist regimes passed through as they faced different challenges over time. In this study, I focus only on the strand of Jowitt's work that deals with developmental changes, and I argue that some of the same tasks and uncertainties identified by Jowitt in Leninist regimes also occur in most other kinds of dictatorship and lead to some of the same kinds of systematic changes over time that Jowitt noted in Leninist regimes.

In a seminal article written several decades ago, Jowitt articulated the implicitly evolutionary argument that successful Leninist regimes would have different sets of traits during different stages of their existence.[1] During the chaotic period of power seizure, when considerable popular support was needed in order to gain political control, Jowitt emphasized that two characteristics would contribute to regime survival: collegial relationships within the party that left cadres with the autonomy and discretion to respond to rapidly changing circumstances, and a responsive attitude toward the populace. A different set of traits, however, would contribute to survival during the post-seizure period when the drive to consolidate political power led leaders to try to destroy potential bases of opposition in society, including cadres who had previously developed local bases of popular support. During this time, hierarchy within the party and a more combative relationship with the populace would aid regime survival. Leninist regimes would evolve yet another set of traits when the society and economy had been successfully transformed and the regime could afford a less security-oriented stance toward citizens.

In this essay, I build on Jowitt's insights about Leninist regimes to make several arguments about typical developmental stages in other kinds of dictatorships. First, Jowitt's observations about Leninist regimes at the time political power is seized accurately describe most other authoritarian regimes as well, and for exactly the reasons Jowitt identified. Second, the consolidation stage Jowitt describes in Leninist regimes is one possible outcome of the narrowing processes and leadership struggles that occur in all authoritarian regimes after the seizure of power. Finally, some of the characteristics Jowitt identifies as part of the inclusion stage are less problematic and far less conflictual in other kinds of authoritarian regimes than in Leninist regimes, though others challenge the survival capacity of any authoritarian government. In making these arguments, I draw on standard rational choice ways of thinking about the world, and information I have collected about more than 170 authoritarian regimes,[2] as well as Jowitt's analysis. Although many, including Jowitt himself, find the rational choice idiom and worldview dissonant, an amalgam of apparently conflictual

approaches, like charisma and organization in Leninist parties, can sometimes be fruitful.

During the drive for control of political power, which may take years of
armed struggle either before or after the seizure of the organs of the state,
Jowitt argues that the critical task of a Leninist party is to "eliminate the
political and military capacity of opposition elites."[3] To accomplish this in
a turbulent and unpredictable environment, cadres must have the autonomy to make decisions in the field in response to whatever conditions arise.
They must take risks and try new strategies. The need for cadre initiative
and discretion during the struggle thus limits the centralization and hierarchy that can be maintained in the party, despite its commitment to principles of democratic centralism. Consequently, Leninist parties tend to be
relatively collegial during what Jowitt labels the transformation stage. To
secure power, the party also needs support from the populace and thus must
be somewhat responsive to popular aspirations. It needs to be able to draw
manpower and other resources from the society in order to keep up the
struggle, and it cannot do this entirely through coercion. Instead, it must
make credible promises of a better life after the ouster of the old regime.
It makes these promises credible by actually providing some benefits.
During the period of struggle, for example, both Soviet and Chinese communists carried out popular land reforms in areas they controlled. They
did not collectivize—a profoundly unpopular policy—until after they had
secured full military and political control.

Non-Leninist parties and other groups that aspire to seize political power
have many of the same characteristics during the struggle for power. The
group may embrace the principle of democratic centralism (many non-
Leninist parties have copied this aspect of Leninist organization) or military hierarchy, but the leader usually lacks the means to enforce it prior to
the seizure of power. Those who disagree with a leader can simply leave
the party or coup conspiracy, which is one of the reasons that radical parties are so frequently riven by schisms. It is estimated that 90 percent of
those who joined the American communist party, for example, had deserted
it by the end of their first year. In order to maintain the minimum support
needed for effective action, leaders must consult and be somewhat responsive to the ideas and interests of members of the group. The leader has little ability to enforce conformity. He usually has no police apparatus at his
disposal and little ability to intimidate. Consequently, leaving the party or

coup conspiracy entails few costs for the one who leaves. In contrast, the loss of comrades can be quite costly to remaining conspirators, who may be left with too few allies for effective action and who may even be betrayed by their former comrades.

The same kinds of considerations affect the relationship between the group and the populace. A group bent on seizing power does not need majority support, but it needs some support. It needs manpower and other resources if a prolonged struggle is required. Regardless of the mode of seizing power, it needs the "contingent consent" of the ruled.[4] No regime can rely on coercion for everything.

As an abstract summary of this situation, the bargaining power of followers relative to leaders and of ordinary members of the community relative to the seizure group are much stronger before the seizure of power than after. They are also stronger in the immediate aftermath of the seizure, when the regime is still uncertain of its grip and reliant on much of the pre-seizure bureaucratic and military apparatus, than they are later, when the implementing arms of government have been transformed into loyal instruments of the new leadership.

For these reasons, success is more likely for somewhat collegial seizure groups that: (1) articulate an ideology or point of view attractive and intelligible to many ordinary people and make credible promises of a better life after the transition; and (2) choose a moment to intervene when disgust with incumbents has spread through much of the populace. When both these conditions have been fulfilled, seizure groups can attract broad, though often temporary, public support. Various elite groups as well as ordinary citizens often support a seizure of power simply because they want to oust the old order, which they deem incompetent, venal, or self-serving. Most authoritarian regimes have begun with widespread popular support.

Fidel Castro's march into Havana, for example, was initially supported by many of those who subsequently moved to Florida. His public ideological stance had become more and more moderate from the time of the attack on the Moncada Barracks until the actual seizure of power—to the point where what he advocated at the time of the march on Havana was indistinguishable from the statements of other nationalistic opposition movements.[5] Meanwhile, Fulgencio Batista's government first demonstrated its incapacity to defeat even such a small and amateurish force as Castro's and then disintegrated, leading to a further withering of support for it. In consequence, although most Cubans had only superficial knowledge about Castro before he took power, they supported his overthrow of Batista.

Similarly, much of the Nicaraguan elite, as well as many workers and peasants, supported the Sandinistas against Anastasio Somoza. That broad coalition of support developed in response to Somoza's very visible venality in handling the aid money that poured into the country after the Managua earthquake. The brutality and ineffectiveness of his effort to defeat the Sandinistas increased opposition still further.

Most African single-party regimes rode the wave of popular nationalism to power. With colonial rulers as the foe, it took remarkably little time and organization to mobilize widespread popular support behind a nationalist party or particular leader.[6]

Very few public opinion surveys are taken in the immediate aftermath of authoritarian seizures of power, but those we have indicate widespread public support. Over 60 percent of the Argentine public supported the military coup of 1966.[7] During the administration of a singularly unsuccessful and uncharismatic elected president, the Argentine military appealed to the public by claiming that they would return the country to prosperity and order. An even higher proportion of Peruvians supported Alberto Fujimori's *autogolpe* in 1992.[8] Fujimori promised to end the rebellion led by Sendero Luminoso and carry out economic reforms that would restore growth. In both cases, attractive promises in a context of widespread anger about the current situation led to broad popular support for a coup.

The general point is that even military coups need and usually have quite a bit of civilian support at the time of intervention. To get that support, military seizure groups typically make promises to restore things nearly all citizens want, such as public order and growth. Other kinds of seizure groups make promises like "peace, bread, and land."

Where the struggle to oust the old regime has been prolonged and the seizure group has needed to maintain popular support for some years and also to draw manpower and other material resources from the population, successful groups have generally provided more than promises. As Samuel Popkin has noted, change-oriented organizations are more likely to succeed in attracting a mass base if they can provide real benefits to those they seek to organize.[9] Since their material resources are usually quite limited, as is their ability to tax, they often provide public goods such as land reform and organization for self-defense in the areas they control, along with individual benefits that require cadre labor but little money. Literacy and vaccination campaigns are common strategies. These benefits are highly valued by the recipients and create loyalty that ideology and promises alone could not elicit. Leninist parties in China and Vietnam relied heavily on these strategies during the years prior to the seizure of power, as did Sendero Luminoso in Peru.[10] Popkin describes similar strategies used by the Cao

Dai, Hoa Hao, and Catholic missionaries in Vietnam,[11] and nationalist parties pursued similar strategies during the struggle for independence in several African countries.

In summing up the argument so far, let me make Jowitt's implicit evolutionary argument explicit. Many are called to the revolutionary vocation, but few succeed. Although hierarchy contributes to discipline and secrecy—both of which are useful to the survival of revolutionary groups in a hostile environment—too much centralization creates vulnerability to several potentially fatal ills. Over-centralized out-of-power organizations can fail because of an inability to maintain the loyalty of militants, lack of responsiveness toward potential supporters, or decapitation. As noted above, out-of-power party leaders cannot usually impose heavy costs on cadres who desert the cause. Consequently, if a leader demands too much obedience and subordination from militants, they may simply desert, leaving the group too small to accomplish the task.

In most political movements, militants, whose activism is required for revolutionary success, favor more extreme policies than do potential followers, whose support is also needed.[12] The need to maintain the support of activists pushes seizure groups toward extreme ideas (such as collectivization and reliance on violence), but unresponsiveness to popular needs can cut the group off from crucial information about both the enemy and ordinary people. Without good information, a guerrilla strategy cannot succeed. Popular hostility also makes it much harder and more costly to recruit manpower and collect the food needed to keep a revolutionary army on its feet. Hostile peasants have betrayed many a potential revolutionary to authorities. The fates of Che Guevara and the pre-Leninist Russian revolutionaries are well-known examples.

In addition, extremely hierarchical revolutionary groups can be destroyed by decapitation, as the rapid disintegration of Sendero Luminoso after the capture of its leader Abimael Guzmán shows. For these and other reasons, extremely hierarchical groups that espouse ideological positions and practical strategies opposed to the interests and values of ordinary people are unlikely to succeed in seizing power. Those groups that do succeed are thus more likely to have somewhat more collegial relationships among cadres and leaders and to be somewhat more responsive to popular will—prior to their accession to power—than disquisitions on democratic centralism or military hierarchy would lead one to expect. The more centralized and unresponsive groups tend to die out during the struggle.

The selection mechanisms that favor collegial and responsive traits are always at work on groups that aspire to seize power, but they work more

BARBARA GEDDES

forcefully on groups that must undertake long struggles and groups reliant on ordinary people for resources. In contrast to these groups, military coup plotters already have the weapons and manpower they need and so can seize power with less popular support, though they need some support—along with consensus within the officer corps and a propitious moment. Seizure groups that can fund their military effort by picking up alluvial diamonds from streambeds need even less popular support. They can buy or coerce manpower and elite cooperation. They can survive for a long time without popular support, and even take power sometimes, though decapitation is still a danger.[13]

THE CONSOLIDATION OF POWER

Jowitt argues that once a seizure group has succeeded in conquering political power, the Leninist party elite tries to insulate cadres from potentially contaminating societal and familial interests in order to safeguard the regime's transformative capacity. That leads them to put a high premium on cadre obedience. In the stable environment created by the successful conquest of power, daring, autonomous cadres able to use their own judgment in response to unpredictable situations no longer help the party to succeed. Instead, party elites shift their concern to bringing under control partially autonomous cadres who may have begun to develop their own regional bases of popular support. Because they face the task of creating a new set of radically different economic and societal institutions in a hostile and unreconstructed traditional society, Leninist party leaders then want to recruit ideologically trustworthy cadres who will follow central directives. Jowitt labels this period the consolidation stage.

In its dealings with society, instead of responding to popular aspirations, the party tries to reshape not only the economy but also popular culture and societal norms in ways most ordinary people oppose. Party ideology and policy become dogmatic rather than responsive. In the effort to accomplish these tasks, the party becomes more centralized and hierarchical. Leadership narrows and becomes more personalized, according to Jowitt, which limits the points of access for members of society. The security forces become the most important instrument of the regime, and violence is used against cadres and supporters, not just enemies.

Jowitt argues that the consolidation stage distinguishes Leninist regimes from other post-revolutionary regimes. Based on the cases I have examined, it appears that although the particular constellation of features Jowitt attributes to the consolidation stage is uncommon in non-Leninist regimes, a general narrowing of both the regime elite and its societal bases of support occurs after seizure in most other dictatorships, as does a struggle over the personalization of leadership. The consolidation stage Jowitt describes is one possible outcome of this narrowing process, but not the most frequent one. In all kinds of dictatorship, once the seizure group has captured political power, the various incentives that had tended to keep the group collegial change, as do those incentives that impelled the group to maintain broad popular support. As soon as the group is securely in power, the costs of hierarchy are reduced. This does not mean that hierarchy necessarily contributes to regime survival, but only that since it no longer dramatically reduces survival chances, it will tend to develop because it often serves the interests of individual leaders.

CHANGED INCENTIVES FOR LEADERS AND CADRES

When a leader can tax his subjects and controls the state's coercive apparatus, the bargaining power of the leader relative to members of the seizure group increases. The cost to the leader of losing cadres all but disappears; in fact, typically, converts and opportunists flock to groups in power, so deserting cadres can easily be replaced. The cost to cadres of desertion, however, rises. They may lose leadership positions and jobs; they may be harassed, beaten, and jailed; they may have to go into exile; they may even be killed. In short, the relative bargaining power of the leader and cadres is reversed.

At the same time that the ruling group is becoming more disciplined and centralized, the logic of minimum-winning coalitions also asserts itself, even in authoritarian settings.[14] In democratic theory, politicians are expected to form minimum-winning coalitions rather than larger ones if the policies being voted upon involve distributive goods. Each member of the coalition can get more for his or her constituents if the number across whom the benefits have to be spread is as small as possible, though above the majority needed to win the vote. An analogous logic applies in authoritarian settings. Rulers need some support—though there is no magic 51-percent rule—and they have to provide some benefits to their supporters. To the extent that the kinds of benefits the government is able to distribute to supporters are limited to private or individual goods, the coalition has a strong incentive to keep itself as small as it can while still surviving in power. The minimum-winning logic is the same: the smaller the number of individuals to receive distributive goods, the more each can have. It is thus very

　　　　　　　　　　　　　　　　　　　BARBARA GEDDES

common to see the regime alliance narrow as it becomes more sure of its control.

This narrowing affects the elite, support groups, and the beneficiaries of economic policy. A seizure group that promised something vague and attractive like increased growth must, after coming to power, select a particular set of policies that inevitably advantage some citizens and hurt others—usually some of those who initially supported them. Any choice of economic policy concentrates benefits in some groups while reducing the income of others, and these changes are highly visible.

Analysts have given lots of attention to the radicalization of economic policy in leftist regimes, which causes elite supporters to desert the coalition, as in postrevolutionary Nicaragua and Cuba.[15] The selection of economic policies not advertised before the seizure of power is also characteristic of both personalist dictatorships carrying out state interventionist policies and right-wing military regimes defending Western Christian culture from the communist threat. For example, Hastings Banda, the autocratic ruler of Malawi for more than three decades, achieved power at the head of a nationalist movement, but, to the dismay of allies and fellow party members, pursued conservative economic policies that included only moderate Africanization of the economy and bureaucracy. In Chile, few of the officers or citizens who supported the military intervention of 1973 expected or supported the extreme economic liberalization carried out by the Pinochet government. Many manufacturers of import-competing goods, who had been among the supporters of the coup, were driven into bankruptcy by these policies. As in both of these examples, a regime's choice of economic policy often causes many erstwhile supporters to desert it.

THE PERSONALIZATION OF LEADERSHIP

The narrowing of the coalition base after seizures of power occurs concurrently with another standard feature of post-seizure consolidation: the struggle for leadership within the seizure group. These struggles vary depending on how the regime came to power. Autonomous authoritarian regimes come to power in three principal ways. Most colorfully but least frequently, they defeat incumbents in a revolutionary insurgency or civil war. The most common means of coming to power is the military coup. Authoritarians can also come to power via internal transformation of a constitutional government. Elected ruling parties or leaders can engineer rule changes that outlaw opposition parties and close or purge other branches of government. This was the strategy used by most African single-party regimes. They initially came to power in competitive elections, but then changed the rules in ways that guaranteed their indefinite control of high office.

If they do not seek merely to replace one civilian government with another, military interventions usually aim to initiate rule by the military itself as an institution.[16] Typically, single-party rule follows either revolution or the illegalization of opposition parties. Changes in the formal and informal rules that define these regime types often occur during the first years after a seizure of power, however. These can result in the personalization of political power in either military or single-party regimes. Personalization occurs because of the changes in relative bargaining strength of leaders and cadres described above.

Members of seizure groups rarely intend or expect personalization. Early leaders are often elected or chosen by consensus. Top cadres or officers often make rules about who should help the leader make policy and how these lieutenants should be chosen. They also often make rules about rotation of leadership and how succession should be handled.

Professionalized militaries, which tend to be legalistic and rule-bound, may negotiate quite detailed rules about consultation and succession prior to coups—especially if they have had past experience with the post-seizure personalization of power by an erstwhile colleague.[17] They respect established military hierarchy, but nevertheless try to make rational decisions about which among the set of top active or retired officers should be chosen to head the government. They often consciously choose an individual considered uncharismatic and legalistic to reduce the likelihood of personalization. It has been reported that Augusto Pinochet, a latecomer to the Chilean coup conspiracy, was chosen for that reason. Experience shows, however, that personality traits exhibited in a constraining and rule-bound institution like the military do not predict behavior very well in the much less rule-bound situation facing the paramount leader of an authoritarian regime.

Out-of-office parties have standard ways of choosing leaders, making strategy choices, and delegating tasks. In general, members seem to assume that the same procedures will be followed after the seizure of power, so they engage in less explicit negotiation beforehand than do militaries.

After the seizure of power has occurred, however, most paramount leaders seek to remain at the top, regardless of the rules to which they have previously agreed. The impulse to consolidate personal power is not universal, but it seems to be quite common among those who scramble to leadership

BARBARA GEDDES

positions in seizure groups. Among the 172 authoritarian regimes I have examined, initial leaders voluntarily maintained fairly collegial consultative bodies and handed power to a successor not selected by themselves in only a few cases.

From the desire to secure their position from challenges—both those arising from within the ruling group and those from outside—a number of behaviors flow. Leaders seek to gain more individual discretion over policy decisions and more control over other party members. In short, they seek to concentrate power and resources in their own hands.

Once in power, the leader's interests diverge somewhat from those of his lieutenants, and their respective bargaining power becomes more unequal, as noted above. A stylized version of this bargaining takes the following form. After coming to power, the leader decides whether to stick to the procedures established before the seizure, or to renege on the implicit or explicit agreement with supporters. The leader controls some discrete amount of goods and powers that both he and other members of the seizure group value highly. These include material goods, such as monopoly rights to import certain products, and also control over various aspects of policy and the choice of personnel for high and low office. These goods are valuable both to have and to be able to give to clients to help build one's own political base. The leader decides how to distribute these goods to best secure the adherence of needed supporters.

After the leader has demonstrated the way he intends to handle the resources associated with his office, members of the seizure group can accept the distribution of power and resources the leader has proposed or challenge it. Opposition is costly, not only to those who take the risk of overtly expressing disagreement but also to the leader, because disagreement and factionalization weaken the whole group's hold on power. If some of the group oppose the leader's proposal, he can either offer members a larger share of goods and decision-making authority or punish his opponents. Punishment can be very costly to opponents. They will almost certainly be demoted; they may be sent to live in the poverty-stricken countryside, jailed, or exiled; or they may be killed. Punishment is also costly to the leader, because it expends resources, weakens the regime, and creates enemies who will surface as soon as they deem it safe. Whichever way the leader responds, cadres can either acquiesce or try to depose him.

Trying to remove authoritarian leaders is always risky, and no one plotting such a course can be certain of success. Serious consequences follow the discovery of plots. Consequently, fewer lieutenants plot than are dissatisfied with their share. If a dissatisfied faction could oust the current leader and take his place, they would of course achieve a larger share of power and resources. Factors affecting the likelihood of plotting are discussed below.

Plots are also risky for leaders. How serious the consequences of a successful plot are varies depending on regime type and other characteristics of the political situation. In military regimes, ousted leaders are usually allowed to retire in peace, so the cost of ouster is moderate. Ousted single-party leaders may also be allowed to retire, though not if they are perceived as potential focal points for later opposition. The cost to leaders can be very great, however. Sometimes they are killed, along with members of their families and close allies. Jail and exile also affect their retirement plans.

To sum up this section, authoritarian leaders bargain with their lieutenants over the distribution of both material advantages associated with high office and also discretion over policy. All leaders need some support, which they must reward, but the desire to remain at the top gives them strong incentives to concentrate resources and decisions in their own hands. When the leader succeeds in concentrating everything in his own hands, observers label the regime "personalistic." Lieutenants want to share the spoils and power, but have little bargaining power beyond the threat to withdraw support and replace the leader. Failure to agree on a distribution is costly to both leaders and lieutenants.

Authoritarian regimes vary enormously in levels of repression, distribution of costs and benefits across societal groups, policies followed, and ideological justification. Nevertheless, the impulse toward narrowing and personalization is common to all types. This observation suggests that the transformative capacity of Leninist regimes was a by-product of a more general process of post-seizure consolidation interacting with ideology. For Stalin, all good things went together.

Factors That Affect the Personalization of Power

In all the complexity and detail of particular authoritarian experiences, thinking about the strategic interaction between leaders and lieutenants within the seizure group helps to highlight the areas we need to understand if we want to figure out when personalization is likely to succeed and when other members of the seizure group will be able to resist it. Three factors systematically affect the likelihood of personalization: the prior organization (or not) of lieutenants into a disciplined organization, lieutenants' autonomous control over armed and trained forces, and the control and competence of the security apparatus.

If lieutenants have little prior organization and leaders can make separate bargains with individuals, lieutenants will compete with each other for the leader's favor and drive the price of support down. Unorganized individual lieutenants also face a collective action problem when plotting to overthrow the leader, which makes plots both more costly and more risky, but also makes the threat of overthrow less credible during bargaining. For these reasons, leaders facing lieutenants in recently organized undisciplined parties made up of the clienteles of multiple "big men" or unprofessional militaries riven by ethnic factions can drive a harder bargain with lieutenants. They can concentrate more resources and power in their own hands. In short, they can personalize the regime, as did a number of African leaders who initially came to office as heads of nationalist parties or military conspiracies.

In contrast, where leaders have to bargain with a unified and disciplined party or a professionalized military with its hierarchy intact, the threat of ouster is much more credible and the price of support is likely to be higher. Leaders in this situation face a unified group which, like a labor union, can drive a harder bargain than can the individuals who make it up. In these circumstances, leaders usually find it expedient to consult with brother officers or the party politburo, and they usually distribute resources of various kinds broadly within the support group. In short, the prior organization, unity, and discipline of the seizure group affect the likelihood of later regime personalization.

Thinking about the relationship between leaders and lieutenants in this way has two theoretical consequences. First, it helps explain why the concentration of power in one individual's hands is so common in authoritarian regimes, even those with an egalitarian ideology and earlier history of collegial leadership. Second, it directs attention precisely to the characteristics of seizure groups and political situations that affect the kind of regime that tends to emerge during consolidation. Where professionalized militaries or disciplined parties with a history of prior effective action leading a mass struggle head authoritarian regimes, lieutenants are likely to be able to resist extreme personalization. Where instead militaries are incompletely professionalized or recently indigenized and riven by factions, or where parties are recent creations by the leader himself or amalgams of multiple jostling factions, personalization of rule usually occurs.

In a dictatorship, the key question that must be asked if the leader reneges on promises to consult or to allow himself to be succeeded after a certain period of time is, can his lieutenants remove him? In a military regime, they usually can. When the military rules as an institution, the leader cannot monopolize the means of force. Coups against the leaders of military regimes are relatively easy because the plotters have ready access to guns and troops. Coups that oust a military president without destabilizing the regime are common; they are analogous to votes of no confidence in parliamentary systems.

Where a party organization has developed prior to the seizure in which able lieutenants have made their careers, possibly developed regional bases of support, and command the loyalty of men who fought under them, party members also have greater ability to constrain and, if necessary, replace leaders. In some single-party regimes, the politburo actually has the power to remove unwanted leaders, though such institutions are among the first that leaders try to change. Leaders who have just acceded to office after the death of an incumbent can be removed relatively easily because they have not yet managed to consolidate their personal hold over the party, military, and state apparatus.

In general, leaders who themselves control the security apparatus are more difficult to remove. A competent and loyal security service increases the chance of discovering plots. If the likelihood of successfully ousting the leader is low, no one will plot, because the costs of detection are so very high. Where plots are likely to fail, the implicit threat of overthrow that underlies lieutenants' bargaining power is not credible. When both leaders and lieutenants understand that plots are likely to fail, the leader will concentrate additional resources and power in his hands, and lieutenants will acquiesce.

It is easier for leaders to gain control over the security apparatus in some situations than in others. Typically in professionalized militaries, a separate security apparatus is controlled by each force, which helps to prevent the personalization of control—though in a few instances military leaders have established personal control via the appointment of loyalists to head these agencies. This is more likely if the paramount leader of a military regime is allowed to continue as active-duty commander in chief, as Pinochet was. In most military regimes, however, generals must retire before taking office as head of state.

Parties do not generally have security organizations before they achieve power unless they have fought civil wars. Instead, they take over the state police and military, with more or less success depending on their own prior history as well as the state's. Parties that have led revolutionary insurgencies and independence movements have some cadres specialized in security and violence, but only those that have fought lengthy civil wars are likely to have the specialized organization and personnel that would allow them to take over and/or replace state security services rapidly and thoroughly. More frequently, partly unreconstructed military and security services

BARBARA GEDDES

remain a problem for single-party leaders after they achieve power and reduce their ability to rely on force to induce change. A number of African single-party leaders tried to resolve this difficulty by creating militias, president's guards, or paramilitaries. These paramilitary forces, usually drawn from groups or regions especially loyal to the leader, can help to maintain a leader in power, but they are often undisciplined and venal. In addition, their existence further alienates the established military; the creation of these forces has precipitated coups against many African dictators.

Where a military or single-party leader does gain personal control of the security apparatus, as, for example, General Pinochet did, the leader has taken a giant step toward personalization of rule, even in countries with a professionalized military or well-developed party. In such settings, control of the security apparatus will not be enough to transform the regime completely; the military was marginalized in Chile, but continued to serve as a bulwark of the regime, as did the Communist Party during Stalin's rule in the Soviet Union. In countries in which the military is incompletely professionalized prior to seizure or the party was recently founded and scarcely exists outside big cities, however, there is no countervailing force within the regime to limit the leader's impulse to concentrate power in his own hands. In such regimes, leaders only become susceptible to overthrow as they become old or infirm and lose the ability to keep the security apparatus under tight personal control.

In light of this analysis, the Leninist regimes Jowitt analyzed can be seen as the outcome characteristic of seizures of power carried out by parties that varied from somewhat to highly developed as a result of prior political and revolutionary experience. The Russian Leninist Party was disciplined and dedicated before the seizure of power, but small and limited in reach. It developed into a much larger and more penetrating entity while Lenin lived, but the overwhelming need for cadres to man the state apparatus and fight in the civil war led to a rapid and uncontrolled expansion of membership during the first years after the seizure of power. Many made quick and superficial conversions at that time, and many joined for opportunistic reasons. Thus by the time Stalin began to consolidate personal power at the party's expense, the party was large but less capable of defending itself. The commanders of irregular troops during the civil war had been demobilized and dispersed or incorporated into the closely controlled Red Army so they could no longer effectively oppose personalization.

Parties that fought prolonged civil wars before achieving power and/or mobilized an effective underground resistance to occupying forces have developed more capacity to moderate the centralizing tendencies of leaders and even, at times, to remove them from decision making when their policies have failed. Mao Zedong's eclipse after the disastrous Great Leap Forward is an example, although Mao eventually mobilized his own supporters for a comeback.

To sum up this section, whether power becomes personalized in the hands of a single man during the aftermath of an authoritarian seizure of power depends on the outcome of a struggle between the group's leader and his lieutenants. Among the 172 cases upon which the generalizations in this analysis are based, more than half of all the authoritarian regimes initiated by militaries, parties, or a combination of the two had been partly or fully personalized within three years of the initial seizure of power. In about a third of the cases, the leader had succeeded in full personalization.

The outcome Jowitt describes as the consolidation stage of Leninist regimes, in which one man monopolizes most decision making and personally controls the security apparatus but nevertheless maintains a functioning party to run the state apparatus and channel the distribution of resources, can occur when the party is disciplined and cohesive but lacks control over the means of force. This amalgam characterized a number of Leninist regimes at early stages, but has also occurred elsewhere. In the set of authoritarian regimes used for this study, ten non-Leninist cases exhibit this amalgam of personalist and party-centric characteristics. Such an amalgam may well be useful for carrying out a transformative mission, as Jowitt has argued, but it also occurs in the absence of such a mission, because most leaders attempt to consolidate personal power even when pursuing more modest goals.

INCLUSION

What Jowitt labels the inclusion stage involves the reestablishment of legal and institutional predictability after the consolidation of a seizure of power, along with the extension of limited participation rights to citizens and the transition to a more consultative style of interacting with economic and cultural elites. Inclusion has proven difficult for Leninist regimes to implement because consultation with experts and responsiveness toward citizens inevitably generate pressures toward economic rationality, which threatens regime survival. Some of the elements Jowitt sees as needed at this stage have also posed difficulties for non-Leninists, but others are unproblematic for them.

Economic rationality and consultation with experts and economic elites usually pose no threat to non-Leninist regimes. In fact, most noncommunist authoritarian governments consult with them from the beginning and try to co-opt and accommodate them, which Jowitt refers to as premature inclusion. Regimes that seek survival rather than breakthrough turn co-optation into an art form.

Seizure groups need the cooperation of economic elites in order to survive, just as democratic governments do. In capitalist countries, one of the surest roads to economic crisis and consequent political instability is capital flight. This is an especially threatening political weapon because it need not be coordinated or organized. Hundreds of individuals making self-interested rational decisions can, without any effort at collective action, undermine a government simply by refusing to invest and instead sending their money abroad.

Seizure groups thus need an effective way to manage the always latent threat of capital flight. Leninists deal with the threat by confiscating all assets and delegating their management to party loyalists. At the other extreme, some regimes try to devise policies to keep private investors happy and thus maintain their support for the regime. Private business owners and investors are notoriously fickle and ungrateful, however, and governments can only control some of the forces that affect economic outcomes, so the second strategy is quite risky in practice. The majority of authoritarian governments have chosen an in-between strategy: partial state ownership, heavy regulation, and the creation of private-sector opportunities for themselves and loyal allies. Despite intense international pressure to liberalize their economies since the 1980s, most current authoritarian regimes continue to pursue modified state interventionist strategies that benefit those parts of the private sector that support the regime. It has proved as politically risky for other kinds of dictators to liberalize their economies as it was for the Leninists.

Limited popular participation, identified by Jowitt as a feature of the inclusion stage, occurs in many authoritarian regimes. In single-party regimes, including Leninist, directed popular participation has been allowed, indeed required, from the beginning; in other regimes, elites often initiate such participation after they have created parties to support themselves. It is common for secure authoritarian regimes to allow some degree of competition, either from toothless opposition parties or within the single party, for local office or seats in the legislature. Such electoral authoritarian regimes can be stable for many decades.

Not all elements that characterize the inclusion stage are equally easy to manage, however. The reinitiation of some legal rights and the concomitant reduction in violence and other arbitrary punishments can cause the regime difficulties. This change in regime norms occurs when some regime elites believe that power has been safely consolidated and society no longer threatens their hold on office. They advocate a more legalistic and predictable form of authoritarianism to increase the predictability and security of their own lives and careers. In a number of historical instances of regime decompression, we have evidence that reformist members of the elite sought specifically to reduce the power of a security apparatus that was beginning to threaten even them. They sought to limit the discretion of security personnel by giving courts more powers and reintroducing legal rights such as habeas corpus. Relaxing media censorship can also help rein in the security apparatus; atrocities and abuses of power are less likely to occur when they are reported in the media, which leads to demands for punishment of offenders. Roused public opinion can threaten authoritarian leaders even when no institutionalized method of removing individuals from office exists.

Relatively few authoritarian regimes have hit upon a formula for successful and stable inclusionary authoritarianism. Mexico under the rule of the Partido Revolucionario Institucional (PRI), stable and inclusionary from 1937 to 1987, is probably the best known and longest lived. The Franco regime in Spain, the Salazar regime in Portugal, rule by the Parti Socialiste in Senegal, and Chama Cha Mapinduzi (CCM) rule in Tanzania are others. In many cases, however, attempts to routinize, legalize, and increase participation without losing control have created cracks in the dam through which the floodwaters of democratization eventually poured. During the last twenty-five years, numerous regimes, including the long-lived and apparently stable ones in Mexico, Spain, and Senegal, have moved from the inclusion stage to democratization despite the best efforts of regime elites. Tanzania has also held free and fair competitive elections, although the CCM has not lost one yet.

Although regime insiders introduce the legal and institutional changes underpinning the inclusion stage in order to increase their own security, these reforms also reduce the risks of opposition for regime opponents. Once the risks of open opposition have been lowered and censorship has been relaxed, events that reflect badly on the government—such as economic crisis or defeat in a minor war—are likely to lead to more widespread opposition. What was once largely symbolic electoral opposition permitted by the regime can then be used to express public discontent, even if rules have been devised to prevent the opposition from winning. During the recent "third wave" of democratization,[18] controlled opposition in a number of these previously stable inclusionary systems has become uncon-

BARBARA GEDDES

trolled, leading to the loss of power by incumbents. In other words, the inclusion stage carries with it considerable risk.

Even fewer dictators, however, have found a secure, stable exclusionary formula. Among these 172 cases, only 36 non-Leninist regimes have lasted twenty-five years or more. Of those 36, less than a third failed to institutionalize a more-or-less predictable legal system and somewhat meaningful popular participation. Most of those that did not were led by repressive personalist dictators in very poor countries, such as Rafael Leónidas Trujillo in the Dominican Republic, the Duvaliers in Haiti, Kamuzu Banda in Malawi, Gnassingbe Eyadema in Togo, and Joseph Mobutu in Congo/Zaire. In short, stable exclusionary authoritarian rule seems to be nearly impossible to maintain in countries at moderate-to-higher levels of economic development. Inclusionary authoritarianism tends to survive longer, but becomes vulnerable during economic and other kinds of crises.

CONCLUSION

Certain patterns of change in regime personnel and decision-making style first explained by Jowitt in Leninist regimes also occur, as shown above, in most other kinds of authoritarian rule. Most authoritarian regimes come to power at the barrel of a gun. New rulers seize control either during a military coup or a revolutionary uprising. Less frequently, constitutionally chosen leaders engineer rule changes that outlaw other parties and close or purge other branches of government. Generally, as Jowitt noted, the first months of a new dictatorship are fairly chaotic. Leadership within the junta or other governing entity tends to be collegial, with hierarchies and routines for making and implementing decisions not yet established; personnel within the junta often change in rapid succession; citizens, especially those with personal links to members of the governing group, often have considerable access and ability to influence decisions. Jowitt labels this early period the transformation stage in Leninist regimes, and his insights about that stage are equally valid for non-Leninist authoritarian regimes.

Seizure is followed by the consolidation stage, during which Leninist elites centralize and reduce their responsiveness both to party cadres and to other citizens. A similar phenomenon occurs in non-Leninist regimes. Within about three years, if the regime survives, a clear hierarchy will have been established, and decision making within the junta or politburo will have become less collegial. This narrowing in non-Leninist regimes is a consequence of minimum-winning coalition logic. That is, members of the regime alliance want enough elite support to survive in power, but no more, because the larger the number of individuals or groups over which resources must be spread, the less there is for each one. At the same time, struggles within the ruling elite among members attempting to consolidate their own individual power may personalize the regime as well as narrow it further. These efforts to personalize power succeed about half the time. While these struggles are occurring within the elite, it is also common for large numbers of citizens to abandon the coalition supporting the dictatorship as they discover how its policies will really affect them. The regime's support base thus also narrows and becomes more ideologically defined.

Once their hold on power seems secure, voices from within non-Leninist regimes will arise, as they do in Leninist regimes, to advocate a more rule-bound, more predictable, and less violent political climate—what Jowitt calls the inclusion stage. In both kinds of regime, these advocates of institutionalization or decompression (*distensão,* as it was called during military rule in Brazil) are motivated by the desire for more secure and predictable lives themselves. They often seek by means of legal changes and relaxation of media censorship to rein in a threatening security apparatus. Hardliners within the regime, especially those in the security apparatus, oppose such changes, as they have in Leninist regimes, but in most single-party and military regimes moderates have eventually prevailed. Such voluntary changes emanating from within the regime elite have in some instances resulted in stable long-lived authoritarian regimes like that of the PRI in Mexico. At other times, the same kinds of changes have instead reduced the risk of expressing opposition and thus opened the way for an orderly return to democracy, as in Brazil, although regime elites did not initially intend that result. No matter how the effort to develop a more legalistic, predictable, and inclusionary regime turns out, however, the impulse to move in that direction is motivated by the same perceptions and concerns in both Leninist and non-Leninist regimes.

When Jowitt first wrote about Leninist regimes, they were confident political entities boldly striding through history, apparently enjoying an indefinite lifespan. Very few of them, however, have survived the "Leninist extinction."[19] Yet many of Jowitt's ideas about them have survived better than the regimes themselves. His analysis of the stages of development traversed by Leninist regimes illuminates a common pattern of development in non-Leninist authoritarian regimes as well. Although non-Leninist dictatorships have not carried out economic and cultural transformations equivalent to those carried out by Leninists, the desire of all regime elites to survive in office and benefit from control of the levers of power, the drive of many individual leaders to amass personal power, and the wish of ordinary cadres for a secure and predictable life are characteristic of both types of regime. Although specific outcomes have varied, these similar motivations have led to generally similar patterns of development in both Leninist and non-Leninist authoritarian regimes.

NOTES

1. Kenneth Jowitt, "Inclusion and Mobilization in European Leninist Regimes," *World Politics* 28, no.1 (October 1975): 69–96.

2. Empirical generalizations in this article are based on information about nearly all authoritarian regimes of three-years duration or more at any time between 1946 and 2000. Monarchies and regimes in countries created after 1989 or with populations under one million are excluded. For more details on the data, see Barbara Geddes, *Paradigms and Sand Castles: Theory Building and Research Design in Comparative Politics* (Ann Arbor: University of Michigan Press, 2003), chap. 2.

3. Jowitt, "Inclusion and Mobilization," 69.

4. Phrase coined by Margaret Levi, *Consent, Dissent, and Patriotism* (New York: Cambridge University Press, 1997).

5. Theodore Draper, *Castroism: Theory and Practice* (New York: Praeger, 1965), 15.

6. See, among many others, descriptions in Aristide Zolberg, *Creating Political Order: The Party-States of West Africa* (Chicago: Rand McNally, 1966), and Samuel Decalo, *The Stable Minority: Civilian Rule in Africa, 1960–1990* (Gainesville: Florida Academic Press Books, 1998).

7. Guillermo O'Donnell, *Modernization and Bureaucratic-Authoritarianism: Studies in South American Politics* (Berkeley: Institute of International Studies, University of California Press, 1973).

8. Susan Stokes, *Mandates and Democracy: Neoliberalism by Surprise in Latin America* (New York: Cambridge University Press, 2001).

9. Samuel Popkin, *The Rational Peasant: The Political Economy of Rural Society in Vietnam* (Berkeley: University of California Press, 1979).

10. See Chalmers A. Johnson, *Peasant Nationalism and Communist Power: The Emergence of Revolutionary China, 1937–1945* (Stanford: Stanford University Press, 1962), for descriptions of the organization of self-defense and literacy campaigns in China; see Cynthia McClintock, *Revolutionary Movements in Latin America: El Salvador's FMLN & Peru's Sendero Luminoso* (Washington, DC: U.S. Institute for Peace Press, 1998), for a useful description of the early strategies of Sendero Luminoso.

11. Popkin, *The Rational Peasant*, 1979.

12. See James DeNardo, *Power in Numbers* (Princeton: Princeton University Press, 1985) for a thoughtful analysis of this tension.

13. Charles Taylor of Liberia is the classic example. The capture of Foday Sankoh, leader of Revolutionary United Front (RUF), which seems to have finally ended the

civil war in Sierra Leone, is an example of the vulnerability of this kind of movement to decapitation. On the relationship between the availability of lootable resources and civil war, see Michael Ross, "How Does Natural Resource Wealth Influence Civil Wars? Evidence from Thirteen Cases," *International Organization* (forthcoming), and "What Do We Know about Natural Resources and Civil War?" *Journal of Peace Research* (March 2004): 337–56; and William Reno, *Warlord Politics and African States* (Boulder, CO: Lynne Rienner, 1998).

14. In theories of democratic politics, "minimum-winning coalition" refers to the idea that members of a coalition prefer that their alliance include only as many members as are needed to win a vote, usually a bit more than 50 percent. The implicit assumption is that benefits secured as a result of votes taken will be shared among coalition members, so the fewer the number of members, the larger the share for each one.

15. See Forrest Colburn, *Post-Revolutionary Nicaragua: State, Class, and Dilemmas of Agrarian Policy* (Berkeley: University of California Press, 1986), for an insightful analysis of Sandinista economic policy and its consequences.

16. In some well-known instances, the leader has in effect chosen the group; that is, he founded and organized the group and has maintained his central position despite the vicissitudes of the struggle. In such cases, followers do not make a separate leadership choice, but rather choose the leader along with the group they have chosen to support. In other cases, however, the group either has a less-defined hierarchy before the seizure of power or the original leader dies during or shortly after power is secured. In these situations, cadres select leaders.

17. See the description in Andrés Fontana, "Political Decision-Making by a Military Corporation: Argentina, 1976–83" (Ph.D. diss., University of Texas, 1987), of the months-long negotiation over rules within the Argentine military before the 1976 seizure of power.

18. Samuel Huntington, *The Third Wave: Democratization in the Late Twentieth Century* (Norman: University of Oklahoma Press, 1991).

19. Kenneth Jowitt, *New World Disorder: The Leninist Extinction* (Berkeley: University of California Press, 1992).

9

FROM NEOTRADITIONALISM
TO NEOFAMILISM

Responses to "National Dependency"
in Newly Industrialized Countries

YONG-CHOOL HA

INTRODUCTION

A quarter of a century ago, Ken Jowitt made the following observation, "Taking the general notion of backwardness, [Alexander] Gerschenkron developed a challenge-response pattern that on the basis of several empirically based indicators enabled him to predict and explain the particular institutional form industrialization would take in a country. . . . Lenin offered a Gerschenkronian solution to the challenge of creating a class form of organization in a non-Western peasant society."[1]

The above quotation speaks clearly of the ongoing academic concerns of Ken Jowitt. Jowitt approached Leninism and socialist efforts from the perspective of overcoming backwardness through an organizational novelty that Jowitt called "charismatic impersonalism." Following from this broad interest, Jowitt has been keenly interested in the process of the emergence of the socialist version of modernity, which is distinctly different from the Western version. As much as he might have wished for a successful emergence of socialist modernity, history betrayed his hope. What he saw long before the actual collapse of the Soviet Union was the degeneration of the socialist system into a by-now well-known "neo-traditionalism," where the party evolved into an institution that was mainly interested in maintaining its status, having completely lost its heroic tasks.

With this broad insight on the historical trajectory of socialist institutional evolution in mind, Jowitt proposed stimulating concepts, approaches, and theoretical frameworks to understand its dynamics. One of these is to demonstrate the intricate interaction patterns between tradition and modernizing tasks such as industrialization. Jowitt's seminal article on an organizational approach to culture in the 1974 APSR succinctly and successfully demonstrated how traditional cultural values were unintentionally reinforced in building socialism. It was at the time when the tradition-modernity dichotomy was fiercely criticized as being artificial and false, without any concrete conceptual alternative to overcome it. The following is an attempt to extend Jowitt's understanding of the interaction between tradition and modern tasks in the context of late-industrialized countries like South Korea.

QUESTIONS RAISED

The main focus of political economy for the past several decades has been on understanding different paths for overcoming economic backwardness. The common thread of all these efforts has revolved around explaining the role of the state in economic development. Thus, while the role of the state in overcoming backwardness has been amply demonstrated, what have been conspicuously absent are efforts to understand the impact on social changes of state involvement in economic development. The state was brought back in to explain late industrialization but stopped short of reaching the societal level. The upshot is a considerable discrepancy between political economic studies and political sociological studies of late-industrializing countries: while the prominent role of the state is considered in understanding the process of late economic development, conventional Western sociological categories and conceptual frameworks have been applied to analysis of its social consequence industrialization.

One reason for the discrepancy is the prevalent assumption that industrialization, regardless of its different timings and patterns, brings about universal social consequences. Following Gerschenkron, much effort has been made to understand the different paths of overcoming economic backwardness. Studies of late industrialization have focused on the role of the state in economic development, bringing the state back into the mainstream of social analyses. In contrast, social implications of state-led industrialization have been given scanty attention, rendering analyses of impacts of the state short of reaching societal level. One reason for that is the prevalent assumption that industrialization brings about universal social consequences. Another reason is that before the emergence of newly

YONG-CHOOL HA

industrializing countries, the number of late-industrializing countries was very limited, and because each late-industrializing country is unique, it is difficult to establish any general conceptual frameworks.

How is backwardness perceived and translated into institutional and policy-making processes, and what are the sociological implications? What is the process whereby, in the course of its initiation and implementation of economic goals and policies, the state affects social changes?

One may study the role of the state in reinforcing traditional social relations by using empirical evidence from South Korea during the period of industrialization from the mid-1960s through 1980. Analyzing state economic policy and the interactions between government, industry, and society in Korea, one can see that during industrialization (1) certain traditional primary social ties were unintentionally reinforced rather than weakened; (2) neofamilism's major source is the role of the state—in particular, the ways in which the state interacted with the economy and society; and (3) in place of class, new social units—amalgams of modernity and tradition—were created, which I call "neofamilism." Because these new social units were systemic and socially decisive, not intermittent, partial, or anecdotal, understanding how they arose and function is a prerequisite to understanding Korean society both socially and economically.

NEOFAMILISM DEFINED

"Neofamilism" denotes the dynamic process of reinforcement of a social ethos and social relations based upon primary solidarity. The prefix "neo" emphasizes that traditional relationships have been revived and transformed in an industrial setting. "Familism" does not refer to the conventional family, but is an inclusive term incorporating broader primary ties based on kinship, region, or school.[2] But familism denotes a narrower and thus more specific structural configuration than a broader concept like "traditionalism."

Neofamilism can be understood at three levels: as an identity marker, as a survival strategy, and as a social and institutional outcome. Neofamilism as an identity marker means that people define their identity and social relations primarily in terms of familial, school, and regional ties. Familial ties can cover the range from the immediate nuclear family to the clan. School ties may include those established from primary school through university, although high-school ties are perceived as strongest. Regional ties include those of the village. With neofamilism, class identity and functional or role identity are overshadowed by neofamilial identity bases.

As a survival strategy, neofamilism refers to people's use of neofamilial ties to promote their socio-economic interests. Rather than playing by the rules, people can mobilize neofamilial ties to promote their own personal interests. This behavior negatively affects the application of universal norms and predictability in administrative and legal operations.

Finally, neofamilism at the institutional level is the consequence of the other two aspects of neofamilism: identity and survival strategy. It refers to the effects of neofamilial identities and their uses as life strategies on institutions. The social consequence of the development of small (neofamilial) units is that society loses its structural configuration and develops only weak impersonal modes of institutional operation.

Neofamilial phenomena have frequently been regarded as anecdotal, transient, and partial ties that eventually disappear. Western macro-sociological frameworks often treat them as aberrations or partial continuations of traditional social behavior. Korean neofamilism is systematic and thorough at the identity, life-strategy, and social and institutional levels, and is a unique social process of Korean-style industrialization.

THE KOREAN CASE IN COMPARATIVE PERSPECTIVE

The Korean case shares with other late-industrializing countries the leadership's strong sense of backwardness and need for rapid industrialization. Like Japan and Prussia, Korea recruited officials based on merit, though in Korea merit-based recruitment was severely compromised. Unlike in Prussia, in Korea and Japan officials were not tied to a particular organized social group or class, and thus were relatively autonomous. However, at the time of industrialization the Japanese bureaucracy was internally more secure and stable than Korea, with stronger bureaucratic institutions.

In Germany strong opposition to industrialization existed, while in Japan and South Korea opposition to industrialization was either weakened or destroyed. In Germany the Junkers held many important bureaucratic positions. The Junkers' base was in land. They occupied local administrative and political positions, and they were the main recruitment sources for the officer corps and for higher administrative positions at the federal level. At the local level, they operated more or less autonomously. Thus, industrialization had to be pursued by the king and by the petite bourgeoisie and bureaucrats who were recruited by the king through merit-based principles.[3]

In Japan there was no counterpart to the Junkers. The samurai were deprived of landownership since the seventeenth century, and increasingly built close relationships with merchants. With the Meiji restoration, the

YONG-CHOOL HA

samurai became important sources of recruitment for bureaucrats or entrepreneurs, and they, unlike the Junkers, were eager to support state industrialization efforts. An exam-based merit system of recruitment highly insulated the samurai-turned-bureaucrats from politics and society. At the same time, Meiji politicians, officials, and intellectuals made judicious efforts not to lose Japanese tradition in the course of industrialization.[4]

In South Korea the traditional social structure was either deliberately destroyed or lost political significance owing to colonial rule, war, and land reform. Korea's political leaders were not as keen on the invention of tradition as their Japanese counterparts. In short, South Korean state-led industrialization was unique. Like other late-industrializing countries such as Germany and Japan, Korea felt a strong backwardness and need to change, and its government was heavily involved in pursuing economic development. As in Japan, Korean industrialization did not face strong social resistance, and state bureaucrats were not tied to land or any economic interests, and thus not tied to any strong social groups or classes, as were state bureaucrats in Germany. Korean bureaucrats were formally recruited based on merit, but, unlike in Japan, the administrative structure was only weakly bureaucratic. With the breakdown of the traditional social structure, political leaders and intellectuals were not especially influenced by traditional values and institutions. This created the myth that as traditional structures such as the landlord system broke down, industrialization would only bring about modernity. What was lacking were attempts to understand the mechanisms of social change in a country like Korea. A new conceptual framework is needed before one can conclude that the breakdown of a social structure will lead to modernity.

Understanding the social implications of industrialization in Korea, where the traditional social structure broke down and political leaders presented no blueprint for rescuing traditional values and institutions, is not possible without analyzing the interactions between state and nonstate actors. This analysis sheds light on the conscious and unconscious reinforcement of social forces and units even after macro-structural elements lost their political and economic significance. In other words, the influences of tradition do not disappear because one social class (such as landlords) disappears; because of the speed of the industrialization effort, traditional values and institutions still affected the process.

Therefore, research should focus first on the nature of society at the time of industrialization. Rather than analyzing Korean society in structural terms and thus arguing that the absence of a landlord class or any other class provided the basis for state autonomy, we need to understand the interactions of nonstructural social and economic forces. Given the importance of who was recruited into the bureaucracy under existing Korean social conditions, the relationship between the political leadership and the bureaucracy and between modes of recruitment and the internal institutional dynamics of the bureaucracy should be analyzed. Also, the interaction patterns of non-state actors, such as business with the state, should be examined for their social implications.

THE EMERGENCE OF A SCHOOL-REGIONAL NEXUS

The regime of Park Chung Hee set a new agenda. Parks' explicit economic goals departed from the vague political and ideological goals of Kores's past. He recognized the country's profound backwardness and felt deep shame about Korea's past and its lack of effort to industrialize. He attributed these problems to the lack of resoluteness of past political leaders:

> Retreat, crudity and stagnation have marked our 5,000 years of history beginning from prehistoric Ancient Chosun and continuing through the era of the Three Kingdoms, Unified Shilla, and the 500 years of the Yi dynasty. When did our ancestors, even once, dominate the territories of others, seek foreign civilization in order to reform our national society, demonstrate our power of unity to the outside world and act with independence in the face of others? Always, it has been we who have been mauled by big powers, assimilated by foreign cultures, impeded by primitive forms of industry, indulged in fratricidal squabbles. Ours has been a history of stagnation, idleness, complacency, accommodation, and feudalism. . . . Unless we can establish an "economy first" consciousness, our dream of building a strong nation state will end in a dream and nothing more.[5]

Park set ambitious development goals, developed an export-oriented strategy, offered economic incentives to business, and pursued an interventionist policy in economic management. Whereas gross national product growth under previous regimes had been on the order of 4.1 percent (1953–55 to 1960–62), Park set a goal of 7 to 9 percent annual growth. Park's second five-year economic plan made an export-oriented strategy a central part of the larger economic developmental strategy.[6]

The most important social implications resulted from the many economic incentives to business. In finance, to promote exports and foreign investment, the state manipulated exchange rates, established special tax

YONG-CHOOL HA

incentives, offered loan guarantees for borrowed foreign capital, reduced corporate taxes, and designated industrial sites as free economic zones. Overall, it offered thirty-eight different incentives to promote exports.[7] In encouraging development, Park was faced with three serious problems. He relied heavily on the military because he had taken office in a military coup d'état. Economically, the country was too poor to launch a rapid economic development program. And administratively, Park had been bequeathed a corrupt administrative apparatus.

Park's reliance on the military brought a large number of the ex-military into state-administrative and state-controlled agencies. In 1961 some 14.08 percent of higher civil servants had been in the military immediately before joining the civil service. This percentage increased in the higher ranks; in 1965, 56.12 percent of those between the ages of thirty-six and forty were ex-military.[8] Between 1963 (the beginning of the new civilian government) and 1967, 40 out of 95 cabinet officials had professional military backgrounds. Ten out of 11 directorships of independent regulatory commissions and 32 of 59 ambassadorial posts were held by inactive military officers. In the National Assembly, 36 out of 174 seats in the sixth assembly (1963–68) and 37 out of 175 seats in the seventh assembly (1967) were held by retired military figures. In the economic sphere, in 1969, 33 of 42 major publicly financed industrial establishments were headed by former military officers.[9]

But what is important is that among these officers those from the southeastern region were heavily favored. Of 19 Ministry of Commerce and Industry officials who were above section-chief level, 6 came from the southeast, 4 from Seoul, 3 from North Korea, 3 from Chungnam, 2 from Kyunggi, and 1 from Chunbuk. Conspicuously unrepresented was Chunnam (a southwestern province).[10]

Park seemed to kill two birds with one stone by appointing former military to civilian posts. On the one hand, he paid a political debt by providing them with new appointments and making them politically innocuous. On the other hand, he expected the military discipline and modern management skills they allegedly possessed to contribute to the new administrative apparatus.[11]

Park also attempted to install a new administrative structure to cope with new economic tasks. He instituted organizational reform and reshuffled personnel. A new economic planning board centralized the dispersed economic functions of the administration, such as budgeting, planning, and policy coordination.

In personnel, Park had to consider both competency and loyalty.

Employing only the competent would not allow full implementation of his policies, while using only the loyal might lead to an inappropriate formulation of policy and the distortion of information. Park tried to resolve this problem by continuing the tradition of hiring midlevel bureaucrats on the basis of their performance on a highly competitive examination. But he also seemed to favor people from his own region. One finding shows that the regional representation of those from the southeast increased significantly under the Park regime, from 18.8 percent of all ministerial-level officials during the first republic to 30.1 percent under the regime. This was a tremendous change from the first republic, when the southeast had been underrepresented.[12]

The same trend developed in the Ministry of Commerce and Industry. Of 171 officials who were newly appointed to section chief and higher between 1963 and 1975, 55 (32 percent) were from the southeast, a much higher proportion than the 19 percent of the national population. In contrast, before the coup d'état in 1961 no regional overrepresentation was visible. Of 51 who were recruited on merit, 45 percent were from the southeast.[13]

Twenty-three of 55 who were recruited from the southeast between 1963 and 1975 took high civil service examinations, and 8 entered public service after some kind of non-career path examination, constituting 57 percent of the total. Twenty-nine graduated from Seoul National University. Only five of the best-known regional high schools produced 24 of those 29. These numbers reflected efforts to combine merit and loyalty based on examinations and school and regional ties.[14]

The core positions directly related to economic policy planning, implementation, taxation, and staffing were filled predominantly by people from the southeast. Between 1961 and 1990, southeastern elites occupied 33.2 percent of the ministerial positions on the Economic Planning Board and 35.5 percent of the ministerial positions in the Ministry of Finance. In collecting and spending agencies from 1962 to 1972, chiefs of the National Tax Office, the Office of Government Supply, and the Customs Office were either entirely or mostly residents of the southeast. Of the seven major commercial banks, 32.3 percent had southeastern presidents between 1961 and 1984, and 46.2 percent of the board of the central bank were from the southeast (in 1986).[15]

A FAMILY-SCHOOL-REGIONAL NEXUS: THE BUSINESS SECTOR

Korean business ownership is heavily concentrated in the hands of family members of the founders. The next managerial layer consists largely of top university graduates with regional ties to the owners. At the lowest level, solidarity among average workers is based largely on regional ties.

It is well known that Korean *chaebols* (Korean business conglomerates) are owned and managed by the family members of their founders. When a family enterprise is defined as one that includes the participation of stock-owning family members in management, one survey showed that out of 137 big enterprises with more than 300 employees, 121 (93.75 percent) were family owned and managed. Family ownership and management could mean management by father and son, male siblings, or sons-in-law. The same survey found that out of 69 small- and medium-sized enterprises, 55 (79.7 percent) were family owned and managed.[16] Of 100 sons in 34 *chaebols*, 40 were presidents, managing directors, executive directors, or directors, and another 10 were directors or department chiefs of filial companies of *chaebols*. Of 31 sons-in-law in 19 *chaebols*, 12 were presidents, managing directors, or directors, and another 3 were directors or department chiefs.[17] Of 71 brothers of the founders of 30 *chaebols*, 51 were presidents or managing directors of filial companies, and 2 were directors or department chiefs of the companies under *chaebols*. This heavy family ownership indicates *chaebols'* efforts to cope with highly uncertain economic and political situations and to keep secrets.[18]

Among white-collar employees who entered *chaebols* and later became high-ranking managers, most were graduates of Seoul National University, Yonsei University, or Korea University. Of 3,987 who were board members of the 347 member companies of the Korean Federation of Industrialists, 35.2 percent were Seoul National University graduates, and 8 percent were graduates of Yonsei and Korea universities, respectively.[19] Other findings confirm this. Among executive officers of the 10 largest *chaebols* above managing director level, 48.7 percent were graduates of Seoul National University, 7.1 percent of Korea University, and 11.5 percent of Yonsei University. This roughly corresponds to the distribution of elites within the government bureaucracy. Among high-ranking bureaucrats in the three major economy-related ministries (Finance, Industry and Commerce, and the Economic Planning Board), 53.8 percent graduated from Seoul National University, 6.7 percent from Yonsei University, and 13.4 percent from Korea University. More detailed statistics are not available, although college graduates' high-school ties constituted core subcategories of these groupings, as one business executive remarked:

> During the 1960s and the third republic the southeastern regions were favored, and this cannot be denied. In lobbying, school and regional ties are important

to get more from the state. I graduated from SNU College of Commerce and from Taegu Commercial High School. . . . in the past the number was very small. Thus graduates of the SNU College of Commerce know each other well.[20]

What is also significant is the high regional affinity between owners and high-ranking managers of the 100 *chaebols*. Of 2,243 high-ranking managers who were not blood-related to founders or owners from the southeast, 57 percent were from the southeast; when owners were from the Southwest, 60.7 percent of high-ranking managers were also from the southwest.[21] As discussed below, similar recruitment patterns between governmental and business sectors indicate business efforts to deal with the government in a highly volatile environment in the course of industrialization.

At the company level, "much of the stock of its member companies was held by this kin group, many of whom occupied several of the highest managerial positions both in these companies and in the *chaebol's* own management."[22] And in recruitment of new white-collar employees, despite open competition, personnel managers of major companies sought to cultivate good relations with faculty members, especially those at the more prestigious business schools. Companies also demonstrated some regional discrimination in the selection process: those from the southwestern Cholla Province were especially disadvantaged.[23]

The same pattern was visible among small- and medium-sized business enterprises. Of 69 small- and medium-sized manufacturing businesses, 79.7 percent were family owned. In 1975, 59.2 percent of the financing of such enterprises was provided by outside sources, such as family and relatives.[24] In addition, these enterprises favored workers from the same regional origins as the company owners.[25]

Among factory workers (especially those on production lines), regional ties were quite strong. Because recruitment patterns were based on regional ties, workers from a particular region continued to recruit others from the same region. Even more important, such regional ties were regarded as a survival mechanism. During the 1960s and 1970s, most factory workers were left without state welfare protection. Workers, especially women, organized various means of self-support, such as the traditional Korean rotating financing scheme based on trust and regional ties. But such region-based solidarity, though conducive to the smooth functioning of labor unions, also aggravated regional antagonism:

The regional tensions between Kyongsan Province and Cholla Province are acute. . . . Kyonsang people look down on [Cholla people] and regard them as

YONG-CHOOL HA

backward and dishonest. People from Cholla Province, on the other hand, feel that they are victims of hundreds of years of government neglect.[26]

INTERACTIONS BETWEEN ADMINISTRATIVE OFFICIALS AND BUSINESS

It is only natural that in the process of rapid economic development, government decisions were frequently changed. The process was characterized by pragmatism and particularism. Pragmatism refers to a willingness to change in order to achieve set goals. Realistically, this means making quick decisions, and frequently changing those decisions. For example, it was reported that the law on restraining real estate investment was written after a twenty-four-hour study, and the 1973 law on price stability after only three days of preparation.[27] The export-oriented strategy, as well as the inexperience of both government and business in implementing it, led to many hasty, and ill-considered, decisions. One unintended consequence of such a hectic administrative operation was a deterioration of organizational integrity and government-business relations.

"Particularism" refers to the "practice of making policy decisions with a low level of generality: for example, with application to only a single firm at a particular time." The decision may be codified in a measure, directive, order, or other legal form, but is often so highly specific that the outcome may be characterized as more of a "rule of men" than a "rule of law."[28] This enhanced the discretionary power of bureaucrats enormously and opened wide the possibility of bureaucratic arbitrariness and corruption:

> Korean bureaucrats of economic affairs are undoubtedly geniuses of extemporization. They come up with new measures, institutions and regulations in a dizzying speed only to change them almost daily afterwards. Korean bureaucrats deserve to be called actors of thinking while running. . . . It is not unusual for them to formulate policies without thorough evaluation and preparation. Consequently, trial and error processes are repeated under the name of measures of modification of original ideas and sometimes basic directions are repeatedly changed only to confuse concerned parties. This is the reason why the economic bureaucrats can dominate the business world.[29]

Such decision-making and implementation styles reflect the extremely uncertain environments in which both the state and business had to work. One high-ranking official remarked that there were no precedents for the state's decisions, or any guarantees that those decisions would succeed. Nobody knew for sure what to do or whether they would be successful:

> We fought a life-and-death struggle to make things work. Nobody knew the way, so we acted as if we were in the middle of the wild forest. Faith comes from confidence, but there was no faith. We did our best and prayed for best results. . . . There were so many problems and a high degree of uncertainty. Nobody knew what was coming the next day.[30]

With pressure from the top leader to achieve quick and visible results, state officials had to mobilize all possible means of realizing their economic goals. Internally, this meant increasing informal networks for gathering the information necessary to make and implement decisions. Because business planning, financial resources, and marketing were weak, the state had to set targets and strategies and sometimes provide management support. One former official noted that the state even had to create a market. Even within the state apparatus, school and regional ties were ubiquitous and were frequently invoked on individual cases and in an organized fashion.[31]

However, unlike in socialist countries, because the Korean state was not itself a producer of goods, it depended on business to be successful. There thus developed a spontaneous, mutually reinforcing dependency between the state and business: the state was in charge but dependent on business for success and, ultimately, for the regime's survival. This commanding dependency often encouraged fabrication and exaggeration (on each side and jointly) about the records.

Business felt a high degree of uncertainty about its activities, given its lack of experience, scarce financial resources, and the competitive and unpredictable international market. Business needed financial resources from the state, as well as information that would allow it to make plans and become competitive. It also needed approval for new projects and assistance in solving temporary difficulties. Unlike in Japan, there were no established norms for securing access to state favors, so every big business used any means possible. As one former businessman remarked, "Connections with the government are essential in starting factories. It is not difficult to understand the reasons for collusion, and collusion does not happen without a reason; it arises simply because the government controls financial sources. Without connections no business can succeed."[32]

It was only natural for business people to establish connections through blood, school, and regional ties; government and business shared a com-

YONG-CHOOL HA

mon personnel pool. Former big-business managers all acknowledged the importance of these ties in contacting bureaucrats: "In Korea we all know each other through introductions based on school, regional, and blood ties. Business systematically uses these. If you become a high-ranking manager, you have to submit the list of people who you know through these ties."[33] Consequently, recruitment patterns in business sectors were heavily influenced by changes in government agencies. None of the three ties had priority. School ties were used most frequently, but in many cases they overlapped with regional ties.[34]

At the beginning of industrialization, the interactions between business and the state through school, regional, and blood ties were not as dysfunctional as one might think. Each side needed the other in pursuit of the same goals. And, at the beginning, there was little difference among competing enterprises, so decisions based on school ties were in fact not particularly discriminatory. Most bureaucrats thought that decisions based on school ties had merit because most of them had graduated from top universities and thus trusted their classmates. Also, as mentioned, export records acted as a checking mechanism. As long as exports improved, decisions could be justified.

However, as the economy became more complicated in scale and structure, major *chaebols* competed for expansion rather than efficiency, which caused false record keeping,[35] *yasaengmahyunsang* (literally, "a wild-horse phenomenon," the irregular intervention by business into regular bureaucratic decision making, usually through political influence), and a bandwagon phenomenon.

Ties can take different forms: temporary, dyadic, collective, or a combination of the three. These ties are based on reciprocity and can be easily invoked whenever necessary, even after a long break. Business may try to establish direct contacts with government by using a third party or invoking school ties between businessmen and officials. Officials interviewed reported various forms of the "wild-horse phenomenon"—extreme cases of decision making in which outside influences overpower the normal bureaucratic process, thus weakening bureaucratic autonomy.

One survey supports the prevalent perception that government support is essential to business success: 64.7 percent of those surveyed said that the relationships with bureaucrats affects business success; 90.5 percent said that government policies affect strategy; 75.5 percent said government support helps business growth; 63.9 percent said lobbying is necessary for management success; but only 26.7 percent said business influences government policies.[36]

The late industrialization of South Korea led to unique social and institutional consequences not normally associated with industrialization. The breakdown of the traditional social structure before industrialization, Park Chung Hee's recruitment style of using merit mixed with regionalism, the availability of isomorphic recruitment pools between business and the state, and the high level of dependency of business on the state all contributed to the reinforcement of neofamilial ties at the levels of identity formation, survival strategies, and institutional outcomes.

Although the dynamics among the political leadership, the bureaucracy, and the business community contributed to neofamilism, the relationship between the state and the masses was also important for its rise. Park's industrialization drive changed the expectations of the masses by proposing economic goals and providing the leadership and the means to accomplish them. The import-substitution economy of the Rhee regime had produced prosperity and opportunity for a small group of businessmen and government officials, but the export-oriented economy expanded the possibilities of advancement. As the masses began to change their perception of the state, their aspiration for upward mobility became intense, especially since the traditional social structure had vanished. Those who could sought access to state power through kinship, regional, or school ties, some becoming part of the neofamilial core, others having only differential access to the state-business nexus. Those weakly linked to state power formed peripheral neofamilial groups to make up for the lack of state protection.

Therefore, contrary to the conventional expectation that industrialization brings about universal social and institutional consequences, such as class society, bureaucratization, or civil society, Korean-style industrialization brought about a society in which neofamilial units were reinforced. Because neofamilism is a source of identity and survival, it is unlikely to disappear, as many Western sociological studies on informal organizations have argued it would.[37] In fact, neofamilism operates at the macro and micro levels. At the macro level, neofamilism discourages the creation of class-based units, as seen in rampant regionalism in Korean elections at all levels (legislative and presidential).[38] In what is perhaps Korea's most industrialized city, Ulsan, no workers' representative has been elected for the past twenty years. In one newly emerged industrial city, contrary to expectations, the number of hometown meetings, alumni associations, and clan associations rapidly increased throughout industrialization.[39]

At the micro level, in public bureaucracies, transfers and promotions are based largely on school and regional ties. Blood, school, and regional ties are also salient features in the business management structure. Survey data also corroborates this phenomenon: without exception, everyone surveyed practiced or wanted to practice neofamilism.[40] Thus, other institutional consequences of industrialization should be reconsidered: prevalent assumptions about the existence of a coherent middle class, the emergence of civil society, and bureaucratization all require serious revision. The Korean middle class shares only an income level; otherwise they are isolated from each other according to their means of gaining access to the state. In fact, the whole society is divided by degree of accessibility to state power. With regard to bureaucratization, contrary to the prevalent observation, Korean bureaucracy has been hollowed out, losing its bureaucratic elements. The blurring of boundaries between business and state bureaucracy was one of the requirements of rapid industrialization.

NOTES

1. Ken Jowitt, *The Leninist Response to National Dependency* (Berkeley: Institute of International Studies, University of California, 1978), 2.

2. D. Kulp Jr., *Country Life in South China* (New York: Bureau of Publications, Teachers College, Columbia University, 1925), 29.

3. Reinhard Bendix, "Preconditions of Development: A Comparison of Japan and Germany," in *Aspects of Social Change in Modern Japan*, ed. R. P. Dore (Princeton: Princeton University Press, 1967), 36–44. On the Junkers' efforts to occupy administrative positions, see Lysbeth W. Muncy, *The Junker in the Prussian Administration under William III, 1888–1914* (Providence, RI: Brown University, 1944), chap. 5.

4. On the invention of tradition, see *The Invention of Tradition*, ed. E. J. Hobsbawm and Terene Ronger (Cambridge: Cambridge University Press, 1984), and in Japan, W. Dean Kinzley, *Industrial Harmony in Modern Japan: The Invention of a Tradition* (New York: Routledge, 1991); Yasusuke Murakami, "Ie Society as a Pattern of Civilization," *Journal of Japanese Studies* 10, no. 2 (Summer 1984): 279–363.

5. Chung Hee Park, *The Country, the Revolution and I* (Seoul: Hollym Corp., 1970), 245, 248–49.

6. Kwangha Kang, *Five-Year Economic Plans: Goals and Evaluations of the Implementation* [in Korean] (Seoul: Seoul National University Press, 2000), 46ff.

7. Youngil Lim, *Government Policy and Private Enterprise: Korean Experience in Industrialization* (Berkeley: Institute of East Asian Studies, University of California, Berkeley, Center for Korean Studies, 1981), 18.

8. Suk-Jun Cho, "The Bureaucracy," in *Korean Politics in Transition*, ed. Edward R. Wright (Seattle: University of Washington Press, 1975), 73.

9. Se-Jin Kim, *The Politics of Military Revolution in Korea* (Chapel Hill: University of North Carolina Press, 1971), 161–66.

10. These statistics are from my own analysis of 171 officials above the section level at the Ministry of Commerce and Industry who were hired between 1965 and 1975 (Yong-Chool Ha, "An Analysis of Personnel Policy of Ministry of Commerce and Industry of Korea," unpublished research memo, March 2001).

11. Hanbin Lee, *Developmentalist Time and Leadership in Developing Countries* (Bloomington, IN: Comparative Administrative Group, 1965), 19–21.

12. Man-Heum Kim, "A Study on Regionalism in Korean Politics" (Ph.D. diss., Seoul National University, 1991), 81.

13. Yong-Chool Ha, "An Analysis of Personnel Policy," unpublished research memo, 2001.

14. Kwangho Lee, interview with author, May 12, 2001, Seoul.

15. Yong-Hak Kim, "Regional Differences," 274–75.

16. Ki-dong Pak, "A Study of Korean Family Enterprises" (Ph.D. diss., Dong-A University, 1980), 60–61.

17. Ibid., 62–67.

18. Jung-ja Kong, "A Study of Chaebol Families' Conjugal Connections" [in Korean] (Ph.D. diss., Ewha Women's University, 1989), 49–50.

19. Ibid., 202–3.

20. Youngse Yi, interview with author, December 29, 1999, Seoul.

21. Hee Park, "A Study of Organization Management in Korean Chaebols and Labor Relations with a Focus on Impacts on Familism" [in Korean] (Ph.D. diss., Yonsei University, 1993), 127.

22. Roger L. Janelli with Dawnhee Yim, *Making Capitalism: The Social and Cultural Construction of a South Korean Conglomerate* (Stanford: Stanford University Press, 1993), 90.

23. Ibid., 136.

24. Ki-dong Pak, "A Study of Korean Family Enterprises," 59, 84.

25. Wangim Hong, interview with author, November 24, 1999, Yongin, Korea.

26. Seung-Kyung Kim, *Class Struggle or Family Struggle? The Lives of Women Factory Workers in South Korea* (New York: Cambridge University Press, 1997), 34–35.

27. Il Sagong and Leroy P. Johns, *Government, Business, and Entrepreneurship in Economic Development: The Korean Case* (Cambridge, MA: Harvard University Press, 1980), 60–61.

28. Ibid., 64–65.

29. Ibid., 63.

30. Wonchul Oh, interview with author, April 13, 2001, Chungpyong, Korea.

31. Taewhan Seo, interview with author, March 7, 2001, Seoul.

32. Jonggyu Park, interview with author, June 3, 2001, Seoul.

33. Yongwhan Kim, interview with author.

34. Yi interview.

35. Oh interview.

36. Jongwha Han, "Characteristics of Macro-Management and Strategies" [in Korean], in *Characteristics of Management of Five Korean Chaebols,* ed. Yoo-keun Shin (Seoul: Sekyungsa, 1995), 42–43.

37. L. Wirth, "Urbanism as a Way of Life," in *New Perspectives on the American Community,* ed. R. L. Warren and L. Lyng (Homewood, IL: Dorsey Press, 1983), 36–42.

38. Man-Heum Kim, "A Study on Regionalism in Korean Politics," 108–31.

39. Mun Woong Lee, "Research on the Workers' Life Style and Job Adaptation" [in Korean], 86-4 (research paper, Institute of Korean Studies, 1986), 129–61.

40. Yong-Chool Ha, "An Analysis of Survey Results on Neofamilism" (unpublished research memo, March 2002).

10

LENINISM, DEVELOPMENTAL STAGES, AND TRANSFORMATION

Understanding Social and Institutional Change
in Contemporary China

CALVIN CHEN

In the field of communist studies, the work of Ken Jowitt offers some of the most theoretically compelling insights into the birth, development, and death of what he calls the "Leninist phenomenon." While other scholars have catalogued and analyzed the various attributes of Leninist regimes, few have matched Jowitt's ability to explain the significance of Leninism's most novel and essential features. His analytical framework, with its focus on "elite-designated core tasks and stages of development,"[1] is crucial to the field in that it presents a considerably more dynamic and comprehensive view of Leninist regimes than those offered by the universalist, essentialist, and exceptionalist schools. In his writings, Jowitt provides a powerful means for understanding not only the interconnections between elite goals, actions, and results, but also how and why new tensions within and without the party arise in relation to shifting organizational imperatives.

While the utility of Jowitt's analytical framework has been recognized in Soviet and post-Soviet studies, it has been somewhat underappreciated in the China field, especially in analyses of the post-Mao reform period.[2] While some scholars see current policies as analogous to "self-strengthening" efforts that date back to the previous century; others see the decline but persistence of work-unit or *danwei* practices as evidence of the regime's desperate attempt to maintain its Leninist orientation; and still others see the expansion of China's market economy as the potential cause of an eventual "Leninist extinction."[3] Although these studies have captured critical trends and developments in post-Mao China, few have provided a thorough explanation of institutional change that links these recent trends to the logic of Leninist development. Instead, current debates have centered on whether or not the Chinese party-state can prevent challenges to its authority or will ultimately follow in the footsteps of Leninist regimes in the former Soviet Union and Eastern Europe.[4]

Jowitt's theory of developmental stages helps us better understand institutional and social change in post-Mao reform China, especially the rise of local organizations such as township and village enterprises (TVEs). My assessment is based on a study of two major TVEs, Phoenix and Jupiter, that I conducted in Wenzhou and Jinhua (two locales in China's Zhejiang province) in 1997, 1998, and 2004.[5] In contrast to Jowitt's transformation, consolidation, and inclusion stages, I describe the developmental stages of TVEs as survival, expansion, and reintegration. In applying Jowitt's framework to TVEs, I argue that its focus on process—how and why decisions are made as well as their consequences—is especially useful in overcoming many of the pitfalls associated with the property rights debate and the limited understandings regarding the internal operations of Chinese enterprises that permeate the scholarly literature.[6] With its sharper focus on organizational dynamics and structure, Jowitt's work helps move the academic debate on TVEs beyond the simple assumptions made about actor preferences and organizational behavior. In explaining how and why enterprise leaders change their strategies of work organization, recruitment, and personnel management, his framework provides deeper insights not only into how the logic of Leninist development and organizational growth are intertwined, but also how they can sometimes contradict each other.

JOWITT'S DEVELOPMENTAL STAGES FRAMEWORK

What does Ken Jowitt's theory of developmental stages entail? In his essay "Inclusion and Mobilization in European Leninist Regimes," Jowitt argues that the elite-designated core task is the critical factor that precipitates an array of responses and developments. Specifically, the core task produces "a particular locus of political uncertainty and generates a particular regime structure."[7] Once a core task has been defined and established, party cadres act to fulfill it within a specific social and political milieu, but in so doing create the possibility for "social and organizational turbulence," especially in the first stage of transformation, where unanticipated contradictions within the party as well as between regime and society are sometimes produced. It is precisely these changes that force the party elite to revise the "rationale and format" of the regime and subsequently begin the definition of a new core task. This process takes place in each of the three developmental stages Jowitt lays out in his work: transformation, consolidation, and inclusion.

What is particularly noteworthy about Jowitt's conception is its clear linkage of elite goals, the nature of the social and political environment in which these objectives are to be realized, the organizational structure of the regime, and the consequences of success or failure. This approach takes process seriously without assuming that a particular outcome is preordained. The intentions and perceptions of leaders are also treated seriously rather than being caricatured as a simple reflection of totalitarian tendencies. Of course, this does not mean that Jowitt accepts party announcements as "truth"—far from it. Rather, by acknowledging the elite-designated task as meaningful, he establishes a basis for analyzing how these goals are pursued and how they affect on party behavior and identity.

Moreover, Jowitt's framework goes beyond developments at the elite level and includes a trenchant analysis of how social groups respond as well. Under inclusion, for example, Jowitt suggests that the party's attempt to expand membership in the regime involves the attempted co-optation of new social elites, the professional and skilled groups who are the by-products of the party's success in attaining developmental goals. The problem here, though, is that the unconditional support of these social elites for the party is uncertain because there is a mismatch between the party's insistence on maintaining its charismatic status and dominant role over society and its shift towards using manipulation rather than domination as the primary means of managing regime-society relations.[8] As a result of this change, the likelihood of the party successfully realizing inclusion decreases and the chances of organizational corruption or neotraditionalism setting in increases.[9]

Although Jowitt brilliantly captures how and why Leninist regimes failed to achieve inclusion, he never described an organization that made any progress towards achieving this goal. In large measure, this stemmed from the inability of firms in the Soviet bloc to generate the resources necessary for economic success in the long run. In other words, Jowitt never had the opportunity to examine what an even partially successful inclusion would look like or mean because the Soviet Union and Eastern Europe never reached this level of relative material abundance. Despite this, what makes his framework so valuable is that it nevertheless allows us to explore that development in another Leninist context, post-Mao China.

In profitable TVEs especially, high earnings have increased the availability of "slack resources," which enterprise managers have used in an attempt to shape the attitudes and behavior of employees.[10] Yet even under these circumstances, inclusion is not easily achieved. The massive increase in a company's workforce in just a few years (Phoenix, for example, went from 3,000 employees to over 13,000 in six years) complicates the process of integration in that enterprise leaders face the challenge of adapting new personnel to new and unfamiliar roles and practices even as they try to accommodate their interests. In essence, they are plagued by a perceived need to return to the core task designated under expansion even as they move forward with reintegration. Although Jowitt did not describe such a scenario, his theory of developmental stages nevertheless provides a solid foundation for investigating the emergence of such trends at the micro level in contemporary China.

ENTERPRISE SURVIVAL

Applying Jowitt's framework to the TVEs I studied, I suggest that their development and organizational dynamics can be characterized in the following way. Under enterprise survival, the core task designated by enterprise leaders is the establishment of an organizational structure that advances production while also minimizing social friction among enterprise members. This task mirrors that of "transformation," in that the goal is to break through the various historical, ecological, and political constraints that previously prevented the full development of TVEs in Wenzhou and Jinhua, respectively. This process began in the unpredictable political environment of the early 1980s, when the direction and permanence of the Deng Xiaoping–initiated reforms was still unclear.[11] To deal with this situation, enterprise leaders relied heavily on kinship and social ties to provide the material and social inputs necessary to launch and sustain their companies.

In a sense, utilizing family and social networks to achieve economic ends is hardly novel.[12] However, in Wenzhou and Jinhua, such ties became an effective means of building solidarity in regions where securing local state support was an arduous, if not impossible task; this situation contrasts sharply with those in more prosperous locales like the Sunan area in Jiangsu province where local cadres were effective catalysts for economic growth.[13] Yet what makes the relatives and fellow natives at Phoenix and Jupiter stand out is their resemblance to the "heroic cadres" of the Leninist party. They operated under the broad auspices of the enterprise founders and demonstrated high levels of competence, initiative, and resolve over a protracted period of time, all of which helped company leaders weather turbulence both within and without their organizations.

This was evident in the organization and execution of production. At both firms, technically skilled personnel drawn from kinship networks were placed in strategic positions throughout the factory. This move not only improved oversight of the production process, but it also increased the likelihood of compliance with higher-level orders. Moreover, a relatively flat authority structure and high levels of personal interaction between manager and worker prevented widespread incidents of slowdowns, strikes, absenteeism, and sabotage. The personal presence of the founders and their inner circle of heroic cadres on the shop floor inspired workers (and made them fearful on occasion) and strengthened the bonds between members of the factory community. Working side by side reduced the perception of unbridgeable social distance between worker and manager and generated a rough sense of egalitarianism that led to a higher degree of cohesion and harmony among enterprise members.

In fact, for some of the managers, fostering camaraderie and "human feeling" *(renqing)* seemed like the most natural and effective way to oversee factory affairs. A plant manager at Phoenix, widely regarded as one of the most caring and upstanding men in management, explained his approach this way:

> I don't like to use a tough, cold approach. If I have a problem with a worker, I call that person into my office and we talk. I discuss the problem and ask how the worker feels. It's a discussion, not a scolding. I would never discuss anything in the workshop. The worker would "lose face" *[meiyou mianzi]*, and this would cause serious emotional problems. I try to treat people in such a way that if they leave the factory, they leave on good terms. It's impossible to work without some "human feeling.". . . If you think the worker is here to serve the factory and the factory has no need to serve the worker, the factory will eventually fail. You can't go around ordering people to do whatever you want them to do.[14]

At the same time, the success of this approach depended heavily on the individual assessments of the managerial staff, as was the case with party cadres during the stage of transformation. For one of the plant administrators at Jupiter, this ability is what separates successful enterprises from unsuccessful ones. He emphasized that

> management is not a dead science; you don't follow the rules in every case. A manager needs to be flexible and understand that workers have very different personalities. For some employees, you have to explain what they did wrong and be courteous. They'll listen because they want to improve, and feel embar-

rassed. Others won't listen at all unless you scold them. They won't be motivated unless there is a chance they'll lose their jobs. We have to realize that workers aren't stupid and that we cannot treat them like robots.[15]

In contrast to managers at foreign-owned or joint-venture plants, enterprise managers at Phoenix and Jupiter were paternalistic, but not overbearing; they cared less about how work was conducted and more about its completion. They seldom exercised their authority in the harsh manner reminiscent of the "foreman's empire"[16] and, in the process, stabilized labor and social relations within the enterprise.

ENTERPRISE EXPANSION

Despite the early success of Phoenix and Jupiter, increasing competition from rival firms during the late 1980s and early 1990s convinced enterprise leaders to shift to the new task of enterprise expansion.[17] In launching the expansion and rationalization of production and management, enterprise leaders sought to increase control and efficiency without undermining the reciprocity and trust that characterized labor relations during enterprise survival. In addition, enterprise leaders sought to recruit new personnel as well as reshape the extant habits and mentalities of its current employees.[18] This effort was partly a response to the more stable political environment that emerged during the late 1980s (with the exception of Tiananmen in 1989) and the slow consolidation of a "socialist market economy." However, this new policy, with its emphasis on specialization, standardization, and impersonal norms, produced an increasingly bureaucratic organizational structure whose logic conflicted with the more personal managerial approach that existed under enterprise survival. As in Jowitt's consolidation stage, enterprise expansion privileged those most willing to follow the directives of top management, and precipitated new social conflicts between old and new groups within both enterprises.

Realizing the core task of expansion was also difficult for the following reasons. First, the benefits of the new assembly line approach were limited. At Phoenix, many of the transformers and relays the company produced contained small screws and bolts whose insertion into compact spaces was more difficult and time-consuming under an assembly-line orientation than assembly by one individual. Applying assembly-line methods to such products often resulted in bottlenecks at critical stations on the line, leaving some workers idle while others struggled furiously to keep up. In contrast, at Jupiter's textile operations, only the first stages of garment production—the preparation, cutting, and bundling of cloth—stood to benefit (and only marginally) from the application of production-line techniques. The task of sewing various pieces into pants and sweatshirts remained in the hands of the individual worker operating the sewing machine.

Rationalization efforts were affected by substandard production supplies. A technical chief at one of Phoenix's plants analyzed the situation in these terms:

> Our product quality has been fairly consistent, but sometimes our subcontractors create problems [for us]. Sometimes they cut down on the copper content or they reduce the thickness of some parts. That creates problems when electricity is turned on. It changes the performance capabilities of the products, and it's because they "cut corners" [tougong jianliao] and think they can make a little more this way. It's difficult for us to control this because we use lots of different parts. It would take too long to check all of these parts, so we just spot-check them when [new shipments] come in. Sometimes we receive bad parts. . . . We can only complain and hope our subcontractors improve the quality of their output.[19]

For some subcontractors, variability in product quality was unavoidable, for the technology they employed in manufacturing components was often outdated and unreliable. Kinship relations were also intimately linked to substandard components, since the suppliers were often relatives of key enterprise members seeking to profit from the enterprise's success. A technical-parts designer at one of Phoenix's newer factories highlighted the essential dynamic driving the relationship:

> I know that much of their collective success is based on involving as many family members in the enterprise as possible. They may not all work at the same factory, but if they need a part for their product, they'll order from the wife's side of the family or from a cousin. Later on, they may part ways, but only after they've made some money.[20]

However, for reasons of familial harmony, managers accepted these components, even though product quality was obviously poor. These problems persisted. "How can the founder [of Phoenix] argue with the subcontractor?" one plant official cracked, "That guy's his uncle. How do you tell an elder that his factory is producing poor quality products?"[21]

Just as production methods shifted, so too did authority relations at

CALVIN CHEN

Phoenix and Jupiter. Under enterprise expansion, these relationships became more formal and bureaucratic with decision-making authority increasingly vested in a small but growing managerial class that coordinated enterprise activities from central offices. While managerial authority was disproportionate to the size of the staff (managers rarely exceeded 10 percent of the total workforce), it was clearly expressed in the power to force workers to meet pre-determined levels of performance. The new impersonal schemes both firms utilized not only made the worker more responsible for his earnings, but more clearly distinguished good workers from less productive ones. Piece rates *(jijian)*, which compensated workers for each product completed, were instituted instead of timed wages *(jishi)* in the vast majority of plants. The head of Phoenix's trade union explained that this actually benefited workers because "most of the managerial staff received differentiated pay, but there was no way to give workers a chance to earn more. We didn't want to be like the state-owned enterprises, where you receive the same pay whether you did a little or a lot of work. Through piece rates, workers now have an opportunity to earn more based on their own ability and hard work."[22]

In other instances, some managers tried to secure compliance through fines and public shaming. One vice-manager at Phoenix emphasized that the fine itself was not important. Rather, the public posting of violations allowed "everyone [to see the problem] and learn from it. It's embarrassing to have your name on the blackboard for everyone to see, so workers will try to avoid another violation."[23] This policy was the direct opposite of the informal and less public reprimands managers had handed out in the past, and it often generated worker resentment, in contrast to the relative harmony of enterprise survival.

Astonishingly, enterprise management went even further and sought to reshape and regulate the personal habits and lifestyles of its workers. In his analysis of evolving managerial structures in American industry, Richard Edwards points out that through the effective employment of sanctions, workers were forced to exhibit the traits of the "good worker," qualities that did not have an immediate bearing on worker productivity.[24] This too is what managers in rural factories strove to achieve under expansion. Punctuality, for example, was rewarded with a monthly bonus if the worker punched in on time every day of the month. One "tardy" during the month, however, would disqualify the worker from receiving the bonus. At some of Phoenix's other plants, the employee was fined one *yuan* for each minute he was late. Even more important than punctuality was the demonstration of proper attitudes and behavior. Unbecoming conduct such as vulgar speech or crass acts routinely resulted in fines of ten *yuan* and more. At Jupiter, managers indirectly promoted "family values," banning cohabitation among unwed employee couples under penalty of a two hundred *yuan* fine.[25] This intrusiveness into workers' lives, previously unheard of at Phoenix and Jupiter, underscored a growing rift in core values between management and the rank and file.

At the factory level, managerial staff at both Jupiter and Phoenix sometimes ignored or resisted the new strategy. To them, the new rules increased the likelihood of social conflict. Many members of the managerial staff sympathized with workers, since many still remembered the demanding conditions under which they had previously labored. One workshop director expressed strong reservations about her duty to punish in this way:

> We hardly ever fine workers now. Although I have the authority to fine them, I usually don't dock their wages when pay day arrives. . . . I just don't feel good about fining them. I used to be an assembler myself, and I still remember how bad it felt to be fined. Everyone works hard for their money, so I'm reluctant to take it away from them. I guess I'm just not ruthless enough.[26]

In plants where work rules were strictly enforced, the "factory regime" (as Michael Burawoy calls it), appeared almost tyrannical in comparison.[27] Despite worker protestations, the managers in these factories were less affected by the social considerations that contributed to a more relaxed atmosphere elsewhere. One of the toughest managers at Phoenix justified his view in the following manner:

> Some people have criticized me for my strict approach to management. I impose stiff fines, and some people say I should also give out rewards for good work. But my rules should be seen in the same way as traffic rules. Do you reward each person individually for stopping when the light is red? . . . The reward comes on a broader level. When everyone follows the rules, everyone arrives at their destinations quickly and easily. It's the same in the workshops.[28]

For this manager, the only way productivity could be improved was to divorce production demands from social concerns whenever possible. For workers, though, these fines represented an utter disregard for their financial well-being and, more importantly, an assault on their dignity. Public shaming in particular was a sore point, leading one shop director to conclude that "you have to give workers some 'face' *[mianzi]*. If they think they've been humiliated, they won't listen to you next time."[29]

196   CALVIN CHEN

Despite their dissatisfaction, workers rarely engaged in any overt or organized acts of resistance. For instance, in factories where workers shared a stronger rapport with their superiors, workers aired their grievances directly with the manager, hoping to resolve their differences through dialogue and persuasion. When workers failed to attain their goals, they expressed their frustration by using what James Scott describes as "weapons of the weak."[30] For example, employees often spread vicious rumors about managerial staff members, snubbed them, or excluded them from social activities. At other times, workers disrupted the flow of work by turning work rules against managers. Workers often refused to assemble products unless all the components met the enterprise's standards for quality. Others stuck carefully to their "job descriptions" and would not help with other tasks when deadlines were pressing or the factory was understaffed. The most disaffected simply quit and sought employment at a different enterprise.

Changes in workforce composition further complicated the logic of expansion as unprecedented numbers of outsiders *(waidiren)* joined both companies. Just as New York in the nineteenth century and Shanghai in the early twentieth were transformed by waves of new immigrants, so too were Wenzhou and Jinhua. During expansion, two distinct waves of migrants altered the social terrain at Phoenix and Jupiter. Whereas the first wave consisted predominantly of better-educated, highly skilled, and generally middle-aged personnel, the second wave consisted mostly of less-educated, less-skilled, and generally younger workers. Although the increasing diversity of the workforce strengthened production capabilities in key areas, it also accelerated the fragmentation of the enterprise community by altering status distinctions and frames of identity.

The first wave of skilled employees were laid-off workers or retirees drawn largely from state-owned enterprises. Still in their early forties and fifties, these former state employees possessed the critical skills TVEs needed and were open to working a few more years at rural firms and earning some extra income. However, their arrival upset the previous company hierarchy by simultaneously displacing locals from technical positions and carving out a new occupational niche for outsiders.[31] Outsider dominance in these areas soon became overwhelming. At Phoenix, for instance, outsiders filled nearly 70 percent of all technical and design positions.[32] At Jupiter's newer plants where advanced machinery was in use, the number of outsiders in technically skilled positions assumed similar proportions. Under these changed circumstances and despite the general observation expressed by one Jupiter administrator that "whether we like it or not, we need outsiders because they have skills we don't have,"[33] locals were slow to accept outsiders as equals. Earlier, advanced skills had been tightly intertwined with local identity: locals had been able to handle all technical challenges on their own. However, under expansion, advanced skills became increasingly associated with people who were unfamiliar and threatening.

The second wave of migrants accentuated these antagonisms. Compared with the first wave of outsiders, these nonlocals were different in that they possessed no special skills or knowledge, were generally less cosmopolitan, and originated from extremely impoverished areas such as Jiangxi, Anhui, Hunan, and Sichuan.[34] Offering raw, physical labor, these laborers held the same status that Irish immigrants once did when they first migrated to Lowell, New York City, and Jersey City in the 1800s, and evoked the same nativist reactions from local residents.[35] They could only take assembly positions in the workshops and enjoyed few benefits or privileges within the enterprise.[36] Despite their modest backgrounds, these nonlocal laborers nevertheless managed to divide the enterprise further because of their willingness to work long hours and take on dangerous tasks. One Phoenix factory manager expressed these views in the following manner:

> Eighty percent [of the 140 workers in my factory] are *waidiren.* To be honest, this factory would not be what it is without them. They do most of the dirtier and more dangerous work. Locals won't do that anymore because they can now leave that work to outsiders. It's not uncommon for outsiders to lose fingers or get hurt in some other way while operating the machines.[37]

Although he himself was a local, this manager found the outsiders employed at his plant more reliable and more cooperative than locals. He intimated that locals were spoiled by their own success and were no longer willing to put out the effort necessary to sustain the factories they had so painstakingly built. Some managers liked outsiders so much they even made use of outsider networks to recruit additional workers for their plants. In these factories, outsiders commonly comprised 50 percent or more of all production workers. Other managers, however, clung to prevailing stereotypes, concluding that outsiders were no more than thieves and thugs and thus unworthy of joining their community.[38] In these factories, locals typically outnumbered outsiders by a ratio of two to one.

These splits hurt relationships among production workers as well. While local workers did not feel threatened in the same way as locals in technical positions, they nevertheless felt that outsiders pressured them to work harder than before. Many locals simply concluded that "outsiders are different from us. They'll do anything to make extra money. We work hard too, but they're always looking for more work. I bet they wouldn't sleep if they had the chance to work 24 hours a day."[39] At Jupiter, the contempt locals displayed assumed more personal overtones: "Outsiders have different habits than we do . . . most outsiders are dirtier. They won't pick up any garbage even if it's in front of their rooms. A local will remove that trash."[40]

Together, these waves of outsiders left an enduring imprint on both enterprises. Although locals initially unleashed a torrent of resentment against outsiders, the occupation of some of the most exalted and the lowliest positions in the company by newcomers raised serious questions about their work experiences. Locals eventually began to ask whether it was the outsiders or the enterprise leaders who were most responsible for the inequities of their situation. Locals began to wonder if native-place solidarity meant anything at all to firm leaders and whether perhaps they shared more in common with outsiders working alongside them than they first thought. Although both enterprises had improved their productive capabilities and increased their income, many of those gains were tempered by the erosion of the social trust and goodwill that had previously distinguished Phoenix and Jupiter from their rivals.

ENTERPRISE REINTEGRATION

The conflicts that afflicted Jupiter and Phoenix during enterprise expansion reminded enterprise leaders that improvements in output and productivity without adequate attention to the social concerns of their members would not enhance their long-term competitiveness or stabilize labor relations. Reflecting on their recent experiences, enterprise management realized that pulling back from the excesses of expansion and recapturing the spirit of cooperation and camaraderie that marked their earlier histories would be vital to their lasting success. This realization caused a shift to the new core task of enterprise reintegration, where the goal was to preserve and deepen the production gains made under enterprise expansion while reviving the bonds of community that characterized enterprise survival. This current stage, in which both firms have been engaged since the mid–late 1990s, is characterized not only by the continuing rationalization of production but also by greater organizational flexibility and a drive to bridge status distinctions through the creation and manipulation of a new fictive kinship-based company identity. This attempt at accommodating social concerns mirrors Jowitt's inclusion stage with one exception: the companies' financial success provides them with the necessary resources for enterprise-wide activities that promote an "enterprise family" orientation.

Both Phoenix and Jupiter have reorganized their operations along the lines of multidivisional firms, with their central offices focusing more on setting broad financial and production targets, and plant-level managerial staff handling the day-to-day management of production. This reorganization has resulted in the wholesale elimination of a number of departments even as new ones are being created. In trying to streamline their organizations, leaders were taking the first cautious steps towards reducing some of the status distinctions that had emerged during expansion. At the factory level, plant managers have kept their supervisory staff to a minimum in order to contain costs and close the formal distance between worker and manager. In some of Phoenix's plants, for example, these efforts have resulted in a cutback in managerial personnel, a drop from 10 percent of the total workforce to 5 or 6 percent.

In addition, during the late 1990s, the differences in official salaries were reduced considerably; in fact, the gap between the highest and lowest salary in the factory is in principle not to exceed a three-to-one ratio. At both enterprises, workshop directors and those of similar rank earned on average two hundred *yuan* more than workers (approximately 900 *yuan*), and higher-level staff, including the factory manager, earned a few hundred more than their subordinates, thus dropping the ratio to roughly two to one. It should be noted, though, that these targets are easily undermined. Since 2000, Phoenix's rapid growth in workforce and output has actually reversed this trend and the gap in income between the lowest- and highest-paid plant employee is now approximately seven to one. In addition, skilled staff and managers routinely receive larger year-end bonuses than unskilled workers, but the actual sums are kept strictly confidential for fear of creating major social dissatisfaction. Based on interview data I collected in 2004, I discovered that the ratio in year-end bonuses can be over 150:1 (500,000 *yuan* for a manager to 3,000 *yuan* for a line worker).

Although these restructuring efforts were initially well-received at both enterprises, they did not eliminate informal status differences. Despite declarations that job assignments would be determined by merit, kinship and native-place connections continue to affect personnel choices. Managers still prefer candidates they know well and see as more trustworthy; this favors kinsmen and locals over nonnatives. At Phoenix, although a few outsiders serve as factory vice-managers, only one outsider occupied the position of factory manager in 1998, and that was only by virtue of his long-standing personal friendship with the enterprise founder. In the central offices, only

CALVIN CHEN

one nonlocal occupied the position of department head; all other positions were staffed by locals. Since 2000, more outsiders have been heading key departments, but their numbers have not surpassed 10 percent of the total number of senior managerial staff.

Enterprise leaders have tried instead to shift attention away from these status distinctions through a focus on the "enterprise family." By promoting a sense of fictive kinship, management hopes that all members of the enterprise will see that personal status should be subordinated to the broader concerns and well-being of the enterprise. Now, employees are "brothers and sisters" in Phoenix's and Jupiter's families first, and natives of Wenzhou, Jinhua, Shanghai, and Beijing second. This new stance serves as the basis of the new "enterprise culture" *(qiye wenhua)* and is designed to alter the orientations of company employees. Compared to IBM's and Toyota's near-legendary efforts at building corporate culture, these attempts do not appear particularly striking, but they are innovative for two reasons.

First, leaders at both firms are attempting to distill the most critical attributes of their early success and reconfigure them to fit the new circumstances in which they find themselves. They have taken membership in kinship and native-place networks, both exclusive modes of association, and redefined them to be more inclusive without fundamentally altering the principles which govern their operation. This shift tacitly acknowledges the unifying power of kinship ties as well as its corrosive effects. If these ties only bind together specific segments within the enterprise and exclude others, division, not solidarity, results. To avoid this outcome, firm leaders have thus enlarged the definition of membership in their groups but kept intact the requirements and responsibilities of membership.

Second, this new policy is notable because of the mechanism that management is using to implement it: the Chinese Communist Party (CCP). The party, long considered a major obstacle to the effective functioning of Chinese factories, is now serving as management's junior partner in improving coordination and rebuilding trust and social harmony. Recently retired local cadres have joined both firms, not only because they possess valuable connections and knowledge of government policies but because "they are very good at coordinating the work of different departments . . . [and] this helps us improve our overall efficiency."[41] Even a young party member at Phoenix noted that the company's desire to work with the party was a surprising move:

> By inviting the CCP into the enterprise, the company is doing precisely the opposite of what other companies are doing. A lot of enterprises fear the party's presence in the enterprise. They think it's bothersome, or they think party activities

will hurt operations. It's true that in the past we would stop work to carry out party activities, but we can't do that anymore.[42]

More critically, leaders at both firms believe that the party stands above kinship and native-place loyalties and they want to use this position and the party's expertise in organization to legitimize their new enterprise family orientation and to restabilize labor relations. Working in tandem with the party, enterprise management is attempting to break the conflation of privilege and social identity. For management, the enterprise family embodies a general commitment to all segments of the organization over the particular interests of specific groups within the firm. As Jowitt would have predicted, enterprise leaders have relied almost exclusively on manipulation rather than domination to make this point. Still, the leaders' interest in building a partnership with the CCP has translated into only a complementary role for the party in the enterprise. Although party institutions—the trade union, the Women's Federation, the Communist Youth League—have been replicated throughout the enterprise, politics and production remain separate. If the two come into conflict, the demands of production always take precedence. This is partly reinforced by the party's dependence on the enterprise for funding; little to no money is disbursed for party-related activities unless the enterprise's economic viability is first ensured.

This new enterprise-party partnership has led to a broad program to make membership in the enterprise family tangible, beneficial, and attractive. Towards this end, expanding employee benefits has been one of the most critical steps taken so far as both enterprises try to convince employees that the well-being of all members of the enterprise family matters, regardless of the employee's background. Phoenix's management, for instance, has worked to ensure that every employee enjoys a minimum level of fringe benefits. Sodas and bottled water are distributed regularly during the summer months, when "cool drinks" *(lengyin)* are in high demand to beat the sweltering heat. On special holidays like the lunar New Year *(chunjie)*, gifts such as fruit baskets, clothing, and even red envelopes *(hong-bao)* stuffed with small amounts of cash are distributed. At Jupiter, factories periodically hand out a range of daily necessities like laundry detergent, bars of soap, towels, and cooking oil. More recently, the trade union at Phoenix successfully lobbied for the extension of subsidized meals to workers, a benefit previously guaranteed to only the managerial staff. Since 2002, employees have been allotted free uniforms each year. Phoenix's current agenda combines proposals to improve workers' material situations with efforts to "improv[e] the lifestyle, the nonwork activities of company employees."[43] With the completion of a small library in 2001 and fitness/weight rooms planned for the near future, managers hope workers will have better outlets for reducing work-induced stress and a means of better resisting the temptations of late-night card playing and mahjong.[44]

These steps have been followed by an assortment of events and contests that are loosely known as *biwu* (matches of skill). These events run the gamut from bicycle races, Chinese chess, and tug-of-war to cooking and typing competitions, karaoke, basketball games, and speech contests.[45] Under the direction of the party, these activities are not only contests of individual prowess, but also a combination of mass campaign and large-scale "party." Party officials encourage employees' participation and seek to imbue these activities with the electricity and high purpose of party-backed rallies. For management, these seemingly ordinary events are not mere diversions or entertainment: they are opportunities to reinforce identification with the enterprise over other social allegiances. Although these affairs often contain a competitive strain, they emphasize enterprise unity over individual rivalry. During my research at Phoenix in 1997, I was also drawn into this process, playing on Phoenix's basketball team against the teams of other local firms. This not only reaffirmed Phoenix's identity vis-à-vis the other firms, but also underscored their willingness to expand membership in the enterprise community, even to a foreign researcher.

Enterprise executives believe these activities can buttress the new family orientation and lead to greater stability at both the individual and collective levels over the long haul. Singing and speech contests in particular have become a means of didacticism and molding the "political thought" of the employee. Here, participants mostly sing songs with socialist or revolutionary themes and speak about how experiences at the enterprise have transformed them. At Jupiter, "the most important thing about such events is that it's an opportunity to teach, [an opportunity] to talk about the company and personal goals, and what we should try to achieve."[46] Even so, while memories of unfairness and native-place discrimination have faded to some extent, they still persist in the minds of many employees. Despite significant progress made towards reintegration stemming from increasing slack resources, both enterprises have not yet fully replaced those memories with new ones of social harmony and inclusion.

CONCLUSION

Ken Jowitt's theory of developmental stages provides an elegant and powerful explanation of how and why change took place under Leninist regimes in the Soviet Union and Eastern Europe. What makes his theory even more useful, though, is the analytical leverage it affords in studying social and institutional change in contemporary China, especially in relation to TVEs. Many analyses of rural enterprises emphasize that enterprise success hinges on the low cost of their products and their systematic, if not ruthless, exploitation of labor.

There is certainly compelling evidence for this, but such views ignore the organizational and social dimensions of these institutions—the impact of shifting organizational imperatives; the construction and redefinition of labor relations; the centrality and fragility of trust and reciprocity; and the personal backgrounds, values, and expectations of enterprise personnel. Jowitt's framework overcomes these deficiencies through its focus on core tasks, the social and political environments in which these goals are pursued, and regime structure. In linking these elements together, Jowitt provides a sophisticated way for capturing and comprehending organizational dynamics and tracing not only how broad goals are translated into policies but, more importantly, how actors perceive and respond to such initiatives and what they win or lose in the process. In resisting the temptation to blackbox organizational behavior, Jowitt's approach represents true respect for the actors studied—for the challenges they face, their aspirations, and their actions. Indeed, for this reason as well as the analytical rigor of his path-breaking approach, Ken Jowitt's work should and will continue to illuminate and inspire scholars wrestling with understanding the evolution, and, perhaps, the eventual extinction of Leninism in China.

NOTES

1. Ken Jowitt, "Inclusion and Mobilization in European Leninist Regimes," in *New World Disorder: The Leninist Extinction* (Berkeley: University of California Press, 1992), 88.

2. Andrew Walder's *Communist Neotraditionalism* (Berkeley: University of California Press, 1986) is a notable exception, but his definition of the concept differs considerably from Jowitt's original understanding. Although Walder skillfully explains how Chinese workers became economically and politically dependent on their enterprises, his focus on clientelism ignores Jowitt's view of Leninism as an innovative recasting of mutually exclusive orientations (i.e., individual heroism and organizational impersonalism) and how organizational corruption emerges when the party's general interests are not distinguished from the particular interests of its members. See Jowitt, "Neotraditionalism," in *New World Disorder*, 121.

CALVIN CHEN

3. See Vivienne Shue, *The Reach of the State* (Stanford: Stanford University Press, 1988); Lü Xiaobo and Elizabeth Perry, eds., *Danwei* (Boulder, CO: Westview Press, 1998); Andrew Walder, "The Quiet Revolution From Within: Economic Reform as a Source of Political Decline," in Andrew Walder, ed., *The Waning of the Communist State: Economic Origins of Political Decline in China and Hungary* (Berkeley: University of California Press, 1995), 1–24.

4. See the essays in the *Journal of Democracy*, v. 14, no. 1 (January 2003), such as Bruce Dickson's "Threats to Party Supremacy," 27–35.

5. Phoenix and Jupiter are fictitious names that I created to protect the identities of the companies and individual respondents I interviewed. My conclusions are derived from participant observation when I worked alongside workers on the production line and from personal interviews conducted with over 130 individuals.

6. See, for example, Jean C. Oi and Andrew G. Walder, eds., *Property Rights and Economic Reform in China* (Stanford: Stanford University Press, 1999).

7. Ken Jowitt, "Inclusion," 88.

8. Ibid., 92–93, 96.

9. Jowitt, "Neotraditionalism," 121–58.

10. On slack resources, see Richard Cyert and James March, *A Behavioral Theory of the Firm* (Englewood Cliffs, NJ: Prentice-Hall, 1963).

11. For Phoenix, this stage began in 1984 and ended in the late 1980s. For Jupiter, it started in 1975 and ended in the mid-1980s.

12. For a review of the role these ties play in the economic development of East Asia, see Gary Hamilton, ed., *Asian Business Networks* (New York: Walter de Gruyter, 1996).

13. Keith Forster highlights Zhejiang's difficulties during the Maoist era in *Zhejiang Province in Reform* (Honolulu: University of Hawaii Press, 1998). Also see Yia-Ling Liu, "Reform From Below: The Private Economy and Local Politics in the Rural Industrialization of Wenzhou," *China Quarterly*, no. 130 (June 1992): 293–316. For an analysis of this development in Jiangsu province, see Samuel Ho, *Rural China in Transition: Non-agricultural Development in Rural Jiangsu, 1978–1990* (Oxford: Clarendon Press, 1994). On Shandong, see Jean Oi, *Rural China Takes Off* (Berkeley: University of California Press, 1999).

14. Respondent #6, interview with the author, July 9, 1997, Wenzhou, China.

15. Respondent #105, interview with the author, July 13, 1998, Jinhua, China.

16. See Daniel Nelson, *Managers and Workers: Origins of the New Factory System in the United States, 1880–1920* (Madison, WI: University of Wisconsin Press, 1975).

17. For Phoenix, expansion lasted from the late 1980s until the mid-1990s. For Jupiter, this period lasted from the mid-1980s to the early 1990s.

18. See Richard Edwards, *Contested Terrain: The Transformation of the Workplace in the Twentieth Century* (London: Basic Books, 1979), especially 111–62.

19. Respondent #20, interview with the author, July 28, 1997, Wenzhou, China.

20. Respondent #12, interview with the author, July 17, 1997, Wenzhou, China.

21. Respondent #82, interview with the author, April 22, 1998, Wenzhou, China.

22. Respondent #21, interview with the author, July 28, 1997, Wenzhou, China.

23. Respondent #26, interview with the author, August 1, 1997, Wenzhou, China.

24. Edwards, *Contested Terrain*, 147–52.

25. To put this in perspective, a production worker's average monthly salary at Jupiter at this time was approximately 700 *yuan*. Thus, a workers stood to lose nearly 30 percent of his or her monthly salary for this infraction.

26. Respondent #86, interview with the author, April 28, 1998, Wenzhou, China.

27. Michael Burawoy, *The Politics of Production: Factory Regimes Under Capitalism and Socialism* (London: Verso, 1985).

28. Respondent #10, interview with the author, May 8, 1998, Wenzhou, China.

29. Respondent #43, interview with the author, August 16, 1997, Wenzhou, China.

30. James Scott, *Weapons of the Weak: Everyday Forms of Peasant Resistance* (New Haven, CT: Yale University Press, 1985).

31. These developments follow Elizabeth Perry's observations regarding the structure of labor markets in Shanghai, although the distinction between "northerner" and "southerner" was not as crucial in my cases. See *Shanghai on Strike: The Politics of Chinese Labor* (Stanford: Stanford University Press, 1993), 32–64.

32. Respondent #18, interview with the author, July 24, 1997, Wenzhou, China.

33. Respondent #103, interview with the author, June 18, 1998, Jinhua, China.

34. Dorothy Solinger analyzes the plight of migrant workers in *Contesting Citizenship in Urban China: Peasant Migrants, the State, and the Logic of the Market* (Berkeley: University of California Press, 1999). Although Solinger focuses on the urban setting, the dynamics she describes are similar to those in rural environments.

35. See Milton Cantor, "Introduction," in *American Workingclass Culture: Explorations in American Labor and Social History*, ed. Milton Cantor (Westport, CT: Greenwood Press, 1979), especially 16–21.

36. A particularly good parallel to this situation appeared in the nineteenth-century American mining industry and involved Irish, English, and Welsh mine workers. See Anthony Wallace, *St. Clair: A Nineteenth Century Coal Town's Experience with a Disaster-Prone Industry* (Ithaca, NY: Cornell University Press, 1981), 133–38.

37. Respondent #3, interview with the author, July 6, 1997, Wenzhou, China.

38. Respondent, #7, interview with the author, July 9, 1997, Wenzhou, China.

39. Respondent #64, interview with the author, September 1, 1997, Wenzhou, China.

40. Respondent #98, interview with the author, June 1, 1998, Jinhua, China.

41. Respondent #2, interview with the author, August 19, 2004, Wenzhou, China.

42. Respondent #85, interview with the author, April 28, 1998, Wenzhou, China.

43. Respondent #21, interview with the author, July 28, 1997, Wenzhou, China.

44. Respondent #21, interview with the author, September 5, 1997, Wenzhou, China.

45. Respondent #104, interview with the author, June 19, 1998, Jinhua, China.

46. Ibid.

IV *Methodological Orientations*

11

WEBER, JOWITT, AND THE DILEMMA
OF SOCIAL SCIENCE PREDICTION

STEPHEN E. HANSON

For those of us who have worked for many years within the neo-Weberian theoretical framework developed by Ken Jowitt, one of its most appealing features is its ability to generate almost prophetically accurate predictions of future trends—both within the former Leninist world, and more generally.[1] Jowitt's trenchant analysis of the "neo-traditionalism" that emerged in the USSR during the Brezhnev era, for example, has been amply borne out by the continuing importance of *blat* (reliance on personal connections), patron-client relations, and corruption throughout most of the post-Soviet world.[2] In the early 1990s, when the vast majority of social scientists studying postcommunist societies were enamored of the optimistic metaphor of successful "transition" to democracy and the market, Jowitt argued instead that a culture of cynicism about and alienation from politics would likely endure in the region for a long time.[3] Recently, careful evaluation of survey evidence by Marc Howard shows that, over a decade since communism's collapse, citizens throughout Eastern Europe remain significantly less willing to participate in civic organizations than their counterparts in postauthoritarian societies elsewhere—let alone in the established democracies of Western Europe.[4] Jowitt's prediction that "movements of rage" based on hatred of the West would likely emerge to fill the gap left by the collapse of communism and the withdrawal of the Soviet Union from the Third World—a view essentially ignored by mainstream political scientists—also appears, after the events of 9/11, to have been precisely accurate.[5] More recently, Jowitt's prewar prediction that U.S. intervention in Iraq would more likely be a "poison dart" for democratization in the region than a "magic bullet" seems already to have been confirmed by the chaotic aftermath of the fall of Saddam Hussein.[6]

One might think that a theory that has generated so many accurate predictions might quickly take the political science discipline by storm, inspiring generations of young scholars to refine, expand, and promote it. This manifestly has not occurred. Indeed, even political scientists well disposed to Jowitt's paradigm—sadly, not by any means a majority at present—seem curiously unwilling to concede its predictive accuracy. Reviewing Ken Jowitt's *New World Disorder: The Leninist Extinction* in 1994, for example, Ellen Comisso argued that the real value of Jowitt's work lies in its "diagnostic" features rather than its "predictions." Indeed, Comisso went further, arguing that

> each time an essay strays into the realm of prediction . . . it is simply wrong. If we accept mainstream social science's account of itself, according to which the test of a theory is its ability to predict, Jowitt—along with just about every other student of leninist systems—is a failure as a theorist.[7]

Similarly, in a volume of essays devoted to reviewing the relative merits of arguments by Jowitt and others about the importance of the "Leninist legacy" versus the "imperatives of liberalization," the overwhelming majority of contributors concluded that the latter had played the greater role in the 1990s, contrary to Jowitt's predictions.[8] While I too proposed some refinements of Jowitt's original argument—in particular, emphasizing the importance of geographic proximity to the West and disaggregating the specific legacies of Marxist ideology, Leninist politics, and Stalinist socioeconomic institutions—no one else in this volume took Jowitt's theoretical framework as a productive starting point for further research.[9]

In short, Jowitt's approach, despite having one of the most easily documented records of successful prediction over the past few decades, has only a handful of supporters in the contemporary political science discipline. Meanwhile, other theorists who have ostensibly more embarrassing records of predictive inaccuracy are accorded far more scholarly attention.[10] Obviously, explaining this odd situation is of some personal importance to those of us still committed to Jowitt's neo-Weberian approach. But, on a more detached level, the professional marginalization of successfully predictive theories and the professional promotion of predictively inaccurate

STEPHEN E. HANSON

theories represent an interesting intellectual puzzle that demands theoretical attention.

At least one important reason no one has noticed the predictive accuracy of neo-Weberian theory is that, contrary to Comisso's assumption, there is actually no consensus at all among contemporary political scientists about the role of empirical prediction in testing theories. Indeed, a substantial number of scholars in the field have (explicitly or implicitly) given up the idea that what actually happens in the world has any role to play in evaluating a social-scientific theory's value. Detached from the anchor of empirical testing, the political science discipline floats in a sea of abstractions, with little relevance to "science" as it has been understood in the modern world since the Enlightenment. Ironically, at the same time, scholars interested in real-world political phenomena have increasingly tended to reject the ideal of "political science" altogether—thus ceding the symbolically crucial term "science" to the disciplinary mainstream.

In what follows, I will first outline several contemporary views on the role of prediction in political science methodology, showing how few scholars now formally accept the idea that repeated incorrect predictions must necessarily falsify a theory. I will then argue for an alternative Weberian approach to understanding the three main ideal types of "prediction"—traditional "wisdom," charismatic "prophecy," and rational-legal "scientific testing"—each tied to a particular conception of time. I'll then conclude by showing how Jowitt's theory of "regime evolution" succeeds so well in generating specific, testable hypotheses about future developments in global politics.

POLITICAL SCIENCE AND PREDICTION

Comisso's notion that most political scientists accept the accuracy, or inaccuracy, of empirical predictions as the ultimate test of a theory's worth reflects the dominance of this viewpoint in the 1960s, when Carl Hempel's argument for "covering law" explanations of social and historical outcomes and Karl Popper's related conception of "falsification" as the engine of scientific progress became widely popular in the social sciences.[11] Simply put, a "covering law" is a statement of empirical correlation that takes the form "If x, then y"—in all times and places. Thus, if one can find evidence of x in some social setting, one should be able accurately and unfailingly to predict the presence of y as well. Social science, from Hempel's perspective, must strive to establish the existence of such "laws" in order to become more like the successful natural sciences. Popper's argument that science progresses largely through the disconfirmation of attempts to establish such laws helped further to popularize the notion that social scientists (presumably like natural scientists) should develop falsifiable hypotheses about future outcomes, and then seek to disconfirm them. From this "deductive-nomological" point of view, prediction indeed plays a central role in the social-scientific enterprise.

But the Hempel-Popper perspective long ago came under attack, for a variety of reasons. As Thomas Kuhn famously argued, even within the natural sciences, the methods and standards used to judge what counts as a successful prediction are themselves dependent upon shared "paradigms" among working communities of scientists concerning the nature of good scientific research.[12] Scientists whose predictions are incorrect will be highly unlikely to toss aside a successful paradigm in the face of a single, or even several, wrong predictions; negative results that might challenge fundamental paradigmatic assumptions can always be explained as a result of faulty procedures or poor research design. If Popper's notion of falsifiability seems unworkable even within the natural sciences, then surely it is even less applicable to the social sciences, which in Kuhn's terms are still "pre-paradigmatic": that is, agreement among researchers about basic issues of ontology and methodology is still absent.

Kuhn's critique seriously weakened the appeal of the Hempel-Popper "deductive-nomological" approach to falsification. Still, many philosophers of science—and philosophically sophisticated social scientists—objected to Kuhn's insistence on the "incommensurability" of competing paradigms, which seemed to imply that no rational reason for accepting or rejecting any particular scientific paradigm could exist. If so, "progress" in the natural sciences was impossible—and the pre-paradigmatic social "sciences" were doomed to total irrelevance. For these reasons, Imre Lakatos's philosophy of science, which aims to transcend the Popper-Kuhn divide, has become extremely popular among social scientists. Lakatos fully agreed with Kuhn that the simple Popperian perspective on falsification was "naive": "Contrary to naive falsificationism, *no experiment, experimental report, observation statement or well-corroborated low-level falsifying hypothesis alone can lead to falsification. There is no falsification before the emergence of a better theory.*"[13] Scientific "research programs," Lakatos argued, could be analyzed as containing both a "hard core" of unchallengeable assumptions and a "protective belt" of auxiliary hypotheses; only the latter were directly subject to empirical testing, and even here scientists could legitimately "adjust" the interpretation of such tests in order to preserve a research program's "core."[14] The key to preserving the integrity of the scientific enterprise, according to Lakatos, is a commitment among researchers to abandon "degenerating" research programs—ones in which the adjustments of auxiliary hypotheses take place primarily on an ad hoc basis—for "progressive" research programs which explain all the empirical content of their predecessors while explaining "novel facts" as well.

But Lakatos's theory does not satisfactorily establish the criteria by which scientists should decide just when a research program has started to "degenerate." He had in mind here groups such as Lamarckian biologists after the victory of Darwinism, or defenders of classical Newtonian physics after the development of Einstein's theory of relativity. In cases such as these, the ability of new research programs to explain all of the old facts while pointing the way towards novel ones seems reasonably clear. Applied to the social sciences, however, Lakatos's views can seemingly justify the defense of just about any research program. Since social scientists have established no (or very few) robust causal theories that produce reliable empirical predictions, the Lakatosian demand that competing scholars produce a "better theory" before current research programs be abandoned makes it impossible in practice to mount an effective challenge to currently dominant research traditions on the basis of disconfirming empirical evidence. Moreover, defenders of dominant paradigms can shrug off their own poor predictive records as irrelevant to the status of the paradigm's "core," as long as that core can be presented as possessing some internal logical consistency.

The influence of Lakatos's approach to science can be seen in a wide variety of contemporary political science understandings of the (highly limited) role of prediction in evaluating theories. The authors of *Analytic Narratives*, for example, see their empirical case studies essentially as illustrations of abstract models derived from "core assumptions" of rational choice theory.[15] But, as Margaret Levi admits, "even when a rational choice analysis offers a logical story consistent with the facts, this hardly constitutes a validation of the explanation."[16] Gary King, Robert Keohane and Sidney Verba, who are often described as straightforward defenders of the Hempel-Popper approach, in fact also describe the role of prediction in political science in essentially Lakatosian terms:

> We have suggested that the process of evaluating theories and hypotheses is a flexible one: particular empirical tests neither confirm nor disconfirm them once and for all. When an empirical test is inconsistent with our theoretically based expectations, we do not immediately throw out the theory. We may do various things: We may conclude that the evidence may have been poor due to chance alone; we may adjust what we consider to be the range of applicability of a the-

ory or hypothesis even if it does not hold in a particular case and, through that adjustment, maintain our acceptance of the theory or hypothesis. Science proceeds by such adjustments; but they can be dangerous. If we take them too far we make our theories and hypotheses invulnerable to disconfirmation. The lesson is that we must be very careful in adapting theories to be consistent with new evidence. We must avoid stretching the theory beyond all plausibility by adding numerous exceptions and special cases.[17]

Here, as in Lakatos, the integrity of science seems to lie in a commitment by scholars to abandon degenerating research programs—but the authors provide no criteria for distinguishing between legitimate "adjustment" and illegitimate "stretching" of a theory. This indeterminacy and the remarkably poor predictive record of most social science theories over the past few decades combine in practice to set the bar for empirical testing of political science theories exceedingly low.[18]

Contemporary critics of Lakatosian approaches to social science, unfortunately, have few workable alternatives to propose. Margaret Somers, for example, after persuasively criticizing the nonfalsifiability of rational choice approaches to historical sociology, proposes the adoption of what she calls "relational realism." But her alternative conception of how to test social science theory against empirical evidence is hopelessly vague: "Theorizing convincingly about mechanisms, then, is a task requiring neither pure induction nor pure deduction but one that demands devising diverse and creative ways . . . to answer the question of whether the theoretical entity being hypothesized can actually be demonstrated to have a relational effect on a specific problem."[19] Meanwhile, other contemporary critics of mainstream social science often deny the "scientific" pretensions of the field altogether; for them, the goal of prediction should be discarded altogether in favor of "interpretation" or "explanation."

Ironically, then, Comisso's attempt to support Jowitt's contribution to social science by dismissing the importance of his predictions ends up diminishing the impact of Jowitt's challenge to mainstream social science approaches. Comisso's notion that social science can at best develop competing "scenarios" of the future actually is the dominant view in the field—not the idea that empirical evidence can be used in any reliable way to confirm or deny theories or hypotheses. Thus, it should not surprise us to see that even political scientists whose empirical predictions have failed utterly and spectacularly—while so many of Jowitt's predictions have come true—can simply shrug off the implications of this for their favored theoretical approaches.

STEPHEN E. HANSON

As this review of the literature implies, it seems to me that any coherent account of the social-scientific enterprise simply has to include successful prediction of future outcomes as an important criterion for the evaluation of competing theories. Otherwise, there remains literally no scientific check on the ability of empirically incorrect, but deductively consistent, theories to endure indefinitely. By no means does this mean that we should beat a full retreat to Popperian positivism, of course; the critiques of Kuhn and others of "naive falsificationism" are persuasive ones. The problem is to find an alternative conception of prediction that takes into account the peculiar subject matter and reflexivity of the social, as opposed to the natural, sciences.

Here Weber's methodological contributions are particularly helpful. In particular, "social science" prediction itself must be analyzed in comparison with other, more common social forms of foretelling the future. In this respect, we can follow Weber's theory of the three ideal types of legitimate domination and distinguish among traditional, charismatic, and rational-legal ideal types of prediction. Each of these types of legitimacy, as I have argued elsewhere, can be seen as reflecting the acceptance of a particular conception of time—and hence, of the "future" that is supposed to be foretold.[20] "Traditional" forms of prediction are intimately tied to a conception of time as based on the concrete flow of events, usually interpreted as cyclical in nature. In this manner, sages and elders in traditional settings predict that historical outcomes will repeat themselves ineluctably, and insist that acceptance of one's fate constitutes "wisdom." Such advice may, in fact, be highly appropriate and accurate in traditional settings.

"Charismatic" forms of prediction are tied to the belief that time (and space) is actually an illusion, and thus those with extraordinary or divine insight can see the "future" as "present." "Prophecy," in the true sense, thus involves communication by the charismatic prophet to his followers of what is "already true" about the future. The experience of successful prophecy—paradigmatically illustrated by the Oedipus myth—has an identity-transforming effect on the recipient of the message.

Finally, "rational" prediction—the sole form that is "legitimate" within the institutional context of modern science—is based upon acceptance of the notion that time (and space) are abstract, forming a grid that extends infinitely and linearly from the past to the present to the future. As Weber himself puts it, "The stream of immeasurable events flows unendingly toward eternity."[21] To predict concrete future outcomes within this framework of rational time requires logical, impersonal procedures designed to ascertain causes at one point in time that can be reliably shown to bring about effects at later points of time. The classic institution of modern science, of course, is the laboratory, where controlled experiments in principle allow the scientific researcher to abstract entirely from particular historical and geographical contexts in order to arrive at "pure" causal relationships. However, the notion of abstract time that lies behind modern notions of scientific prediction is conceptually separable from the specific institution of the laboratory; hence nonexperimental sciences such as cosmology and evolutionary biology can be accepted as fully scientific to the extent that they also strive to verify causal relationships in linear time.[22]

This ideal typical scheme already helps to pinpoint one reason for the confusion among social scientists about the role of empirical prediction: far more frequently than social scientists realize, the sorts of prediction they are interested in are traditional or charismatic, rather than rational. Weber points to both of these confusions in his methodological essays. To the extent that social scientists enter the profession in order to "prove" the superiority of particular social arrangements, they unwittingly conflate the task of scientific (linear/causal) prediction with the defense of inherited, traditional values. In contemporary social science scholarship, too, the study of history is often motivated by a search for "lessons" about the past that can reveal timeless "wisdom" about the human condition; such scholars "predict" that abstract schemes to improve the human condition will necessarily fail due to their rejection of local knowledge, but they do not embrace the search for testable hypotheses about causal relationships linking antecedent conditions to future outcomes.[23] To the extent that scholars attempt to use the lecture hall to dispense "academic prophecy," they conflate the tasks of science with those of spiritual leadership. One can see this conflation at work among scholars who explicitly claim that their goal is to engage in "social engineering" by mastering the laws of social "physics"; success in this endeavor would implicitly place social scientists in the role of charismatic leaders, issuing infallible prophecies about the results of particular efforts at institution building and "designing" institutions with perfectly predictable results.[24]

Even in the natural sciences, where laboratory methods allow much more reliable empirical confirmation or disconfirmation of predictive hypotheses, the potential to conflate rational prediction and charismatic prophecy exists as well. Indeed, the conception of the successful natural scientist as "charismatic prophet" still has a certain amount of purchase among laypeople and scientific practitioners alike; the quest for a unified general

STEPHEN E. HANSON

theory in physics that would account for all empirical data throughout time and space is one product of this essentially spiritual "mission."

Yet natural scientific predictions of the future, however impressively they are confirmed, can for most people be easily compartmentalized and generally have little direct impact on their identities. Adopting an ideal typically rational approach to prediction in social science, by contrast, would have immense and, for many, unwelcome implications for the self-understanding of social scientists. To begin with, an abstract and linear view of the unfolding of human history would firmly have to embrace Darwinian evolutionary theory as providing the "scope conditions" under which social science is even possible. As Weber well understood, a science of interpretive beings—the subject matter that makes social science a distinct field of inquiry—can only exist where, empirically, creatures with the capability of abstract symbolic communication have emerged from the evolutionary process.[25] Beyond this, however, a truly "rational" social science would have to place all religions, ideologies, and scientific paradigms themselves on the abstract time line in order to examine in a procedural and impersonal manner the reasons for their emergence, institutionalization, and disintegration.[26] Thus efforts to establish theoretically the superiority or inferiority of particular "civilizations" or cultural traditions are, from this point of view, necessarily unscientific. Meanwhile, from the Weberian point of view, the position of would-be "institutional engineers" becomes not so much immoral or wrongheaded but logically impossible: the first questions one would have to ask about abstract designs for human institutions would be, under what empirical conditions are analysts likely to arrive at these conclusions about which institutional rules are best? And how likely are such designs to be accepted by empirical political actors under the social conditions actually characteristic of the contemporary world? Since scientific (as opposed to ideological or religious) answers to these questions must necessarily indicate the high likelihood of something short of full acceptance and implementation of proposed incentive systems by all human beings, the utopian dream of social-scientific engineering must, from a Weberian point of view, be abandoned.

Yet Weber continues to insist that prediction is a crucial element of the social-science enterprise. Indeed, in nearly every respect, Weber argues, the logical procedures for establishing causal linkages in social science are no different from those used in natural science—since all modern science, as we have seen, must accept a "rational" conception of time. The only real difference between prediction in the cultural sciences and in the natural sciences is that the social scientist, given the nature of the subject matter, must always consciously place his or her own cultural values into the historical "timeline." As Weber puts it, "the causal analysis of personal actions proceeds logically in exactly the same way as the causal analysis of the historical 'significance' of [important events], i.e., by isolation, generalization, and the construction of judgments of possibility." This procedure must logically be applied even to one's own actions: "The valid answer to the question: why did I act in that way, constitutes a categorically formed construct which is to be raised to the level of the demonstrable judgment only by the use of abstractions. This is true even though the 'demonstration' is in fact here conducted in the mind of the 'acting person' himself."[27]

Adopting this perspective, however, forces the social scientist to assess the "causes" of his or her own epistemological, ontological, and methodological stances—including the reasons for his or her very commitment to the modern scientific enterprise. Thus, a certain degree of "subjectivity" is introduced into the social-scientific enterprise that need not be present—or at least, need not be made conscious—among natural scientists. Once one faces the demonstrable fact that modern science is itself a social activity—a collective product of interpretive beings—then there is no way to escape the conclusion that one's choice of profession and of subject matter must reflect on some level the subjective value orientations that one brings to scientific activity as a predictable result of one's upbringing and socialization in a particular historical and geographical context. And yet the logical operations involved in proving or disproving hypotheses about the ideal typical "developmental tendencies" of interpretive beings are not thereby changed.[28]

In sum, Weberian interpretive sociology arms the analyst with three crucial conceptual tools for engaging in scientific prediction. First, Weberian analysis, uniquely among major social-scientific paradigms, emphasizes the causal importance of the subjective orientations of social actors in determining the course of institutional development and broader cultural change—a factor often downplayed or ignored by competing theoretical approaches. Second, Weberian social scientists will tend to be especially sensitive to their own subjective biases, and thus be better prepared to guard against the human tendency to let these biases unconsciously color the conclusions of scientific analysis. Third, forearmed with a clear understanding of the conceptual distinctions among prophecy, wisdom, and scientific prediction, Weberians should, in principle, have an easier time admitting when their favored hypotheses do fail, since they make no claims to prophetic infallibility or traditional authority that might be damaged by

STEPHEN E. HANSON

honesty in this sphere. "In science," Weber emphasizes, "each of us knows that what he has accomplished will be antiquated in ten, twenty, fifty years. That is the fate to which science is subjected; it is the very meaning of scientific work. . . . Every scientific 'fulfillment' raises new 'questions'; it asks to be 'surpassed' and outdated. Whoever wishes to serve science has to resign himself to this fact."[29]

CONCLUSION

This brings us back to the question with which this essay began: why, exactly, have Jowitt's predictions of outcomes in the Leninist and post-Leninist world frequently been so accurate? In fact, Jowitt's explicit embrace of Weber's nonsociobiological Darwinian perspective on social evolution makes his theory scientifically far more "rational"—in the sense described above—than is typical of the contemporary social science mainstream. Jowitt's analysis is almost always deductively derived from his general abstract theory (derived from Weberian sociology) about how human belief systems emerge, are consolidated against environmental threats, and then either reproduce themselves over time or go "extinct."[30] In brief, Jowitt's theory states that only charismatic leaders who successfully convince their followers that their principles are "timeless" and "spaceless" ever manage to create enduring new rituals in turbulent social environments ("frontiers"); that such charismatic movements can survive and generate social power only to the extent that they successfully define and institutionalize "boundaries" of some sort against alternative ways of life; that most charismatic movements tend at some point in their development to define their boundaries rigidly and coercively, creating "barricades" against perceived hostile elements; that only a few charismatic movements succeed ultimately in relaxing their "barricades" in order to create stable and tolerant regimes; and, finally, that informal "cultural" responses to formal institutional orders may endure long after those orders themselves disappear. These "laws" of human history generate a wide range of quite testable empirical hypotheses about social development—with the rise, consolidation, and collapse of Leninist regimes being an ideal environment for testing them.

That "democratic and capitalist transitions" in postcommunist Europe would likely remain incomplete due to the cultural legacies of Leninism throughout the region, Jowitt predicted scientifically from the law that links the endurance of informal cultural values to earlier imposition of rigidly bounded regime types; this law makes the continuing evidence of "neo-traditionalism" in much of the former Soviet Union unsurprising. That "movements of rage" with radical anti-Western ideologies would emerge after the end of the cold war, and that after the Soviet invasion Afghanistan in particular would become a danger to the entire world, Jowitt predicted scientifically from the law that links the emergence of new charismatic movements promoting radically novel ways of life (such as the Taliban) to turbulent frontier environments. Finally, Jowitt's predictions about the low likelihood of postwar "democracy" in Iraq highlight both the cultural aftereffects of Baathist autocracy and the apparent absence of any charismatic movement or principle that could unite the disparate cultures, ethnicities, and religions of the country into a coherent civic polity.

The predictive success of all these risky, falsifiable hypotheses seems to be more than enough reason for future scholars to join Jowitt in further development of the Weberian social-scientific paradigm. Is this likely to occur? Along the lines suggested in this essay, we can approach this question, too, scientifically. In fact, the embrace of a truly scientific social science seems scientifically unlikely. First, the incentive structures currently entrenched in academic institutions do not tend to reward value-free scholarship: powerful figures in the social science mainstream continue, consciously or unconsciously, to promote younger scholars who share their particular political value commitments, while many students and broader public audiences continue, as in Weber's time, to reward academic social scientists who try to provide prophetic insights rather than simply apply and explain scientific procedures. Instrumentally rational graduate students will thus likely continue to gravitate toward currently dominant social science approaches.

Thus the further spread of Jowitt's neo-Weberian paradigm depends upon the very unlikely "charismatic conversion" of a core group of scholars to a viewpoint that is fundamentally at odds both with the usual charismatic promise of time transcendence and with the embrace of "traditional" conceptions of the good life. Weber's own famous attempt to wrestle with this paradox concluded that science "as a vocation"—that is, as a charismatic personal mission—meant facing the "disenchantment of the world" starkly ("like a man"), since science could never answer the central question of how we should live. Instead, the main value of social science would be its ability to produce "self-clarification." Nearly a century after Weber argued this, Weberian social science remains in a distinctly marginal position. The evidence suggests that institutional disincentives, as well as the psychological discomfort necessarily involved in embracing the Weberian theoretical perspective, make it nearly impossible for Weberians to attract mass professional support. If Weberian theory is right, then, I predict that

STEPHEN E. HANSON

Weberian social science, despite its predictive accuracy, will remain a minority viewpoint.

NOTES

I wish to thank Michael Bernhard, David Waldner, Laurence McFalls, Steven Pfaff, and Rudy Sil for their helpful comments on this essay.

1. As I argued in 1995, "The turbulent nature of the post-Leninist genesis environment has been confirmed rather spectacularly. Writing in 1989 and 1990, Jowitt successfully predicted the outbreak of civil war in what used to be Yugoslavia, the appearance and at least partial success of diverse demagogic politicians such as Tymninski, Mečiar, and Zhirinovsky, and the general political turbulence throughout the post-Leninist region. . . . Whereas we have gotten used to these phenomena since the breakup of the Soviet bloc, Jowitt was emphasizing them before many analysts in the field were ready even to entertain them as possibilities." See Stephen E. Hanson, "The Leninist Legacy and Institutional Change," *Comparative Political Studies* 28, no. 2 (July 1995): 307–8.

2. See "Neotraditionalism," in Ken Jowitt, *New World Disorder: The Leninist Extinction* (Berkeley: University of California Press, 1992); Alena V. Ledeneva. *Russia's Economy of Favours: Blat, Networking, and Informal Exchange* (Cambridge and New York: Cambridge University Press, 1998); Stephen Kotkin, "Trashcanistan: A Tour Through the Wreckage of the Soviet Empire," *The New Republic,* April 15, 2002.

3. See "The Leninist Legacy" in Jowitt, *New World Disorder.* Article originally published in *Eastern Europe in Revolution,* ed. Ivo Banac (Ithaca, NY: Cornell University Press, 1992), 207–24.

4. Marc Morjé Howard, *The Weakness of Civil Society in Post-Communist Europe,* Cambridge and New York: Cambridge University Press, 2003.

5. Ken Jowitt, "The Leninist Extinction," in *New World Disorder.* Article originally published in *The Crisis of Leninism and the Decline of the Left: The Revolutions of 1989,* ed. Daniel Chirot (Seattle: University of Washington Press, 1991), 74–99.

6. Ken Jowitt, "Rage, Hubris, and Regime Change," *Policy Review,* no. 118 (April–May 2003): 33–42.

7. Ellen Comisso, "Comments on a Ken Jowitt Retrospective," *Slavic Review* 53, no. 1 (1994): 187. Of the four specific predictions Comisso cites as being "wrong," two are arguably right after all: the "return to mobilization" in Leninist regimes Jowitt predicted in the early 1970s was in fact very much the motivation behind Gorbachev's perestroika, and "the 'global danger' of the Soviet invasion of Afghanistan" became manifest to everyone after 9/11. A third "failed prediction," according to Comisso— Jowitt's argument that Gorbachev's "exceptional commitment" to Eastern Europe would not diminish over time—is specifically acknowledged in an author's postscript in the updated text of *New World Disorder.* Comisso fails to mention this, or to engage

with Jowitt's theoretical defense of his original hypothesis. This leaves only Jowitt's hypothesis that a "strong, not absolute 'Giolittian' presidency" would emerge under Gorbachev in 1990 as a clear predictive failure.

8. Beverly Crawford and Arend Lijphart, *Liberalization and Leninist Legacies: Comparative Perspectives on Democratic Transitions.* (Berkeley: International and Area Studies, University of California, 1997).

9. Stephen E. Hanson, "The Leninist Legacy, Institutional Change, and Post-Soviet Russia." In *Liberalization and Leninist Legacies: Comparative Perspectives on Democratic Transitions,* ed. Beverly Crawford and Arend Lijphart (Berkeley: International and Area Studies, 1997), 228–52.

10. The work of the eminent political scientist David Laitin—whose work, I should emphasize, is a model of intellectual integrity—provides one example. In 1991, Laitin predicted (in an article written four months before the August coup and published in October) that the USSR would not collapse along the lines of its national republics; and in 1998, Laitin predicted in an article written four months before the August coup and published in October) that Russian-speakers in the non-Russian former Soviet republics would increasingly embrace a new political identity as "the Russian-speaking population." Yet no one argues that rational-choice theory should be rejected because of Laitin's predictive failures. See Laitin, "The National Uprisings in the Soviet Union." *World Politics* 44, no. 1 (1991): 139–77; and Laitin, *Identity in Formation: The Russian-Speaking Populations in the Near Abroad* (Ithaca, NY: Cornell University Press, 1998).

11. Carl Hempel, *Fundamentals of Concept Formation in Empirical Science* (Chicago: University of Chicago Press, 1952); Karl Popper, *The Logic of Scientific Discovery* (London: Hutchinson, 1959).

12. Thomas Kuhn, *The Structure of Scientific Revolutions* (Chicago: University of Chicago Press, 1962).

13. Imre Lakatos, "Falsification and the Methodology of Scientific Research Programs," in *Criticism and the Growth of Knowledge,* ed. Imre Lakatos and Alan Musgrave (Cambridge: Cambridge University Press, 1970), 119; emphasis in original.

14. Ibid.

15. Robert Bates et al., *Analytic Narratives* (Princeton, NJ: Princeton University Press, 1998).

16. Margaret Levi, "A Model, a Method, and a Map: Rational Choice in Comparative and Historical Analysis," in *Comparative Politics: Rationality, Culture, and Structure,* ed. Mark Irving Lichbach and Alan S. Zuckerman (Cambridge: Cambridge University Press, 1997), 33.

17. Gary King, Robert O. Keohane, and Sidney Verba, *Designing Social Inquiry: Scientific Inference in Qualitative Research* (Princeton: Princeton University Press, 1994), 104. For an analysis of King, Keohane, and Verba as defenders of the Hempel-Popper approach, see, e.g., Timothy McKeown, "Case Studies and the Statistical Worldview: Review of King, Keohane, and Verba's 'Designing Social Inquiry: Scientific Inference in Qualitative Research,'" *International Organization* 53, no. 1 (1999).

STEPHEN E. HANSON

18. An admirable exception to this trend is John Gerring: "A theory that is able to predict election results six months in advance of an election is superior *(ceteris paribus)* to one that can predict results only a week ahead. . . . The closer one moves to the outcome of interest, the less useful a prediction is likely to be. Earthquake warnings that arrive seconds before the earthquake itself are scarcely predictions at all, in the normal sense of the term. Comets, eclipses, and other natural occurrences, on the other hand, have been predicted decades, sometimes even centuries, in advance of their occurrence. These are better." Gerring, *Social Science Methodology: A Criterial Framework* (Cambridge: Cambridge University Press, 2001), 126.

19. Margaret Somers, "'We're No Angels': Realism, Rational Choice, and Relationality in the Social Sciences," *American Journal of Sociology* 104, no. 3 (November 1998): 773.

20. Stephen E. Hanson, *Time and Revolution: Marxism and the Design of Soviet Institutions* (Chapel Hill: University of North Carolina Press, 1997).

21. Max Weber, "'Objectivity' in Social Science and Social Policy," in *The Methodology of the Social Sciences,* ed. Edward A. Shils and Henry A. Finch (New York: Free Press, 1949), 84.

22. Jack A. Goldstone, in his critique of Somers, rightly emphasizes the importance of scientific "laws" to evolutionary biology— contrary to the assumptions of many historical institutionalists. See Goldstone, "Initial Conditions, General Laws, Path Dependence, and Explanation in Historical Sociology," *American Journal of Sociology* 104, no. 3 (November 1998): 829–45.

23. See, for example, James C. Scott, *Seeing Like A State: How Certain Schemes to Improve the Human Condition Have Failed* (New Haven, CT: Yale University Press, 1997).

24. See, for example, Peter Ordeshook, "Engineering or Science: What Is the Study of Politics?" in *The Rational Choice Controversy: Economic Models of Politics Reconsidered,* ed. Jeffrey Friedman (New Haven, CT: Yale University Press, 1995), 175–88.

25. Max Weber, *Economy and Society,* trans. and ed. Guenther Roth and Claus Wittich, 2 vols. (Berkeley: University of California Press, 1978), 15–17.

26. This, by the way, is the step not taken by sociobiology, which, in its assumption that strictly genetic mechanisms are responsible for all forms of social change, implicitly leaves relatively short-term changes in political ideologies and regimes (such as the rise and fall of the USSR, which quite obviously cannot be explained by changes in the gene pool) out of the realm of scientific analysis. In this way, sociobiology, despite its scientific pretensions, is actually less threatening to the pride and sense of autonomy typical of contemporary Homo sapiens than would be a thoroughgoing rational social science.

27. Max Weber, "'Objectivity' in Social Science and Social Policy," 177.

28. Stephen Kalberg, *Max Weber's Comparative-Historical Sociology* (Chicago: University of Chicago Press, 1994).

29. Max Weber, "Science as a Vocation," in *From Max Weber: Essays in Sociology,* ed. H. H. Gerth and C. Wright Mills (New York: Oxford University Press, 1953), 138. Some readers may object that Weber's ideal-typical description of scientific modesty

merely amounts to an unenforceable call to abandon "degenerating" research programs that in the end differs little from Lakatos's position. It is true, of course, that no philosophy of science can guarantee the scientific integrity of those who formally embrace it. The emergence of a corrupt, hegemonic Weberianism whose leading figures fail to admit their predictive errors is admittedly a sociological possibility. It is my contention, however, that the extreme degree of scholarly self-consciousness required by Weber's reflexive sociology acts as a serious check on the tendency of social scientists to justify the endless refining of established "theoretical" propositions without engaging in sustained empirical testing or admitting predictive failure.

30. Ken Jowitt, "The Leninist Extinction."

STEPHEN E. HANSON

12

THE EVOLVING SIGNIFICANCE OF LENINISM IN COMPARATIVE HISTORICAL ANALYSIS

Theorizing the General and the Particular

RUDRA SIL

Although Ken Jowitt did not write anything explicitly advocating any particular methodological approach, his lectures and seminars regularly made reference to the importance of grasping both the *general* and the *particular* significance of any phenomenon. Jowitt's own effort to do this with regard to communism, together with his perceptive and potent critiques of then-prevalent approaches to communist studies, reveal a systematic application of a variant of the comparative method.[1] It is this method that enabled Jowitt to develop his own conception of "Leninism" as a category alongside a theoretically compelling account of the distinctive challenges it faced at different stages of its development. The same strategy later allowed Jowitt to employ the notion of the "Leninist legacy" to anticipate and characterize particular obstacles to postcommunist transformation that did not seem to garner much attention in new debates over "reform" and "transition."

Against the backdrop of recent discussions of the trade-offs across various strategies of comparative analysis,[2] the first section suggests how Jowitt's approach to defining and analyzing the Leninist universe may be understood as an original and eclectic effort to combine John Stuart Mill's methods of agreement and difference. This strategy enabled Jowitt to do two things:[3] (1) distinguish the *general* features of Leninist organizational culture and development trajectories everywhere from the *particular* features of individual Leninist regimes that paved the way for distinctive outcomes, and (2) identify the *particular* challenges of engineering a "revolutionary breakthrough" in a hostile social environment from the *general* tasks of development and nation building confronting most of the world. The second section considers Jowitt's ambivalent reaction to the alleged failure to predict what he called "the Leninist extinction," challenging the notion that the event should have been predicted on the basis of what was known, but criticizing the field for theoretical weaknesses that prevented it from recognizing the mechanisms at work. The same comparative strategy evident in Jowitt's conception of Leninism also enabled him to articulate the significance of the "Leninist legacy" as a useful category for examining important questions ignored or marginalized in new debates on post-communist studies. The following section notes that Jowitt's approach, while valuable in overcoming theoretical blind spots in the field of post-communist studies, came with some trade-offs that can now be mitigated so that the category "Leninism" can continue to be exploited fruitfully for new insights about institutional change across time and space. In this regard, I specifically call for more systematic historical comparisons between (post)Leninist and non-Leninist developmental experiences, and between the Leninist legacies and transitional experiences of individual postcommunist countries.

THE "LENINIST RESPONSE" TO COMMUNIST STUDIES: BEYOND UNIVERSALISM AND ESSENTIALISM

Jowitt's conception of Leninism may be viewed as part of a distinctive strategy of comparative-historical analysis in response to the simplifications evident in the debates between "essentialists" and "universalists" in communist studies. The former emphasized the peculiarity of communist totalitarianism and dismissed the notion that there was anything genuinely "modern" about totalitarian regimes. The latter sought to downplay the distinctiveness of communist regimes and focused on the increasingly "modern" features emerging out of the processes of economic, social, and political development. Neither approach was capable of illuminating what Jowitt would come to see: that Leninism was a world-historical phenomenon that had features that were both "genetic" and "developmental," distinctive yet replicable, cosmopolitan yet revolutionary. Making analytic sense of these dualisms required a creative eclectic approach that simply was not conceivable given a priori assumptions about either the uniqueness of communist totalitarianism or the universality of the developmental imperatives and processes driving change in communist regimes.

RUDRA SIL

The essentialists found in Stalinist "totalitarianism" not only a counterpart to Nazi Germany, but a static system of political control that was
unreformable and a hindrance to anything resembling economic, social,
or political transformations that had taken place elsewhere. Some essentialists viewed the emergence of such a system in Russia and Eastern Europe
as facilitated by a political culture in these regions that was supposedly recep-
tive to hierarchical patterns of authority.[4] Others viewed communist rule
as a tragic interruption of the distinctive modernizing processes unfolding in Russia and Eastern Europe, but nevertheless viewed the steeply hierarchical structure of totalitarianism as the essence of communism.[5] While
the differences between these two characterizations spurred vigorous
debates among historians, for those seeking to understand the political
dynamics of communist regimes, what mattered was the common treatment of the Bolshevik revolution as a seizure of power that produced an
essentially static and unreformable system of terror, atomization, ideological
rigidity, and steeply hierarchical political control. Such a system could be
nothing more than a terrible historical aberration and could not be meaningfully compared or contrasted with "normal" or "ordinary" social orders
evolving elsewhere.

Such an approach required that essentialists ignore the distinctive aims,
institutions, and transformations that characterized Leninism and distinguished it from Nazism and other models of autocracy established previously in Russia and Eastern Europe. As Jowitt noted, "With its Platonic
emphasis on an essentially fixed ideological and political reality, totalitarianism provided no real leverage for analyzing the contingent leadership
and developmental features of Leninist regimes."[6] Moreover, the essentialists failed to provide any explanation for the shared institutional
configurations adopted by Leninist regimes (such as in China, Yugoslavia
and Cuba) that remained outside the Soviet bloc and that had quite different historical inheritances and political cultures. Neither the diversity
of Leninist regimes nor the diverse socioeconomic conditions under which
Leninism appeared were deemed relevant in view of the supposedly more
fundamental realities of power, control, and atomization that constituted
totalitarian rule. In effect, as Jowitt put it, "the theory of totalitarianism
actually made the empirical study of Leninist regimes superfluous" while
performing "the civic and ideological function of identifying and isolating
the enemy."[7]

The scholars I label "universalists" recognized and challenged the ideological underpinnings of essentialist treatments of communism. Under
the twin influences of modernization theory (in the 1960s and 1970s) and

the revisionist turn in social history (in the 1970s and 1980s), universalists sought to highlight changes in Soviet-type societies and interpreted these changes as increasingly being shaped by the same developmental imperatives that had led to the emergence of modern industrial societies elsewhere. Whereas the essentialists sought to view totalitarianism as a unique phenomenon that defied meaningful comparison, the universalists chose to emphasize historical processes, institutional dynamics, and social trends that could be more comfortably interpreted in terms of narratives and conceptual frameworks constructed on the basis of Western history. Perhaps one of the most overt and deliberate examples of this was Jerry Hough's examination of the growth of bureaucratic rationalization and "institutional pluralism" in Soviet politics during the 1960s and 1970s.[8] Others sought to employ such familiar categories as "corporatism" and "social contract" to suggest that the post-Stalin Soviet regime was coping with essentially the same dilemmas of labor incorporation and state-society relations that advanced industrial societies had once had to overcome.[9] In addition, revisionist social historians set out to plot social processes and historical trends that demonstrated the fluidity of Soviet society and identified the social groups on which the regime relied for legitimacy and support. Where some traced the upward mobility of an increasingly educated urban proletariat, others saw Stalinist terror as partly an unintended consequence of chaotic and uncontrolled social processes, and still others went on to demonstrate the growth of a progressively more mature "civil society" characterized by politically articulate actors with distinct sets of skills and interests.[10]

These universalist interpretations of communism did erode the dominance of the "totalitarian school," but they also betrayed a tendency to ignore or minimize the differences between Leninist systems and "ordinary" responses to the imperatives of modernization.[11] Quoting Leon Trotsky, Jowitt saw this tendency as the result of scholars attempting to "seek salvation from unfamiliar phenomena in familiar terms."[12] Thus, Jowitt took Hough to task, arguing that he "regularly assimilates the unfamiliar into the familiar by neglecting or slighting the differences between Western and Leninist institutional settings." Others were criticized for deliberately using familiar concepts and vocabularies in a manner that simply could not grasp either "the institutional peculiarity" of Leninism or the novelty of Leninism's historical attempt to "hierarchically fuse the conflicting roles of state leadership and public citizenship" within the party-state apparatus.[13] And, in spite of his respect for the work of many of the revisionist social historians, Jowitt referred to Moshe Lewin's *The Gorbachev Phenomenon* simultaneously as an "outstanding sociological essay" and as "conceptually one-legged in its determinist neglect of the intervening role of institutions in mediating social change and political outcomes."[14] In sum, the universalists were no more successful than the essentialists in grasping the amalgam of features that made Leninism a distinct category in the study of order and change.

Jowitt's own conceptualization of order and change in the Leninist universe reflected a self-conscious effort to avoid the pitfalls and simplifications characteristic of essentialist and universalist approaches. As Jowitt himself put it: "A one-dimensional emphasis on either the essential or developmental features of Leninist regimes remains an obstacle to a more generous theoretical grasp of Leninism's novelty as a historical and institutional phenomenon."[15] In methodological terms, we might say that if the essentialist perspective implicitly favored a one-dimensional application of Mill's method of difference to highlight the peculiarity and immutability of communist totalitarianism, and if the universalist approach implicitly favored the method of agreement to accentuate the equivalence of developmental patterns found within and beyond the communist universe, then Jowitt's treatment of Leninism may be viewed as an eclectic combination of Mill's methods of agreement and difference that enabled him to recognize both the general and particular, as well as the relationships between them.

The method of agreement enabled Jowitt to identify general aspects of Leninism that simply could not be rendered intelligible in the simplified framework of the totalitarian model. One set of general aspects concerned the remarkably similar institutional features that accompanied Leninist breakthroughs across diverse social settings. Whereas the totalitarian school focused largely on the Soviet Union and viewed other regimes as effectively controlled by Moscow, Jowitt's conception of Leninism suggested that the appearance of remarkably similar institutional configurations across vastly different social settings could not be explained away as the result of a singular kind of political culture or an aberrant sequence of historical accidents. What made Leninism recognizable from China and North Korea to Yugoslavia and Cuba was not simply the expanding power of Soviet totalitarianism but the deliberate replication of a mode of organization and development intended to simultaneously engineer social revolution and economic modernization by means of a party distinguished by its "charismatic impersonalism."

The method of agreement also enabled Jowitt to deal with change over time in a way that the essentialists could not. In contrast to the essentialists' assumption that communism stood in the way of modernity, Jowitt was able to identify genetic as well as developmental features in Leninist regimes that could be meaningfully compared (and contrasted) to patterns of development seen in other "modern" countries. These features included the impersonal quality of interpersonal relations suggested by the use of the term "comrade," the assertion of the party's "vanguard role" in terms of its authoritative grasp of the laws of science and history, and, I would add, the vigorous effort to redeploy in socialist settings technologies and systems of production borrowed from advanced capitalist economies.[16] These were all constituent elements of Leninism that could only be identified by implicitly comparing features of communist and non-communist regimes, comparisons that proponents of the totalitarian model did not consider, given their a priori view of communism as an accidental or culturally specific phenomenon. Thus, while their fixed ontology prevented the essentialists from doing anything more than declaring by fiat that communist totalitarianism was an essentially atomizing and unreformable phenomenon,[17] Jowitt was able to anticipate the key challenge that the Leninist party would set for itself once it felt secure in its social environment: to "integrate itself with, rather than insulate itself from, its host society."[18]

While Jowitt and the universalists converged in rejecting the view of communist regimes as static, antimodern systems of totalitarian oppression, Jowitt did not fall into the trap of assimilating the common transformations he saw across the Leninist universe into existing models of development and modernization. It is here that the method of difference enabled Jowitt to develop a quite distinctive understanding of the particular features of Leninist parties and Leninist modes of development. Thus, where the universalists opted to focus almost exclusively on developmental processes that they found to be the equivalents of trends identified in Western economic and social modernization, Jowitt recognized that comparability did not mean similarity. In fact, applying the method of difference, Jowitt discerned that the "modern" aspects of Leninism were only a part of an amalgam that included a "charismatic" organizational culture linked to the heroic quest for building a new social order in a hostile environment. Moreover, while the universalists tended to privilege processes of change, Jowitt continued to pay attention to the genetic features at the heart of the category of Leninism and to how these were affected by the political, economic, and social transformations taking place at various points in time. Thus, whereas Jowitt may have agreed with his universalist colleagues that the party was seeking to redefine its relationship with a changing society, he also recognized that this process would lead to new problems and tensions, not to unidirectional, evolutionary change (as suggested by the universalists' use of such commonplace concepts as "corporatism" or "institutional pluralism" to describe change across communist systems).

Significantly, the method of difference ultimately led Jowitt to recognize and theorize a crucial dynamic that neither the essentialists nor the universalists could make sense of within their respective analytic templates: the emergence of "neotraditional" political corruption that was a by-product of Leninist regimes seeking to renegotiate their relationship with previously excluded social actors in the absence of a combat task. This relationship, far from resembling anything like corporatism or interest-group pluralism, came to be marked by the spread of "pariah" activities and networks of *blat* (personal connections) that increasingly blurred the divide between the public and private domains. In other words, Lenin's "party of a new type," which once combined revolutionary heroism with the quest for social transformation on the basis of impersonal scientific laws, gradually became a mafia of "the old type," with its original combat task giving way to the mundane quest for gain through personal networks and informal modes of social exchange. Thus, there *was* a transformation of the relationship between party and society, but the result was an invidious relationship between a "parasitic" party and a "scavenger" society that Yuri Andropov and Mikhail Gorbachev ultimately failed to restructure.[19]

In general, Jowitt's approach constitutes a truly original and eclectic comparative approach to communist studies in that it privileged neither continuity nor change, neither the essentialism of the "totalitarian school" nor the universalism of modernization theorists and revisionist historians (see fig. 1). This eclectic comparative strategy enabled Jowitt to do three things that other students of communism had by and large neglected to do. First, it bounded the Leninist universe in a new way—not in terms of the ideology and policies followed by parties embracing a "communist" worldview but in terms of the organizational culture of a party seeking nothing short of a revolutionary transformation of its environment while seeking to institutionalize a novel amalgam of "charismatic" and "impersonal" features. Second, Jowitt drew attention to the distinctions and relationships between Leninism's genetic features (related to the organization, self-image, status, and purpose of the party) and its developmental features (related to distinctive sets of core imperatives and associated challenges as the regime took power, consolidated its position, and then sought avenues for integrating society). And, third, the framework sought to draw a clear distinction between the Leninist mode of development and other developmental projects that did not require a problematic redefinition of the relationship between regime and society in the way that Leninist parties had to in response to changing organizational imperatives and social environments. While there were certainly many incisive writings on specific aspects of

FIG. 1. Jowitt's Eclectic Characterization of Leninism

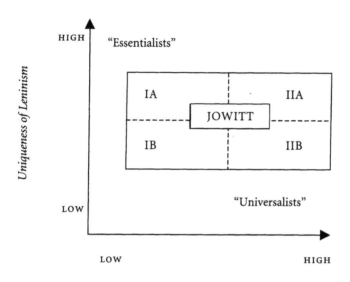

Significance of Change Over Time

Constituent elements of Jowitt's approach to continuity and change in Leninist systems:

I. Genetic features of Leninism as a historically novel amalgam, but one that can be grasped through (Weberian) categories

    IA. "Charismatic" aspects of Leninism (emphasis on revolutionary heroism)

    IB. "Rational-legal" aspects of Leninism (emphasis on impersonalism, science)

II. Developmental features of Leninism as a novel mode of transformation, but one with some recognizable imperatives and processes

    IIA. Features linked to changing core tasks in the course of transforming society

    IIB. Features linked to standard tasks of production and distribution

Leninism and on individual Leninist regimes, these three contributions in Jowitt's work collectively constituted what Jowitt himself characterizes as "a theory of Leninist institutional identity and development."[20] This was a highly original and enormously powerful intellectual breakthrough that many in the field of communist studies would come to recognize but fail to build on.

POSTMORTEM AND ADAPTATION: THE "LENINIST LEGACY" IN POSTCOMMUNIST TRANSITIONS

Following the extinction of Leninism, neither the essentialists nor the universalists had the confidence to directly contest the popular perception that the events of 1989 (and, later, the break up of the USSR) represented "a dismal failure of the predictive power of political science."[21] Whereas most of the field either reacted to this charge with embarrassment or defensiveness, Jowitt boldly proclaimed, "The most powerful theory would not have predicted the singular quality of the events of autumn 1989."[22] Certainly, there were good reasons to identify tensions and problems that could spiral out of control—and Jowitt's analysis of the "neotraditional" corruption of Leninism was among the most compelling articulations of these tensions and problems. There were also good reasons to anticipate the unintended consequences of various reform strategies in a Leninist context—and, again, Jowitt was among the few scholars to offer a theoretical account of how Gorbachev's particular attempt to rescue Leninism would have the unintended consequence of "relativizing" the party and effectively bringing about the end of Leninism. But, beyond pointing to these problematic dynamics and escalating tensions, any specific prediction of the fall of communism would have been mere "prophecy" for Jowitt, borne not out of theoretically informed comparative analysis but of ideological conviction.

Such a view was pointedly *not* intended to serve as a vindication of the field. In fact, Jowitt agreed that the field of communist studies *had* failed, not because it could not predict the events from 1989 to 1991 but because it had failed to develop a theoretical grasp of the distinctive institutional characteristics and dynamics of Leninism. Quoting Trotsky's writings on the 1905 revolution, Jowitt noted, "The question was not of the date of the revolution but of the analysis of its inner forces and of foreseeing its progress as a whole."[23] This did not happen with the field of communist studies because, although it produced a number of illuminating studies, the field failed to generate an analytic framework within which the observations in these studies could be directly compared and synthesized. Reversing Sherlock Holmes's observation that "there are fifty who can reason synthetically for one who can reason analytically," Jowitt noted that quite the opposite was true in communist studies: "We have any number of good analyses of issues and developments in Leninist regimes, and all too many fail to relate their disaggregated findings to the institutional matrix shaping the expression and meaning of phenomena."[24] Had the field been less dominated by the sterile debates between universalists and essentialists, and had it encouraged more eclectic comparative frameworks of the sort Jowitt embraced, then, perhaps, we might have had a shot at grasping the "inner forces" leading to the Leninist extinction, even if we may not have been able to specify the particular sequence of events.

In the first few years following the "velvet revolutions" of Eastern Europe, the theoretical failure of communist studies came to be compounded, not remedied, in the nascent field of postcommunist studies. Jowitt was deeply disturbed by the haste with which the empirical work produced by students of communism was jettisoned, and by the singularly uninformative debate between "transitologists" and specialists focusing on countries of the former Soviet bloc. Those seeking to employ uniform frameworks for studying democratization worldwide did not bother to create a theoretical category to make sense of the distinctive challenges and dynamics of political transformation in postcommunist settings. Challenging Adam Przeworski's claim that institutional traces from the past "can be gradually wiped away" in the course of transitions, Jowitt noted that most transitologists "failed to adequately recognize and conceptualize the coexistence and persistence of competing organizing principles in political, social, and economic life."[25] On the other hand, area specialists focusing on postcommunist countries offered programmatic assertions of the inattentiveness of transitologists to the unique challenges facing postcommunist reformers. In the process, they produced illuminating studies of institutions, leaders, and policies in selected countries, drawing attention to the peculiarities of transition in each case. But there was little attempt to articulate a coherent theoretical framework that could focus attention on the dimensions along which transformation processes could be systematically compared and contrasted across postcommunist and other settings. Thus, as in the case of communist studies, the dualism emerging in the first few years of postcommunist studies reflected the familiar inability to simultaneously appreciate the *general* challenges and characteristics of "transitional" processes alongside the *particular* features of post-Leninist transitions, with the result that neither transitologists nor most specialists in the postcommunist region could agree upon a useful analytic framework for bounding, differentiating, and explaining patterns of postcommunist institutional change.[26]

Once again, Jowitt chose to bypass this stale debate and provided a crucial conceptual breakthrough by developing and applying the concept of a "Leninist legacy."[27] While the notion of "legacy" is a familiar one in historically oriented comparative studies, Jowitt's conception of the "Leninist legacy" was designed to not merely point to the relevance of the past but to bound and articulate the common dilemmas and dynamics linked to a quite uncommon institutional inheritance shared by postcommunist countries. As Jowitt put it, "There is a powerful rationale for treating the countries that experienced Leninism (or socialism) as an area. The Leninist legacy enables us to theoretically bound, not strangle, the diverse developments in the area."[28] Jowitt's point was not that characteristics associated with Leninism were certain to uniformly and indefinitely shape post-Leninist societies; it was that the historical novelty of Leninism requires a concept such as the "Leninist legacy" that can serve as a focal point for a set of crucially important questions that neither area specialists nor transitologists were capable of formulating in view of their respective blind spots. In effect, the "Leninist legacy" provided a plausible and powerful rationale for extending the style of comparative-historical analysis that Jowitt had brought to bear in the study of Leninism. In Millean terms, the notion of a "Leninist legacy" pointed to the application of the method of difference to suggest why transitologists could not grasp some of the distinctive challenges and dynamics of liberalization in postcommunist contexts; it simultaneously pointed to the application of the method of agreement to reveal certain common constraints and modes of behavior that were missed by those focusing solely on the "diverse paths of extrication" from communism in particular countries.[29]

Now, more than a decade after the Leninist extinction, the category of "the Leninist legacy" continues to point to the vast analytic middle ground between the turfs marked off by the overly universalistic templates for charting political and economic transitions and the overly historicist accounts of the peculiarities of change in postcommunist countries. Perhaps this is why many among the new generation of scholars have continued to look to Jowitt's work in search of intellectual vistas that were initially obscured by the stagnant debates between transitologists and postcommunist specialists. Even as these scholars move on to explore events and processes that are now further removed from the extinction of Leninism, they have been explicitly or implicitly building on Jowitt's notion of "Leninist legacy" to develop new arguments and interpretations about sources of continuity, change, and variation along different dimensions of institutional change across postcommunist settings.[30] This suggests that the category "Leninism" remains an analytically useful one, both in demarcating the distinctive experience of post-Leninist societies and in drawing attention to the implications of specific aspects of ideology, organizational culture, and regime-society relations for pathways of transformation.

By privileging particular dimensions of comparison at the expense of others, Jowitt was able to analytically accentuate certain crucial aspects of the Leninist phenomenon that could not be grasped by mainstream approaches in the field. At the same time, it is necessary to recognize that Jowitt's approach came with its own set of intellectual trade-offs. For one, although Jowitt recognized that aspects of Leninist and post-Leninist development were akin to processes of institutional change unfolding elsewhere, he was not in a position to undertake systematic comparisons to explore the range of mechanisms contributing to similarities and differences across the Leninist and non-Leninist universes. Moreover, although Jowitt paid close attention to the distinctive interactions between Leninism and the particular sociocultural milieus in which it took root, the theoretical status of variation across Leninist regimes was clearly not the same as that accorded to the novelty of Leninism as a world-historical phenomenon. While these choices helped Jowitt to "consolidate" his approach in the intellectual environment he was writing in, perhaps the time has come for a more "inclusive" strategy of comparative-historical analysis, without anxiety about contamination from the one-dimensional approaches that once dominated (post)communist studies. In practice, this requires two distinct avenues of comparative-historical analysis that Jowitt did not systematically pursue, but would, I think enthusiastically encourage: (1) direct historical comparisons of (post)Leninist and non-Leninist societies, and (2) variation-finding historical comparisons within the (post)Leninist universe. Each of these axes of comparison takes seriously the category of Leninism, but each allows for the further development of theoretical frameworks to explore questions about institutional change that Jowitt's work pointed to without systematically investigating.

Comparing Patterns of Change across (Post)Leninist
and Non-Leninist Contexts

Jowitt's emphasis on the historical novelty of Leninism was largely a response to universalistic perspectives on unilinear modernization and to the more generalized notion of an "end of history."[31] In this context, it made sense to sharply distinguish Leninist "revolutionary break-throughs" and "Leninist legacies" from other efforts at development and transition. However, in light of recent trends in both the postcommunist world and the social sciences writ large, it makes sense to specify the extent to which (post)Leninist societies have diverged from the experience of other countries that embarked upon grand programs of economic, social, and political transformation within the same international environment. This requires direct, systematic comparative-historical studies across (post)Leninist and non-Leninist experiences with development and transition. I am not challenging the notion that Leninism and its legacy represent historically novel forces with a set of peculiar institutional dynamics. What I am suggesting is that it is possible to recognize the novelty of Leninism and encourage comparisons of (post)Leninist and non-Leninist experiences to generate fresh insights about how, when, and to what extent the peculiarities of Leninism actually matter in relation to particular aspects of institutional change.

As Jowitt was quite aware, Leninist regimes and non-Leninist late-developers did share certain common developmental objectives as well as certain common influences and pressures brought to bear by their external environments. Postcolonial countries in the global periphery—such as Brazil, India, and Korea—may not have been pursuing revolutionary break-throughs, but they did promote ambitious strategies of "state directed development"[32] and periodic attempts at social engineering in the hope of raising their status and influence in the international order. While Leninist regimes harbored far more ambitious visions of revitalizing economic production, reorganizing society, and restructuring the global order, they still had to address at least *some* set of concerns that all late-developing states had to cope with: how to promote rapid industrialization without repeating the problematic experiences of early industrializers; how to maintain social order while coping with large-scale social mobilization; how to maintain discipline in new "modern" institutions in the face of the persistence of "neotraditionalism"; how to assimilate technologies and organizational techniques that have proven effective elsewhere while rendering these authentic; and how to challenge, engage, and learn from referent societies considered to be economically or militarily "advanced" while preserving a distinctive sense of political community.[33]

A comparison between post-1868 Japan and Soviet Russia is instructive in this regard. In spite of differences in ideology and organizational culture, Meiji elites sought to combine "Western learning" with "Japanese spirit" just as the Bolsheviks sought to combine "American efficiency" with "Russian revolutionary sweep." The fact that "Japanese spirit" evoked past traditions while "Russian revolutionary sweep" suggested a vision of the future should not keep us from recognizing the fundamental dilemma of reconciling claims of distinctiveness with the borrowing of foreign organizational forms and techniques. An argument evaluating the Leninist and Japanese responses does not contradict Jowitt's analytic framework in the least, but it does point to the value of open-ended historical comparisons designed to specify the implications and limits of Jowitt's categories for different aspects of institutional change beyond the Leninist universe.[34]

Similarly, in the post–cold war era, it makes sense to investigate and specify when, where, and how the Leninist legacy matters by directly comparing the dynamics of reform in post-Leninist and non-Leninist late-developers. Both sets of countries are engaged in efforts to transform institutions that were once deeply embedded in their respective types of societies. Both are coping with new political pressures generated by the gap between new groups of "winners" and "losers." And both are coping with new economic pressures stemming from an increasingly open international environment. We cannot hope to understand what all this means for the long-term distinctiveness of post-Leninist societies unless we design systematic historical comparisons explicitly aimed at revealing the extent and significance of the divide between post-Leninist and other late-developers along different dimensions of institutional change.[35] In the case of industrial relations, for example, while the legacy of communist trade unionism certainly creates distinctive challenges for labor mobilization in response to reduced wages and diminished job security, some of the most powerful obstacles to an influential labor movement are essentially the same in both Leninist and non-Leninist late-developers—notably, the growing stratification of the labor force, the competitive pressures for more "flexible" forms of employment, and the dependence of the most desperate workers on informal labor markets and employer paternalism.[36]

Variation-finding Historical Comparisons
within the (Post)Leninist Universe

A second avenue for adapting Jowitt's comparative strategy requires theoretically informed historical comparisons aimed at explaining variation across different countries (or groups of countries) within the (post)Leninist universe.[37] Jowitt recognized quite early on the "developmental interaction" of different social settings with Leninism.[38] Indeed, this is precisely why Jowitt was able to construct a compelling account of why the Solidarity movement arose in western Poland, and to consider how the effects of the Leninist legacy were mediated by different regional forces in different parts of the Leninist universe.[39] However, the theoretical status accorded to the mechanisms of variation across (post)Leninist societies was relatively low, given the priority Jowitt placed on articulating the genetic and developmental features of Leninism as a distinctive category of world-historical significance. This priority is certainly justified and to some extent empirically validated by work done by Jowitt's students, as in the case of Marc Howard's convincing demonstration of how the differences in civic participation across post-Leninist countries remain relatively small compared to the differences between Eastern and Western Europe.[40] However, considering that initially small differences may reflect mechanisms capable of generating larger differences over time, it is necessary to make room for systematic variation-finding comparative studies aimed at exploring the diversity of the postcommunist universe through general categories that transcend the peculiar "developmental interaction" of particular locales with Leninism and its legacy.

One area where we might do this is in systematically exploring the implications of a fact that Jowitt himself pointed out, that while Leninist regimes came to power through indigenous revolutions in a few places, in most of Eastern Europe they were "based on political replication of a Soviet 'sacred center.'"[41] One could not expect Jowitt to take it upon himself to lay out the full significance of this difference over time, but there are some important dimensions of comparison worth revisiting. These include the character of membership in a Leninist party that did not experience civil war, the dilemmas faced by Leninist regimes attempting to include previously excluded social actors without first having carried out a sustained cultural revolution, the level of industrialization evident across different parts of the Soviet Union and regions that later joined the Soviet bloc (including the Baltics), and the different ways in which preexisting elements of national identity were synthesized with the cosmopolitan quest for world communism in different countries.[42]

This is related to the need for a more systematic analysis of the variations in the developmental transformations of Leninist regimes, particularly in regard to the timing and scope of efforts to consolidate the regime's identity, power, and vanguard role in society. Jowitt recognized how the shift to inclusion in the Soviet Union generated severe problems for relations with a Maoist China still in the midst of consolidating its power, and he appreciated the significance of Nikita Khrushchev's "Aquinian" view for regime individuality within the Soviet bloc.[43] But what remained to be more systematically explored was the long-term consequence of the comparatively small amount of time, violence, and social dislocation associated with the consolidation of Leninist parties in Eastern Europe. For example, Central European countries, having experienced a much shorter period of communist rule and a relatively less traumatic and less disruptive period of cultural revolution, managed to retain some "institutional memory" of capitalism and even allowed for the direct transmission of familiar alliances between churches and parties from pre- to postcommunist periods.[44] Moreover, while all Leninist regimes witnessed the emergence of "neotraditional" networks of *blat*, the greater pervasiveness of corruption in post-Soviet Russia compared to Central Europe may well be the result of the fact these networks had been cultivated over a much longer period of time, going back to the 1930s, when cohorts of workers and managers formed "circles of protection" to manipulate information and evade the pressures and penalties associated with Stalinist forced industrialization.[45]

It is also worth considering more carefully and systematically the implications of Jowitt's recognition of the special status and special responsibilities conferred upon the Soviet Union as the center and protector of the "Leninist regime world" in the wider international arena.[46] This meant that economic activities and military ambitions became fused as part of a giant military industrial complex in the Soviet Union in a way that was neither necessary nor encouraged in Eastern Europe. A comprehensive account of the different trajectories of economic transformation in the former Leninist world will have to take into account the complications accompanying the "legacy of a militarized economy" inherited by post-Soviet Russia.[47] By the same token, it is significant that the Leninist party in China, while harboring ambitions for expanded influence among postcolonial socialist regimes, expended a much smaller part of its resources and productive capacities on military activities worldwide. Paradoxically, this may have something to do with why China was able to engineer sustained economic growth and emerge as a new challenger to U.S. hegemony in the same period that saw the Soviet Union break up and Russia embark upon a troubled transition.

Finally, it is worth paying closer attention to the specific processes through which individual countries experienced the exit from Leninism, as this may give us clues into the particular mechanisms through which legacies of the past are reinforced or diffused. On this point, Jowitt himself laid out the different patterns of "extinction" for different clusters of Leninist regimes, ranging from the dynamics of Gorbachev's reforms in

Soviet Union to the role of an emergent Solidarity-led "public" in Poland and the "pseudoextinction" of Leninist regimes in Romania and Bulgaria.[48] Moreover, we should add that the end of Leninism in China followed an entirely different process altogether, involving neither the relativization of the Leninist party nor the collapse of an empire but rather a series of incremental adaptations culminating in the decision to extend market production and admit capitalists into the upper echelons of the Chinese Communist Party. These differences have implications for the extent to which, and the manner in which, institutions once set up by Leninist parties can be restructured to meet a different set of imperatives in a different environment. And this, in turn, has implications for the mechanisms through which Leninist legacies can be meaningfully reproduced or diffused in varied institutional contexts.

CONCLUSION

In view of the simplifications accompanying the universalist-essentialist debates through the early 1990s, Jowitt necessarily put a premium on methodologically and theoretically accentuating (1) the distinctiveness of Leninism and post-Leninist transformation vis-à-vis more commonplace processes of development and transition worldwide, and (2) the common features and legacies of Leninism vis-à-vis experiences of individual societies in which Leninist parties came to power. In the process, Jowitt was able to develop a set of powerful concepts and categories that, in turn, enabled him to identify aspects of institutional change that most of the field failed to recognize. Now, in an intellectual climate that is somewhat different from the one in which Jowitt was writing, it is up to a new generation of scholars to adapt Jowitt's eclectic style of comparative analysis more creatively and expansively in order to address unresolved and emerging issues concerning the extent and sources of continuity and change across the post-Leninist universe and beyond. To this end, we need to simultaneously preserve the category of "Leninism" and encourage comparative-historical studies that focus on (1) the sources of similarities and differences that either correspond to, or cut across, the boundary between (post)Leninist and non-Leninist experiences with development and transition, and (2) the extent, sources, and implications of diversity along different dimensions of institutional change within the (post)Leninist universe. Without rethinking the relationship between the general and the particular in light of these kinds of questions, the field of postcommunist studies will fare no better than its predecessor, and we will have failed to take full advantage

of the analytic and methodological leverage afforded by Jowitt's conceptualization and analysis of "Leninism."

NOTES

1. This is most clear in Jowitt's highly insightful and provocatively titled article,
"Weber, Trotsky and Holmes on the Study of Leninist Regimes," *Journal of International Affairs* 45, no. 1 (Summer 1991): 31–49.

2. See, e.g., Henry Brady and David Collier, eds. *Rethinking Social Inquiry: Diverse
Tools, Shared Standards* (Lanham, MD: Rowman & Littlefield, 2004); James Mahoney
and Dietrich Rueschemeyer, eds. *Comparative-Historical Analysis: Achievements and
Agendas* (New York: Cambridge University Press, 2003); Charles Ragin, *Fuzzy-Set Social
Science* (Chicago: University of Chicago Press, 2000), especially 21–145; and Rudra Sil,
"The Division of Labor in Social Science Research: Unified Methodology or 'Organic
Solidarity'?" *Polity* 32, no. 4 (Summer 2000): 499–531.

3. John Stuart Mill, *A System of Logic* (New York: Harper and Row, 1888).

4. Richard Pipes, for example, sees the Bolsheviks as simply grafting Marxism
onto "the sturdy stem of Russia's patrimonial heritage"; see Pipes, "Did the Russian
Revolution Have to Happen?" *American Scholar* (Spring 1994): 215–38, 227. This view
may also be found in Zbigniew Brzezinski's treatment of the Bolshevik revolution as
an "act of revitalized restoration" in Brzezinski, "Soviet Politics: From the Future to
the Past?" in *The Dynamics of Soviet Politics,* ed. Paul Cocks et al. (Cambridge, MA:
Harvard University Press, 1976), 340. See also Richard Pipes, *Russia and the Old Regime*
(New York: Scribner's and Sons, 1974); and Pipes, *The Russian Revolution* (New York:
Vintage, 1990). The classic statement on the "totalitarian model" is, of course, Zbigniew Brzezinski and Carl Friedrich, *Totalitarianism Dictatorship and Autocracy* (Cambridge, MA: Harvard University Press, 1956).

5. Martin Malia, *Russia Under Western Eyes: From the Bronze Horseman to the
Lenin Mausoleum* (Cambridge, MA: Belknap Press of the Harvard University Press,
1999); Sergei Pushkarev, *Self-Government and Freedom in Russia* (Boulder, CO: Westview, 1988); Aleksandr Solzhenitsyn, "Misconceptions about Russia Are a Threat to
America," *Foreign Affairs* 58, no. 4 (1980): 797–834; and Solzhenitsyn, *The Russian Question: At the End of the Twentieth Century,* trans. Yermolai Solzhenitsyn (New York:
Farrar, Straus and Giroux, 1995). More recently, this view has been resuscitated in
arguments that suggest that postcommunist democracy could be expected to flour-
ish in Russia and elsewhere as a result of precommunist trends towards democracy
and civil society. See, e.g., Nikolai Petro, *The Rebirth of Russian Democracy: An Interpretation of Political Culture* (Cambridge, MA: Harvard University Press, 1995); and
Viktor Sergeyev and Nikolai Biryukov, *Russia's Road to Democracy: Parliament, Communism, and Traditional Culture* (Brookfield, VT: Elgar, 1993).

6. Jowitt, "Weber, Trotsky and Holmes," 35.

7. Jowitt, "Weber, Trotsky and Holmes," 35–36.

8. Jerry Hough, "The Soviet System: Petrification or Pluralism," *Problems of Communism* (March–April 1972), and Jerry Hough and Merle Fainsod, *How the Soviet Union is Governed* (Cambridge, MA: Harvard University Press, 1979). Hough explicitly viewed his interpretation as nested in the grand theories of modernization that had been employed to analyze standard imperatives and processes of political, economic, social, and cultural development; see *The Soviet Union and Social Science Theory* (Cambridge, MA: Harvard University Press, 1977).

9. Valerie Bunce, "The Political Economy of the Brezhnev Era: The Rise and Fall of Corporatism," *British Journal of Political Science* 13 (April 1983): 129–58; and Peter Hauslohner, "Gorbachev's Social Contract," *Soviet Economy* 3, 1 (1987).

10. For a general discussion of revisionist treatments of the Stalin era, see Sheila Fitzpatrick, "New Perspectives on Stalinism," *Russian Review* 45, no. 4 (October 1986): 357–73. Examples include Sheila Fitzpatrick, *Education and Social Mobility in the Soviet Union, 1921–1934* (Cambridge, MA: Harvard University Press, 1979); J. Arch Getty, *Origins of the Great Purges: The Soviet Communist Party Reconsidered, 1933–1938* (Cambridge: Cambridge University Press, 1985); Moshe Lewin, *The Gorbachev Phenomenon* (Berkeley: University of California Press, 1988); and Lynne Viola, *The Best Sons of the Fatherland: Workers in the Vanguard of Soviet Collectivization* (New York: Oxford University Press, 1987).

11. In addition to Hough, *The Soviet Union*, see Francis Fukuyama, "The Modernizing Imperative: The USSR as an Ordinary Country," *The National Interest* no. 32 (1993): 10–19.

12. Jowitt, "Weber, Trotsky and Holmes," 38; quote from Leon Trotsky, *The Revolution Betrayed* (New York: Merit, 1965), 245.

13. Jowitt, "Weber, Trotsky and Holmes," 40–41.

14. Jowitt, "Weber, Trotsky and Holmes," 43, note 38.

15. Jowitt, "Weber, Trotsky and Holmes," 38.

16. On the significance of the language of "comradeship," Jowitt frequently cited Ezra Vogel, "From Friendship to Comradeship: The Change in Personal Relations in Communist China," *China Quarterly* no. 21 (January–March 1965): 1–28. On the widespread and deliberate borrowing of Western technologies and methods of production, see my discussion of the bolsheviks' assimilation of Taylorism in Rudra Sil, *Managing "Modernity": Work, Community, and Authority in Late-Industrializing Japan and Russia* (Ann Arbor: University of Michigan Press, 2002), ch. 4.

17. See the famous statement by Z [Martin Malia], "To the Stalin Mausoleum," *Daedalus* 119, no. 1 (1990): 295–344.

18. Jowitt, "Inclusion and Mobilization in European Leninist Regimes," reprinted in *New World Disorder: The Leninist Extinction* (Berkeley: University of California Press, 1992), 91.

19. The most clear articulation of the character and dynamics of neotraditional corruption is in Jowitt, "Soviet Neotraditionalism: The Political Corruption of a Leninist Regime," reprinted in *New World Disorder*, chap. 4. The discussions of the "para-

sitic" party's mafia-like characteristics and its ties to a "scavenger" society are from Jowitt, "Gorbachev: Bolshevik or Menshevik?" in *New World Disorder*, 224–28.

20. Jowitt, "Weber, Trotsky and Holmes," 46.

21. Adam Przeworski, quoted in Jowitt, "Weber Trotsky and Holmes," 32, note 4.

22. Jowitt, "Weber, Trotsky and Holmes," 32, note 6.

23. Jowitt, "Weber, Trotsky and Holmes," 32; quote from Leon Trotsky, *My Life* (New York: Pathfinder Press, 1980), 181.

24. Jowitt, "Weber, Trotsky and Holmes," 42.

25. Ken Jowitt, "Challenging the 'Correct' Line," *East European Politics and Society* 12, no. 1 (Winter 1998), 87; the reference to Przeworski is Adam Przeworski, *Sustainable Democracy* (New York: Cambridge University Press, 1995), 48.

26. See the exchange between Valerie Bunce, "Should Transitologists Be Grounded?" *Slavic Review* (Spring 1995): 111–27; and Terry Lynn Karl and Philippe C. Schmitter, "From an Iron Curtain to a Paper Curtain: Grounding Transitologists or Students of Postcommunism?" *Slavic Review* (Winter 1995): 965–78.

27. Jowitt, "The Leninist Legacy," in *New World Disorder*, chap. 8; see also Marc Howard, "The Leninist Legacy Revisited," in this volume.

28. Jowitt, "Challenging the 'Correct' Line," 106.

29. See, e.g., David Stark and László Bruszt, *Postsocialist Pathways: Transforming Politics and Property in East Central Europe* (Cambridge: Cambridge University Press, 1998), 4.

30. On the relevance of the Leninist legacy for civil society, see Marc Morjé Howard, *The Weakness of Civil Society in Post-Communist Europe* (Cambridge: Cambridge University Press, 2003). On nationalism, see Cheng Chen, "The Roots of Illiberal Nationalism in Romania: A Historical Institutionalist Analysis of the Leninist Legacy," *East European Politics and Societies* 17, no. 2 (Spring 2003): 166–200. In the case of labor relations, see Rudra Sil and Calvin Chen, "Communist Legacies, Post-communist Transformations, and the Fate of Organized Labor in Russia and China," presented at the 2003 Annual Conference of the Central and East European International Studies Association (CEE-ISA), Budapest, Hungary, June 2003. For a variety of studies examining the effects of Leninist legacies on different kinds of institutions in different countries, see Grzegorz Ekiert and Stephen E. Hanson, eds., *Capitalism and Democracy in Central and Eastern Europe: Assessing the Legacy of Communist Rule* (New York: Cambridge University Press, 2003).

31. Francis Fukuyama, *The End of History and the Last Man* (New York: Free Press, 1992).

32. This useful category is taken from Atul Kohli, *State Directed Development: Political Power and Industrialization in the Global Periphery* (New York: Cambridge University Press, 2004).

33. In this context, note the connections drawn between "neotraditionalism" and Korean "neofamilism" in Yong-Chool Ha's contribution to this volume, "From Neotraditionalism to Neofamilism: Responses to 'National Dependency' in Newly Industrialized Countries."

34. See Sil, *Managing "Modernity,"* which grew out of a dissertation chaired by Jowitt.

35. See, e.g., Neil Munro, *Different Dynamics for Contrasting Legacies: South Korea and Russia Compared* (Glasgow: Center for the Study of Public Policy, University of Strathclyde, 2004).

36. See Rudra Sil and Christopher Candland, "Institutional Legacies and the Transformation of Labor: Late-Industrializing and Post-Socialist Economies in Comparative-Historical Perspective," in *The Politics of Labor in a Global Age*, ed. Christopher Candland and Rudra Sil (Oxford: Oxford University Press, 2001), 285–308.

37. Arguably, the most significant effort to do this is the volume edited by Ekiert and Hanson, *Capitalism and Democracy in Central and Eastern Europe;* see especially the chapter by Ekiert and Hanson, "Time, Space, and Institutional Change in Central and Eastern Europe."

38. Ken Jowitt, "An Organizational Approach to the Study of Political Culture in Marxist-Leninist Regimes," reprinted in *New World Disorder*, chap. 2.

39. See, respectively, Jowitt, "The Leninist Extinction," in *New World Disorder*, 253–54; and Jowitt, "A Research Agenda for Eastern Europe," *East European Politics and Society* 4, no. 2 (Spring 1990): 193–97.

40. See Howard, *The Weakness of Civil Society*.

41. Jowitt, "Moscow 'Centre,'" reprinted in *New World Disorder*, 175.

42. On the latter point, see the excellent comparative-historical study recently completed by Cheng Chen, "Illiberal Nationalism in Post-Leninist States: Russia, China, Hungary and Romania" (Ph.D. diss., University of Pennsylvania, 2003).

43. Jowitt, "Moscow 'Centre,'" 180–85, 192–94

44. On the relevance of the "institutional memory" of capitalism, see Vladimir Gimpelson and Douglas Lippoldt, *The Russian Labour Market: Between Transition and Turmoil* (Lanham, MD: Rowman & Littlefield, 2001), 2–3. On the transmission of church-party ties, see Jason Wittenberg, *Crucibles of Political Loyalty: Church Institutions and Electoral Continuity in Hungary* (New York: Cambridge University Press, 2006).

45. The best study on this phenomenon is Joseph Berliner, *Factory and Manager in the USSR* (Cambridge, MA: Harvard University Press, 1957). For a more brief discussion, see my *Managing "Modernity,"* 238–40. On how Russia compares to Central Europe on levels of corruption today, see the *2005 Transparency International Corruption Perceptions Index*, available at http://ww1.transparency.org/cpi/2005/cpi2005.sources.en.html.

46. Jowitt, "Moscow 'Centre,'" passim.

47. See Clifford Gaddy, *The Price of the Past: Russia's Struggle with the Legacy of a Militarized Economy* (Washington, DC: Brookings Institution, 1996).

48. Jowitt, "The Leninist Extinction," in *New World Disorder*, 253–60.

v *The Big Picture*

13

CONJURING UP A BATTLEFRONT
IN THE WAR ON TERROR

STEPHEN HOLMES

O n September 11, 2001, a multinational team of hijackers struck the United States. In response, after "running out of targets" in Afghanistan, the United States invaded Iraq. To explain this swivel of the cannon, commentators often draw a sharp distinction between mere pretexts and the real reasons for the Iraq war. To bring along the American electorate, the administration initially drew on two powerful impulses, retaliation and self-protection. Many Americans supported the United States' invasion of Iraq, first, to avenge the 9/11 attack, and, second, to prevent the United States from being struck without warning by Iraqi weapons of mass destruction (WMDs) delivered by stealth to U.S. shores. When the feebleness of these two reasons for the war became evident, the administration switched to a "humanitarian" justification for the invasion, stressing America's moral obligation to overthrow a malignant dictator who had tortured and gassed his own people. To this purely humanitarian consideration, the invasion's apologists added a complicated theory about the contribution that an Arab democracy, imposed by American might, would make to U.S. security.

Because the original rationales were so flimsy and the backstop rationales were so far-fetched, some critics have assumed that the real reasons for the war must lie elsewhere, in secret plans, such as setting up permanent military installations to facilitate swift access to Gulf oil infrastructures in case of a fundamentalist power grab in Saudi Arabia or deposing

Saddam Hussein to improve the security position of Israel. But what if 9/11 itself had a decisive psychological impact on the interagency coalition that took the United States into war?

The distinction between secret schemes to promote unspoken interests and official rationalizations designed to gull the public has a lot to be said in its favor. But a sharp appearance/reality dichotomy is probably too schematic in this case. More generally, the cynical use of disinformation provides no proof of underlying rationality. There is no reason why a successful manipulator cannot also be psychologically disturbed. Even a purveyor of bogus intelligence can sometimes commit himself to risky action on the basis of supposed evidence that he has not bothered to double-check simply because it neatly corroborates his preconceptions. In other words, the real motivations for the Iraq war may have resembled the public justifications more than is commonly believed. The former, too, may have included a sincerely held conviction that invading Iraq was an "appropriate" response to 9/11. The hawks' hidden thinking may have been just as clouded by fixation, autism, escapism, and tunnel vision as the rationales they improvised for public consumption. This would not be especially surprising, since immense power has never freed its wielders from hallucination.

CORPORATISM AND REVENGE

Only sketchily informed about Saudi and Egyptian politics, most Americans seem to have believed that the 9/11 attacks came "from nowhere." They may have therefore approved their government's decision to strike back just about "anywhere" because of their limited capacity to distinguish one place from another. They certainly gave their government a blanket authorization to do "whatever it takes." This blank check drew upon a widespread desire to "do something" in response to a cruel exposure of American vulnerability. That is to say, the uncomplicated emotional basis of initial support for the Iraq war lay in the public's craving for revenge, and that necessarily means for collective punishment. Strong corporate identities, as Ken Jowitt has explained, help people suppress lingering guilt when engaging in acts of violence. Corporate identity does this because it numbs people engaged in inflicting pain and death on others to their victims' individuality. A shadowy group of Arabs flew airplanes into American buildings and killed thousands of anonymous Americans. The revenge instinct, in response, fueled an American desire to desecrate the skyline of a representative Arab city and dole out misery to generic Arabs. It did not matter, for the logic of revenge, that the Arabs whom Americans attacked were not the same Arabs who attacked America. What matters, in a blood feud, is that some members of the same group who harmed us are harmed by us. We can inure ourselves to their individual plight by imaging them to be blood kinsmen of the hijackers or by erasing their humanity as "collateral damage."

By misleadingly blurring together the image of transnational terrorists and the image of Iraqi insurgents, the administration has enlisted an archaic longing for revenge in building support for its counterinsurgency in Iraq. To use the umbrella term "terrorists" is to disguise the fact that Iraqi insurgents are not members of Al Qaeda, and that killing Sunni guerrillas who resist a Shiite takeover of Iraq (under the cover of "Western-style democracy") will do nothing to avenge 9/11 or stop Al Qaeda cells from plotting an American Hiroshima.

To some of his supporters, Bush may symbolize less the president who prays than the president who never reads the newspaper and who therefore implicitly frees them from thinking about the complexity of the world. But Bush aside, the promoters and architects of the Iraq war presumably knew the difference between Saudis, Egyptians, and other Arabs volunteering for global jihad and Iraqis thrust into a local insurgency by a military invasion. When they set out to blur that distinction in the public's mind, they did so deliberately, in order to achieve by ruse what they could not achieve by persuasion. Speaking of "the terrorists," they memorably claimed that it would be better to fight "them" over there rather than over here, even though any neutral observer would have pointed out that two very different "thems" were involved. So was their reasoning cynical or delusional?

To admit the importance of a distinction between the Iraqis whom we attacked and the Saudis, Egyptians, and others who attacked us would spoil the logic of revenge and undermine the emotional basis for public support of the war. To call our Iraqi attackers insurgents or rebels, in fact, would be to weaken their image as terrorists. They cannot be "evil" if they are exercising a right well known to American history, namely, the right of rebellion. To describe them with nonpejorative terms is to suggest that those killing U.S. troops are "freedom fighters" engaged in armed conflict for a just cause, that is, to expel a foreign army from their country. To think of America's Iraqi attackers as rebels, rather than terrorists, is additionally disagreeable to the war party, because it suggests that Iraq is a rerun of Vietnam, a conflict in which the United States was bloodied and defeated. The "terrorist" label, by contrast, may help repress the politically damaging thought that the United States is entangled in a bloody counterinsurgency that will be immensely difficult to prosecute successfully.

In any case, some Americans who longed for vengeance after 9/11 supported the invasion of Iraq because they confused Iraq and Al Qaeda (or Saddam Hussein and Osama bin Laden). But what about those government officials who deliberately purveyed this confusion in order to build popular support for a war they desired on other grounds? Their action was rational or irrational depending on the rationality or irrationality of the thought processes that led them to advocate the war in the first place. We cannot aspire to a definitive account of the real motive behind the Iraq war. Many actors, with conflicting motives, were involved in the decision-making process. The decision to invade resulted from what philosophers call an "overlapping consensus." No single subgroup inside the executive branch, with a clear reason for supporting the invasion, could have launched the war on its own. That a sufficient number of them gave the go-ahead for war does not imply that they all agreed upon a single overriding objective. It implies only that everyone who approved the decision believed that the invasion served some important interest. There were many such interests besides helping Israel and securing access to Gulf oil. These no doubt included completing the unfinished Gulf War of 1991, discouraging minor powers from defying the United States, experimenting with smaller and swifter invasion forces, decamping from Prince Sultan airbase in Saudi Arabia, showing that the United States could absorb military casualties without flinching, and violently destabilizing the Middle East to overcome decades of stalemate and then "to see what happens." So, different rationales brought different decision makers on board. If this account is valid, then the invasion lacked a single dominant rationale.

But such an account does not exclude the possibility that obscure psychological pressures, triggered by 9/11, also played a role. War fever might have been stoked, inside the administration, by an incoherent pluralism of emotions and fixations as well as an incoherent pluralism of reasons.

DELUSIONS OF THE POWERFUL

Before exploring further the unbalanced thought processes that may have contributed to the decision to invade Iraq, it will help to look briefly at the budgetary and bureaucratic interests of the American defense establishment, including both the Pentagon and the arms industry. Why has the Bush administration chosen a predominantly military solution to a problem that lends itself better to a mixed strategy with greater emphasis on international police and intelligence cooperation and the tightening up of nonproliferation treaties than on military invasion and occupations? At the

STEPHEN HOLMES

end of the cold war, the U. S. defense establishment was faced with the question of how to retain high levels of defense spending in the absence of a militarily powerful enemy state. The Department of Defense's civilian leadership found an unanticipated answer to this question on 9/11. If the military could wrest primary control in "the war on terror" from law enforcement and intelligence agencies, it could justify massive defense spending. The only problem with this plan is that the Department of Defense is not well positioned to lead the war on terror. True, the Pentagon could and did pour discretionary resources into standing up highly mobile hunter-killer teams. But this certainly accounts for only a tiny percentage of our national-defense spending, most of which goes for programs designed to defend against no-longer-existent threats. Moreover, the Department of Defense has little or no experience in collaborating with law-enforcement and intelligence establishments around the world, where most of the professionals knowledgeable about radical Sunni terrorism work. The war on terrorism depends, above all, on accurate intelligence, and accurate intelligence requires deep cultural and political knowledge about remote lands and peoples. The Pentagon did not, and still does not, have inside its own bureaucracy anything like the level of detailed and accurate knowledge of the world necessary to conduct an effective counterterrorism strategy. But the Department of Defense nevertheless won the interagency power struggle. By so doing, it foisted on the country its interpretation of the terrorist threat, an interpretation that, against any reasonable assessment, made a loose-knit terrorist network appear especially vulnerable to a concentrated military strike.

To justify taking a lead role in the war on terror, the civilian leadership at the Department of Defense and their White House supporters came up with the "hand-off" scenario. A rogue state, they hypothesized, might secretly transfer a WMD to a terrorist group who could, in turn, use it against the United States. Such a state sponsor of terrorism could be effectively taken out by the Department of Defense. What is most striking about this little narrative is that, if a nuclear hand-off from a rogue state were the major threat facing the United States, then the agency to take the lead in counterterrorism would logically be the Department of Defense. This coincidence suggests that the bureaucratic interest of the Department of Defense's civilian leadership influenced their decision to depict the terrorist threat in a certain way. Their depiction was not based on a neutral assessment, but rather tailored to advance the interests of one government agency over its rivals.

Before 9/11, some members of the administration planned to invade Iraq to prevent Saddam Hussein from developing WMDs, which he could then use to blackmail neighbors and even the United States in his search for domination of Gulf oil reserves. At that stage, however, proponents of war with Iraq doubted that the need to forestall nuclear blackmail by an anti-American dictator would suffice to kindle political support. They therefore planned to invoke "humanitarian" reasons as well, rehearsing a litany of Saddam's sickening crimes. Bush's own electorate may not have been especially keen to save a distant people from a distant tyrant. But many influential American opinion makers, of a liberal-internationalist persuasion, could be co-opted or at least silenced by stressing the humanitarian rationale for war.

The attacks of 9/11 changed the political landscape and opened up new opportunities for proponents of war with Iraq. For one thing, 9/11 provided two powerful new pretexts for war (revenge and immediate self-defense) alongside of the rather weak rationales of long-term self-defense and humanitarianism. These new rationales would obviously be sufficient to ready the public for invasion. Riding this wave, the administration began to stress the possibility that Saddam would pass his WMDs to a terrorist group. That is to say, it replaced a blackmail scenario, which assumed that Saddam would keep his WMDs, with a hand-off scenario, which assumed that he would give them away.

But this fine-tuning of the storyline may have had several causes. Bureaucratic interests can no doubt generate a skewed assessment of threats. But an additional impulse to war may have come from a deep psychological urge, what Jowitt himself might call a visceral desire to re-imagine an impalpable threat as a palpable threat. This, at the very least, is a hypothesis worth exploring further. Oil reserves, Israel, and Pentagon budgets were weighty factors. But the invasion may have never taken place were it not for "battlefront nostalgia." We can discern signs of such a longing for a palpable battlefront, where an elusive enemy can be confronted and defeated, in Vice President Dick Cheney's startling claim that Iraq is "the geographical base of the terrorists" who attacked the United States on 9/11 ("Meet the Press" interview by Tim Russert, aired on NBC, September 14, 2003).

President George W. Bush, too, has repeatedly said that Iraq is *the frontline* in the war on terror. The problem with this statement is that the war on terror, by definition, has no battlefront. Our terrorist foes are dispersed and highly mobile. After the Afghan operation, they had no obvious geographical base. This is why they cannot be conclusively defeated by a concentrated military onslaught. This is why our massive military superiority is not decisive in the war on terror. It is immensely frustrating, admittedly,

254   STEPHEN HOLMES

for the world's only superpower to be faced with an enemy whom it cannot crushingly defeat. But the psychological stress our vulnerability causes can be relieved, to some extent, by a fantasy drawn in the air. For instance, we might imagine that our highly dispersed enemies will decide to concentrate their forces in one place where we can destroy them. Talk like this was common in administration circles during the run-up to the Iraq war. The claim that Iraq is not simply part of the war on terror but actually the central battleground in the war on terror could simply be a ploy to reassure the public that its elected leaders are destined to prevail. But it might also evince something equally human, namely, wishful thinking. The hardheaded advocates of war may have unconsciously misinterpreted an impalpable threat as a palpable threat because they needed, for psychological reasons, to reassure themselves.

THE WHIMSIES OF PREEMPTION

To prepare for a storm when the sea is still calm asks a great deal of human nature. The doctrine of preemption is based on the empirically sound observation that the U.S. government, in particular, tends to let problems fester and usually manages to respond only when a crisis erupts. It would be more rational to deal with problems when they first appear, before they deepen and become more difficult to manage. The Afghan training camps operating freely during the 1990s are a case in point. The existence of camps where Islamic militants vowing to kill Americans were being trained to use explosives was well known. But it was politically impossible, at the time, to rouse political support for decisive military action. After 9/11, the Bush administration declared that it was changing the ground rules. Henceforth, threats would be nipped in the bud.

This seems rational enough. But appearances can be deceptive. The danger of preparing for the wrong storm, or for a storm destined to dissipate on its own, may be just as great as the danger of not preparing for a storm at all. Without better intelligence than it apparently has at its disposal, the United States will be condemned to one wild-goose chase after another. Operationalized, "preemption" means that the United States need not explain its threat assessment to any other nation (this would apparently signal a betrayal of U.S. sovereignty) and, by extension, that the administration need not explain its threat assessment to Congress, the courts, the press, or the public. But if the executive branch stops giving reasons for its actions, it may eventually begin to act without having reasons for its actions. Something similar may have already occurred. In any case, as Jowitt again has suggested, the doctrine of preemption opens the process of prioritizing threats to arbitrary intuitions, cognitive biases, and profiteering interests. Moreover, "preemption" also means, in practice, that no intelligence agency can suffer greatly for providing rotten intelligence, because punishment would make agents reluctant to stick out their necks and make guesses on the basis of flimsy, patched-together evidence. So the administration has committed itself doctrinally to increasing its unfiltered intake of disinformation.

That the underlying motives driving the architects and promoters of the Iraq war may have been less than perfectly rational is also suggested by their neglect of opportunity costs. At the very root of the administration's counterterrorism strategy lies the following thought. To know how to behave in our new security environment, we must multiply the probability of the threat by the gravity of the threat. Thus, even a very small chance of a catastrophic event (especially a nuclear bomb exploding in an American urban center) requires immediate aggressive action by the United States. We cannot wait until we are sure that the threat is real. We must "prespond," not merely respond. When we are dealing with nuclear terrorism, false negatives are infinitely more dangerous than false positives. This is why counterterrorism forces us to abandon that pillar of due process, the presumption of innocence.

Such worst-case reasoning suggested that Saddam Hussein must be toppled immediately because he might possibly have WMDs, or might possibly be able to acquire them, and might possibly hand such devastating weapons over to a terrorist group that, in turn, might possibly use them on the United States. This is an exceedingly roundabout justification for the use of lethal force. In domestic law, for example, you cannot invoke a right to self-defense by claiming that you were only defending yourself when you killed someone because he, in the future, might have sold a gun to someone else who, in turn, might at some unspecified time have murdered you. Rather than pleading "necessity" after acting on such reasoning, a preemptive self-defender would be better off pleading insanity. But analogous reasoning seems to have played an important role in the decision to invade Iraq. Preemption was not simply a pretext invented to gull the public. A 1-percent chance of a mass casualty event provides greater reason for unleashing lethal force than a 99-percent chance of a modestly harmful event. The problem with this "logic" is that there existed, in 2002, a small possibility of a catastrophic event in dozens of other places in the world as well. Worst-case reasoning, in other words, does not help establish priorities (why Iraq before North Korea?) or dictate where to apply scarce

STEPHEN HOLMES

resources most effectively. This is why worst-case reasoning becomes a Trojan horse for pre-rational commitments, immunizing them from rational examination and critical oversight.

If our enemy is dispersed and the gravest threats we face can come from any direction at any time, it cannot possibly be rational for the United States to tie down 90 percent of its national-security assets in one place. We cannot know in advance where the next danger may emerge. Therefore, we must always keep some of our powder dry and have a considerable reserve force at the ready. The possibility of catastrophic terrorism does not suspend the laws of scarcity. It is unwise to shoot first and aim afterwards, which is what preemption in effect requires, for the simple reason that our supplies of ammunition are never unlimited. Giving the executive branch a blank check to respond in any way it wishes to any possible national-security threat will have the same effect as institutionalizing soft-budget constraints. It will encourage irrational, excessive, and misplaced spending. The Iraq war has shown how an unrivaled military can be overstretched and, indeed, almost broken. This is why the danger of acting may sometime be greater than the danger of not acting, even in an age of nuclear terrorism.

REAWAKENING TO A NUCLEAR NIGHTMARE

What about the self-defense rationale for the war? It turned out that Saddam Hussein had no significant stockpiles of chemical and biological weapons. Nor did Iraq have an ongoing program to produce nuclear weapons. Because of the obvious threat from Iran, moreover, Iraq had reasons to engage in a clandestine disinformation campaign, bluffing to suggest that it did perhaps have WMDs even though it did not.

If Saddam had held large stockpiles of chemical and biological weapons under his tight control, then what would have happened once the U.S. military broke the back of the Baathist regime? Massive quantities of biological and chemical toxins would have sluiced through the smuggling routes that crisscrossed Iraq's borders. They would have quickly found their way into the international clandestine arms market, as have the high-yield explosives, automatic weapons, and shoulder-fired ground-to-air missiles looted from unguarded Iraqi storage depots after the invasion.

But the administration's failure to take precautions against a possible postwar proliferation catastrophe does not mean that self-defense from WMDs had nothing to do with the decision to invade. It is perfectly possible, even probable, that key decision makers in the administration thought that the real urgency in attacking Iraq was political, not military. They were in power at the time and knew that they might not be in power later on. Immediately after 9/11, they also realized, presumably, that public support for military action would never be greater. How could they let this brief window of opportunity slip by? Perhaps they had to mislead Congress and the public into believing that the threat from Saddam was genuinely imminent. But such a white lie is only what higher patriotism demands.

This version of administration gaming seems plausible enough. But it downplays several puzzling factors. First of all, why would an administration that declares itself intent on preventing nuclear materials from falling into the hands of terrorists have paid so little attention to the grave danger posed by loose nuclear materials strewn across the former Soviet Union? Indeed, it initially reduced the funding of the Nunn-Lugar program devoted to addressing this problem. Moreover, Bush has proposed creating a whole new generation of small-size nuclear bombs that would be ideal for sneaking into an urban center if they ever fell into terrorist hands.

So why would an administration that has behaved so casually about proliferation simultaneously act as if it were panicked by the thought of proliferation? Perhaps the political pressure to respond violently to 9/11 was so overpowering that it blinded the war party to sources of proliferation that could not be associated with Arab-Islamic anti-Americanism and that could not be taken out by a military strike. Formulated differently, 9/11 may have interacted with a preexistent fixation on Iraq to crystallize a vague fear about nuclear terrorism that was previously intuited but not strongly felt.

After 9/11, moreover, our top leaders began to be reminded, at every morning briefing, that the city in which they live with their families might be incinerated without warning at any moment. Speeches by key members of the administration, strikingly enough, suggest that they do not associate 9/11 with New York City. They see it, instead, as a decapitation strike aimed to kill the nation's leaders. (They know about decapitation strikes, having planned one against Iraq.) So, they took the 9/11 attacks quite personally. Listen to Vice President Cheney describe the enemy:

> And they know no restraint. There's no reason in the world why they would hold back and not use something like that [chemical, biological, or nuclear weapons] if they could get their hands on it. So the biggest threat we face today is the possibility of a terrorist cell setting up shop inside one of our own cities, with one of those truly deadly weapons—a biological agent of some kind, say, or even a nuclear weapon— that cost perhaps hundreds of thousands of lives, not just 3,000, if they were to launch such an attack. It's a whole different scale

STEPHEN HOLMES

of threat, a different kind of problem than we've had to deal with in the past [Remarks and question-and-answer session at a Town Hall meeting, Embassy Suites Hotel, Des Moines, Iowa, September 7, 2004].

What psychologically destabilized those in the administration's innermost circle was the realization, previously banished to the periphery of consciousness, that nuclear weapons might actually be used, and used against them.

The threat of a nuclear decapitation strike, because it cannot be deterred, may shake the leaders of a superpower to the core and even drive them to the brink of unreason. Al Qaeda exposes our helplessness and vulnerability in a way that the much more powerful Soviet Union did not. Here lies the essence of asymmetrical war: Al Qaeda can use a nuclear weapon against the United States to devastating effect, while the United States cannot return the favor. What 9/11 almost immediately brought to the minds of top officials, we now know, was the terrible possibility of a suitcase nuke in the nation's capital. The resulting panic, in turn, may have triggered an irrational response, namely, a lashing out at a despised dictatorship which had repeatedly defied the United States but had little capacity to fight back. Lashing out allowed the administration to send a signal to the American electorate that it was doing something dramatic in response to 9/11. It may also have provided psychological solace to the decision makers themselves. How could they be expected simply to sit and wait for the delivery of a nuclear inferno to their own "home base"?

Another reason why the nightmare scenario of a suitcase nuke in Washington, D.C., did not make administration officials act consistently, across the board, to slow down proliferation was that they could have done this only by strengthening the international treaties on arms control and nonproliferation, treaties they were ideologically devoted to dismantling. So dogmatism may also have played a role. In any case, the fear of a suitcase nuke apparently introduced a strain of edginess and jumpiness into their foreign policy. The urgency of the need, mixed explosively with the unlikelihood of ever feeling safe again, may have provided the last indispensable push to war.

ASSIMILATING THE UNKNOWN TO THE KNOWN

Is the United States, once again, at war with "totalitarianism"? Are we facing "Islamic fascism," as some neoconservatives contend? Do we find ourselves once again in a global struggle between freedom and tyranny? Did the 9/11 terrorists attack us because we are a democracy? This last possibility is unlikely for several reasons, not the least of which is that these same terrorists who attacked us have singled out for their most intense hatred Saudi Arabia, a country that is certainly not a democracy.

Tyranny and terrorism are not the same. Nor will a war with one resemble a war with the other. One signal that the administration has adapted only shakily to the post-9/11 security environment it that it is still endeavoring to assimilate the war on terrorism with the war on communism. When trying, not long after 9/11, to reassure Americans that we would respond forcefully to the 9/11 attacks, Under Secretary of Defense Paul Wolfowitz said that dictators always underestimate America's strength. What is remarkable about this statement is Wolfowitz's seemingly unthinking leap from terrorists to dictators.

The takedown of Saddam's statue in Baghdad was stage-managed to evoke memories of the spontaneous toppling the statue of Felix Dzerzhinsky in Lubyanka Square in August 1991. The televised reenactment helps us understand why the administration shifted U.S. forces from the chase after Osama bin Laden to the invasion of Iraq. It is not merely that Iraq had more targets than Afghanistan. Rather, Saddam made a much better target than Osama. For one thing, as the leader of a state, Saddam had statues that could be pulled down. No state has erected statues in honor of Osama; in compensation, his image is emblazoned on millions of T-shirts throughout the Muslim world. The problem for Wolfowitz and the others was obvious. The United States could topple a statue, but it could not topple millions of T-shirts.

Searching for a new "paradigm" to help orient American policy makers after the cold war, Samuel Huntington famously suggested that Americans should transfer their existential enmity from the now-defunct USSR to the "upsurging" Muslim world. American minds had been imbued with Manichaeanism by the cold war. They naturally understood the world as a battleground between good and evil. It was only a matter of placing the international Islamic community into the slot vacated by world communism. Huntington's "musical chairs" approach to shifting geopolitical threats to the United States closely tracks American policy after 9/11. The administration did not respond to 9/11 by tearing up the rulebook and radically rethinking U.S. national security policy. Rather, it clung to old patterns of thought and action and tried to pour the new terrorist danger into the old bottle of antidemocratic tyranny.

The exaggerated focus on rogue states, in other words, may also have an ideological source. States that harbor terrorists, the administration

STEPHEN HOLMES

announced in the immediate aftermath of 9/11, will be held fully responsible for the terrorists they harbor. This is reasonable, as far as it goes. But it may also express mental rigidity, wishful thinking, and the persistence of cold war habits of thought in the face of changed realities. True, states are still the most important actors in international affairs. But terrorist organizations such as Al Qaeda may have evolved to a point where they have little further need of extensive or ongoing state sponsorship. Al Qaeda, as Jowitt reminds us, does not have global power, but only global reach. Moreover, it obtained its global reach not from rogue states but from us. Far from pacifying violent conflicts at the periphery, globalization provides a new vehicle for spreading them to the center. We cannot turn back the clock and pull the global transportation, communication, banking, and arms-sales networks out from beneath our vowed enemies' feet. In addition, terrorist gangs are probably more dependent today on private religious charities and the unregulated arms market than on rogue states. While the Pentagon is well-equipped to destroy rogue states, it is no better equipped to destroy rogue religious charities and rogue arms markets than it is ready to roll back globalization. Ideology also enters the picture. This is because the worldview of this administration cannot easily admit that private religious charities and unregulated markets pose serious problems for American national security. Its entire public philosophy assumes that the world will be better off with more private religious charities and more unregulated markets. To admit that both are Trojan horses for "evil" would explode its conservative worldview.

LAW AS WEAKNESS

In his January 20, 2004, State of the Union address, Bush said, "After the chaos and carnage of September the 11th, it is not enough to serve our enemies with legal papers." Implicit in this pronouncement is a theory about the relation between law and security. The basic idea here is that law is a completely inadequate instrument for confronting terrorism. This is because law, allegedly, makes the government weaker. Due process is said to reduce flexibility and tie the government's hands. Legal rules designed to protect individuals, for example, are blamed for preventing government agencies from cooperatively sharing information about terrorists. Anti-legalists in the administration generally present procedural safeguards for individuals as making the country less safe. The terrorists who tried to knock down the World Trade Center in 1993 were prosecuted and tried to the full extent of the law. But this legal treatment did nothing to deter a second and successful attack. Law is of little use in fighting terrorism, according to this line of thought, because law is backward-looking, designed to punish perpetrators for past misdeeds. True, law enforcement managed to incapacitate some twenty-nine terrorist supporters and conspirators in the 1990s. But during the same period training camps in Afghanistan managed to spawn 70,000 more. This is an unacceptable ratio. What we need today, therefore, is a forward-looking approach, designed not to punish perpetrators but to prevent future attacks.

But how plausible is this analysis? Does law actually make government weak? That legalism can sometimes be used to paralyze the executive branch and interfere with its ability to respond to threats from abroad was made obvious by the Republicans' impeachment of Bill Clinton. But can we reasonably blame law itself for such a partisan use of law?

The administration's aversion to legalism has several sources. One of the most important is its commitment to "preemption." Preemption means that we must unleash lethal force on the basis of hearsay testimony, that is, before alleged facts have been double-checked and sketchy rumors have matured into reliable evidence. Legalism would permit no such thing. Nor would it give government the right to execute suspects, which is what American hunter-killer squads are now doing around the world. Even JAG lawyers object to this activity. They protest especially about the inevitable cases of mistaken identity. But the stakes are so high, administration supporters argue, that we must drop our ordinary scruples. We should simply view those unlucky individuals who are mistakenly assassinated as collateral damage in the war on terror.

Putting the wisdom of extra-judicial executions aside, there is no reason to accept the unrealistic picture of law implicit in this general approach. Historically, law has seldom been a tool of the weak. On the contrary, it has almost always been a tool of the strong. ("Corporations do not break laws, they make laws" is not the whole story, but it points in the right direction.) If law sometimes sets limits on the discretion of law-enforcement personnel, this is presumably because powerful forces in society have wanted to subject armed law-enforcement personnel to a strict discipline, for fear agents of power might otherwise use their discretion for ends ultimately damaging to the powerful themselves.

The political imperative to "connect the dots" entails intense pressure to act on the basis of fragmentary evidence. It will necessarily result, some of the time, in misconnecting the dots and constructing imaginary castles in the air. It will give teeth and claws to paranoia. It will send police officers on wild-goose chases, preventing a rational allocation of scarce manpower.

It will discourage arresting officers from separating the wheat from the chaff at the point of capture, thereby filling detention centers such as Guantánamo Bay with low-level prisoners of no intelligence value. The cognitive challenge of detective work is to discriminate, at the outset, between promising and unpromising leads. Preemption, whatever it means, cannot erase the practical importance of this discrimination.

But does law not tie the hands of the police in their attempt to catch and kill terrorists? Not exactly. The main tool in the arsenal of counterterrorist officials, to cite Jowitt yet again, is not the gun but the snitch. The key to counterterrorism is timely and accurate information. This insight leads to a revaluation of law's role in fighting terrorism. One of the main objects of criminal procedure is to protect the system against disinformation stemming from witness malice. Many of the rights of the accused—including the right to counsel, the right to "discovery," the right to compulsory process and to cross-examine adverse witnesses, and so forth—are meant to filter out disinformation. If the Department of Justice announces that it will put people in jail and throw away the key on the basis of anonymous tips that it does not bother to double-check, guess what will happen? The police will be flooded with false tips motivated by personal rivalry or animosity. Procedures designed to winnow out disinformation take into account the elasticity of supply of crackpot informants. Throwing normal evidentiary standards to the winds will not make the police more "flexible." It will drown the police in a sea of disinformation.

Admittedly, the United States was not prepared for 9/11. But the fault for this lack of preparedness cannot be fairly laid at the door of law or excessive liberalism in criminal procedure. The country was not prepared because of a universal complacency about the gathering threat that afflicted both parties, the press, and the public at large. The country was unprepared because of a lack of Arabic fluency inside intelligence and law-enforcement communities. The country was unprepared because of turf wars inside the executive branch, interagency conflicts having nothing to do with judicial or legislative oversight. There is no point in blaming "law" for these deplorable flaws.

SOVEREIGNTY AS AUTISM

International law cannot settle the world's conflicts. But neither is it possible to enhance U.S. security without voluntary cooperation from other countries. There is no such thing as unilateral antiproliferation. There is no such thing as unilateral counterterrorism. These are contradictions in terms. To fight terrorism, the United States needs extensive linguistic and cultural knowledge about remote and inaccessible parts of the world. This knowledge exists, but most of it resides in the heads of non-Americans, whose cooperation we must assiduously seek. The limited capacity of Americans to communicate effectively with the rest of the world therefore poses an inadequately recognized danger to our national security.

All politics are local. Viewed from the locality of Washington, D.C., the debate between unilateralists and multilateralists is a struggle between the Pentagon and the State Department for control of U.S. foreign policy in "the age of terror." The Pentagon has decisively won this interagency power struggle. It has therefore succeeded, as already mentioned, in imposing its unusual interpretation of the terrorist threat on the administration and the nation. Department of Defense dominance in America's approach to terrorism has created considerable strains with Europe, the region of the world currently most at risk of transnational terrorist attacks. One source of the tension is that everywhere in Europe counterterrorism is managed by law enforcement and intelligence, not by the military.

Indeed, nowhere is the administration's failure to adapt to the new post–cold war security environment more visible than its repeated insinuations that Europe is a "security pygmy," incapable of bringing anything to the table in the war against terrorism. True, Europe is a military pygmy. But it is not a security pygmy, because the principal threats that face the West cannot be countered militarily. Having survived the cold war under an American military umbrella, the Europeans channeled most of their security spending into law enforcement and intelligence. After the end of the superpower standoff and the beginning of the war on terror, this nonmilitary investment has paid off. To dismantle terrorist networks, it greatly helps to have highly trained counterterrorist units with deep cultural and linguistic knowledge. The Europeans, and especially the French, are far ahead of the United States in this field. To scorn their cooperation would be so self-defeating that the United States and France continue to cooperate quietly on a police level in the war on terror. But the Iraq war has nevertheless introduced serious and growing strains into European-American relations.

Jowitt argues persuasively that the growing divide between the United States and Europe is a form of cultural self-mutilation. America and Europe share a common cultural heritage and common liberal-democratic principles. Even taken together, he argues, they are a tiny cultural minority that controls much of the world's wealth. It would be self-crippling for them not to work together to protect their common interests in a turbulent world.

STEPHEN HOLMES

But Jowitt delves even deeper into this issue. An individual who lives alone and never communicates with others, he analogizes, becomes autistic and disconnected from reality. Self-insulation, for nations too, is unlikely to breed realism. Only revivified relations with our "cultural kin" in Europe can provide a reality check and save us from a debilitating autism. Only such civilizational partners can provide the emotional support the United States needs to think straight about complex and evolving threats. American television has shown a completely different Iraq war than was seen on European television (not to mention Arab satellite TV). How can the United States act intelligently in the world if American citizens have a picture of the world that bears no resemblance to the picture of the world that their counterparts in allied nations have in their minds? It is a question not of submitting to the opinions of others but of having some modest understanding of what others, enemies as well as allies, think and why.

BLITZKRIEG DEMOCRACY

Does the administration want to hurt Arabs or help them? Luring Al Qaeda terrorists into Iraq so that we can fight them on Iraqi streets rather than on American streets does not seem the best way to build a model democracy. Wars of punishment and prevention make much more sense, Jowitt argues, than wars of conversion by occupation. Defeating and disarming Saddam was a reasonable goal. But spreading American values at gunpoint was not. Coercing the Iraqis to conform their outward behavior to an American political model verges on the unintelligible, although it has the advantage of allowing the administration to associate the novel war on terror with a more familiar war on tyranny.

Bernard Lewis has accused of being a racist anyone who doubts that Iraq can become a democracy. But obstacles to Iraqi democracy stem from history, not biology. Iraq will be hard to democratize for the same reason that it was easy to conquer militarily. It is very difficult, in a pluralistic society, to establish a government that is simultaneously representative and coherent. Saddam's government achieved some degree of coherence precisely because it was not representative of the entire society but was rather based on a Sunni subgroup, in fact, a Tikriti clan. That a political system which is both coherent and representative will be extraordinarily difficult to create in Iraq is the least that might be said.

This is not to deny the sophistication of the theory behind the administration's announced plan to democratize the Middle East. One of the principal functions of democracy is to channel social grievances inside the system so that they can be processed in a peaceful way without endangering the lives of the rich and powerful. If grievances are left to fester outside the system, they may explode in uncontrollable forms of wildcat or even revolutionary violence. In the Middle East, if social grievances are left unattended to, angry young men may channel their frustration into an international jihad against the United States. Two-tiered societies, Jowitt says, are ripe for what he calls "movements of rage." It will be much better for America if the infuriating elite/mass gap is somewhat reduced and groups hostile to the status quo are given a "political horizon." The idea is to coax oppressive regimes into gradual reform, giving those who feel aggrieved a chance to vent their complaints and receive some remedy inside their domestic political order. If successful, such reforms will take the wind out of bin Laden's sails.

For a seminar in democratic theory, this is undoubtedly an interesting argument. But it is not very useful as a guide to practice. For one thing, no agency in the U.S. government has any idea how to promote democracy. For another thing, U.S. influence in weak states and backward economies depends essentially on an elite/mass gap. This is especially true now, when the terrorist threat has led the United States to jack up its support for nontransparent and unaccountable security apparatuses around the world.

Moreover, even if elections are held throughout Iraq, there is virtually no chance that a system will emerge in which distinct nationwide parties will peacefully enter and leave office on a rotating basis. Democracy is not only about periodic elections. It is also about rotations of power. It therefore requires the country to be organized in a certain way. Incumbents have to feel confident that they will not suffer excessively in their persons and property once they relinquish office. This is a historically rare state of affairs. As a result, democracy is a historically rare political regime.

Rotations of power, what the French call *l'alternance,* are also unlikely to become routine in a society with a fixed Shiite majority and a Sunni minority. The fault line in Iraq is not between terrorism and democracy. Instead it lies between a traditionally dominant but now politically shattered Sunni minority and a traditionally subordinate but now on-the-rise Shiite majority. The Shiite obviously view elections as a pathway to Shiite domination. The Sunnis view it the same way. That is why the Shiites seem devoted to popular government, while the Sunnis continue to plant roadside bombs.

A sign that the administration has not managed this issue very successfully is its attempt to produce a multidenominational and multiethnic police and military in Iraq by means of "training." Training can affect skill, but

STEPHEN HOLMES

it is unlikely to effect loyalty. What will stop the newly trained recruits from running off with their weapons to join their tribal or ethnic or religious leader? The chances for creating a highly cohesive militarized branch of the state bureaucracy, whose members will dutifully follow the central government and ignore the wishes of their own clan or group, are very small. The proof is that Iraq's extremely weak central government today has to put up with perfectly independent Kurd and Shiite militias.

Finally, something more should be said about the mixed motives of the United States in promoting Iraqi democracy. That some democratization advocates are perfectly sincere is neither here nor there. All that a skeptic need point out is that certain key actors on the American side, such as Dick Cheney and Donald Rumsfeld, do not seem like proselytizers on fire with Jowitt's "holy grail zeal." Their commitment to a missile shield signals a desire to separate the United States from the world, not to remake the world in the United States' image. They have shown little inclination to invite the inhabitants of near or distant ghettos to their banquet. Converting Iraqis to the American way of life is certainly less vital to them than preventing foreign governments from defying U.S. wishes. They are more concerned to police the jungle than to civilize it.

If we take this line of argument to its logical conclusion, we might conclude that "democracy" has a hidden meaning in the administration's vocabulary. It may be a stick with which to beat the enemy, rather than a blueprint with which to reconstruct the enemy's polity. This is the way "democracy" functioned in the thought of hawks during the cold war. There is no special reason to believe that hawks think about it any differently today.

A JOWITTIAN QUESTIONNAIRE

Can the West fight radical Islamic terrorism and remain true to its core principles? Can an open society protect itself from the threat of WMD terrorism without closing its gates to talented and knowledgeable foreigners, thereby undermining the very sources of its wealth, social effervescence, and military strength? Will fear of contamination lead the United States to replace Jowitt's supple "boundaries" with impassable "barricades," isolating itself from the skills and energies of the rest of the planet? Will unreasoning faith in the universality of American values foster destabilizing military adventurism in the name of democracy? Will a fundamental misunderstanding of our new security environment further erode America's psychologically stabilizing relations with Europe? Will the prominence of the terrorist threat gradually transform the U.S. executive branch into a giant counterterrorist organization, silencing the judiciary and turning the legislature into a rubber stamp? Will our largely liberal public philosophy be replaced with a largely antiliberal public philosophy?

After some ups and downs, America managed to maintain its liberal identity behind the barricades of the cold war. But the United States held onto its liberalism together with its Western allies, while remaining open to much of the world. The ultimate threat posed by the terrorism of our nightmares today is mimetic antiliberalism, the possibility that we will become, as George Kennan warned in a different context, as "intolerant, secretive, suspicious and cruel" as our enemies. Bets are still out. There is much we cannot predict. But the principal question we want answered is now fairly clear: Will the shock of 9/11, filtered through the distorting lenses of partisan interests and individual psychology, end up enshrining dogmatic megalomania into an American virtue and demoting a skeptical sense of limits into an American vice?

STEPHEN HOLMES

14

THE POWER OF IMAGINATIVE ANALOGY

Communism, Faith, and Leadership

DANIEL CHIROT

en Jowitt's outstanding quality is his ability to grasp the essence of
a political situation and find an analogy, a verbal image that so perfectly captures its meaning that his listeners or readers will immediately understand. His are not merely colorful phrases—though they are
often that, too. They are flashes of profound insight that clarify very complex
situations and, at their best, suggest whole models that even demanding
positivists can use to explain and predict. This is what Vladimir Tismaneanu,
Rudra Sil, and Stephen E. Hanson want to tell us in their essays, by pointing out that Ken's imagination is actually one of the best guides in contemporary comparative political analysis, and also a remarkably successful
way of predicting outcomes.

When I met him in Bucharest in 1970, Ken Jowitt was a junior professor; I was a graduate student trying to understand Romania's troubled history and murky politics. Ken was more sympathetic to leftist third-world
causes then than he would be later, although even then his sense of realism kept him free of the mindless Marxism that was infecting our generation of social scientists. He was never blind to the realities of what was
happening in the communist world. He did believe that these kinds of
regimes were undergoing a critical breakthrough to modernity, and that
Romania could be a model for other third-world socialist autocracies, but
he was never fooled into believing that Marxist class analysis could shed
much light on the process.

"It's nationalism and the Soviet development model together," he explained when I told him that I was puzzled by the contradictions in Nicolae Ceauşescu's foreign and domestic policies. Later everyone came to understand that Leninist regimes could obtain a measure of legitimacy and survive only by playing up hypernationalism. At that time, however, this had not yet been understood by many analysts, who, based on their different analyses of Marx, still thought that there were doctrinal differences between different communist regimes rather than simply conflicting nationalist agendas. That was particularly so on the academic left, which at that time was engaging in arcane debates about what Marx had really meant and whether or not Franz Fanon had correctly interpreted the "holy texts."

On the other side, in 1970, many policy makers and supposedly informed experts had somehow come to believe that because he was occasionally mildly anti-Soviet and pro-Western, the Romanian dictator was a liberal reformer. I don't think Ken was ever fooled. He was one of the first to recognize that, on the contrary, communist Romania's brand of nationalism was, if anything, more fiercely autarkic and totalitarian than that of the more cynical bloc countries like Hungary who were quite willing to bow down to the Russians as long as they didn't have to bully their own population too much. Ceauşescu had no particular affection for liberalism or Western development models, and his anti-Sovietism was a reflection of his disgust with what he thought were Soviet failures to maintain the right model.

As Katherine Verdery and Gail Kligman point out in their essay, Romania was a revolutionary regime, collectivization was essential to accelerate progress, and so-called liberal reforms were a sham. They were meant to attract Western political support, investment, and technology, but at home it was more important to win over Romania's intellectuals and professionals, whose right-wing xenophobic views fit so well Ceauşescu's own. The population was meant to receive a few tidbits, but the real aim was full socialist development, not a gradual slide into the kind of semi-market reforms being tried by the Hungarians and Poles.

Later, in the 1980s, when it became obvious that Ceauşescu was in no sense a liberal, Ken was not surprised, though it would take the State Department years more to figure it out.

Shortly after Ceauşescu's visit to North Korea in 1971, I heard Ken utter a phrase which was later picked up by many, though never properly attributed. More than a decade after he first used it, I saw it in *The Economist*: "It's socialism in one family," Ken exclaimed, slyly parodying Stalin's famous phrase. "That's why Ceauşescu so likes Kim Il Sung." Indeed, Kim

Il Sungism combined the fierce nationalism of a small, insecure, and some-what marginalized communist power with total state control, total autarky, and god-like personal rulership. Marxism was somewhat beside the point. At the time I was taken aback. That was not what Leninism was supposed to be about—xenophobic patrimonialism—was it? Was Ken seeing some-thing everyone else was missing, that perhaps Stalin had come to under-stand, but that all the Marxist intellectuals in the West were completely missing? The modernizing patina concealed the truth from most of our eyes until much later, though I think that Ken understood it well before others. The purpose of this kind of modernization was to create national and personal power, not to move towards capitalist consumer economies.

In the event, Kim Il Sung succeeded in passing the throne on to his son. Ceauşescu failed, but not for lack of trying. It was his misfortune that his chosen heir was a drunken lout and that in 1989 Romania was surrounded by communist regimes in a state of collapse. By then, outside his family, almost no one believed in him. His fall, by the way, had one major effect far away. It convinced Kim Il Sung's inner circle and family that if they ever lost power, they would be slaughtered like their Romanian friend and admirer, so it was better to hold on at any cost than to compromise. By so doing, North Korea has succeeded in entering the "axis of evil" while Roma-nia prepares to enter Europe as the European Union's Balkan mendicant little cousin.

In the 1980s, Ken's use of his deep knowledge of Catholic theology increasingly shaped his analysis. The analogy between Marxism and reli-gion had been perceived before, by Mircea Eliade among others, but rarely by political scientists. Ken's professional peers were too blinded by their own secularism to see, as he did, that ultimately all deeply held ideology requires faith over reason. Marxism in particular requires not only impas-sioned belief to sustain itself but, for those not used to the fine points of Thomist or Augustinian philosophical debates, the arcane disputations among Marxists were assumed to be ones that could be resolved by mar-shalling social scientific arguments and data. Nothing could be further from the truth! But Ken's insights were deeper than this. Thomas Aquinas was serious about his religion, and so were the original Marxists, if not the sec-ond and third generation, who merely repeated the phrases without usu-ally believing them. Those revolutionary Marxists once in power had to combine rather abstract principles into something that could reconcile the perplexed to the discrepancies in the world. As Oleg Kharkhordin points out in his essay, this resulted in a worldview that privileged abstract revo-lutionary virtue over principle, thus justifying or at least excusing arbitrary evil in the name of a higher truth. This is precisely what the liberal Enlightenment fought against, and what the Rousseauist revolutionaries share with pre-Enlightenment Christian theological despotism. As Kharkhordin shows, it is the mode of thought that prevails in Russia today and makes genuine liberalism there impossible. To be sure, Marxism's god never promised an afterlife, so, as successive generations saw that the revolution was failing to fulfill its promises, they could not be persuaded to sustain the faith. For a time, however, the analogy with medieval Christian theology was perfectly appropriate and more insightful than either the Kremlinology or the naive acceptance of claims about successful modernization that prevailed in the field at the time.

There are few communist regimes left today, and Marxism has lost its mystical appeal, but Ken's way of understanding politics through analogies with medieval Christian philosophy is probably more important than ever. There are and will be other revolutionary dictatorships, and many will be overtly religious. This will be the case in the Islamic world, and in some parts of Christendom as well. Our analysts are generally as unable as ever to understand the profundity of faith and the importance of philosophical disputations among the intellectual elite of any faith-based movement. We could do worse to understand our troubled new world than go back to Ken's analogies. To call such extremism irrational, or criminal, is simply to miss the point of the religiosity and considerable philosophical thought that lies behind it.

One of Ken's major insights (that, unfortunately, has not been picked up but should be) also stems from his appreciation of faith. The great charismatic thinkers who created major revolutionary movements were only dimly understood by the majority of their followers. They may appear to be magically inspired, but they are hard to follow because of their originality and incomprehensible genius. Thus, they need interpreters—practical disciples who can explain the holy genius's program and execute it. This is the basis of Ken's fascination with Sherlock Holmes and his ordinary but understanding disciple Dr. Watson. The good doctor is to Holmes as Saint Paul was to Christ, as Abu Bakr and Umar were to Muhammad (they were the first two Umayyad caliphs who turned the prophet's vision into a functioning empire by interpreting his word and cementing his role as the final prophet). Hitler needed a Goebbels to explain him to the masses, a coldly calculating Himmler to turn racial hatred into the reality of mass murder, and, ultimately, the practical architect Speer to run his military industry. It was the prosaic Stalin who turned Lenin's vision into a functioning military power. Indeed, just as the practical administrative and mil-

DANIEL CHIROT

itary abilities of the Umayyads did not appeal to Ali, who wanted to continue the charismatic tradition of Muhammad, so did Stalin's administrative competence disgust Trotsky's followers, who believed in genius more than in explaining Leninism in simple terms to the new cadres and actually making the system work. Marx himself had needed the practical Engels to make his wilder predictions and historical leaps seem reasonable.

I don't think Ken was able to persuade many of his own followers that this analogy to Sherlock Holmes was more than an amusing sideline, but, actually, it remains useful and important. Who will be the charismatic revolutionaries of the twenty-first century? We already have one, Osama bin Laden, whose Dr. Watson is Dr. Ayman al-Zawahiri. This pattern has occurred over and over again, and we would do well to understand it better in order to predict what will happen to movements originated by mystical fanatics.

When Ken entitled a collection of his essays *New World Disorder,* I don't think that phrase had been used yet. We were still celebrating the new world order brought about by the fall of communism. Now the phrase is commonplace. At the same time, Ken was using the expression "movements of rage" to predict the movements that would bring about this new disorder. Today hardly anyone would deny that this is exactly what has happened, and many of our most farsighted analysts think it is going to get a lot worse. What led Ken to see this before the vast majority of his peers was that he saw the end of the cold war as the collapse of a whole era, like a geological mass extinction, that was sure to be followed by a long period of unsettled chaos. This was another of his far-fetched analogies that turned out to be prescient. Marc Morjé Howard points out that not all of Ken's dire predictions about chaos in the postcommunist world turned out to be true, largely because of the European Union's beneficial influence over most of Eastern Europe. Ken did point out how necessary this would be to avoid catastrophe, although he did not think the Europeans would understand what they needed to do. That they did, however, points to the wider fact that the West is unable to intervene in enough places with enough money or influence to avoid the spreading disorder that besets us. Ken was wrong about the future of Central Europe, but right about much of the rest of the former Soviet lands, and even more right about the future of the world in general.

Finally, in recent years Ken has been fascinated by the Normans, whose combination of Viking ruthlessness, medieval Christianity, and French feudal organization allowed them to conquer vast empires, from the British Isles to Palestine. He bemoans the lack of such an inspired, unifying movement in the West. It is, of course, politically incorrect to say something positive about the burst of European energy that produced the Crusades as well as the start of modern political organization in Europe. Ken has never been bothered by being politically incorrect. Indeed, his insight that this was the period that laid the groundwork for the later "European Miracle" that allowed the Europeans to create the modern world may be correct, although there are few academics today willing to celebrate that accomplishment.

It may be his thinking along these lines, reminiscent in some ways of Arnold Toynbee's grandiose thinking about civilizations, that finally drove Ken to abandon Berkeley and to give up trying to engage the combination of boring positivism and conformist, muddled leftism that dominate the academic social sciences. In many ways this is a loss for all of us, because today he preaches to those who love his mocking dismissal of academics but who barely understand the profound analysis that lies behind his speeches and writing.

Too many of Ken's brilliant insights are scattered in various articles, speeches, conversations, and the wonderful lectures that entranced a whole generation of Berkeley students. He now needs his own Dr. Watson to systematize and bring together all those wonderful ideas. He will not do this himself, because to someone like him that work is too tedious, but we can only hope that one of his students or a later follower will. It would be a worthwhile endeavor. Perhaps this volume is a start in that direction. Its excellent essays certainly point the way.

DANIEL CHIROT

SELECT BIBLIOGRAPHY

Amis, Martin. *Koba the Dread: Laughter and the Twenty Million.* New York: Hyperion, 2002.

Antonić, Slobodan. *Zarobljena zemlja: Srbija za vlade Slobodana Miloševića.* Belgrade: Otkrovenje, 2002.

Aron, Raymond. *Main Currents of Sociological Thought: Durkheim, Pareto, Weber.* New York: Basic Books, 1967.

Artemiev, Aleksei. *Dobrodetelnaia dusha, ili Nravouchitelnyia pravila v polzu i nauchenie iunoshestva.* St. Petersburg, 1777.

Ashley, Maurice. *England in the Seventeenth Century.* Baltimore: Penguin, 1967.

Banac, Ivo, ed. *Eastern Europe in Revolution.* Ithaca, NY: Cornell University Press, 1992.

Bates, Robert, et al., eds. *Analytic Narratives.* Princeton, NJ: Princeton University Press, 1998.

Bendix, Reinhard. "Preconditions of Development: A Comparison of Japan and Germany." In *Aspects of Social Change in Modern Japan,* ed. R. P. Dore. Princeton: Princeton University Press, 1967.

Berlin, Isaiah. *The Crooked Timber of Humanity: Chapters in the History of Ideas.* New York: Knopf, 1991.

Berliner, Joseph. *Factory and Manager in the USSR.* Cambridge, MA: Harvard University Press, 1957.

Berman, Harold. *Justice in the USSR.* 2nd ed. Cambridge, MA: Harvard University Press, 1962.

Berman, Paul. *Terror and Liberalism.* New York: Norton, 2003.

Besançon, Alain. *The Rise of the Gulag: The Intellectual Origins of Leninism.* New York: Continuum, 1981.

Bobbio, Norberto. *Thomas Hobbes and the Natural Law Tradition.* Chicago: University of Chicago Press, 1989.

Bonner, Elena. "The Remains of Totalitarianism." *New York Review of Books,* March 8, 2001.

Bourdieu, Pierre. "Legitimation and Structured Interests in Weber's Sociology of Religion." In *Max Weber, Rationality, and Modernity,* edited by Scott Lash and Sam Whimster. London: Allen & Unwin, 1987.

Brady, Henry, and David Collier, eds. *Rethinking Social Inquiry: Diverse Tools, Shared Standards.* Lanham, MD: Rowman & Littlefield, 2004.

Brzezinski, Zbigniew. "Soviet Politics: From the Future to the Past?" In *The Dynamics of Soviet Politics,* edited by Paul Cocks. Cambridge, MA: Harvard University Press, 1976.

Brzezinski, Zbigniew, and Carl Friedrich. *Totalitarianism Dictatorship and Autocracy.* Cambridge, MA: Harvard University Press, 1956.

Budding, Audrey Helfant. "Serb Intellectuals and the National Question, 1961–1991." Ph.D. diss., Harvard University, 1998.

———. "Systemic Crisis and Nationalist Mobilization: The Case of the Memorandum of the Serbian Academy." In *Cultures and Nations of Central and Eastern Europe: Essays in Honor of Roman Szproluk,* edited by Zvi Gitelman et al., 49–69. Cambridge, MA: Harvard Ukrainian Research Institute, 2000.

Bulanin, Dmitrii M.. *Antichnye traditsii v drevnerusskoi literature XI–XVI vv.* Munich: Otto Sagner, 1991.

———. *Perevody i poslaniia Maksima Greka.* Leningrad, 1984.

Bulanin, Dmitrii, ed. *Slovar' knizhnosti i knizhnikov Drevnei Rusi.* Vol. 2, part 1. Leningrad: Nauka, 1987.

Bunce, Valerie. "The Political Economy of the Brezhnev Era: The Rise and Fall of Corporatism." *British Journal of Political Science* 13 (April 1983): 129–58.

———. "The Political Economy of Postsocialism." *Slavic Review* 58, no. 4 (1999): 756–93.

———. "Should Transitologists Be Grounded?" *Slavic Review* (Spring 1995): 111–27.

———. *Subversive Institutions: The Design and the Destruction of Socialism and the State.* Cambridge: Cambridge University Press, 1999.

Burawoy, Michael. *The Politics of Production: Factory Regimes Under Capitalism and Socialism.* London: Verso, 1985.

Burg, Steven. "Political Structures." In *Yugoslavia: A Fractured Federalism,* edited by Dennison Rusinow. Washington, DC: Wilson Center Press, 1988.

Burks, R. V. *The Dynamics of Communism in Eastern Europe.* Princeton, NJ: Princeton University Press, 1961.

Bushkovitch, Paul M. *Religion and Society in Russia: The Sixteenth and Seventeenth Centuries.* Oxford: Oxford University Press, 1992.

Bynum, Caroline Walker. *Docere verbo et exemplo: An Aspect of Twelfth-Century Spirituality.* Missoula, MT: Scholars Press, 1979.

Cantor, Milton, ed. *American Workingclass Culture: Explorations in American Labor and Social History.* Westport, CT: Greenwood Press, 1979.

Čavoški, Kosta. *Slobodan protiv slobode.* Belgrade: Dosije, 1991.

Chen, Cheng. "Illiberal Nationalism in Post-Leninist States: Russia, China, Hungary and Romania." Ph.D. diss., University of Pennsylvania, 2003.

———. "The Roots of Illiberal Nationalism in Romania: A Historical Institutionalist Analysis of the Leninist Legacy." *East European Politics and Societies* 17, no. 2 (Spring 2003): 166–200.

Chirot, Daniel, ed. *The Crisis of Leninism and the Decline of the Left: The Revolutions of 1989.* Seattle: University of Washington Press, 1991.

———. "What Was Communism All About?" Review essay on *The Black Book of Communism. East European Politics and Societies* 14, no. 3 (Fall 2000): 665–75.

Cho, Suk-Jun. "The Bureaucracy." In *Korean Politics in Transition,* ed. Edward R. Wright. Seattle: University of Washington Press, 1975.

Christensen, Kit R. *The Politics of Character Development.* Westport, CT: Greenwood, 1994.

Clark, Elizabeth A. *Clement's Use of Aristotle: The Aristotelian Contribution to Clement of Alexandria's Refutation of Gnosticism.* Lewiston, NY: Edwin Mellen Press, 1977.

Clark, Katerina. "Socialist Realism With Shores: The Conventions for the Positive Hero." In *Socialist Realism Without Shores,* edited by Thomas Lahusen and Evgeny Dobrenko. Durham, NC: Duke University Press, 1997.

Cohen, Lenard. *Serpent in the Bosom: The Rise and Fall of Slobodan Milošević.* Boulder, CO: Westview Press, 2001.

Colburn, Forrest. *Post-Revolutionary Nicaragua: State, Class, and Dilemmas of Agrarian Policy.* Berkeley: University of California Press, 1986.

Comisso, Ellen. "Comments on a Ken Jowitt Retrospective." *Slavic Review* 53, no. 1 (1994): 187.

———. "Prediction Versus Diagnosis: Comments on a Ken Jowitt Retrospective." *Slavic Review* 53, no. 1 (Spring 1994): 186–92.

Conquest, Robert. *Reflections on a Ravaged Century.* New York: Norton, 2000.

Cooper, John M. "Political Animals and Civic Friendship." In *Friendship: A Philosophical Reader,* edited by Neera Kapur Badhwar. Ithaca, NY: Cornell University Press, 1993.

Courtois, Stéphane, ed. *Du passé nous faisons table rase! Histoire et mémoire du communisme en Europe.* Paris: Robert Laffont, 2002.

Crawford, Beverly, and Arend Lijphart. *Liberalization and Leninist Legacies: Comparative Perspectives on Democratic Transitions.* Berkeley: International and Area Studies, 1997.

Cyert, Richard, and James March. *A Behaviorial Theory of the Firm.* Englewood Cliffs, NJ: Prentice-Hall, 1963.

Damaskin, Ioann. *Polnoe sobranie tvorenii.* St. Petersburg, 1913.

Decalo, Samuel. *The Stable Minority: Civilian Rule in Africa, 1960–1990.* Gainesville: Florida Academic Press Books, 1998.

De George, Richard T. *Soviet Ethics and Morality.* Ann Arbor: University of Michigan Press, 1969.

DeNardo, James. *Power in Numbers.* Princeton: Princeton University Press, 1985.

Deutscher, Isaac. "Marxism and Primitive Magic." In *The Stalinist Legacy: Its Impact on 20th Century World Politics,* edited by Tariq Ali. Harmondsworth, UK: Penguin Books, 1984.

Diggins, John Patrick. *Max Weber: Politics and the Spirit of Tragedy.* New York: Basic Books, 1996.

Dinkić, Mladjan. *Ekonomija destrukcije.* Belgrade: Stubovi kulture, 1997.

Di Palma, Giuseppe. *To Craft Democracies: An Essay on Democratic Transitions.* Berkeley: University of California Press, 1990.

Djurić, Mihailo. "Smišljene smutnje." *Anali pravnog fakulteta u Beogradu* 3 (May–June 1971): 230–33.

Dobrincu, Dorin, and Constantin Iordachi, eds. *Țărănimea și puterea: Procesul de colectivizare a agriculturii în România, 1949–1962.* Iasi, Romania: Editura Polirom, 2005.

Dola, Kazimierz. "Kosciol Katolicki na Opolszczyznie w Latach, 1945–1965." *Nasza Przeszlosc* 22 (1965): 105.

Dragović-Soso, Jasna. *Saviors of the Nation: Serbia's Intellectual Opposition and the Revival of Nationalism.* London: Hurst and Company, 2002.

Draper, Theodore. *Castroism: Theory and Practice.* New York: Praeger, 1965.

Edwards, Richard. *Contested Terrain: The Transformation of the Workplace in the Twentieth Century.* London: Basic Books, 1979.

Ekiert, Grzegorz. *The State Against Society: Political Crises and Their Aftermath in East Central Europe.* Princeton: Princeton University Press, 1996.

Ekiert, Grzegorz, and Stephen E. Hanson. "Time, Space, and Institutional Change in Central and Eastern Europe." In *Capitalism and Democracy in Central and Eastern Europe: Assessing the Legacy of Communist Rule.* New York: Cambridge University Press, 2003.

Ekiert, Grzegorz, and Stephen E. Hanson, eds. *Capitalism and Democracy in Central and Eastern Europe: Assessing the Legacy of Communist Rule.* New York: Cambridge University Press, 2003.

Erikson, Erik H. *Young Man Luther.* New York: Norton, 1958.

Fish, M. Steven. "Democratization's Requisites: The Postcommunist Experience." *Post-Soviet Affairs* 14, no. 3 (1998): 212–47.

Fitzpatrick, Sheila. *Education and Social Mobility in the Soviet Union, 1921–1934.* Cambridge, MA: Harvard University Press, 1979.

———. "New Perspectives on Stalinism." *Russian Review* 45, no. 4 (October 1986): 357–73.

Florovskii, Georgii. *Puti russkago bogosloviia.* Paris, 1937.

Fontana, Andrés. "Political Decision-Making by a Military Corporation: Argentina, 1976–83." Ph.D. diss., University of Texas, 1987.

Forster, Keith. *Zhejiang Province in Reform.* Honolulu: University of Hawaii Press, 1998.

Freeze, Gregory. *The Russian Levites: Parish Clergy in the Eighteenth Century*. Cambridge, MA: Harvard University Press, 1977.

Fukuyama, Francis. *The End of History and the Last Man*. New York: Free Press, 1992.

―――. "The Modernizing Imperative: The USSR as an Ordinary Country." *The National Interest*, no. 32 (1993): 10–19.

Gaddy, Clifford. *The Price of the Past: Russia's Struggle with the Legacy of a Militarized Economy*. Washington, DC: Brookings Institution, 1996.

Gawlik, Wiesław. "Poznanie Boga przez sumienie u Newmana." *Znak*, no. 179 (1969): 172–73.

Geddes, Barbara. *Paradigms and Sand Castles: Theory Building and Research Design in Comparative Politics*. Ann Arbor: University of Michigan Press, 2003.

Gerring, John. *Social Science Methodology: A Criterial Framework*. Cambridge: Cambridge University Press, 2001.

Getty, J. Arch. *Origins of the Great Purges: The Soviet Communist Party Reconsidered, 1933–1938*. Cambridge: Cambridge University Press, 1985.

Gimpelson, Vladimir, and Douglas Lippoldt. *The Russian Labour Market: Between Transition and Turmoil*. Lanham, MD: Rowman & Littlefield, 2001.

Goldstone, Jack A. "Initial Conditions, General Laws, Path Dependence, and Explanation in Historical Sociology." *American Journal of Sociology* 104, no. 3 (1998): 829–45.

Gorbachev, Mikhail, and Zdenek Mlynař. *Conversations with Gorbachev on Perestroika, the Prague Spring, and the Crossroads of Socialism*. New York: Columbia University Press, 2002.

Grabowski, Tomek. "Breaking Through to Individualism." Ph.D. diss., University of California, Berkeley, 2002.

―――. "Nowy Światowy Nieład: Rozmowa z Kenem Jowittem." *Gazeta Wyborcza*, February 27–28, 1993, 12.

Halfin, Igal. *From Darkness to Light: Class, Consciousness, and Salvation in Revolutionary Russia*. Pittsburgh: Pittsburgh University Press, 2000.

Hamilton, Gary, ed. *Asian Business Networks*. New York: Walter de Gruyter, 1996.

Han, Jongwha. "Characteristics of Macro-Management and Strategies" [in Korean]. In *Characteristics of Management of Five Korean Chaebols*, edited by Yoo-keun Shin. Seoul: Srkyungsa, 1995.

Hanson, Stephen E. "The Leninist Legacy and Institutional Change." *Comparative Political Studies* 28, no. 2 (1995): 306–14.

―――. "The Leninist Legacy, Institutional Change, and Post-Soviet Russia." In *Liberalization and Leninist Legacies: Comparative Perspectives on Democratic Transitions*, edited by Beverly Crawford and Arend Lijphart, 228–52. Berkeley: International and Area Studies, University of California, 1997.

―――. *Time and Revolution: Marxism and the Design of Soviet Institutions*. Chapel Hill: University of North Carolina Press, 1997.

Hassner, Pierre. "Par-delà l'histoire et la mémoire." In *Stalinisme et nazisme: Histoire et mémoire comparées*, edited by Henry Rousso. Paris: Editions Complexe, 1999.

Hauslohner, Paul. "Gorbachev's Social Contract." *Soviet Economy* 3, no. 1 (1987).

Heller, Mikhail, and Aleksandr Nekrich. *Utopia in Power: The History of the Soviet Union from 1917 to the Present.* New York: Summit Books, 1986.

Hempel, Carl. *Fundamentals of Concept Formation in Empirical Science.* Chicago: University of Chicago Press, 1952.

Ho, Samuel. *Rural China in Transition: Non-agricultural Development in Rural Jiangsu, 1978–1990.* Oxford: Clarendon Press, 1994.

Hobsbawm, E. J., and Terene Ronger, eds. *The Invention of Tradition.* Cambridge: Cambridge University Press, 1984.

Horton, John, and Susan Mendus. *After MacIntyre.* Notre Dame, IN: University of Notre Dame Press, 1994.

Hough, Jerry. "The Soviet System: Petrification or Pluralism." *Problems of Communism* (March–April 1972).

———. *The Soviet Union and Social Science Theory.* Cambridge, MA: Harvard University Press, 1977.

Hough, Jerry, and Merle Fainsod. *How the Soviet Union is Governed.* Cambridge, MA: Harvard University Press, 1979.

Howard, Dick. *The Specter of Democracy.* New York: Columbia University Press, 2002.

Howard, Marc Morjé. *The Weakness of Civil Society in Post-Communist Europe.* Cambridge: Cambridge University Press, 2003.

Huntington, Samuel. *The Third Wave: Democratization in the Late Twentieth Century.* Norman: University of Oklahoma Press, 1991.

Jaeger, Werner. *Early Christianity and Greek Paideia.* Cambridge, MA: Belknap, 1961.

Janelli, Roger L., with Dawnhee Yim. *Making Capitalism: The Social and Cultural Construction of a South Korean Conglomerate.* Stanford: Stanford University Press, 1993.

Janos, Andrew C. *East Central Europe in the Modern World: The Politics of the Borderlands from Pre- to Postcommunism.* Stanford: Stanford University Press, 2000.

Johnson, Chalmers A. *Peasant Nationalism and Communist Power: The Emergence of Revolutionary China, 1937–1945.* Stanford: Stanford University Press, 1962.

Jović, Dejan. *Jugoslavija: Država koja je odumrla.* Zagreb: Prometej, 2003.

———. "Yugoslavism and Yugoslav Communism: From Tito to Kardelj." In *Yugoslavism: Histories of a Failed Idea, 1918–1992,* edited by Dejan Djokić. Madison: University of Wisconsin Press, 2003.

Jowitt, Ken. "Challenging the 'Correct' Line." *East European Politics and Society* 12, no. 1 (Winter 1998).

———. "Inclusion and Mobilization in European Leninist Regimes." *World Politics* 28, no. 1 (October 1975): 69–96.

———. *The Leninist Response to National Dependency.* Berkeley: Institute of International Studies, University of California, 1978.

———. *New World Disorder: The Leninist Extinction.* Berkeley: University of California Press, 1992.

———. "An Organizational Approach to the Study of Political Culture in Marxist-Leninist Regimes." *American Political Science Review* 68, no. 3 (September 1974): 1171–91.

————. "Rage, Hubris, and Regime Change." *Policy Review,* no. 118 (April–May 2003).

————. "A Research Agenda for Eastern Europe." *East European Politics and Society* 4, no. 2 (Spring 1990): 193–97.

————. *Revolutionary Breakthroughs and National Development: The Case of Romania, 1944–65.* Berkeley: University of California Press, 1971.

————. "Soviet Neotraditionalism: The Political Corruption of a Leninist Regime." *Soviet Studies* 35, no. 3 (July 1983): 275–97.

————. "Weber, Trotsky and Holmes on the Study of Leninist Regimes." *Journal of International Affairs* 45, no. 1 (Summer 1991): 31–49.

Kalberg, Stephen. *Max Weber's Comparative-Historical Sociology.* Chicago: University of Chicago Press, 1994.

Kalugin, Vasilii. *Andrei Kurbskii i Ivan Groznyi.* Moscow: Iazyki russkoi kultury, 1998.

Kang, Kwangha. *Five-Year Economic Plans: Goals and Evaluations of the Implementation* [in Korean]. Seoul: Seoul National University Press, 2000.

Karl, Terry L., and Philippe C. Schmitter. "From an Iron Curtain to a Paper Curtain: Grounding Transitologists or Students of Postcommunism?" *Slavic Review* (Winter 1995): 965–78.

————. "Modes of Transition in Latin America, Southern and Eastern Europe." *International Social Science Journal,* May 1991, 269–84.

Kenney, Padraic. *Rebuilding Poland, 1945–1950.* Ithaca, NY: Cornell University Press, 1997.

Kerčov, Sava, Jovo Radoš. and Aleksandar Raiš. *Mitinzi u Vojvodini 1988 godine.* Novi Sad: Dnevnik, 1990

Kharkhordin, Oleg. "Reveal and Dissimulate: A Genealogy of Private Life in Soviet Russia." In *Public and Private in Thought and Practice,* edited by Jeff Weintraub and Krishnan Kumar. Chicago: University of Chicago Press, 1997.

————. "The Soviet Individual: Genealogy of a Dissimulating Animal." In *The Global Modernities,* edited by Roland Robertson. New York: Sage, 1995.

Kideckel, David. "The Socialist Transformation of Agriculture in a Romanian Commune, 1945–62." *American Ethnologist* 9 (1982): 320–40.

Kim, Man-Heum. "A Study on Regionalism in Korean Politics." Ph.D. diss., Seoul National University, 1991.

Kim, Se-Jin. *The Politics of Military Revolution in Korea.* Chapel Hill: University of North Carolina Press, 1971.

Kim, Seung-Kyung. *Class Struggle or Family Struggle? The Lives of Women Factory Workers in South Korea.* New York: Cambridge University Press, 1997.

King, Charles. "Post-Postcommunism: Transition, Comparison, and the End of 'Eastern Europe.'" *World Politics* 53, no. 1 (2000): 143–72.

King, Gary, Robert O. Keohane, and Sidney Verba. *Designing Social Inquiry: Scientific Inference in Qualitative Research.* Princeton: Princeton University Press, 1994.

Kinzley, W. Dean. *Industrial Harmony in Modern Japan: The Invention of a Tradition.* New York: Routledge, 1991.

Kitschelt, Herbert, Zdenka Mansfeldova, Radoslaw Markowski, and Gábor Tóka. *Post-*

Communist Party Systems: Competition, Representation, and Inter-Party Coopera-tion. Cambridge: Cambridge University Press, 1999.

Klibanov, Alexander. *Dukhovnaia kultura srednevekovoi Rusi.* Moscow: Aspekt Press, 1994.

Kligman, Gail. "Crearea autorității comuniste: Luptă de clasă și colectivizare la Ieud, Maramureș." In *Țărănimea și puterea: Procesul de colectivizare a agriculturii în Româ-nia, 1949–1962,* edited by Dorin Dobrincu and Constantin Iordachi. Iași, Roma-nia: Polirom, 2005.

———. *The Wedding of the Dead: Ritual, Poetics and Popular Culture in a Transyl-vanian Village.* Berkeley: University of California Press, 1988.

Kohli, Atul. *State Directed Development: Political Power and Industrialization in the Global Periphery.* New York: Cambridge University Press, 2004.

Kolakowski, Leszek. *Main Currents of Marxism.* Vol. 3, *The Breakdown.* Oxford: Oxford University Press, 1978.

Kominek, Bolesław. *W sluzbie Ziem Zachodnich: Z teki posmiertnej.* Wrocław: Wydawnictwo Wrocławskiej Ksiegarni Archidiecezjalnej, 1977.

Kondratieva, Tamara. *Bolcheviks et Jacobins: Itineraire des analogies.* Paris: Payot, 1989.

Kong Jung-ja. "A Study of Chaebol Families' Conjugal Connections" [in Korean]. Ph.D. diss., Ewha Women's University, 1989.

Kopstein, Jeffrey S. "Postcommunist Democracy: Legacies and Outcomes." *Com-parative Politics* 35, no. 2 (January 2003).

Kopstein, Jeffrey S., and David A. Reilly. "Geographic Diffusion and the Transfor-mation of the Postcommunist World." *World Politics* 53, no. 1 (October 2000): 1–37.

Kotkin, Stephen. "Trashcanistan: A Tour Through the Wreckage of the Soviet Empire." *The New Republic,* April 15, 2002.

Krichevskaia, Liubov. *Slepaia mat', ili nagrada ispytannoi dobrodieteli: Drama.* Kharkov, 1818.

———. *Dobrodetelnoi volshebnik: Dramaticheskaia opera v piati deistviiakh.* Moscow, 1787.

Krucina, Jan. "Formacja teologiczna alumnow." In *Piecdziesiat lat Wyzszego Semi-narium Duchownego we Wrocławiu,* edited by Ignacy Dec and Krystyn Matwijowski. Wrocław: Instytut Historyczny Uniwersytetu Wrocławskiego, 1997.

Kuhn, Thomas. *The Structure of Scientific Revolutions.* Chicago: University of Chicago Press, 1962.

Kulp, D., Jr. *Country Life in South China.* New York: Bureau of Publications, Teach-ers College, Columbia University, 1925.

Laitin, David. *Hegemony and Culture: Politics and Religious Change Among the Yoruba.* Chicago: University of Chicago Press, 1986.

———. *Identity in Formation: The Russian-Speaking Populations in the Near Abroad.* Ithaca, NY: Cornell University Press, 1998.

———. "The National Uprisings in the Soviet Union." *World Politics* 44, no. 1 (1991): 139–77.

Lakatos, Imre. "Falsification and the Methodology of Scientific Research Programs." In *Criticism and the Growth of Knowledge*, edited by Imre Lakatos and Alan Musgrave. Cambridge: Cambridge University Press, 1970.

Lakatos, Imre. "Falsification and the Methodology of Scientific Research Programs." In *The Methodology of Scientific Research Programs*, edited by John Worrall and Gregory Currie. Cambridge: Cambridge University Press, 1978.

Lal, Deepak. *Unintended Consequences: The Impact of Factor Endowments, Culture, and Politics on Long-run Economic Performance*. Cambridge, MA: MIT Press, 1998.

Lampland, Martha. *The Object of Labor: Commodification in Socialist Hungary*. Chicago: University of Chicago Press, 1995.

Lazič, Mladen. *U susret zatvorenom društvu*. Zagreb: Naprijed, 1987.

Ledeneva, Alena V. *Russia's Economy of Favours: Blat, Networking, and Informal Exchange*. Cambridge: Cambridge University Press, 1998.

Lee, Hanbin. *Developmentalist Time and Leadership in Developing Countries*. Bloomington, IN: Comparative Administrative Group, 1965.

Lee, Mun Woong. "Research on the Workers' Life Style and Job Adaptation" [in Korean], 86-4. Research paper, Institute of Korean Studies, 1986.

Lefort, Claude. *La complication: Retour sur le communisme*. Paris: Fayard, 1999.

Levi, Margaret. *Consent, Dissent, and Patriotism*. New York: Cambridge University Press, 1997.

———. "A Model, a Method, and a Map: Rational Choice in Comparative and Historical Analysis." In *Comparative Politics: Rationality, Culture, and Structure*, edited by Mark Irving Lichbach and Alan S. Zuckerman. Cambridge: Cambridge University Press, 1997.

Levy, Robert. "Primul val al colectivizării: Politici centrale şi implementare regională, 1949–1953." In *Ţărănimea şi puterea: Procesul de colectivizare a agriculturii în România, 1949–1962*, edited by Dorin Dobrincu and Constantin Iordachi. Iaşi: Editura Polirom, 2005.

Lewin, Moshe. *The Gorbachev Phenomenon*. Berkeley: University of California Press, 1988.

Lih, Lars T. "How a Founding Document Was Found, or One Hundred Years of Lenin's *What is To be Done?*" *Kritika: Explorations in Russian and Eurasian History* 4, no. 1 (Winter 2002): 5–49.

Lim, Youngil. *Government Policy and Private Enterprise: Korean Experience in Industrialization*. Berkeley: Institute of East Asian Studies, University of California, Berkeley, Center for Korean Studies, 1981.

Linz, Juan J., and Alfred Stepan. *Problems of Democratic Transition and Consolidation: Southern Europe, South America, and Post-Communist Europe*. Baltimore: Johns Hopkins University Press, 1996.

Liu, Yia-Ling. "Reform From Below: The Private Economy and Local Politics in the Rural Industrialization of Wenzhou." *China Quarterly*, no. 130 (June 1992): 293–316.

Lukes, Steven. "On the Moral Blindness of Communism." *Human Rights Review* 2, no. 2 (January–March 2001).

Macfarlane, Alan. *The Origins of English Individualism*. Oxford: Basil Blackwell, 1978.

MacIntyre, Alasdair. *After Virtue*. London: Duckworth, 1981.

Madsen, Douglas, and Peter G. Snow. *The Charismatic Bond: Political Behavior in Time of Crisis*. Cambridge, MA: Harvard University Press, 1991.

Mahoney, James, and Dietrich Rueschemeyer, eds. *Comparative-Historical Analysis: Achievements and Agendas*. New York: Cambridge University Press, 2003.

Malia, Martin. *Russia Under Western Eyes: From the Bronze Horseman to the Lenin Mausoleum*. Cambridge, MA: Belknap Press of the Harvard University Press, 1999.

———. *The Soviet Tragedy*. New York: Free Press, 1994.

Marek, Ryszard. *Kosciol rzymsko-katolicki wobec Ziem Zachodnich i Polnocnych* (Warsaw: PWN, 1976).

McClintock, Cynthia. *Revolutionary Movements in Latin America: El Salvador's FMLN & Peru's Sendero Luminoso*. Washington, DC: U.S. Institute for Peace Press, 1998.

McKeown, Timothy. "Case Studies and the Statistical Worldview: Review of King, Keohane, and Verba's 'Designing Social Inquiry: Scientific Inference in Qualitative Research.'" *International Organization* 53, no. 1 (1999).

Micewski, Andrzej. *Cardinal Wyszynski*. San Diego: Harcourt Brace Jovanovich, 1984.

Mihailović, Kosta, and Vasilije Krestić. *Memorandum SANU: Odgovori na kritike*. Belgrade: SANU, 1995.

Mill, James Stuart. *A System of Logic*. New York: Harper and Row, 1888.

Milošević, Slobodan. *Godine raspleta*. Belgrade: BIGZ, 1989.

Morawska, Ewa. "The Polish Roman Catholic Church Unbound." In *Can Europe Work?* edited by Stephen E. Hanson and Wilfried Spohn. Seattle: University of Washington Press, 1995.

Mrkšić, Danilo. *Srednji slojevi u Jugoslaviji*. Belgrade: SSO Srbije, 1987.

Muncy, Lysbeth W. *The Junker in the Prussian Administration under William III, 1888–1914*. Providence, RI: Brown University Press, 1944.

Mungiu-Pippidi, Alina, and Gérard Althabe. *Secera și buldozerul. Scorniceşti şi Nucşoara. Mecanisme de aservire a ţăranului român*. Iasi: Polirom, 2002.

Munro, Neil. *Different Dynamics for Contrasting Legacies: South Korea and Russia Compared*. Glasgow: Center for the Study of Public Policy, University of Strathclyde, 2004.

Murakami, Yasusuke. "Ie Society as a Pattern of Civilization." *Journal of Japanese Studies* 10, no.2 (Summer 1984): 279–363.

Nelson, Daniel. *Managers and Workers: Origins of the New Factory System in the United States, 1880–1920*. Madison, WI: University of Wisconsin Press, 1975.

Oblak, Jan. "Dzieje diecezji warminskiej w okresie dwudziestolecia (1945–1965)." *Nasza Przeszlosc* 22 (1965).

O'Donnell, Guillermo. "Delegative Democracy." *Journal of Democracy* 5, no. 1 (1994): 55–69.

———. *Modernization and Bureaucratic-Authoritarianism: Studies in South American Politics*. Berkeley: Institute of International Studies, University of California Press, 1973.

O'Donnell, Guillermo, Philippe C. Schmitter, and Laurence Whitehead, eds. *Transi-*

tions from Authoritarian Rule: Comparative Perspectives. Baltimore: Johns Hopkins University Press, 1986.

Offe, Claus. "Capitalism by Democratic Design? Democratic Theory Facing the Triple Transition in East Central Europe." *Social Research* 58, no. 4 (1991): 865–92.

Oi, Jean. *Rural China Takes Off.* Berkeley: University of California Press, 1999.

Oi, Jean C., and Andrew G. Walder, eds. *Property Rights and Economic Reform in China.* Stanford: Stanford University Press, 1999.

Onişoru, Gheorghe. *Instaurarea regimului comunist în România.* Bucharest, 2002.

Ordeshook, Peter. "Engineering or Science: What Is the Study of Politics?" In *The Rational Choice Controversy: Economic Models of Politics Reconsidered,* edited by Jeffrey Friedman. New Haven, CT: Yale University Press, 1995.

Pak Ki-dong. "A Study of Korean Family Enterprises." Ph.D. diss., Dong-A University, 1980.

Papaioannou, Kostas. *Marx et les marxistes.* Paris: Gallimard, 2001.

Park, Hee. "A Study of Organization Management in Korean Chaebols and Labor Relations with a Focus on Impacts on Familism" [in Korean]. Ph.D. diss., Yonsei University, 1993.

Park, Hee Chung. *The Country, the Revolution and I.* Seoul: Hollym Corp., 1970.

Perry, Elizabeth. *Shanghai on Strike: The Politics of Chinese Labor.* Stanford: Stanford University Press, 1993.

Petro, Nikolai. *The Rebirth of Russian Democracy: An Interpretation of Political Culture.* Cambridge, MA: Harvard University Press, 1995.

Pipes, Richard. "Did the Russian Revolution Have to Happen?" *American Scholar,* Spring 1994, 215–38.

———. *Russia and the Old Regime.* New York: Scribner's and Sons, 1974.

———. *The Russian Revolution.* New York: Vintage, 1990.

Pirenne, Henri. *Medieval Cities.* Princeton, NJ: Princeton University Press, 1948.

Polan, A. J. *Lenin and the End of Politics.* Berkeley: University of California Press, 1984.

Pop-Eleches, Grigore. "The Enduring Curse of the Past: Initial Conditions and Post-Communist Reform Trajectories." Paper prepared for the 2003 annual meeting of the American Political Science Association, Philadelphia, August 28–31, 2003.

Popkin, Samuel. *The Rational Peasant: The Political Economy of Rural Society in Vietnam.* Berkeley: University of California Press, 1979.

Popper, Karl. *The Logic of Scientific Discovery.* London: Hutchinson, 1959.

Przeworksi, Adam. *Democracy and the Market: Political and Economic Reforms in Eastern Europe and Latin America.* Cambridge: Cambridge University Press, 1991.

Pushkarev, Sergei. *Self-Government and Freedom in Russia.* Boulder, CO: Westview, 1988.

Ragin, Charles. *Fuzzy-Set Social Science.* Chicago: University of Chicago Press, 2000.

Reno, William. *Warlord Politics and African States.* Boulder, CO: Lynne Rienner, 1998.

Roche-Guilhen, Anne de la. *Dobrodetelnaia frantsuzhinka, ili istoriia o Agnesie Soro, zhivshei vo vremia Karla VII.* St. Petersburg, 1791.

Rose, Richard. *A Bottom-Up Evaluation of Enlargement Countries: New Europe Barometer 1.* Aberdeen, Scotland: CSPP Publications, University of Aberdeen, 2002.

Rose, Richard, William Mishler, and Christian Haerpfer. *Democracy and Its Alternatives: Understanding Post-Communist Societies.* Baltimore: Johns Hopkins University Press, 1998.

Ross, Michael. "How Does Natural Resource Wealth Influence Civil Wars? Evidence from Thirteen Cases." *International Organization* (forthcoming).

———. "What Do We Know about Natural Resources and Civil War?" In *Journal of Peace Research* (March 2004): 337–56.

Runia, David T. "Festugiere Revisited: Aristotle in the Greek Patres." *Vigiliae Christianae* 43, no. 1 (1989).

Rupnik, Jacques. "The Postcommunist Divide." *Journal of Democracy* 10, no. 1 (1999): 57–62.

Ryan, W. F. "Aristotle in Old Russian Literature." *Modern Language Review* 63, no. 3 (1968).

———. "Aristotle and Pseudo-Aristotle in Kievan and Muscovite Russia." In *Pseudo-Aristotle in the Middle Ages,* edited by Jill Kraye et al. London: Warburg Institute, 1986.

———. "The Secretum Secretorum and the Muscovite Autocracy." In *Pseudo-Aristotle: The Secret of Secrets,* edited by W. F. Ryan and Charles B. Schmitt. London: Warburg Institute, 1982.

Sagong Il and Leroy P. Johns. *Government, Business, and Entrepreneurship in Economic Development: The Korean Case.* Cambridge, MA: Harvard University Press, 1980.

Scott, James. *Seeing Like A State: How Certain Schemes to Improve the Human Condition Have Failed.* New Haven, CT: Yale University Press, 1997.

———. *Weapons of the Weak: Everyday Forms of Peasant Resistance.* New Haven, CT: Yale University Press, 1985.

Semenov, V., ed. *Drevnerusskaia 'Pchela' po pergammenomu spisku.* St. Petersburg, 1893.

Sergeyev, Viktor, and Nikolai Biryukov. *Russia's Road to Democracy: Parliament, Communism, and Traditional Culture.* Brookfield, VT: Elgar, 1993.

Shleifer, Andrei, and Daniel Treisman. "A Normal Country." *Foreign Affairs* 8, no. 2 (2004).

Shue, Vivienne. *The Reach of the State.* Stanford: Stanford University Press, 1988.

Sil, Rudra. "The Division of Labor in Social Science Research: Unified Methodology or 'Organic Solidarity'?" *Polity* 32, no. 4 (Summer 2000): 499–531.

———. *Managing "Modernity": Work, Community, and Authority in Late-Industrializing Japan and Russia.* Ann Arbor: University of Michigan Press, 2002.

Sil, Rudra, and Christopher Candland. "Institutional Legacies and the Transformation of Labor: Late-Industrializing and Post-Socialist Economies in Comparative-Historical Perspective." In *The Politics of Labor in a Global Age,* edited by Christopher Candland and Rudra Sil, 285–308. Oxford: Oxford University Press, 2001.

Sil, Rudra, and Calvin Chen. "Communist Legacies, Post-communist Transformations, and the Fate of Organized Labor in Russia and China." Presented at the 2003 Annual Conference of the Central and East European International Studies Association (CEE-ISA), Budapest, Hungary, June 2003.

Silber, Laura, and Alan Little. *Yugoslavia: Death of a Nation.* London: Penguin, 1995.

Solinger, Dorothy. *Contesting Citizenship in Urban China: Peasant Migrants, the State, and the Logic of the Market.* Berkeley: University of California Press, 1999.

Solnick, Steven L. *Stealing the State: Control and Collapse in Soviet Institutions.* Cambridge, MA: Harvard University Press, 1998.

Solzhenitsyn, Aleksandr. "Misconceptions about Russia Are a Threat to America." *Foreign Affairs* 58, no. 4 (1980): 797–834

———. *The Russian Question: At the End of the Twentieth Century.* Translated by Yermolai Solzhenitsyn. New York: Farrar, Straus and Giroux, 1995.

Somers, Margaret. "'We're No Angels': Realism, Rational Choice, and Relationality in the Social Sciences." *American Journal of Sociology* 104, no. 3 (November 1998).

Sreznevskii, I. I. *Materialy dlia slovaria drevne-russkago iazyka.* Vol. 1, col. 672. St. Petersburg: Tipografiia Imperatorskoi Akademii Nauk, 1893–1912.

Stambolić , Ivan. *Put u bespuće.* Belgrade: Radio B92, 1995.

———. *Rasprave o SR Srbiji, 1979–1987.* Zagreb: Globus, 1988.

Stark, David, and László Bruszt. *Postsocialist Pathways: Transforming Politics and Property in East Central Europe.* Cambridge: Cambridge University Press, 1998.

Stepan, Alfred. *The Military in Politics: Changing Patterns in Brazil.* Princeton, NJ: Princeton University Press, 1971.

Stokes, Susan. *Mandates and Democracy: Neoliberalism by Surprise in Latin America.* New York: Cambridge University Press, 2001.

Strzeszewski, Czeslaw. "Najbardziej potrzebne czynniki etyczno-spoleczne na Ziemiach Zachodnich." In *Kosciol na Ziemiach Zachodnich,* edited by Jan Krucina. Wrocław: Wydawnictwo Wrocławskiej Ksiegarni Archidiecezjalnej, 1971.

Sztompka, Piotr. "Civilizational Incompetence: The Trap of Post-Communist Societies." *Zeitschrift für Soziologie* 22, no. 2 (1993): 85–95.

———. "The Intangibles and Imponderables of the Transition to Democracy." *Studies in Comparative Communism* 24, no. 3 (1991): 295–311.

Tadić, Ljubomir. *O velikosrpskom hegemonizmu.* Belgrade: Politika, 1992.

———. *U matici krize, 1968–1998.* Belgrade: Čigoja, 1999.

Talmon, J. L. *Myth of the Nation and Vision of the Revolution: Ideological Polarizations in the Twentieth Century.* New Brunswick, NJ: Transaction, 1991.

———. *The Origins of Totalitarian Democracy.* London: Secker & Warburg, 1952.

Tănăsescu, Bogdan. *Colectivizarea între propagandă şi realitate.* Bucharest: Editura Globus, n.d.

Thomson, Francis J. "The Distorted Russian Perception of Classical Antiquity: The Causes and Consequences." Reprinted in *The Reception of Byzantine Culture in Mediaeval Russia.* Ashgate, UK: Variorum, 1995.

Timiş, N. "Demascarea unui mârşav chiabur din Ieud." *Graiul Maramureşului,* July 31, 1949.

Tismaneanu, Vladimir. *Fantasies of Salvation: Democracy, Nationalism, and Myth in Post-Communist Europe.* Princeton, NJ: Princeton University Press, 1998.

Tocqueville, Alexis de. *Democracy in America.* Translated and edited by Harvey C. Mansfield and Delba Winthrop. Chicago: The University of Chicago Press, 2000.

Todorova, Maria. *Imagining the Balkans.* London: Oxford University Press, 1997.

Trotsky, Leon. *The Revolution Betrayed.* New York: Merit, 1965.

Tucker, Robert C. *The Soviet Political Mind.* New York: Norton, 1971.

Turner, Frederick Jackson. *The Frontier in American History.* New York: Holt, 1920.

Urban, Wincenty. *Duszpasterski wklad ksiezy repatriantow w Archidiecezji Wrocławskiej w latach, 1945–1970.* Wrocław, 1970.

Veder, William R. "Old Russia's 'Intellectual Silence' Reconsidered." In *Medieval Russian Culture,* edited by Michael S. Flier and Daniel Rowland. Vol. 2. Berkeley: University of California Press, 1994.

Verdery, Katherine. "Chiaburii vechi şi noi: Închiaburirea şi deschiaburirea ţăranilor din Aurel Vlaicu." In *Ţărănimea şi puterea: Procesul de colectivizare a agriculturii în România, 1949–1962,* edited by Dorin Dobrincu and Constantin Iordachi. Iaşi, Romania: Polirom, 2005.

———. *Transylvanian Villagers: Three Centuries of Political, Economic, and Ethnic Change.* Berkeley: University of California Press, 1983.

———. *The Vanishing Hectare: Property and Value in Postsocialist Transylvania.* Ithaca, NY: Cornell University Press, 2003.

Viola, Lynne. *The Best Sons of the Fatherland: Workers in the Vanguard of Soviet Collectivization.* New York: Oxford University Press, 1987.

Vladisavljević, Nebojša. "Nationalism, Social Movement Theory, and the Grass Roots Movement of the Kosovo Serbs." *Europe-Asia Studies* 54, no. 5 (July 2002): 771–91.

Vogel, Ezra. "From Friendship to Comradeship: The Change in Personal Relations in Communist China." *China Quarterly,* no. 21 (January–March 1965): 1–28.

Volkov, Vadim. *Violent Entrepreneurs: The Use of Force in the Making of Russian Capitalism.* Ithaca, NY: Cornell University Press, 2002.

Vujačić, Veljko. "Institutional Origins of Contemporary Serbian Nationalism." *East European Constitutional Review* 5, no. 4 (Fall 1996): 51–61.

———. "Serbian Nationalism, Slobodan Milošević, and the Origins of the Yugoslav War." *Harriman Review,* December 1995.

Walder, Andrew. *Communist Neotraditionalism.* Berkeley: University of California Press, 1986.

Walder, Andrew, ed. *The Waning of the Communist State: Economic Origins of Political Decline in China and Hungary.* Berkeley: University of California Press, 1995.

Walicki, Andrzej. *Marxism and the Leap into the Kingdom of Freedom.* Stanford: Stanford University Press, 1995.

Weber, Max. *Economy and Society.* Translated and edited by Guenther Roth and Claus Wittich. 2 vols. Berkeley: University of California Press, 1978.

———. "'Objectivity' in Social Science and Social Policy." In *The Methodology of the Social Sciences,* edited by Edward A. Shils and Henry A. Finch. New York: Free Press, 1949.

———. "Science as a Vocation." In *From Max Weber: Essays in Sociology,* edited by H. H. Gerth and C. Wright Mills. New York: Oxford University Press, 1953.

White, Stephen, Alex Pravda, and Zvi Gitelman, eds. *Developments in Soviet Politics.* Durham, NC: Duke University Press, 1990.

Winter, Ella. *Red Virtue: Human Relationships in the New Russia.* New York: Harcourt, Brace and Company, 1933.

Wirth, L. "Urbanism as a Way of Life." In *New Perspectives on the American Community,* edited by R. L. Warren and L. Lyng, 36–42. Homewood, IL: Dorsey Press, 1983.

Wittenberg, Jason. *Crucibles of Political Loyalty: Church Institutions and Electoral Continuity in Hungary.* New York: Cambridge University Press, 2006.

Wójcik, Stefan. *Katechizacja w warunkach systemu totalitarnego.* Wrocław: Instytut Historyczny Uniwersytetu Wrocławskiego, 1995.

———. "Zycie i dzialalnosc Ksiedza Infulata Kazimierza Lagosza." In *Kosciol katolicki na Dolnym Slasku w powojennym 50-leciu,* edited by Ignacy Dec and Krystyn Matwijowski. Wrocław: Instytut Historyczny Uniwersytetu Wrocławskiego, 1996.

Wolfe, Bertram. "Leninism." In *Marxism in the Modern World,* edited by Milorad M. Drachkovitch. Stanford: Stanford University Press, 1965.

Woodward, Susan. *Balkan Tragedy: Chaos and Dissolution After the Cold War.* Washington, DC: Brookings Institution, 1995.

Xiaobo, Lü, and Elizabeth Perry, eds. *Danwei.* Boulder, CO: Westview Press, 1998.

Yakovlev, Alexander. *A Century of Violence in Soviet Russia.* New Haven, CT: Yale University Press, 2002.

Z [Martin Malia]. "To the Stalin Mausoleum," *Daedalus* 119, no. 1 (1990): 295–344.

Zhivov, Victor. "Religioznaia reforma i individualnoe nachalo v russkoi literature XVII veka." In *Iz istorii russkoi kultury.* Vol. 3. Moscow: Iazyki russkoi kultury, 2000.

Zienkiewicz, Aleksander. *Milosci trzeba sie sie uczyc.* Kraków: Wydawnictwo Apostolstwa Modlitwy, 1988.

Zizek, Slavoj. *Did Somebody Say Totalitarianism?* London: Verso, 2001.

Zizek, Slavoj, ed. *Revolution at the Gates: Selected Writings of Lenin from 1917.* London: Verso, 2002.

Zolberg, Aristide. *Creating Political Order: The Party-States of West Africa.* Chicago: Rand McNally, 1966.

Županov, Josip. *Marginalije o društvenoj krizi.* Zagreb: Globus, 1983.

CONTRIBUTORS

CALVIN CHEN is Luce Assistant Professor of Politics at Mount Holyoke College. His research interests include the industrialization of the Chinese countryside, the political economy of East Asia, and labor politics in post-socialist countries. He is currently working on a book-length study of organizational dynamics in China's township and village enterprises.

DANIEL CHIROT is professor of international studies and sociology at the University of Washington. He is the author and editor of books on Eastern Europe, social change, tyranny, and ethnic conflict. His new book, written with Clark McCauley, is entitled *Why Not Kill Them All? The Logic and Prevention of Mass Political Murder* (Princeton: Princeton University Press, 2006). He also works in West Africa on the causes and prevention of war.

BARBARA GEDDES is professor of political science at the University of California, Los Angeles. She works on democratization, authoritarian transitions, and political development with a focus on Latin American politics. Her publications include *Politician's Dilemma: Building State Capacity in Latin America* and *Paradigms and Sand Castles: Theory Building and Research Design in Comparative Politics.*

TOMEK GRABOWSKI is writer, entrepreneur, and assistant professor of European studies and political science at Maastricht University in the Netherlands.

His current research interests include the role of space and geography in cultural transitions. His forthcoming book is *A Freak of Culture: Frontiers and Institutions in the Making of Individualism.*

YONG-CHOOL HA is professor in the Department of International Relations at Seoul National University. His research interests include comparative politics (industrialization and tradition), international politics and social change, and the development of theories of regional politics. He has just published a book on state-led industrialization and social changes in South Korea entitled *Late Industrialization and the Dynamics of the Strong State in South Korea.*

STEPHEN E. HANSON is Boeing International Professor at the University of Washington and the director of the Ellison Center for Russian, East European, and Central Asian Studies at the Jackson School of International Studies. He is the author of *Time and Revolution: Marxism and the Design of Soviet Institutions,* winner of the 1998 Wayne S. Vucinich Book Prize from the American Association for the Advancement of Slavic Studies, and a coauthor of *Postcommunism and the Theory of Democracy.* Hanson specializes in the study of Russian, postcommunist, and comparative politics, and has published numerous articles on these themes.

STEPHEN HOLMES is Walter E. Meyer Professor at NYU Law School. He was the editor in chief of the *East European Constitutional Review* from 1992 to 2003, and has been the director of the Soros Foundation program for promoting legal reform in Russia and Eastern Europe. Holmes's research centers on the history of European liberalism and the disappointments of democracy and economic liberalization after communism. His books include *Benjamin Constant and the Making of Modern Liberalism* (Yale University Press, 1984), *Anatomy of Antiliberalism, Passions and Constraint: The Theory of Liberal Democracy,* and, with Cass Sunstein, *The Cost of Rights: Why Liberty Depends on Taxes.*

MARC MORJÉ HOWARD is associate professor of government at Georgetown University, where he is also a core faculty member of the Center for Democracy and the Third Sector. His research interests address a variety of topics related to democracy and democratization, including civil society, immigration and citizenship, competitive authoritarian regimes, right-wing extremism, and public opinion. Geographically, his research spans both Eastern and Western Europe, with particular focus on Russia, Germany, and France. His publications include *The Weakness of Civil Society in Post-Communist Europe,* which received the 2004 award for best book on European politics from the American Political Science Association, and the 2004 Virginia Hodgkinson Research Prize from Independent Sector.

OLEG KHARKHORDIN is professor at the Faculty of Political Sciences and Sociology, European University at St. Petersburg. He has taught political theory and Russian politics as a visiting professor at Yale, Harvard, and Sciences Po (Paris). His major publications include *The Collective and the Individual in Russia* and *Main Concepts of Russian Politics*. He is currently working on theories of *res publica* and political friendship.

GAIL KLIGMAN is professor of sociology at the University of California, Los Angeles, where she is also director of the Center for European and Eurasian Studies. She has written widely on culture, politics and gender in East Central Europe during and after socialism. Among her books are *The Wedding of the Dead: Ritual, Poetics and Popular Culture in Transylvania, The Politics of Duplicity: Controlling Reproduction in Ceauşescu's Romania,* and *The Politics of Gender After Socialism: A Comparative-Historical Essay,* coauthored with Susan Gal. She is presently coauthoring a book with Katherine Verdery on collectivization in Romania from 1949 to 1962.

GRIGORE POP-ELECHES is assistant professor of politics and international affairs at Princeton University. His research interests include the politics of economic reforms in Eastern Europe and Latin America, comparative democratization and party development, and the role of outside policy conditionality (especially from the IMF) in the political economy of developing countries. His work has been published in *East European Politics and Society, Journal of Democracy,* and *Studies in Comparative International Development.*

RUDRA SIL is associate professor and chair of the undergraduate program in the Department of Political Science at the University of Pennsylvania. His research interests range from methodological and epistemological issues in the social sciences to theories of development and transition, comparative labor relations, and Russian and Asian studies. He is author of *Managing "Modernity": Work, Community, and Authority in Late-Industrializing Japan and Russia.* He has also coedited *Beyond Boundaries? Disciplines, Paradigms and Theoretical Integration in International Studies* (with Eileen M. Doherty) and *The Politics of Labor in a Global Age* (with Christopher Candland). He is also author of several articles and book chapters and is presently working on a monograph on the transformation of labor politics in Russia and other postcommunist settings.

VLADIMIR TISMANEANU is professor of government and politics and director of the Center for Study of Post-Communist Societies at the University of Maryland, College Park. Between 1998 and 2004 he served as editor of the journal *East*

European Politics and Societies, and is currently chair of its editorial committee. He is the author of numerous books, including *Reinventing Politics: Eastern Europe from Stalin to Havel, Fantasies of Salvation: Democracy, Nationalism, and Myth in Post-Communist Europe,* and *Stalinism for All Seasons: A Political History of Romanian Communism.* His book of dialogues with Romania's former President Ion Iliescu *(The Great Shock at the End of a Short Century)* came out in English translation in 2005. His articles have appeared in major American and European journals. He is working on a new book titled *The Devil in History: Communism, Fascism, and the Lessons of the 20th Century.*

KATHERINE VERDERY is Distinguished Professor of Anthropology at the Graduate Center of the City University of New York. Her books include *Transylvanian Villagers, National Ideology Under Socialism: Identity and Cultural Politics in Ceaușescu's Romania, What Was Socialism, and What Comes Next?, The Political Lives of Dead Bodies: Reburial and Postsocialist Change,* and *The Vanishing Hectare: Property and Value in Postsocialist Transylvania.*

VELJKO VUJAČIĆ is associate professor of sociology at Oberlin College. Professor Vujačić's fields of specialization include sociological theory, political and comparative-historical sociology, and social movements, with a special focus on communism and nationalism in the former Soviet Union and Yugoslavia. His articles on these themes and topics have appeared in *Theory and Society, Post-Soviet Affairs, East-European Constitutional Review, The Harriman Review, Research in Political Sociology, The Encyclopedia of Nationalism, The International Encyclopedia of the Social Sciences,* and a number of edited volumes. He is currently working on a large comparative-historical study of Russian and Serbian nationalism and the disintegration of the Soviet Union and Yugoslavia.

INDEX

Bolshevik (Party), 10, 19
Bolshevik Revolution, 19, 227, 242n4
Bolshevism, 5, 8, 19–30
Bosnia, 49, 57, 60, 61, 112, 113, 123
Bourdieu, Pierre, 10, 108–9
Brezhnev, Leonid, 5, 209
Bukharin, Nikolai, 20
Bulgaria, 49, 52, 56, 57, 59, 60, 61,
  241
Bush, George W., 249–68

Cao Dai, 153–54
Cappadocians, 100–101
Castoriadis, Cornelius, 30
Castro, Fidel, 152
Catholic Church, 39; Jowitt's view of,
  38, 39, 50, 55, 132, 271. *See also* Polish
  Church
Caucasus, 40
Ceauşescu, Nicolae, 270–71
Central Asia, 40, 49, 56, 57, 59
Central Europe, 46, 240, 245n45, 273;
  the term, 40, 45n29. *See also* East
  Central Europe
chaebols, 179–85
Chechnya, 59, 63n9
Cheney, Dick, 254, 258, 267
Chernyshevsky, Nikolai, 29
Chetniks, 114, 123
chiabur, 133–42, 144n15, 144n17, 144n19,
  144n24, 145n27, 145n29, 146n53
Chrysostom, Saint John, 98
Civic Forum (Czech), 37; 52
civil servants, 177–78
civil society, 42, 47–63, 228, 242n5
civil war, 57, 59–60, 157, 162–64,
  169–70n13, 221n1
Clark, Katerina, 90
clientelism, 5, 204n2
Clinton, Bill, 262
coalitions, 38, 156
cold war: end of, 6, 220, 253, 273; and
  U.S. mindset, 259–61

collectivization, 21, 154; social dimensions of, 127–42
Comintern, 114
Commonwealth Club, 7
Communist Party, 5, 28, 36, 52, 76, 114,
  163; in China, 201, 241; in Romania,
  81, 85; in the Russian Federation, 29;
  in the Soviet Union, 22; in the United
  States, 151
Communist Youth League, 202
comparative method, 225–42
consolidation (stage), 4, 11, 150, 155–56,
  164, 167, 193
corporatism, 20, 228, 229, 231
corruption, 231, 240; of Communist
  Party, 5; Corruption Perception
  Index, 64nn20–23, 245n45; and
  Korean bureaucracy, 181; and post-
  communism, 54–55
coups, 50, 151–57, 161–62; *autogolpe*
  of 1992 (Peru), 153; coup of 1966
  (Argentina), 153; and Park, 177
Croatia, 56, 57, 58, 59, 60, 61, 111, 113,
  114, 115, 123
Croatian Democratic Union, 53
Czechoslovakia, 37, 38, 39
Czech Republic, 35, 52, 53, 57, 61, 64n20

Dąbrowski, Eugeniusz, 82
danwei, 188–89
Decembrist, 25
Defense Intelligence Agency (United
  States), 7
De Gaulle, Charles, 111
de Maistre, Joseph, 24
democratic centralism, 151, 154
d'Encausse, Hélène Carrère, 27
Deng Xiaoping, 191
Department of Defense (United States),
  253, 264
Deutscher, Isaac, 26–27
Diodorus, 99
Diogenes, 99

Michnik, Adam, 37
Mill, John Stuart, 17, 225, 229, 235
Milošević, Slobodan, 10, 110–24
Ministry of Commerce and Industry
  (Korea), 177, 178, 186n10
Mlynař, Zdenek, 22
mobilization, 5, 108, 121, 122, 237, 238
Mohammed, 272, 273
Mohila, Bishop Petr, 98
Moldova, 38, 51, 58
Mongolia, 57, 58, 61
Monomakh, Vladimir, 99–100
Montesquieu, Baron de, 93
Mount Athos, 95
Movement for a Democratic Slovakia,
  53
Muhammad, 272, 273
Muscovy, 95, 96
muzhiks, 27

Nagorno-Karabakh, 60
The Name of the Rose (Eco), 94, 96
National Assembly (Korea), 177
National Liberation War, 114
National Movement Simeon II
  (Bulgaria), 52
National Salvation Front (Romanian),
  52
NATO, 41, 123
Nazarbayev, Nursultan, 50, 53
Nazi Party, 107
Nazis, 21–22, 27, 104n11, 107, 114, 227
Nechaevism, 23
"neo-traditionalism," 171, 209
New Economic Policy (NEP), 20
New World Disorder (Jowitt), 3, 6, 34–
  35, 47, 210, 273
Nicomachean Ethics (Aristotle), 94, 95,
  96, 100
1917 Revolution, 26, 29, 227. *See also*
  Bolshevik Revolution
Niyazov, Saparmurat, 50
Nunn-Lugar program, 258

O'Donnell, Guillermo, 51
Old Bolshevik, 21
One Step Forward (Lenin), 28
Opole, 70, 82, 83–84
Origen, 100–101

Pannekoek, Anton, 30
Papandreou, 86
Park Chung Hee, 176–78, 184
Parteigenosse, 104n11
Partido Revolucionario Institucional
  (PRI; Mexico), 166
partiinost', 24–25
Parti Socialiste (Senegal), 166
Party Congress (of the Communist
  Party), 90
party-state, 228; in China, 12, 189; in
  Romania, 130, 136, 141, 142, 145n45,
  146n60
paternalism, 20, 53, 238
Paul, Saint, 19
Pavic, Milorad, 96
PAX (Poland), 81
peasants, 69–86, 93, 108, 127–42, 152–
  53, 154
Peripatetic philosophy, 95
Peron, Juan, 111
Petroşani, 139
Philip of Macedon, 99
Pinochet, Augusto, 157, 158, 162, 163
Pipes, Richard, 25, 242n4
Pius XII, Pope, 79
Plutarch, 99
Pobedonostsev, Konstantin, 25
Polan, A. J., 28
Poland, 35, 37, 39, 40, 52, 57, 61, 64n20,
  69–86, 95, 98, 239, 241
Polish Church, 77–85
Politburo, 161–62
Polotskii, Simeon, 98
Popkin, Samuel, 153
post-Leninist period, 5–6, 14, 49, 51, 54,
  60, 219, 221n1, 234–41